MEN IN LOVE

NANCY FRIDAY, THE COURAGEOUS, CANDID AUTHOR OF *MY MOTHER/MY SELF*, EMBARKS ON A BOLD JOURNEY INTO THE SECRET SEX LIVES OF MEN.

"LIBERATING . . . ILLUMINATING . . . THE MOST TALKED ABOUT AND LIFE-CHANGING BOOK OF THE YEAR."

—Michael Korda, author of *Power*

"A LABOR OF LOVE FOR ALL HUMANKIND. NANCY FRIDAY IS STILL ON THE CUTTING EDGE."

—*The Houston Chronicle*

"NANCY FRIDAY'S INTERPRETATION OF MEN'S SEXUAL FANTASIES OFFERS AN IN-VALUABLE NEW WAY OF SEEING MEN. . . . IT IS CRUCIAL THAT THE FANTASIES ARE UN-EXPURGATED, EXACTLY AS SHE RECEIVED THEM; THE WORDS AND IMAGES EMERGE DIRECTLY . . . TELLING US HOW MEN SE-CRETLY FEEL . . . . R AT WOMEN, AT . . . . R UNDERLYING LO . . .

. . . Robertiello, M.D.

BY NANCY FRIDAY

MY SECRET GARDEN

FORBIDDEN FLOWERS

MY MOTHER/MY SELF

MEN IN LOVE:
Men's Sexual Fantasies:
The Triumph of Love Over Rage

JEALOUSY

QUANTITY SALES

Most Dell books are available at special quantity discounts when purchased in bulk by corporations, organizations, or groups. Special imprints, messages, and excerpts can be produced to meet your needs. For more information, write to: Dell Publishing, 666 Fifth Avenue, New York, NY 10103. Attention: Director, Diversified Sales.

Please specify how you intend to use the books (e.g., promotion, resale, etc.).

INDIVIDUAL SALES

Are there any Dell books you want but cannot find in your local stores? If so, you can order them directly from us. You can get any Dell book currently in print. For a complete up-to-date listing of our books and information on how to order, write to: Dell Readers Service, Box DR, 666 Fifth Avenue, New York, NY 10103.

MEN
IN
LOVE

Nancy Friday

A DELL BOOK

Published by
Dell Publishing
a division of
The Bantam Doubleday Dell Publishing Group, Inc.
666 Fifth Avenue
New York, New York 10103

ISBN: 0-440-15903-2

Reprinted by arrangement with Delacorte Press.

Printed in the United States of America

February 1981

20   19   18   17

RAD

Acknowledgments

I wish to thank psychoanalyst Richard Robertiello, M.D., for his professional assistance in reading all the fantasies in this book, and for giving me the benefit of his understanding of their meaning. If I have added my own interpretations to the clarity and brilliance he brought to our discussions, it is because—great teacher that he is—he always encouraged me to question even his opinions.

Further thanks are also lovingly given to two other friends, psychotherapist Dr. Leah Schaefer and psychoanalyst Sirgay Sanger, M.D. Their generosity in giving me so much time, the learning with which they suggested various corrections to my thinking, leave me permanently in their debt.

When I hear other writers deplore the failings of their literary agents, I am always reminded how much I owe my own, Betty Anne Clarke. I may not be able to point to any particular pages of my work and say Betty Anne suggested this idea or that; but without her courageous belief in me during the past six years, perhaps the pages never would have been written.

Happy endings are made all the more poignant by the memory of unhappy beginnings. At a time when few others were interested in my work, Linda Grey came forward with encouragement, advice, counsel— and a contract. My debt to her is one only the most fortunate of writers can understand.

N.F.

Contents

1 / The Masculine Conflict / 11

2 / Masturbation / 27

3 / Sharing and Living Out Fantasies / 55

4 / Oral Sex / 85

5 / Semen / 107

6 / Anal Sex / 133

7 / Starry-Eyed Oedipus / 151

8 / Fetishism / 177

9 / Water Sports / 195

10 / Voyeurs and Exhibitionists / 207

11 / Women with Women / 237

12 / Animals / 259

13 / "She Made Me Do It!" / 275

14 / Sharing the Woman with Another Man / 311

15 / Groups / 339

16 / Straight Men, Gay Fantasies / 359

17 / Bisexuals / 375

18 / Homosexuals / 397

19 / Transvestites / 419

20 / Breast and Vagina Envy / 437

21 / Sadomasochism: The Chains of Love / 451

22 / Virgins / 511

1

The Masculine Conflict

This is a book about men who love women.

Women may not easily recognize that emotion in these pages. These are not conventional valentines. His secret garden is not like mine.

A contemporary confusion is that if the sexes are equal, it must mean they are identical; men often predicted I'd find their fantasies similar to women's. We may seek the same goal in fantasy—sexual excitement—but men and women get there by different paths.

A fantasy is a map of desire, mastery, escape, and obscuration; the navigational path we invent to steer ourselves between the reefs and shoals of anxiety, guilt, and inhibition. It is a work of consciousness, but in reaction to unconscious pressures. What is fascinating is not only how bizarre fantasies are, but how comprehensible; each one gives us a coherent and consistent picture of the personality—the unconscious—of the person who invented it, even though *he* may think it the random whim of the moment.

A man has a reverie of meeting a blond woman in a purple nightgown. He doesn't know why the colors are exciting; his unconscious does, but doesn't bother to explain. The man only knows the blonder, the purple-ier, the more heated he grows. Soon he is inventing scenarios of bare-breasted models hired to test new peroxide hair bleaches, supplied by a company that arbitrarily orders all contestants to wear purple underwear. If the plot seems silly, what does it matter? The erotic has its reasons that reason doesn't know.

Like an Einsteinian equation whose logic would take hours to unravel, a fantasy appears in the mind with the speed of light, connecting hitherto seemingly unrelated and mysterious forces in the internal erotic universe, resolving inconsistencies and contradictions that seemed insuperable before. Nothing is included by accident. If the woman is tall or short, if she forgets her birth control pills and so intercourse carries the risk of pregnancy—*if there is a cuckoo clock on the wall*—it is all meaningful to the inventor's heightened sexuality.

In real life, ambivalence abounds. Women want men, men want women; our dreams of one another, fantasies, not only express our most direct desires but also portray the obstacles that must be symbolically overcome to win sexual pleasure. Fantasy is as close as we will ever come again to the omnipotent joys we once knew as infants. In a moment of rage we say, "I'd like to kill you!" This is a fleeting fantasy, a satisfying violent image which expresses the overheated mood of the moment. But how likely are we to pull a gun and do it? It is important to recognize that not all fantasies are frustrated wishes. This is one of the most common misconceptions about fantasy.

The very courage of fantasies in facing up to, and giving relief to, unconscious horrors, can sometimes make them hard to take. In 1975, I met a man who had written a book on men's sexual daydreams. "The material was so awful and creepy," he said, "I couldn't even talk to my contributors on the phone. I made them speak into an automatic answering machine, and then had the stuff typed up. I couldn't even bring myself to correct the galleys." I had not read his book and was not surprised never to hear of it again.

Beneath their locker room camaraderie and famous mutual support systems, it appeared, men were as sexually restrictive and normative with one another as women have traditionally been with their sisters. Wouldn't a woman who does not see men as competitors or sexual rivals have fewer hurdles in accepting male sexuality, no matter what turns it might take? All my life I'd dreamed of men and sought their company. Even more than the eight years I'd spent researching two books on women's fantasies (*My Secret Garden* and *Forbidden Flowers*), I believed this simple, uninstructed love of men was my best credential for undertaking this work.

I found I had awarded myself the palm too easily.

While the sexual fantasies of many men were a pleasure and easily available to my emotions right from the start, others disgusted or frightened me. Many seemed outpourings from macho braggarts out to shock or trap me in filth. I was like the Victorian husband who encourages his wife to tell all. When she does, he leaves her.

Oh, I'd had a few difficult moments in my earlier books with women who were aroused—for instance—by a loss of bladder control; but on the whole I was able to accept any feminine notion, if only on grounds that it came from a woman. When a woman called a cock a cock, talked of being rammed or reamed, described her cunt juices or the sensation of sucking on a dog's erection, any trepidation I might feel was outweighed by admiration: Our side was breaking through the centuries of female silence at last.

But when men used words like cunt lapping or pussy, they aroused early, primitive fears. Louder than the unabashed sensual love the words were meant to express, I heard the harshness and disdain of the street slang. Long before sex and men had entered my life, a woman had taught me to be a lady. "Excuse my vocabulary," more than one man wrote me. At first I would smile at these apologies. I have come to see that my contributors knew me better than I did.

Ladies. Gentlemen. Cunts. Cocks. To put the four words together is to show how little they seem to have to do with each other. How could I respect a man who wanted to be pissed or shit on? While I felt it was life-enhancing for a woman to dream of sex with two men, I felt compassion for the unfortunate woman married to a man so low he ejaculated to fantasies of showing off her cunt to a stranger.

Something in me could not accept men unless they conformed to dreams of my own. The Fantasy Queen had opened a Pandora's box she could not handle.

I do not necessarily expect sex to be pretty; that is to demean it, attenuate its primitive force. But many of these fantasies were more than I wanted to hear. Why, they were filth! Letter after letter left me with a feeling that I wanted to wash my hands. I often did.

Even as I reached for the soap, I had to laugh at myself. Where was my vaunted objectivity? I watched my disgust with fascination. When my editors suggested I clean up my copy, substitute "excrement" for shit, "sex" for fucking, I objected; if I latinized my writing, drew a sharp line between my text and the four-letter language of fantasy itself, I would be joining the very army of inhibitors I was protesting against. And yet, demanding this freedom for myself, cheering it enthusiastically when it was exercised by women, here I was, objecting to it in men.

Today, while I still find some of this material difficult, I no longer see it as a personal affront. It might be said that familiarity freed me; the third time around, the shock is abated. But that is too simple. It would be more accurate to say I could not come to terms with this book until I had won free of the narcissistic desire to see men in a way that enlarged my own view of myself.

All my life I've been haunted by a little girl's voice within that said women needed men—I needed men—more than they needed us. Men could always go off to Singapore or drink alone in bars, but women ceased to exist in their own eyes when men were gone. I watch the ease with which some women today decide to build a life without men (who never lived up to their expectations anyway) in favor of pursuing newly won autonomy. I can understand the sense of freedom born of ridding oneself of the childish—and ultimately false—security that comes from binding oneself to a man; but I do not believe men could ever abandon women so swiftly. In fact, this book has persuaded me that men want women more than the other way around. Toward satisfying their love, need, desire, lust, men will give up more than women will.

Women call themselves the loving sex; we are always waiting for men, always dreaming of them. We need them to put to rest the gnawing anxiety that comes from never being taught a sense of independent worth or self. *Is this love or is it dependency?* When men do offer love, why is it so often felt to be lacking: "Hold me tighter, never let me go," women beg, unable to find in any man's arms the kind of iron security that dependent, passive people need. The point I want to make is this: Is it the man she really wants, or is it the relief from anxiety which he symbolized?

When women can get their emotional needs satisfied elsewhere, don't they often forget about men? Take the familiar picture of a woman who has found such close-close togetherness with her children that father feels left out. How many men do you know who neglect their wives for their children?

Men are trained to find their security in themselves. Women are their emotional outlet, their main source of love. If, as women believe, men are so lucky, so self-sufficient, so free, dominant, and irresponsible, living in an option-filled man's world, why do they give it all up for marriage? Men may resist, but in the end most do marry because they want women more than anything else; if responsibilities, mortgages, ulcers, child care, and monogamy are part of the package they must buy to get women, they'll do it. The thesis of this book is that men's love of women is filled with rage. Observation shows that in the end love wins out over rage.

In the end, I came to see that even people who wrote in an attempt at aggressive sexual contact with me were also moved by a kind of love and desire for connection with, not really me, but a fantasy of woman in general. Distorted love, ambivalent love, love mixed with rage; love nevertheless.

In fact, my research tells me that *men's love of women is often greater than their love of self*. They worship women's beauty to the unhealthy exclusion of their own narcissistic needs. They discredit the male body as aesthetically displeasing, only to be labeled bestial when they adore women's bodies too openly and too enthusiastically. For women's sake, men give up closeness with their own sex, learn to accept female rules and controls; in marriage they take up the lifelong burden of economic support, often leading to an earlier death; they give their place in the lifeboat to their wife.

Since there is always a question of what love means, let me put it this way: Ultimately, men perform the most gallant act of all. At the heart of even the most shocking S&M

fantasy, we find that more often than not, men in a rage at having given up so much turn their fury not against women but against themselves. Any call girl will tell you that more clients pay to play the victim at a woman's hands than the other way around.

In my books on women's sexual fantasies, the single greatest theme that emerged was that of "weak" women being sexually dominated, "forced" by male strength to do this deliciously awful thing, made to perform that marvelously forbidden act, guiltlessly "raped" again and again.

On the surface, this would seem to be a perfect illustration of the symmetry of desire between the sexes. If women daydream of being overpowered into sex, isn't this desire mirrored in the male fantasy of sexual dominance—the demanding brute who can never get enough women? The answer is no.

Rape or force may be the most popular theme in female fantasy (though I've yet to meet a woman who wouldn't run a mile from a real rapist), but men's fantasies of overpowering women against their will *are the exception.* A closer reading will usually reveal that the woman is a volunteer or has given her consent first. Even in the grimmest S&M fantasy, for reasons to be explained in the appropriate chapter, pain or humiliation of the woman is usually not the goal. They are means toward an end: forcing her to admit to transports of sexual joy she has never known before.

If the cliché were true that men "are only out for one thing," the fact is that masturbation or a homosexual encounter is sex, too; so is sex with an animal or a whore, and this usually accompanied by no tears, no limits, no oaths of lifelong fidelity—no strings at all. But the majority of men still dream of sex with a loving woman. Men love women at any price, love women even though, beginning in childhood, it is the female sex which makes the male feel guilty about what he desires most from them. We will see that one of the reasons men choose the masochistic role is that feeling they are wrong to want sex from women, they accept pain as the symbolic price they must pay. Humiliation is a kind of payment in advance for forbidden pleasures.

This brings us to a closer examination of one of the great "givens" of popular psychology—that boys have a far easier time than girls in sexual development. While infants of both sexes begin by loving, needing, wanting, and being satisfied by the female sex—mother—boys are usually thought to derive an advantage from continuing to love women for the rest of their lives.

I would say this is too simple. It ignores the fact that forever after men sense the forbidding shadow of the primitive, preoedipal mother behind every woman to whom they are attracted. To escape this—and not merely for what are vaguely called "sexist" reasons alone—they are usually attracted to women younger than they. Girls, on the other hand, are never quite so frightened about being in an infantile and/or regressive posture with father/boyfriends.

Nevertheless, girls have the psychologically very difficult problem of crossing over into attraction to the male sex, via the relatively later-learned love of father. It is true there is a risk here for women: By entering into a kind of rivalry with mother for the love of dad (men), the girl risks the danger of losing the love of that all-important first person.

As an explanation of women's notorious problems with sexuality, this is very persuasive. No wonder women have always depended on men to take the sexual lead, to "liberate" the female erotic self, to bring the woman to orgasm. Given their straight-line development, isn't sex far more natural for men?

Today, women are learning that nobody gives you an orgasm, nobody makes you sexual, except yourself. This reevaluation of the feminine position has led to a consequent reassessment of the masculine. While men begin by loving women, this supposed smooth path of development ignores an important and inherent conflict: The male lifelong love affair with women leaves him with desire for someone who stands for such ambivalence, who represents such contradictions of flesh versus spirit, that we begin to understand those early Church fathers who based all their theology on notions of the tempting wickedness of women.

While mother may indeed be the first erotic object in the lives of both girl and boy babies (using erotic to mean the full Freudian gamut of love, tenderness, sensuality, sex, warmth, need, glamour, and desire), she is also the first great inhibitor in our lives. It is her job to impose rules on the baby; hers is the thankless task of toilet training us so strictly that we maintain sphincter control even in sleep; it is she who first removes the playful little hand from the genitals. She takes the breast away when it is time for us to grow up to the next stage, makes us eat our vegetables and do our homework. She teaches us civilization and its discontents. A necessary job, and often done with all the love in the world, but nevertheless one that projects her into the child's unconscious as a curiously divided figure. The female sex is the source of love, but also of inhibition, constraint, and guilt.

Switching over to the male sex may be difficult for the young girl; it is complicated by the fact that she does it trailing mother's introjected sexual inhibitions with her. Women blame men for not living up to childish needs that should have been resolved with mother; they displace onto men old nursery furies. If women break mother's sexual rules, they are devastated if the man does not replace her love with his forever. Many women find it easier to direct their furies against men than show hostility to other women/mother.

And yet, all this having been said, women have one tremendous advantage in sexual development that is usually forgotten: Women rarely need to get angry at men for not allowing them, for not offering them, sex. Women do not spend their sexual lives with the gender that represents the great no sayer of childhood.

Is it any wonder that many women, even in these feminist times, continue to say they feel more comfortable around men? "Women," they say, "are too petty, too critical, too competitive and bitchy." In any generalization so sweeping, it isn't difficult to see not reality, but the shadow of the rule-making mother of childhood.

Both boys and girls, of course, are told in words, body language, and above all, perhaps, by silence, that sex is bad; mother doesn't approve. The little girl wants to be like mother. *That* is how women are. She tamps down her sexual desires and tries to be a lady. Her sexuality remains in conflict with her introjected mother—her all-important niceness—all her life long. That is the subject of another book.

What we are concerned with here is the little boy. *He* doesn't want to be like mother. His body, his anatomy, tells him he is different. He knows mother finds one side of him acceptable: the good boy. The other side is bad, dirty, sexual, willful. This aspect must be hidden—but it is stronger, constantly threatening to overwhelm him.

He wants mother to love him. He swears to himself he will never masturbate again. If mother found out, she would abandon him in a rage. But the difference between the boy and his sister is that while both have taken in mother's antisexual message, the boy wants to accentuate his difference by breaking the rules: He dares to do it anyway. He stands self-convicted: a dirty animal, reveling in his sexuality, angry and forlorn in the knowledge that it is unacceptable to women.

The predicament is agonizing. The boy wants sex but feels he is wrong to want it. Women have placed his body at war with his soul.

Only when he gets out of the house, only when he discovers that other little boys are just like himself, does he get enough reinforcement to bear being *bad:* to experiment with breaking mother's rules, to begin to define himself as separate from her, an individual, a man.

This is how he's going to be, just like the guys, not like silly women and their eternal fussing about don't do this, don't do that. Mother's okay; but after all, she's a woman. What does she know?

In the safety of numbers, and away from mother's censorious eye, boys set out to explore their badness—which has become almost synonymous with masculinity. They talk dirty, spit and laugh and smoke together in vacant lots, play pissing games and show each other their cocks, ever egging each other on to do everything that would horrify mother. And all in secret. "That's bad," sister says, stumbling on her brother writing a dirty word on the wall. She speaks with the assurance of her fully introjected maternal

morality. "I'm going to tell Mom." *The boy is resisting
introjecting the same morality.* That's girl stuff. "Get out of
here!" he says to sis. In the brave new masculine world of
nine and eleven, girls are *out*.

Being accused of liking girls, of wanting all that "lovey-
dovey stuff," is to be accused of not being a man. The boy
at boarding school cries every night because he is homesick
for mother. When she comes to visit him, he pushes away
her kisses. "Don't mind your little friends," she says. "They
wish their mothers were here to kiss them." It's true—but
the boy can't risk his newly emerging masculine identity
for a caress. He would rather have the approval of the
other guys who are watching than his mother's. That feeling of male sexual solidarity is one women have always
envied.

My husband tells a story of sitting under an oak tree on
his twelfth birthday; he vividly remembers telling himself,
"This year was better than last year, and that year was
better than the one before. Will life just keep on getting
better and better?" "Of course," he says, "it didn't." He
had reached puberty.

Suddenly, answering the cry of biology, heterosexuality
reenters the boy's life in the form of young girls. It's almost
as if all the old resentments and dislikes of mother's sex
have been forgotten, so pretty are the girls of adolescence—as full of winning smiles and coquettishness as
mother herself once had been.

Naively, filled with trepidation and excitement—is life
indeed going to keep on getting better and better?—boys
wash their faces, comb their hair, and reach for the phone.
Pretty Sally and Jane may be the same sex as Mom, but
they are younger, livelier, and the signals they send out
seem to say they want what the boys want. Until the boys
get too close. Then it becomes, "Yes, I love you, Johnny,
but not when you do *that*."

Mother's old lesson has received new and powerful expression. How can a man not be in a rage with members of
the sex who make him feel dirty and guilty about the very
desires they have gone to such pains to provoke in him?
The conflict in the male psyche is reinforced. With charac-

teristic refusal to sentimentalize love in any of its aspects, Freud, in a little known essay, "The Most Prevalent Form of Degradation in Erotic Life," sadly concludes that men often find supreme sexual excitement in notions of degrading their wives or lovers.

Please don't interpret me too easily, and nod your head, "Oh, I get it, that's the old madonna/whore split that so many men go in for." That is to take a part for the whole. Something more fundamental and inclusive is being discussed here.

Dividing women into the kind you fuck versus the kind you marry is indeed one of the manifestations of male ambivalence—but only one. The masculine conflict is protean: Like the Greek god who gave us the word, the war of love against rage can take as many shapes as there are fantasies in this book.

Mother used to tenderly tuck you into bed at night, reproving you gently for trying to put your hand on her nightgowned breast. Then she blandly went off to share a bed with dad. Oedipal lover, oedipal furies. Women are wonderful, but they drive you nuts, too. The same man who loves women for their maternal sweetness and warmth will invent scenarios in which feminine hypocrisy is sexually degraded down to the man's own bestial level.

Certain phrases sum up a truth so immediate and universal that even the dullest person responds, "Yes, that's right!" One such phrase has become so overworked that even pop song writers hesitate to use it anymore: "You always hurt the one you love." *It is another way to express the masculine conflict:* love versus rage. Perhaps most revealing about this cliché, for purposes of this book, is this: I have never heard a woman use it.

It is here that we have reached the heart of fantasy's enchantment: No matter what men may do to/with their imaginary lovers, her reactions are just the opposite of mother's—*she loves him for it.* "Yes!" she shouts, "more!" A fantasy woman does not reproach her man for letting other men peep at her, for wanting to share her with another guy, for dreaming of her having sex with a dildo or a dog. Fantasy gives men the love of women they want, with

none of the inhibiting feminine rules they hate. No matter
how wild the man's sexual frenzy, the woman does not
punish, but rewards. Love conquers rage.

But rage does not go away. It is a commonplace that
when children hear their parents making love in the other
room, they think they are fighting. "Daddy is killing
Mommy." This is usually shrugged off with a smile—the
naiveté of children. My own hunch is that the child is intuitively projecting his own infantile sexual rage onto his
grown-up parents: This is what he would be feeling if he
were in their shoes (or bed). Sex, frustration, and hostility
have become associated into one complex of feeling.

Men may love women, but they are in a rage with them,
too. I believe it is a triumph of the human psyche that out
of this contradiction, a new form of emotion emerges, one
so human it is unknown to animals even one step lower in
the evolutionary scale: *passion*. It is notorious that a life of
quiet affection between two people usually puts their sexual
desires for each other to sleep. On the other hand, many
warring couples are known to provoke fights and quarrels
because, consciously or not, they find it heightens their
sexuality afterwards.

There seems to be a need in us not only to recreate—
during sex—our earliest memories of physical touch,
warmth, and communion, but also to extract revenge for
all the pains and frustrations suffered during infancy, too.
It may be dismaying, but it is often true that for some
people the white-hot pitch of obsessive desire that may be
the peak experience sex has to offer is reached when hostility is fused with love.

If I have included my own ambivalences in this text,
spoken of my difficulties in handling some of the material,
it is to help the reader understand why he may or may not
agree with me. Knowing where I stand, he can position
himself to the conservative right or more liberal left, without hastily giving himself a name that leaves him stranded
in some life-depleting sexual corner.

Sexuality is fluent and fluid; there are more overlappings
than strick demarcations. One of the great joys of the
erotic experience should be the emotional freedom it con-

fers for working toward separation, individuality, and independence. For this reason, I am suspicious of self-
proclaimed national surveys on sex. Parades of statistics
and demographic samples aggravate our haste to label ourselves in absolutes: monogamous or guilty, 100 percent
he-male or homosexual. More pigeonholes that reduce the
possibilities of life.

And so, having duly cited my wariness of statistics, let
me offer a few for anecdotal interest. Please read them as
scientific proof of nothing at all. I did not ask my contributors for statistics. Here is the invitation as it appeared on
the last page of *Forbidden Flowers:*

> Nancy Friday is now preparing a new book on men's
> sexual fantasies. Any suggestions, comments and fan-
> tasies can be sent to:
> *(My name and address and a guarantee of anonymity
> followed.)*

Of the over three thousand men from whom I heard,
some volunteered personal data, some did not. The table
below represents whatever data I received from the entire
three thousand, not just the approximately two hundred
whom I felt to be most representative and who are included in these pages.

VOLUNTEERED STATISTICS

AGE	*EDUCATION*
11% in their teens	8% high school students
31% in their 20s	13% college students
26% in their 30s	28% college graduates
14% in their 40s	9% postgraduate degrees
6% in their 50s	42% unknown
2% in their 60s	
10% unknown	

MARITAL STATUS	GEOGRAPHIC DISTRIBUTION
41% married	50% Eastern*
34% single	24% Midwest
12% widowed or divorced	6% Rocky Mountain States
13% unknown	20% Pacific Coast*

* As evidence of how figures conceal at least as much as they reveal, a closer examination of the East Coast figures shows that New York alone accounted for roughly one third of all "Eastern" responses. Of all responses labeled West Coast, fully two thirds came from California; I heard from more Californians than men in any other state.

Over 40 percent of my contributors sent me more than one fantasy, often on several different themes. Sometimes I've included them all. Often space didn't permit. If so, my method was to try to sense in which fantasy lay the greatest emotional intensity, discard the others, and then put the fantasy into whatever category it seemed to fit best. Another person might have arranged these chapters differently. Certain rules for selection were obvious. For instance, the S&M chapter is the longest because I received more responses of this type than any other. I also tried to be guided along objective lines of the most recent psychoanalytic thinking by consulting with various therapists I have come to respect over the years—the most consistently valuable help coming from my old friend and colleague, psychoanalyst Richard Robertiello, M.D.

But is any researcher free of conscious and/or unconscious distortion? Even a computer can work only with data that a human being has chose to feed into it. Nor is it the machine that formulates the questions, chooses what weight to give the replies, and then interprets what the figures "mean."

In an effort to determine just how representative my

contributors were, for a year I edited a monthly column on women's fantasies for a national men's magazine. I did this under another name, and asked male readers for contributions. More than a thousand letters came in. This time my correspondents were magazine readers, not book buyers. A small difference, but nevertheless, an entirely new segment of the male population. Their fantasies mirror those in this book, both quantitatively and qualitatively. The same chords were struck over and over again.

In no way can it be said that the men in this book are typical; the average American male has not read at least one of my two earlier books on women's fantasies, where I asked male readers to contribute to this study.

Would the average man be moved to put his private sexual reveries down in writing and send them off to an unknown woman? Perhaps not, but there were enough interested men so that today, four years later, the mail has not stopped. In most cases, the biographical material was as lengthy as the fantasies themselves—proof, I believe, that my contributors wanted me to believe in them as much as their fantasies. Over 80 percent signed their real names and addresses. "I trust your promise of anonymity," they would say.

It might be, of course, that this frankness was partly exhibitionistic. I would say it was more likely that these men admired the candor of the women who appeared in the pages of my previous books, and were taking them as models. These men wanted me to know they existed, wanted someone to "see" them—not in the sense of the flasher, but rather as expression of a desire to reveal oneself at last, good and bad and warts and all, and to be accepted as such. Like so many of my women contributors, the greater number of men finished their letters, "Thank you for letting me write to you."

Boys and girls meet in adolescence like people from alien planets. It often doesn't get much better as we grow older. This book is one of my efforts to grow up. To be rid of my unreal, romantic—and in the end, coercive—ideals for men: my demand that they show me only the face love wears in my dreams. All my life I've felt threatened or anxious or disgusted by certain vaguely thought-about areas of male sexuality. They may not appeal to me today any more than they ever did, but they no longer take away from my life as they used to. The space in which fear once lived is now available to me.

Women, myself included, have for so long been overwhelmed by the inequity of our passivity and second-class citizenship that we never looked beyond the supposed ease of the male top-dog role. But out of the necessary reappraisal of the feminine condition during the past ten years has come another understanding: Given the way the family and society are set up, is the male role so enviable?

Men will be slower to recognize this than women; while many men have begun to question the value of their traditional power, it is not easy to give up roles and positions society has trained you to see as superior. My own belief is that the greatest help men will get in ridding themselves of their fathers' meretricious attitudes will come from women. We live in a time now when many women are working past their own rage, growing beyond the easy stance of seeing men as "the enemy." Women who care about men will see in these pages—not reflections of their own needs and fears—but people like themselves struggling for sexual gratification and love.

2

Masturbation

"I never fantasize while making love. I use fantasies to masturbate, to turn on my lover, or make an otherwise dull moment an interesting one."

"I always fantasize before and during masturbation. When I'm fucking a partner, I place my full concentration on her satisfaction."

"The last thing I need during intercourse is more stimulation, so I never fantasize about sex while fucking. I have to control myself to her desires, so if I think of anything, I think of dull subjects to slow myself down."

"My feeling is that a fantasy during sex would be an intrusion."

Masturbation without fantasy would be too lonely. The statements above are typical of my contributors.

Clinical evidence shows that male desire has a pattern of sharp rise, a high peak, and sharp decline. Men's fantasies follow a similar line, often taking off from some immediate stimulus. Drake (below) says that when he masturbates he has "the best orgasms by fantasizing about a particularly good-looking woman that I have seen that day." The fantasy moves from climax to climax, in short takes, rarely lingering, always hurrying on toward the inevitable sexual eruption.

Men are more prone than women to acting out sexual daydreams, precisely because they often begin so close to reality. "What if that blonde across the room came over to my table, and she did this, and I do that. Then we're joined by that brunette waitress, and she does this incredible new thing. . . ." Often no scenario is needed at all; just the sight of a naked woman, a photo in a magazine, might be stimulation enough. Hard reality, linked with the fastest route to orgasm, is what male masturbatory fantasy is all about.

The last thing most men need, once they are in bed with a woman, is a fantasy to spur them on to greater heights. On the contrary, rather than dream up erotic images, men tend to focus on bringing their partners to their level. To keep from reaching their own climax too soon, they may even do arithmetical sums in their minds.

Nature is wicked to women. Once the man ejaculates, the species has been served. Nature—often called Mother Nature—doesn't care if women come or not. Reproduction can take place either way. Feminine fantasies tend to follow the same curve as female physiology—a slow buildup, a high plateau, and a slow decline. Woman's training adds reinforcement to her biology; raised on a catalogue of inhibitions, she needs sexual fantasy to give her permission to get past her lifelong habit of saying "No" to sex.

It was not ever so. At the beginning of life, both sexes respond equally to erotic stimulation: It feels good to touch your genitals. At two or three, the little boy approaches the little girl (or vice versa). Hey, there is something about her/his body that's different from mine! The hand goes out. There is no guilt, only attraction and curiosity.

Notice how many men in this book trace their first sexual fantasy/sensation/experiment/experience back to that magic age of four or five. These are the oedipal years when sex is burgeoning. How mother reacts to our doctor games, how she answers our questions, becomes prime data for constructing our lifelong ideas about sex. Nowadays, she knows not to overract, and tries to make her answers warm and comforting, but we hear something missing in her voice. Her gestures, body language, facial expression— all the signs we've learned are more important than what she *says*—declare what mother really thinks: Sex is anxious, guilty business. When she took our hands away from our genitals when we were infants, our guilt was not conscious. Now it is.

We don't like to think of four-year-olds as sexual. However, any observant, honest parent knows better. Classic psychoanalytic thinking was that during the so-called latency years of six to ten, sex went to sleep so that other parts of the psyche would grow. Child psychiatrists now think sex is not so much slumbering as it has learned to hide itself more successfully from mother's anxious eyes. Note how many men in this book cite the ages of eight and nine as the time of their first masturbation, fantasy, or sexual sensation.

Other ages that pop out of these pages like old friends are eleven and twelve, the beginning of adolescence (earlier these days than ever). By now the girl has introjected her mother's example; sex has become something to be avoided. The boy wants to be like his father. What he learns from dad validates and contradicts what mother taught him: When dad cracks off-color jokes, mother looks pained. Dad waits till she's not around to tell them. Sex may not be nice, but men do it and women don't . . . at least, not nice women like mom.

The simple erotic curiosity and pleasure of the three-year-old has changed and begun to run on separate and sexually defined tracks, but what the young boy and girl have in common are feelings of shame and anxiety.

DRAKE

I have always had a conflict, apparently irreconcilable, between sexuality and personal ethics, a conflict which (I now realize) could have been avoided had I not been given in adolescence a view of women's sexuality quite remote from the facts. I was brought up to believe that sex was the expression of married love, and that in courtship the man would lead the girl to marriage and to the realization of her own sexual nature.

Girls I regarded as paragons of purity. Photographs of (not really) nude women revealed beautiful curves, with no ugly penis, and nothing messy. Nothing had indicated that women cultivated sex per se. They wanted to have babies and presumably were prepared to "undergo" intercourse, as they were prepared to undergo the pain of parturition.

Meanwhile, my own experience of myself was different. Semen was messy, but I could not keep from masturbating, from enjoying my penis. I had thoughts in which women actually enjoyed seeing, handling, even receiving my penis. Words came into my mind which no respectable girl would tolerate. So my spontaneous sexuality seemed to involve degrading women, and this went right against my deep conviction that we have no right to treat anybody as less than a person. I felt guilty. I invented symbolic subterfuges, in which garters replaced genitalia.

Very gradually, I have discovered that female reality is not far from male reality, though I can't pretend to have completely shed my instinctive response of guilt. When I first saw a real woman's body, I was amazed to find it as complex and as messy as my own. My wife obviously enjoyed sex and indicated a few things she wanted me to do to give her pleasure, but that was still an offshoot of legitimate lovemaking. It left a lot of my own thoughts unaccounted for.

In the last few months I've had my eyes opened by a long and frank discussion with a woman I have a great deal of respect and affection for, who amazed me by telling me that she goes to bed with men regularly because it's "pleasurable," better than masturbation, which she also enjoys a lot. This inspired me to open the subject with my wife, who told me she masturbates frequently—I had never guessed. Without wishing to change my life-style particularly, I just feel relieved to know that I've no reason to feel guilty about my thoughts and feelings, that I am not degrading women by having them.

Planning this letter has been very useful, too. I have never analyzed my fantasies before, and I've found that doing so has taught me a lot about myself—and also made me more ready to accept myself. I have the best orgasms by fantasizing about a particularly good-looking woman that I have seen that day. When the penis stiffens, prior to ejaculation, the images change radically and are quite uncontrollable.

One incident—a real happening, not a fantasy—brings together many of my fantasy themes. As I walked through the city center on my way home, I felt I just had to relieve myself. So I slipped up a darkened passageway. I had already got my cock in my hand when I realized I wasn't alone: Crouched against the wall was a pretty girl, aged about nineteen, pissing. I was no gentleman on that occasion: I stared transfixed at the sight of panties down, garters, pubic hair and urine, my cock getting fatter every second. She looked at me and said, "Enjoying your fucking self?" I said nothing, but I watched while she pulled her pants up and moved off, trying to look dignified. As she reached the street, she turned round and said loudly, "Fuck off." Two friends were waiting for her; I heard their merry laughter.

This incident has many elements I've used in masturbating fantasies since: underclothing, peeing, and using what was then definitely taboo language.

My fantasies are of three kinds: seeing, conversations, and action.

My sight fantasy has had the same decor for as long as I can remember—a wooded area near a stream, with a grassy bank. Three teen-age girls sit down on the grass. I am watching from behind a tree on the other side of the stream. I very rarely make contact with them, but I watch and listen. Sometimes they take off their stockings or discuss ways of keeping stockings up. One, for example, may be wearing a garter belt, and another separate garters. Sometimes one or more of them pees. Once or twice I have "witnessed" mild lesbianism. Sometimes they masturbate! Sometimes they talk about sex, sometimes they use lewd language. Sometimes they see me; I'm masturbating or peeing. They sit quietly, watching me intently like birdwatchers. Sometimes one of them will call me over. If so, the fantasy becomes type two: conversation.

We talk about what I have seen. They are a bit embarrassed, but not for long. They continue their uninhibited stripping or talking, sometimes asking my opinion. Curiously, though they might talk about sex, they take no notice of my cock, which I'm playing with all the time we talk; and we never fuck.

Conversation fantasies betray my fascination with the liberation scene. I find myself talking to young women about their decisions to screw freely, to use "unladylike" language, etc. Are they self-conscious?

Action fantasies are wilder. I go into a store and tell the young lady I want to buy a cunt. "What size?" "You'll have to measure me." I lay my prick on the counter. She calls her friend, who looks at it and says, "I've got just the right cunt for you, please come this way." We go into a changing booth. She slips her skirt off, she has no panties on, just stockings and a garter belt. My mental screen is then filled with the sight of a cunt. Then I fuck.

Images of shocking the bourgeois are quite common. Standing on a crowded underground train with my cock out. A girl facing me undoes her coat. No skirt, no panties. We kiss, gently masturbating each other.

Or I'm in a park with a girl. Sometimes we lie on the grass, and I play with her clitoris. Passersby notice but don't comment. Or she deliberately provokes people, peeing behind a bush (visibly), or saying in a loud voice, "I'm hot, I'm going to take my fucking knickers off."

Near to climax, I do think of fucking. Nothing very precise, just the sensation of plunging into a vagina and ejaculating. That is pure pleasure.

HARRY

At forty-six and a half years of age, I suppose I fantasize more than many men, but then, I have been doing it practically all my life, even before I knew what sex was all about. Back when I could not understand why my little thingy got hard (at about the age of five) I had fantasies.

The anonymity you guarantee is necessary because I work for a real puritan-type man (although he is of a religion with a history of some sexual freedom) who would really fix my wagon if he knew the things about me which I shall tell you. I am also in the military and the powers that be in Washington would get me, too.

I remember trying to look up women's and girls' dresses while "innocently" crawling around under the table at the age of five or so. I did not then know what a pussy was but

I knew that girls and women were different from men "there" and I wanted to find out how.

Also, at the age of nine or ten, I used to play a little game with a neighbor girl in our garage. I called the game "heinie business" and as the slang name implies it concerned itself with playing with the buttocks of my little charmer. Neither of us knew at that time enough to do anything with her pussy.

My sister, who was four years older than I, heard about my activities and one day asked me to explain and demonstrate the game to her. I did and she liked it, but asked me to stuff some rose petals into her pussy. I did that, but remember being turned off by it as I thought that there was something wrong with hers since there was hair growing around it and there was no hair growing around the lovely little slit of my playmate.

We had extremely repressive parents and after that first experiment, my sister was too scared to cooperate with me openly in my little games. However, on many occasions when the folks were out during the day, Penny (not my sister's real name, of course) would pretend to be asleep in her room for an afternoon nap and I would come in and play with her ass.

I never again thought of playing with her cunt, as I still thought all that hair was disgusting. I know now and even knew then that she was not asleep. Since she was so much older than I she was also much heavier than I and I found it difficult to move her about and get her into the positions necessary to remove her panties. At these times I would just express my wishes aloud, like, "I wish Penny would roll over in her sleep so I could get these panties off." Then, lo and behold, a few seconds after that she would miraculously do in her "sleep" just what I had wished she would do. When she was bare, I sniffed, kissed and licked her asscheeks and gently tickled her asshole and the base of her cunt (where no hair was growing as yet) but never went anywhere near her clit. I didn't even know what one was until years later.

During this whole time I used to fantasize about getting various women and girls I knew with their panties off. These fantasies took the form of daydreams that I had some underground laboratory with a magic sidewalk over it which would enable me to look up the dresses of women and girls as they passed overhead. When a pretty one with nicely shaped legs and ass would pass overhead, I would push the button on my control panel and she would slide down a special chute into my clutches. Then I would reassure the victim that I did not intend to hurt her but wanted her to feel good. She would be placed upon an operating table or examining table like the ones in the doctor's office and her legs would be tied into the stirrups. Then I would remove her panties, slide her skirt up around her hips and just sniff, kiss, and lick her ass and cunt for the longest time. In these daydreams, none of the cunts had hair on them, not even those of the grown women. I had not seen a mature pussy and thought that the one of my sister was sick or something because of the hair.

At thirteen years of age, I accidentally discovered masturbation. I was lying in bed one day and playing with my prick because it felt so nice. At the same time I was having my favorite fantasy about the underground laboratory and got a very very stiff hard-on. I kept playing with it and rubbing the head and all of a sudden, I got this wild funny thrill feeling all up and down my spine and my legs twitched and some eggwhite-looking stuff shot out of the end of my cock all over my belly and hand! Wow!!! It felt better than anything I had ever felt before. I tried it again and again and finally did it four times before I had had enough. These four times were in a total time span of about ten to fifteen minutes at the outside. The thing I noticed was that the later thrills (I did not even know that this was called coming) were more severe and intense than the earlier ones even though there was less stuff that shot out of my dick. In fact, the last one, you might say it just sort of *oozed* out of my prick, but it felt just magnificent.

Another of my favorites was the door-to-door one. I was a newspaper boy and I went from door to door collecting for my paper deliveries (only in the fantasy, unfortunately). Anyway, while I was collecting on my imaginary route, there were some neighbor ladies (who really existed at the time) who would invite me to come inside for a soda pop. While I was there they would keep crossing and uncrossing their legs and getting me real excited so my little prick got hard. I would sit bent over to hide this, but the ladies (each one in a separate fantasy but it was always the same reaction on the part of each) would notice it and ask me if it hurt me. I said it did, just a little, and got real red in the face. The lady then told me not to be upset and that she would fix it for me so it would not hurt. Then she would unbutton my knickers and reach inside and play with my cock the way I did myself in bed. Pretty soon it would start shooting that funny white stuff again and I would come in the fantasy just as I did at the moment since I was busy masturbating while having this fantasy.

I have been having many many fantasies since then. In fact I have one about every attractive girl or woman I meet. I have been jerking off averaging at least once a day every day for the thirty-three and a half years since then. There have of course been some days when I was ill in the hospital when I did not do it at all, but I think that the many days of multiple jerkoffs (in addition to regular sex with my wives and various girl friends) make up for that many times over.

BILL

In general my fantasies are not elaborate (and even less elaborate now than when I was younger and more repressed). I am forty-two. I'm not sexually deprived. My wife and I have a very active sex relationship, and love each other very much. With all this, I still fantasize about being made love to by many women at once. This is probably my only recurring fantasy. One pussy on each finger, one on each toe, and one on my cock, and I'm just lying back watching them all.

When I was a kid I used to masturbate and imagine I had a plastic dick (like Plastic Man) and I'd see a woman on the other side of the street and my dick could come out of my pants and fuck her. Also had a fantasy about doing it on a bicycle with a special seat built so you could fuck while pedaling together. (Her skirt covered it all.)

I seemed to fantasize more when I was an adolescent, but don't seem to need to now as much.

I think women fantasize more because they are less involved in reality and have to find more satisfaction in imagination. They tend to stay home while men are more involved in active things. I also think women have more time to spend on fantasies.

Mother's disapproval of her son's sexuality may drive it underground; but resistance, secret and powerful, is built into the boy's very anatomy. When he sees the girl next door with her skirt up, he knows that no matter what Mom says, it feels good. And he knows where.

Like young Harry (above), he may not recognize why his penis has become erect, but he has a vivid picture to put with that sensation next time he touches himself. And touch himself he does, several times a day, every time he pees. There is no way for a young boy *not to know* what it is that arouses him. Soon he will discover that merely touching that barometer of his sexual psyche increases his excitement. Idly playing with himself in bed one morning, he continues the stimulation until this most extraordinary thing happens: He comes! Now he knows how to make it happen, and also what kind of mental pictures—that little girl next door—put him in the mood. Masturbation and fantasy become inextricably tied with sexuality.

Girls do not have young Bill's easy familiarity (above) with their sexual organs, none of the male's specificity or sense of playfulness. Bill thinks it would be fun to have an extendable "plastic dick" and use it right out in public; but from the start, the little girl doesn't want to think about what is "down there" too explicitly. It's something vague, something to be afraid of, that could be lost or damaged if used. "My greatest treasure."

While the four-year-old girl may be aroused when she first sees a little boy peeing behind a tree, she has no physical indication—in short, no erection—to tell her of her arousal in unmistakable terms. Ten years later there will still be nothing more than a moist vagina to tell her—when, for instance, she reads *The Story of O*—what she is feeling. Her hand doesn't automatically go between her legs. She is not used to touching herself, except when she wipes herself

"clean." *In fact, she has never seen it!* How can she connect the picture of the little boy peeing with some specific
part of her body?

By the time young girls and boys meet in adolescence,
they have entirely different masturbatory/fantasy histories.
A boy may enjoy the idea of strolling in the moonlight
with his girl, but when the touch of her breast on his arm
gives him an erection, he doesn't want to prolong the
moonlight walk. He wants to satisfy that erection. But the
girl wants the moment to last forever, to melt into his arms
in a romantic kiss, to keep the feeling she got the last time
her vagina got moist—which was when she saw Robert De
Niro kiss Liza Minnelli. What has this lovely feeling got to
do with Johnny here, who is grossly putting his hand up
her skirt? He's ruining all her lovely feelings! "What kind
of girl do you think I am, Johnny Brown?"

In women's fantasies the men do not seem real, but ac-
tors sent from M-G-M. They are usually not friends or
lovers from her present or past, but amorous strangers. In
this way, the encounter becomes like the intimate conversation with someone on an airplane: All may be revealed
because you will never see him again. Depriving the fantasy partner of a familiar face, making him wear a mask, or
having everything happen in the dark are some of the most
popular methods women use to handle guilt in fantasy. Editors of the new women's magazines tell me they still have
not solved the problem of how to photograph naked men
in a way that will satisfy their readers. The problem in
part, they say, is technical: Male genitals are hard to photograph. Also, women have no cultural tradition that
makes it okay to look. But I suspect there are reasons that
go deeper into feminine psychology. The definition of the
demon lover for women is that he is never seen with photo-
graphic clarity.

Men react in just the opposite way—hence the great
popularity of the nude in girlie magazines. The more a
man can see, the closer the dream is to reality, the more
specific, the more real the woman—the more exciting.
Most of the fantasies in this book are built upon memories
of real women. It is the boyhood neighbor next door who
lights up a man's imagination, the first woman with whom

he ever had oral sex; he goes over and over his memories of his father's girl friend or the great fuck he had last night, reliving and enhancing actual events until they take on a fantasy quality. The faceless stranger may be the prime feminine sex object, but a man likes to identify whom he is in bed with.

I find this ironic; it neatly turns the tables on the usual idea that only women want (I hate this phrase) "meaningful relationships" while men revel in anonymous one-night stands. Again and again, men write that the casual, unemotional fuck means little. The popular superstition is that bachelors lead the life of healthy rabbits. The fact is that in their fantasies, at least, men who have had a certain amount of experience often shy away from the boredom unto death of hit-and-run sex—an idea fully in accord with the evidence that unattached men consistently rank among the population's highest statistics on depression, breakdowns, and suicide.

Fantasies in which the woman is known, specific, practically tangible (as in a pinup photo)—*that* is the degree to which she arouses desire. Lester (below) tells us that his fantasies are usually about his girl friend or some other specific woman. If she becomes vague, when "sometimes the woman switches identity abruptly," this "tends to turn me off." Allan (below) may remember his first sexual experience because it was so taboo shattering, but he, too, treasures it as a fantasy because the woman is so specific.

For some men, nothing ever captures the intensity of those early masturbatory fantasies. It isn't that a man prefers auto- to heterosex; but before girls entered his life, everything seemed possible. A loving woman is more satisfying than one's own hand, but the teen-age fantasy of the seductive older woman next door inviting you in for more than cookies, is exhilaratingly free of the strings that the real girls he knows attach to sex.

Many women complain, "My husband hasn't had any new erotic ideas since he was sixteen. With him, it's still biff, bam, thank you, ma'am." I would like to say that no man can be more than 50 percent responsible for carrying naive techniques into his mature years. If the woman doesn't tell him what she wants, if she fakes sexual response, if she is too inhibited to try something new, why should he change? Of course his actions will still have the same pace as those first masturbatory fantasies in which his own excitement, his own rush to the goal, was all. He may want to slow down, he may try to work at bringing her along with him; but without some idea of what she really wants, how is he to know that one idea is better or worse than any other? Why make the effort?

ALLAN

When I was a child of five or six years, we had a live-in housekeeper, as my parents worked in their small department store. The housekeeper must have been forty to fifty years old at the time. My earliest recollection was her putting my penis in her mouth and sucking ever so gently after she bathed me, and I was having a thrill like nothing else. She would always ask me if I felt good, when she knew I finished. By the age of thirteen I was having intercourse as well as oral sex with her. At that time, dad hired more help in the store and mother came home to care for me.

When I masturbate I fantasize the woman is around sixty years or so (the older the better), and I am a young child and she fondles me and sucks me and I suck her till her body shudders, and she moans like our old housekeeper did.

To this day, I will only make love to older women (I am forty-five and married) and enjoy sex better, much better than with younger women.

It seems the older the woman, the more experience she has, the more I enjoy it.

LESTER

I'm thirty, a white graduate student in psychology, unmarried, and have lived with a girl friend for three and a half years. I started masturbating when I was about ten or eleven, and still do it (when I have no girl friend) just about every day. When I have reasonably steady sex with a woman, of course I masturbate less often. No feelings of guilt, etc.; it's fun, pleasant, a release. I very rarely fantasize except when I masturbate; then I always do, in fact, I must in order to come. When I'm walking down the street I try not to fantasize because if I do, I get too uncomfortably horny, with no means to satisfy myself. When I'm having sex I concentrate on myself and my partner; a fantasy would be an intrusion during sex.

I usually imagine that my girl friend or some girl that I've seen recently and I are making love, in various positions and places. Sometimes I'm lying in a bed, and she'll come into the room and start taking her clothes off without saying anything, and we'll start running our hands over each other, then start having sex. Sometimes I'll come up behind her (she knows and wants it, but doesn't respond until I touch her) and enter her from the rear. Sometimes we'll be in the shower, outside, etc. Sometimes she's passive, sometimes I am, all depending on my mood. We'll have oral sex, genital, you name it, I'll be on top, she'll be on top, whatever.

Sometimes the woman switches identity abruptly; this tends to turn me off a little, I'm not sure why, perhaps there's a break in concentration. The best sessions of masturbating are those in which I fantasize the woman so well that she's virtually real; I see, feel, even smell her.

I've found that I'm unable to enjoy sex with a woman toward whom I do not at least feel affection. At any rate, they're all straightforward, heterosexual, audienceless encounters, imagined by me while I am lying (usually) on the floor, on my stomach, thrusting myself back and forth (no hands, I've tried it that way, but I can't see the woman clearly enough to enjoy it when I have to pay attention to my hands as well as my cock).

Having a secret from your parents, learning they don't omnisciently know what is on your mind, strengthens the feeling that you have a life of your own. Even the stealth with which masturbation is done works for separation. Adolescence is the classic time of family upheaval, because sex is making a tremendous effort to give us the desire for a life of our own. It is fortunate that the drive is so powerful, because what it must fight—the squelching, suffocating "enemy" we want to escape—is, after all, the family we have always loved. "You used to spend more time at home," mother says. "We used to be such good friends. Now all these secrets. Don't you love your old mom anymore?" How can any private act be done without guilt after a speech like that? Loss of love is once again being threatened as punishment for growing up, becoming ourselves, pursuing our own individuality.

While a son's sexuality may be frightening to mother, it is less so than a daughter's. The adolescent girl reawakens mom's own youthful anxieties. She is a reminder that mom is getting older, that men (dad included) are looking at younger women in a way that mother may never see again. Besides, a girl can become pregnant. Mother becomes even more anxious about the girl's blossoming sexuality, but decides maybe she'd better keep a wary distance from her son's. Men have always been a mystery to her, and she is afraid of doing damage to her boy's still-tender masculinity. An anxiety she communicates to him is further watered down by another message: "Be a man, stand on your own two feet. Don't come running to me with every little problem you have." She is giving him more license for a life of his own than she dares give her daughter.

A boy can afford to do things mother might not like because one of his goals is to establish exactly how *unlike* her he is. When he goes out with his friends, he gets reinforcement from all the other guys—they, too, are fighting identification with mother. Masturbation may be the great female secret, but it becomes a rite in male bonding. Breaking mother's rules and finding that despite her warnings the experience is not awful—you don't go blind, but feel pleasure instead—reinforces the notion that it pays to make up your own mind about what is good or bad. Privacy may be difficult to find at home—mother changes the sheets, launders your clothes, and goes through your bureau drawers—but it is worth fighting for. To be independent pays off directly in sexual pleasure. "I jerked off twice yesterday." "Oh, yeah? Three times for me!" "Let's go behind the garage and do it some more, right now!" No wonder so many men in this book recall early group masturbation with such enormous satisfaction.

Nevertheless, inhibitions established early in life can never be put totally to rest. In fact, I often think proliferation of girlie magazines is a result of this problem. The flagrant covers seem to be saying, "Don't be guilty about a fantasy of naked women and playing with yourself. Millions of other guys who buy this magazine are doing the same thing." It is a message that combines bragging and daring, making the customer feel he's not some poor lonely soul jerking off because no girl is available to him; instead, he's but one of an army of sexy, go-to-hell men who don't mind having a bit of fun any way they can.

We have come a long way from the early part of this century, when masturbation was considered so physically harmful and morally reprehensible that even the Boy Scout manual (1910–1945) warned against it.

And yet if times are changing, I do not believe they are changing as rapidly as most people think. Clifton (below) is only nineteen, born well after World War II—but he describes his parents as "puritanical." Is it surprising he says he is "embarrassed" by his own sexuality? Hal (below), too, is so inhibited that he performs a kind of masturbation I'd only heard about before from women. In a kind of sly maneuver that is obedient on the surface but rebellious beneath, the parental admonition against touching the genitals is taken literally. Lester (above) rubs himself against the sheets. No hands, no guilt. Don (below) goes so far as to tell us his mother would become "hysterical" if she found evidence of his masturbation. Is it surprising that he married "a nice girl" who does not like sex?

If many parents today have learned to speak with a certain tolerance about autoeroticism, one senses that in their gut they feel some of their mother's anxiety. We are all our parents' children. Jud (below) tells us that one of his favorite fantasies is to imagine women applauding his masturbation. A member of the female sex once made him feel guilty about it; to have women "cheer him on" instead, now that he is grown, is supremely satisfying. Research in child rearing today defines masturbation not as an embarrassing phase the child will outgrow if left alone, but as a "normal" part of sexual growth. I have rarely heard even the most enlightened parent recognize masturbation as a mighty force for independence.

CLIFTON

I am a nineteen-year-old college student and I am rather quiet around most people until I really get to know them. I come from a farm and pretty puritanical parents so, even though I have very strong sexual feelings, I always felt somewhat embarrassed by them. I have had two sexual experiences, so I'm not a virgin, but they were emotionless and unfulfilling.

I suppose fantasy has always played an important part in my life. My favorite fantasy is about this girl who lives in my dorm. She lives on the same floor that I live on. Although we've never met, I found out from someone that she kind of digs me because she thinks I look like Elton John (which I do).

My fantasy is that some night, I would walk by her door and hear Elton John music playing real loud inside. I would open the door without her knowledge and see her lying in her bed in only a little light and staring at a picture of Elton John (of course she has no clothes on). She's rocking back and forth to the music and I can tell that he really turns her on.

Gently I take the picture away from her and she's so wrapped up in him that she thinks I am Elton John. She pulls me on top of her. I start kissing her with my tongue and everything and touching her all over her gorgeous little body. She just moans a lot and spreads her legs apart. Then we fuck for all we're worth and I have a shattering climax. When she comes, she screams out "ELTON!!!" loudly and holds on to me tightly.

Even though I have been told before that I look a lot like Elton John, after I found out that she really got off on Elton John, most of my fantasies have centered around being him, on stage, at parties, and in bed.

HAL

My wife asked me to send in the fantasy that I used to have before I knew her or even went to bed with another girl. When I fantasized in my dad's house, I would masturbate stomach down on the bed, rubbing myself on the sheet. I was very quiet so no one might hear and I always felt guilty.

I am twenty and my wife is nineteen. We've been married one year, but had sexual relations for three years.

This was my fantasy: There is a back door to my room where during the night a strange girl happens to slip quietly through. She sneaks slowly across the floor to my bed where I am sound asleep but I wake up as she is carefully lifting the blankets and I feel her presence. I am not sure why she is here so I pretend to be asleep, while she crawls beneath the covers to my hardening cock. I feel intense desire as her hot mouth comes closer and closer until it envelops my dick. She sucks my rod with burning passion until I shoot my semen into her waiting mouth. Then she slips out of the bed with a satisfying look in her eye, turns and leaves as quietly as she came.

DON

Masturbation is gradually gaining social acceptance as a legitimate sexual practice, but I am often amazed by the number of men who feel positively threatened by it, both in themselves as well as in their wives or girl friends.

I am a male of fifty-eight, middle-class background, university, etc., who discovered at age four that the square "trap door" seat in a child's pajama sleeper made playing with himself very difficult. The repeatedly torn-off buttons were the clue which attested to this activity—a near-hysterical mother, the beginnings of perpetual guilt complexes, etc. I'm sure you get the picture. This heavy burden of guilt stayed with me all through childhood and adolescent years until at age twenty-seven, the cloud was miraculously lifted by a girl friend who willingly confided that she had also been enjoying masturbation for years and felt certain that everybody did it.

Now for fantasies. I have never used them during intercourse, but they have always been a necessity for masturbation. At age four or five with no sexual experience to draw on, I used anything that seemed to have (although I didn't know the words then) sexual, anal or genital significance. Over the years, my best fantasies were really nothing more than the memory of a "good" experience or a good experience embellished only slightly. One of the earliest of these and the very first that invoked a female occurred one night when my parents were out and the maid, May, was to bathe me and put me to bed. I had enjoyed the warm slipperiness of her soapy hand around my genitals which she prolonged somewhat more generously than my mother ever did. When she had dried me off and put me into the hated sleeper, my child's instinct made a daring decision. Indicating that she should leave the trap door unbuttoned, I led the way to my bedroom, leaned back against the headboard and unashamedly masturbated to orgasm in front of May, who made no attempt to stop me but simply sat on the foot of the bed and watched. I suppose it took about ten minutes. Being able to get at my cock without the usual restriction of clothing had made it unique. Once, May asked me if it felt nice. When it was over, she tucked me in, kissed me good night, and told me I was naughty but that her girl friend's little brother often did the same thing. She never gave me away to my mother, and the experience was never repeated, but it became my favorite fantasy for masturbation for a long, long time. Only years later did I come to understand the meaning of the flushed avid (envious?) look on May's face as I brought myself off!

Having no sisters, I was always wildly curious about

girls. By the time I got to kindergarten I invented the fantasy of being bathed with another child. (I was in fact often bathed with my kid brother.) In the fantasy, my mother would miraculously leave the bathroom and my little brother and I with our bodies all nicely soapy slippery would stand up and embrace each other, bringing our genitals into opposition with each other. I must have used this fantasy for more than a year. In my mind, I went from my brother to other boys and ultimately to girls. The latter seemed to be the most fun even though at that age, I imagined them to have penises too! Female teachers when they were pretty were finally the greatest turn on, because being older they knew more about it. In these fantasies, I don't recall that my imaginary partner reached climax, but I always did. When I discovered, thanks to a maid who exposed herself to me while urinating, that girls were "different," the fantasy took a whole new turn, even though I didn't know then that girls had a very special place for a penis to fit.

By age twenty, still a virgin, I had had a succession of enchanting teen-age affairs—but since nice girls didn't have sexual organs and certainly didn't fuck, I didn't even attempt to fondle a breast or introduce "French" kissing. I didn't even feel free to fantasize my latest love for masturbation purposes, usually resorting to her sister or one of her less attractive girl friends instead. One's love had to be kept on a special pedestal.

Age twenty-seven was a turning point, however, when I finally discovered that nice girls did have sexual organs, some at least liked to fuck and masturbate, and by thirty I had discovered one lovely girl who in response to my sucking her pussy to orgasm insisted on returning the favor. This incident is still one of my favorite fantasies even though it happened almost thirty years ago. This is particularly true in view of the fact that the girl I ultimately married turned out to have a very low sex drive, would have no part of oral sex—active or passive—and would fuck in only the missionary position. Sexually our marriage went from bad to worse and although it has endured for twenty-seven years, there has been no sex whatsoever for more than five years. Masturbation has been the only thing that saved me from the nuthouse.

In closing, I might say that in general I feel that I am probably "worse" than "most men." On the other hand, while that may be true, there are probably quite a few who are just as "bad" as I am.

JUD

I am fifty-one years old and a widower of three months. I spend a lot of time on the road away from home and naturally resort to masturbation to relieve my sexual tensions, and that's about once a day even at my age. My wife and I had a fairly good sex life, we tried almost everything possible and learned more as time went by.

But enough, for now to my fantasy.

The one most often that comes to mind is thinking why women don't have doe parties like men have stag shows. Then I wonder what a woman's reaction would be if I performed for them. In my mind there are about six or eight women fully dressed (I prefer them in dresses and not in pants). I am totally nude in front of them. They look me over and discuss with each other what they like about a man. Then after a while I spread two sheets of newspaper lengthwise in front of me on the floor and then kneel at one end and the women place their marks on the paper and place a bet on how far I can ejaculate and the one that comes closest wins the bet. I then proceed to masturbate while they watch and cheer me on.

I have realized my fantasy once with my wife. I so enjoyed the look of fascination on her face while she watched me masturbating, that when I finally came, it shot out of me with such force that we were both surprised and the furthest drop away from me was two feet eight inches. I've tried this many times by myself but could not come close to it.

To continue with my fantasy: After this, the women are more relaxed and more eager to look me over and touch me and examine me closer and of course this is needed to get me ready for the next part. When I am ready again, I lay down on a table where all the women can get around and be ready. Now they each take turns in masturbating me for one minute at a time and the one that makes me come when she has her hand on my penis wins the pot.

At times this fantasy varies with me licking their pussies in whatever position they desire while others watch. This is one reason I prefer dresses and if they wear stockings held up by garter belts, so much the better.

If I have no feminine companionship I enjoy masturbation. When I have a chance to relax by myself, I like to be completely nude laying on the bed, reading a good sex book. With one hand slowly jerking and manipulating my penis and at times varying the speed, I can have an erection for hours. Finally when I am ready, I put the book down and fantasize and concentrate on what I am doing and have a real strong ejaculation.

If a marriage is going badly, the husband often throws himself into his work, but may masturbate when alone. Not so his wife. Her therapist may encourage her to masturbate; perhaps she will read one of the new permission-giving books on female sexuality. But she has trouble with the idea. Sex and love have always been synonymous in her mind. Telling her to masturbate now is like telling her to get used to substituting self-stimulation for the love of another person. She also feels let down after all these years of living up to her side of the bargain. She has been a "nice girl," a good wife. Her husband has welched on the payoff. Ergo, she is angry at sex, too.

Instead, she will work harder at home, give even more hours to charity, amassing points for being a good mother and member of the community. (Society never gave her points for being sexual.) She may not enjoy community work, she may be boiling inside and have migraines—but at least she is doing what she was raised for. Her husband may find his hand a lousy substitute for a woman, but he doesn't take masturbation as a sign of his failure as a man. He is angry at her, not at sex.

I remember a summer weekend when I was single. I woke in the night to find my lover was not in bed. I heard noises. When I went into the living room of his summer cottage, I found him lying in the dark, masturbating. I was filled with uncontrollable rage. We'd had sex that night; in fact, our sex life more than anything else held us together.

He tried to placate my anger. Nothing he said could make me feel better. My fury was not only due to him making me feel a failure as a woman, but also because, by stimulating himself, he was making me unnecessary. In those days, the gift of sex was, I thought, my greatest power. I had so little idea of other values in my identity that I saw his masturbation as a total rejection of me.

Women have the notion that any kind of sex is available to any man at almost any time, even if he has to pay for it. This ignores the fact that some people, like Julius (below), are just too shy to approach a woman under any circumstances. He has to make do with masturbation and fantasy. Even highly sexually active men may at times prefer masturbation. For instance, the very notion of walking across a hotel lobby with someone who is not his wife can give a man the shakes. Fears of discovery, shame, guilt (the wife will happen to be in the lobby and spot him), are just too high a price to endure. Fantasy and masturbation are substituted, a safe route to the desired release.

The thought that sexually happy people, like married couples, don't *need* masturbation is puritanical. The italicized word gives it away: only teenagers, maladjusted loners, men in jail, etc., *have to* masturbate; it's no more fun than taking medicine. The truth is that masturbation is simply a choice, a variation, another form of sex, not a substitute for it.

Even men who have half a dozen women available to them may choose to masturbate. Because I would never dream of masturbating with my summer lover in the next room—who *needed* it?—I took his behavior as a comment on my inadequacy.

Burt (below) says he masturbates in secret from his wife once or twice a week. Even though their sex life is good,

"It would upset her if she thought she wasn't taking care of me completely." But what if left over in Burt's imagination was desire for another woman? How could Mrs. Burt take care of that "completely"? Fantasy and masturbation often give our partners something we cannot. To demand that we be all and everything for someone else is inane.

It might be asked, "Is Burt hurting his wife?" No, he is simply doing something for himself. He has been masturbating all his life; of course he feels free to continue to masturbate now, married or not, good sex life or not. He is no more rejecting his wife than if he occasionally went to a movie alone.

In fact, isn't Burt willing to encourage his wife in the same pleasure? If she won't masturbate, it is not his fault. His wife resolutely repeats that *he* is all she needs for good sex. She is not interested in fantasy, not interested in masturbation, "only him." Is this a genuine expression of erotic desire, or another chain of dependency?

Burt is being made to feel he should be grateful, once again, to a woman for all she has done for him. He knows that if his wife found out about his harmless pleasure, she would not be just hurt, but angry. Must not he be angry, too? Here is the masculine conflict again: He likes the erotic charge he gets from masturbation, but his wife makes him feel guilty about it. In choosing not to masturbate herself, despite all Burt's urging, Mrs. Burt is exercising her right, of course. But isn't it self-defeating? She wants to be all the sex her husband needs. She starts out with a no. A story about how two people lose because of one mindless bit of prejudice.

In later chapters we will see that watching a woman masturbate is one of the greatest of all masculine turn-ons. By breaking the rules, the woman has joined the man in expressing unfettered desire. The gap between love and lust has been bridged, the conflict resolved, and only excitement is left.

JULIUS

I was surprised to find out that women have thoughts or fantasies running through their minds, as I do. I thought my fantasies were abnormal, perverted. This made me feel like some kind of monster. I am thirty-four years old, live alone, and never had sex with a girl, due to twenty-two years of guilt and being ashamed of myself. Whenever I start a relationship with a girl it always ends with us being good friends. I figured I had no sex appeal and that women could tell, some way, but I don't know how, of my fantasies. I feel a lot more relieved knowing that some women have just about the same fantasies that I have.

Around the age of twelve I first learned how to masturbate and it was completely by accident. I was taking a bath and for some reason, I guess to wash it, I put my penis under the faucet, letting the warm water splash over it. It started to grow in size as I played with it and all of a sudden I got this great feeling, but had no idea what it was all about. At that age I read comic books a lot, and happened to buy one of a jungle nature, with a Tarzan-type woman as the heroine. Whenever she was captured by the savage natives, they tied her in some way. This gave me a hard-on and I masturbated. I just knew that there had to be something dirty about something that felt so good, and especially having to imagine or see a woman tied up. No one ever told me about sex, I had to learn about it from bits and pieces, sometimes with the wrong conclusions. At the age of sixteen or so I thought I had it all figured out. To make a girl pregnant you fuck her up the ass. I still wonder how I ever believed that! As the years went by I would buy magazines, like the detective ones with women tied up on the covers. The pornography of the day, around 1960, was very mild, but I finally happened on a book with an ad in it for bondage pictures of women to order by mail. Needless to say I ordered some, and have been buying pictures, magazines, and movies of this sort ever since, but always with a deep sense of guilt. During the last four or five years, bondage has finally come out into the open, and the material on it helps me in my fantasies. These fantasies sound pretty wild, but anyone who knows me can tell you that I'm a very gentle person.

Hearing a knock on my door I open it and standing there is a beautiful woman whom I have never seen before. She tells me that she wants me to fuck her, but only if I tie her up. She comes in and we strip one another, both thinking of what is to come and already getting excited. I get some rope nearby and we both go into the bedroom, and she lies down on the bed. With each fantasy I tie her differently, but she is very willing to be tied up each and every time, cooperating all the way. I am getting a terrific hardon as I tie her and she is about to have an orgasm. Finally when both of us can stand it no longer, and depending on how I have tied her, I fuck her, getting and giving the best fuck that any man and woman can have. If I have her tied in such a way that I can't get into her, I use a vibrator or dildo up her cunt and maybe her ass too, to give her an orgasm. I let her have one orgasm after another while I masturbate watching her roped-up body squirm in sexual ecstasy.

Another fantasy along the same lines is wrestling with a woman while both of us are nude, and she overpowers me and ties me up, or I overpower her and tie her up. Then whoever is in control stimulates then masturbates or fucks the other.

What I have tried to convey in this letter is the deep sense of guilt that one can conjure up in his mind and build out of all proportion as I did.

BURT

My wife has always been less interested in sex than I. Could be because her parents were so strict with her. So, right from the beginning, we haven't had sex as often as I'd like to. I have no trouble coming with her—just seeing her nipples jut against her sweater makes me horny.

Sometimes when I wake up with a hard-on and she's too sleepy to get interested, I use a favorite situation to help me get off.

I'm walking along a sunny beach by myself, wearing a string bikini that hides nothing. The cool air is blowing in from the water but I like it that way. Suddenly I see a beautiful woman lying face down on a towel behind a sand dune, out of the wind. She's wearing a very brief two-piece suit with practically nothing but a G-string over her ass.

I walk over and talk to her. When she raises herself up, I realize she has unfastened the top of her suit so she can tan evenly, and I can see all of her beautiful breasts. They're big with rosy-brown tits surrounded by pink dimpled circles. She smiles at me and moves over to let me share her towel.

I straddle her back with my hands cupping her breasts, squeezing and massaging and pinching her nipples until they're hard and engorged. Of course my cock is bulging against my leg. I slide under her and mouth her tits, licking and nipping at them until she really starts to wiggle. She slips off my briefs.

Then I roll her over and kneel over her ready to do a sixty-nine, but first I guide my long cock gently into her open mouth. It's really big and pulsing and alive with excitement. She licks its throbbing purple end and I'm almost ready to spill my load. But I hold off while I slide my lips down her belly and untie her G-string. I bury my face in her soft curly bush. I can smell her cunt and can hardly wait to get into it, but first I let her take my hard cock in her little hands and pull it deep inside her mouth where she slides it up and down, moving the skin, while her nails rake and squeeze my balls. I'm nearly crazy by that time, wanting her.

Finally, I get into her cunt and wow! it's everything I hoped for—all juicy and slippery. I spread her legs as far apart as they'll go and just look at that beautiful pink pussy before I come down onto it with my mouth. I reach out my tongue to lick around the soft lips and slide it in and out of her private opening. I kiss her little clit and nip at it while she squirms and wiggles her ass around under me. Then I really suck at her and I feel all hell break loose when my load comes off in her mouth and she heaves her ass up off the ground and practically drowns me with her sweet juice.

Finally, after sucking and licking her up, I turn back and cuddle her in my arms and we go to sleep with the sun drying the sweat on our bodies.

Often I don't get past the part where she starts licking my cock before I come, but I really like to go all the way through. It's like rockets going off!

My wife and I make it together real good, but she does have some hang-ups about sex. She was reared with the idea she should "save it for your husband." When I met her, she almost wiped out the first time I stroked her clitoris and she had an orgasm. We gradually worked into a good relationship although she is still unable to masturbate. I masturbate about once or twice a week in the shower—I don't think she knows it. I think it would upset her if she thought she wasn't taking care of me completely.

Fantasy always helps me enjoy sex more and to enjoy masturbation. My wife says she doesn't need fantasy—that I am all she needs for good sex (notice that this still is part of the idea "save it for your husband"). In fact, she hardly glanced at your two books. She actually does use fantasy because after reading a porno book on sex, she will be as hot as hell.

3

Sharing and
Living Out Fantasies

Perhaps the greatest misconception about sexual fantasies is that they are suppressed wishes. This confusion between thought and deed is evident in Leon's first words (below). He says he fears he might be "perverted" in actuality because he *imagined* having a homosexual experience and sharing his wife with another man. "I think, therefore I am" may have been true for Descartes; it is not for fantasy.

Out of this confusion is born the urge to share our fantasies with our lovers. "Since this is how I really am, you should know, and I'd feel better if you knew." The subsequent step, of course, is to put these "suppressed wishes" into action. After all, once you've taken the plunge and shared the fantasy in words, isn't it cowardly or puritanical not to experience what you "really" always wanted? No.

An intense inner life is a form of power, a way of defining identity, keeping a place where you live. Some fantasies are best kept forever to yourself. Others? Well, presumably you know your lover well; you know how much he/she wants to hear about what goes on in your secret mind. Even more caution should be taken in deciding which fantasies might well be lived out.

First of all, you have to decide why you want to tell your fantasy. It could simply be for a heightened sexual experience. However, the desire often contains the hope of reversing old hurts. The conflict with parents was how to have a sexual life while retaining their love. The solution was to keep the erotic self hidden. In reaction, now we want to say to our mate, "If you love me, you will accept these bizarre erotic ideas of mine, and not get hurt or angry or stop loving me."

There is a kind of child's blackmail here. Whether your

partner can or cannot accept your fantasies has nothing to do with love. To ask it in the name of love is a throwback to old, infantile desires for symbiosis; the need to feel that mother knows everything you are thinking, *and it is all right*.

One of the reasons we could not trust our parents is that they kept their sexuality secret, giving us no clear model to follow that would let us feel both sexual and safe. It is not surprising, therefore, that most people keep to well-blazed trails: the missionary position, orthodox heterosexuality.

But the sexual force is not interested in safety. Freud called the first stage of life "polymorphous perverse." At birth infants are so undifferentiated that they have the capacity to receive erotic stimulation at every aperture of the body and any area of skin: from either or both sexes; from animals, food, objects, colors, currents of air, gradations of temperature. As we grow older, become socialized, and develop identity, the satisfactions we pursue become more specific.

And yet we live in a world under constant erotic barrage. How can we not find all sorts of notions floating through our minds? Encounters in everyday life, the engines of commerce, the seductions of the movies and TV—all work day and night to seed our minds with startling sexual images. The fact that a man writes solely about one kind of fantasy does not mean he has no others. He may want to reinforce his sexual image of himself by telling me a daydream about the seduction of the Queen of England—and choose not to mention that he also toys with notions of seducing Philip. Some fantasies are suppressed because they do not conform to public ideas of good and bad. Others are repressed—totally forgotten—because they threaten to arouse old oedipal fears. Even in psychoanalysis, where fantasies are one of the prime roads to therapy, patients may keep their most meaningful fantasies (sexual or not) hidden from their doctor for years. How can we be frank with others when we have trouble being frank with ourselves? Deep within this hidden, fermenting jungle, the polymorphous perverse lives on, giving energy, glamour, and that rush of secret, thrilling guilt to our fantasies.

Popular wisdom says nothing should be kept hidden between lovers. "Let it all hang out." Something more primitive—to my mind, something of the ancient wisdom of the race—tells most of us to remain discreet. There is a big difference between contributing sexual thoughts to be published anonymously and sharing them with a lover. Like the straying husband "confessing" to his wife about his latest affair, or one of those "brutally frank" talks in which you inform someone of faults no one else has mentioned, what purports to be honesty may be in the service of making you feel better, not the other person.

Fantasies express the forbidden, and so are exciting. They are taboo, and so are also anxiety laden. Telling them to someone promises to "double the kick but divide the guilt," as I've heard it put. My own feeling is that this is more a clever verbal formula than a description of reality.

Nevertheless, it is a seductive idea to a lot of men. It isn't women's tight togetherness the husband wants; he wants her love, yes—but he wants some freedom, too. While sex makes him feel closer to her, it also gives him a shot of adrenaline. After a wonderful morning of lovemaking, he bounds out of bed, revitalized, and goes off for a Sunday golf foursome with the boys. When the honeymoon is over, she sees his resumption of any relationships that exclude her as betrayal. Little wonder that in a favorite male fantasy, the heroine is not the woman who clings desperately, but one who displays a taste for adventure or freedom, a sexual willingness so insatiable she will masturbate, take a dog to bed, or seduce a stranger on the street. "If you love me," the man says, "we'll answer that ad in the swingers' newspaper for a nice quiet little four-way orgy." It is not that he loves her less; but if she will help him put a little more space and air into the marriage, he will love her more.

To the woman, it's crazy to think she would be showing her love by accompanying him to an orgy. Anything that threatens to divide her from him, that weakens the bonds between them, is frightening. She has been trained in symbiosis, to see her love expressed not by taking an independent road, but by being a faithful partner.

Even his fantasies about imaginary women—she knows what he's really thinking about Charlie's Angels—hurt her feelings. "I suppose you'd really like to have sex with one of them, not me!" she cries, knowing it sounds silly, but unable to contain the fear that any attraction on his part to another woman inevitably means he will desert her.

Oh, she has her own stray and randy thoughts, all right. But the only way she could go to an orgy with him would be if she didn't love him at all.

Ironically, this feminine training that says love is best demonstrated by being tied to the man as tightly as possible can lead women to want to share *their* fantasies with him. She doesn't want to hear his about the blonde next door, because that separates him from her; but to keep something from him as intimate as her erotic reveries—to have any part of her not totally permeated by him—is too lonely. Mrs. Leon (below) feels safe enough with her own fantasies; after all, they are not about leaving Mr. Leon. And even if they were, she knows it is only a passing whimsy and not what she wants in real life. She tells them to him. Leon tells us he was so excited by this evidence that she had a sexual life of her own that he "came as soon as she touched me."

One would think this would be all the encouragement Leon would need to reveal *his* fantasies, but he holds back. Nobody knows Mrs. Leon better than he does, and while something in her felt it would be okay to tell him, something in him senses turn-about might not be a good idea. Sexual fantasies release powerful, unpredictable energies. Once the imp is let out of the bottle, once fantasies are told to someone else, they pass out of your control. The ideas may never be forgiven or forgotten. Leon isn't sure his wife could handle these ideas he has about peeing on her, and about homosexual intercourse. So far he hasn't "had the guts to tell her." I wouldn't call it "guts"—I'd say it is probably wisdom.

LEON

Up until now I worried that I was becoming perverted. I have been married for seventeen years and have enjoyed a satisfactory sex life.

However, last week during a lovemaking session, my wife confided in me about some of her fantasies. At first I thought that it was a joke, but it really turned me on. She admitted that although she was not queer, she often thought of sixty-nine with another woman. While I was at work, she often thought of having her pussy licked by a huge dog. Although she has enjoyed oral sex with me for a number of years, she admitted that she often thought of strangers as she masturbated in the afternoon. She got me so hot, telling me the things that she wanted done to her and the things that she wanted to do to me and the things she wanted to see me do, that I came as soon as she touched me.

Later, she lay in my arms, too tired to do anything but talk. She said that your books made her realize that she was not alone in her erotic thoughts. When she asked me how I felt about it, I was reluctant to tell her some of my fantasies. At her prodding I swallowed my pride and told her what excited me, but had not had the nerve to tell her or anyone. I thought that it was okay for her to suck pussy, because I enjoyed it myself, but sometimes I fantasized that I wanted to suck a cock. I was embarrassed to tell her this, because I was afraid that she would think that I was a homo. She said that she also fantasized that, but was afraid to tell me. I told her that when I wasn't so hot, I rejected the idea. She couldn't see why. Why should I want her to do it, if I thought it was so terrible?

This brought up other thoughts in my mind. Many things I haven't had the guts to tell her. While masturbating, I often think about a cock up my asshole. Although I have done this to her, how would she take the idea? Would she lick my asshole? Let me piss on her and drink it? Take on a couple of my friends while I watched? How would she feel about sharing another girl with me? Maybe in time, I'll be able to confide in her. Until then, these will have to remain my fantasies alone.

What I don't really understand is why do I get these feelings about her, when I can honestly say that I love her more than anything else in the world? She has always been a wonderful wife and mother. When we married, she was a virgin and during our courtship we did little more than pet.

Through the years she has become more attractive to me and my love for her has grown even stronger.

I guess true love is waking up in the morning after a torrid session, and saying, "This is the woman whom I adore, and the mother of my children."

BRYCE'S GIRL, HELEN

Bryce and I are very "outdoor" people. We love parks, camping, nature, and animals. We have a mutual fantasy that was originally Bryce's, and we always end up fucking ourselves silly just by talking about it. He asked me to write it down for you because he is not very good at putting things into words.

We are in a very beautiful mossy, pine-scented woods where there is peace and beauty, untouched by litter or anything at all unnatural. The sun is shining through the pine trees, there is a beautiful clear stream nearby, and we are carrying our clothes because it seems so *right* to be naked in these surroundings. There are signs of our favorite things all around us. Squirrels, birds, and especially complete privacy. Everything is so perfect that the ground seems to pull us downward. We make a "pad" to lie on with our clothes, and Bryce starts to suck me until my clit is bulging. Very gently at first, because after all, what's the hurry? I roll to my side so we can sixty-nine each other and give each other the same pleasure that the surroundings are giving us. He can always make me come very quickly this way, and after I do come, he asks me to stand up. I stand up and he guides me to a smooth-barked tree. At the tree he leans me against it and it feels so cool and sensual on my back. He begins to part my legs and lick up my juices that are still flowing from my first climax. After a few minutes his gentle fingers find their way inside my creamy cunt and asshole, doing their job, until I come and come again, my cunt convulsing against his fingers. Next he tells me to put my hands on his shoulders and when I do he raises me against the tree until I'm at the perfect level to be entered. As he enters, I wrap my legs around him and

he starts to walk toward the nearby stream. He walks right
into the beautiful clear blue water with me nearly out of
my mind wanting him to explode inside me. In the water
about waist-deep, he begins to "dance" as his own climax
comes to him and at the same time I have a very satisfying
one of my own. We fall apart in the water and end our
dream fantasy with a long lazy swim.

VANCE'S WIFE

I'm writing to tell you about my husband's favorite fantasy.
I didn't know he had this fantasy until it happened. He
knows I am writing and doesn't object.

Several days ago, I was reading your book and one of
the letters excited me. The writer spoke about "whacking
off her cunt" which referred of course to playing with her
pussy. I had never heard that expression and I thought I'd
like to read about her whacking off her cunt, while I
whacked off my cunt. My husband wasn't due home for
two or three hours. So I gave no thought of being discovered, my only thoughts were of rubbing my clit and coming.

I keep my pussy shaved because I find I reach orgasm
much more easily and my clit is free to be stimulated this
way. It also keeps my husband more excited. I sat on the
sofa with my legs wide apart. I had a vibrator and my
electric toothbrush beside me, also an ice cube which I rub
my clit with sometimes and in front of me I had a large
mirror. I was jerking off and watching in the mirror, while
my pussy was pouring out juices and bouncing around like
Jell-O. I was engrossed totally with how much I was enjoying myself.

Suddenly, without warning, the door flew open and
there stood my husband. We were both surprised, especially him, because we'd never discussed people playing
with themselves and he had no idea that I did. I couldn't
stop, but I soon saw that he wouldn't want me to. I never
saw a dick get hard so fast. We still hadn't said a word,
and I was still playing with my pussy. He started taking off

his clothes, and he was rubbing his dick while he moved my mirror and stood in front of me. By this time, he was jerking and squeezing his dick and although he rarely ever said a word in bed, he started saying things like, "Fuck that cunt," "Play with that juicy pussy," "I'm beating my peter." I never saw him so excited, his dick was red, his face was red, he was nearly out of breath, his eyes were fixed on my pussy and my hand that was playing with it, and he was jerking his dick off faster and faster until I made it and then his sperm shot out onto my clit. With one hand still on his dick, he kneeled in front of me and rubbed the hot liquid that had just come out of him into my pussy in the same ways that I had been playing with it while he was watching me. I came again and the look on his face was sheer joy.

Later we discussed the episode. He confided that he had often wondered if women really did play with their pussies, and he spent a lot of his time imagining scenes in which he caught a woman beating off. This was usually what he was thinking about when we were in bed. He said he had seen this in stag films and X-rated movies, but it did nothing to confirm in his mind that women really rub their clits. Then when he discovered me, he knew at last. He also said he was thinking of going to a prostitute and paying her to jerk off and let him watch, because then he could tell if she was really enjoying it or not.

Although I'd always thought being caught would be terrible, I'm really glad it happened. We are much more open about our fantasies, and try to act them out now, because neither of us wants the other to look for other partners. His favorite fantasy is still the same, but now instead of becoming obsessed with it, he can enjoy it because we play with ourselves together regularly now. I never imagined I could be so free and my husband says he's now the happiest man in the world and completely fulfilled.

My wife has found reassurance in your books that some of her own sexual fantasies (about which she had felt guilty because of their lesbian character) are a frequent occurrence in the minds of many women.

I am forty-one, my wife is thirty-six, and we have been married twelve years, this being the first marriage for me, the second for her. We are college graduates, employed in our professions—she in teaching, I in industrial art. We are both also quite active in church and civic affairs.

It seems that my wife's preference for masturbating and cunnilingus heightens rather than lessens her sexuality and enjoyment of every variety of sex. What she enjoys most of all is lying on her back with her legs widely spread and my licking her clit and cunt (which she keeps clean-shaven) for sometimes even an hour or longer. Our lovemaking sessions are always very long, often up to two hours (because she doesn't have her first orgasm easily), but after that— wow! While I'm licking her, since I don't see her face, I usually start, after a while, imagining that it isn't her cunt that I'm licking but the cunt of some other women whom I know. I think of some of my friends' wives, my wife's friends; quite often, it is our minister's wife who is quite a sexy female, also Jackie O., Elizabeth T., Sophia L., or another movie star and yes, Nancy, sometimes it's you whose cunt I'm licking. This fantasizing gives me the patience and endurance to lick my wife as long as she needs it for her first orgasm.

After she has come as many times as she enjoys, she usually gets on her knees and shoulders and I fuck her from behind which is the position she prefers. Now, again since I don't see her face, just her ass and cunt, I often fantasize that it's some other woman I'm fucking. By that time my wife's cunt has become dripping wet which always arouses me very much and with the help of my fantasy I need only a few minutes to fill her cunt to the brim.

Lately I at times participate in my wife's lesbian fantasies. While I'm licking and sucking her cunt she describes to me in pretty great detail how she is either sucking the nipples, masturbating or licking the cunt of another woman of our acquaintance or having this done by that woman to her.

I'm pretty sure that my wife fantasizes sexually also about other men, particularly when she masturbates while looking at the naked men in *Playgirl* magazine, which she does quite often. She has, however, never told me about them, just as I don't tell her about my fantasies which I have described to you. I just feel that she might have an adverse reaction and wouldn't be too thrilled to know that while making love with her I am fantasizing about fucking, licking or being sucked off by some other woman. This is also apparently the reason she feels free now to tell me of her lesbian fantasies but never about imagining other men.

I am not surprised that several women sent me their men's fantasies. The ideas may have begun by being his; but now they are shared, the woman sees them as evidence of his trust, his desire to be close. The woman is proud to let the world know that his secrets are mutual property. Helen (above) makes it clear that she and Bryce draw the line very sharply between verbally sharing fantasies and acting them. Their ideas sound harmless and bucolic enough, the line is never crossed: "We just talk."

Lee's wife (above) sometimes takes up to an hour to climax. He uses fantasies to keep both him and her excited. However, he wisely does not tell her those in which other women enter. That would bring her down abruptly and ruin more between them than just one hour of sex. For his part, he enjoys her lesbian fantasies; he assumes she may fantasize about other men, too. He knows better than to ask.

Mr. and Mrs. Lee have my admiration. They are able to give each other the freedom of their bodies without surrendering the freedom of their minds. They intuitively understand the uses and limits of fantasy: To have sex with a real partner while privately imagining that it is with someone else is not betrayal. It is a private excursion of the mind that heightens the physical experience for both.

PENROD

I am thirty-five years old with a graduate, professional degree. My wife is one year younger than me, and also a professional. She was physically and emotionally a virgin when we first screwed; however, I (both before and after our marriage fourteen years ago) have fucked with countless women. Although we have maintained a "satisfactory" and "proper" sex life, I have constantly fantasized about further, additional sexual experiences.

Without getting too Freudian, I must point out that she has always been very orgasmic while still believing (as she was taught) that there is something "dirty" about sex. I almost insisted that she read your two books, but she has never been able to find the time to do so. She indicates impatience when I tell her that I enjoy *Penthouse, Deep Throat,* etc. She will not even consider anal sex. Although she enjoys my going down on her, she considers the thought of giving me a blow job repulsive. While I was able to coerce her into an extramarital affair once in the past, she still approaches fucking as a twice-a-week duty. Please do not misunderstand. Although I consider our marital sex deficient, we have many other qualities in common (including two wonderful children), and I would never consider having such a deep commitment with any other person.

My work requires me to travel all over the country, and this gives me available access for acting out my various fantasies. I have never fantasized a situation I would be unwilling to act out, and, given conducive and nonexploitive circumstances, I am ready to act out any and all of my fantasies.

First, those which I have been able to act out:

—The first was to have an extramarital affair. I was surprised to discover that this not only did not "ruin my marriage," but had no effect upon it.
—Another was to fuck women of different races. Although every partner is slightly different, I now know that there are no discernible racial characteristics.
—Since my wife is rather flat, I dreamed of fucking with a

possessor of enormous tits. Just as with my slightly less than average prick, I learned that size has no relation to competence.

—I always dreamed about receiving a good blow job, and of fucking some woman in the ass. I now enjoy these experiences at every opportunity.

—I had fantasized often about going to a nudist camp. Acting this out was boring, and I learned that sunburned balls smart.

—Still another was to fuck a whore not for money, but because she enjoys me. This has happened with two different ladies and is wonderful for my male ego.

—I have also thought of fucking animals, but the closest I have come is to train my dog to lick my balls and ass while I jack off.

Socially, lesbianism is ignored, while male homosexuality is deplored. While most of us men feel a social necessity to act disgusted at the thought, I suspect that most of us are intrigued at the possibility. I recognize that I would enjoy sucking a cock, and I believe I would enjoy being fucked in the ass. However, I may have to wait some time before the circumstances are conducive for acting out this fantasy.

CHIP

My fantasies stem from the first significant sexual events in my life which occurred during my twelfth and thirteenth years. I had entered puberty then and my sexual apparatus had started to mature and I was beginning to sprout pubic hairs. I was also having a terrible time with unexpected and unbidden erections and was starting to look at girls in a new way.

Up the street a few houses from us lived a girl named Jill who was about a year younger than I. Jill was very pretty and petite with milk white skin, china blue eyes and dark brown hair that fell to her shoulders in fluffy curls. She was also a very nice girl with a pleasant disposition but had started to make a pest of herself by wanting to follow me everywhere I went.

One day I discovered Jill had followed me to a place about a mile from our neighborhood that we called the Jungle. This was a large wooded area with a lot of scrub growth and a rarely used freight track along one side of it. This was where we played all our games of childhood: Cowboys and Indians, War, etc. What I remember about them is that they mainly consisted of imaginarily killing each other off or taking prisoners. I tried to scare Jill off by telling her I would take her prisoner and spank her if she didn't go home. She just stuck out her tongue and dared me to, so I took some cord from my bike kit, tied her wrists behind her and marched her to a small railroad bunkhouse. Instead of being frightened, Jill seemed to relish the adventure, even when I told her I was going to spank her bare-tail. I had to go through with the dare then, so I removed her halter top, shorts and little white panties. She was such a lovely sight with nothing on but her leather sandals that I could hardly control my excitement. I sat on a chair and put her in front of me, telling her that part of her punishment was to have to stand naked in front of me while I inspected her. She, too, was just into puberty with the contours of femininity starting to throw hints around her straight-as-an-arrow body. Her breasts with their rose-pink nipples were just budding, her pubis had formed an enticing little mound and a dark fuzz with a few delicate strands shadowed her pouting sex. I put her over my lap face down and let my hand roam over her smooth back, her sassy round butt and smooth thighs and I didn't care if she could feel my hard-on through my shorts. I ran my hand down her crack between her thighs and she giggled and squirmed against it. Then I began the spanking, gently at first and then harder until her ass was bucking and jerking. Every so often I would stop and put my hand down her crack. Jill told me to keep doing that; spank her some more and then put my hand there again. Jill and I had discovered sexual spanking and, while we didn't know the word for it, I gave her several orgasms.

Jill and I continued that way with our own summer Olympics until her cousin Liz came to visit and soon I had two prisoners to play with. We had great fun and after I was done with each of them, I would have them entertain me by going at each other, a sport they both learned to love.

After a couple of years we moved and Jill and I eventually lost contact but the pattern for my sex life and fantasies had been set. One of my favorite fantasies goes like this:

I am the owner and headmaster of a highly exclusive school for young ladies aged twelve to eighteen. It is very strict but whenever a student has been so unruly as to earn physical chastisement, she is sent to me. The procedure is that immediately after supper, she must prepare for bed. Freshly bathed and brushed, in nightgown, robe and slippers and carrying an envelope containing a description of the behavior she is to be punished for, she must come and knock on the door of my quarters. I receive her sitting in a large thronelike chair and she hands me the envelope with a curtsy. I read the contents while she stands there apprehensively and then I advise her of the seriousness of her offenses. For such behavior she has a choice: She can be sent home in disgrace or accept a physical chastisement from me at once. The thought of being sent home is too humiliating and she opts for chastising. Her only choice then is whether she prefers a spanking, a caning, a birching or a paddling. If she selects an instrument, she must retrieve it from where they hang on the wall and present it to me. She must now remove her robe and nightgown and place them on a table, giving careful attention to properly folding and placing them in accordance with the school's manual. She presents herself to me to have her wrists secured behind her so she can't interfere with the punishment. She must then suffer the indignity and embarrassment of standing before me naked while I lecture her about her misdeeds and study her anatomy. I then position her across my lap if it's a spanking or have her kneel and lie across a padded bench if it's for an instrument. I then proceed inexorably with the chastisement. I am expert so that I know how to give it to her so that she is experiencing pleasure through the pain and I keep it up until I know she is on the verge of getting off. Now I comfort her and brush away her tears, stroking her until my hand reaches her pussy and she gets off like a rocket. She spends the rest of the evening learning how to please me and how I can please her. Sometimes, instead of a student, the culprit is a young teacher who has been judged by her peers.

After reading your last book together, a very dear friend of mine confided to me her favorite fantasy. She thought she would like to see if she would enjoy acting it out. We tried it out successfully and have continued it. Her fantasy is that she is on her way to a very important social engagement but is abducted before she can get there. Her captor takes her to his lair where he loots her of all her valuables and jewelry and strips her of all her finery. He then torments her until she is begging him to use her instead, which he does.

We do the whole thing with complete realism. We select a rendezvous site for that evening, usually a plaza or theater parking lot. At home Laura dresses for the kind of event she's supposed to be going to: cocktail party, formal banquet, theater or dinner dance. She drives to the lot and foolishly parks in a dark and remote corner where I am lurking in the shadows, unseen. She locks her car but before she can take a step, I am upon her, warning her to silence and forcing her into my car. I manacle her wrists, strap her into the seat and put painted-out sunglasses on her until she is safely inside my place. There I take her to a room that I have specially outfitted for these activities. I have a large frame on one wall fitted with heavy duty eyelets that provide for a variety of positions. I place her in a standing position and chain her ankles and her wrists to the frame so that her arms are held away from her body. I start to strip her very slowly, removing one garment at a time and making a ceremony of every single snap, fastening, button or tie. Between each item I stand back and regard her before commencing with the next.

On the opposite wall, there is a full-length mirror and she can watch everything that's happening to her, which she loves to do. By this time Laura is really getting off on her fantasy. She is thinking about this terrible thing that's happening to her instead of being at her important event and of the people who are expecting her and are wondering what's happened to her. When I have removed her last shred and she is naked, I chain her in a spread-eagle position on the frame and run my hands over her, telling her all the things I have in store for her and she is squirming and getting off like mad. I then tease and torment her with a variety of sexual toys from my armamentarium until she is begging and promising to do anything I want. When I let her down we settle in for a grand evening of fun and fucking. We only do this scene once a week or so in order to keep it fresh and so Laura can build up a strong anticipation.

For personal data, I am thirty-eight, average height. I am a university graduate and operate my own enterprise. I am a Catholic and though I am of a type that a pope or prelate would have difficulty discerning, I am one all the same.

LES

I am thirty-seven years old, have been married two and a half years, have no children. I am well educated with B.S. and M.S. degrees and am a public official. I have been masturbating most of my life since I was about twelve years old. In my earlier days, in junior high, I remember masturbating and fantasizing about being tied up to a chair and taunted, sexually, by one of the girls in my class. I have also in more recent years fantasized about fucking some of the girls I knew and was either going out with or wanted to go with. Lately, however, my fantasies have turned to a more homosexual vein, as I have become very sexually excited when corresponding with another male for the purpose of going sixty-nine with him or having him fuck me.

At first I merely fantasized this activity, but in the past few months I have actively sought out this situation, though not very successfully. I have gotten responses from two men I wrote to, after I had sent them Polaroid pictures of my erect penis in various positions, and also tracings of my penis and even some of my juices and cum on my letter. I never did get together with either of these persons, however. My most recent experience took place when I went to another town for a meeting. While I was in a park, I had to use the public washroom and I was immediately turned on by the messages that were written on the walls about people wanting blow jobs and fucking, and wanting to suck someone off. I wrote down my own message and told where to contact me at a motel. I then wrote down some of the phone numbers on the wall. Back at the motel, I excitedly waited for someone to call and fantasized how I would meet them at the door completely nude with a huge hard-on.

When I called the numbers I wrote down, I got completely nude and played with myself. I finally talked with one fellow who was very experienced but really nice about it when I told him that I was not. We never did get together. Later on that evening, about 4:00 A.M., my phone rang and a fellow asked if he could come over and talk about my message and I agreed. I was very excited, but after he came over and we talked awhile, I seemed to get turned off and asked him to leave. After that I masturbated again and had a hard time getting back to sleep.

I have the idea that the fellow that I have sex with should be young and slim and smaller than I am—most of the other persons I contacted in the past were as big or bigger physically than I am (by the way I am six-three and weigh one hundred ninety). I still think I would like to suck someone's dick and feel his hot cum in my mouth as I do in my fantasies. But in the final analysis, I guess my reluctance to really do it relates back to my strong Catholic upbringing and the massive amount of guilt I have experienced most of my life. I enjoy masturbating so much, however, that I have continued it even in marriage. My wife does not know, though I think she suspects it.

WARREN

I am thirty-three years of age, white, divorced and remarried. Throughout my early years, ten to sixteen, I always ran around the house in the nude, whenever I was alone. My real parents were divorced and I was adopted by my grandparents. My first real sexual encounter was with my real mother. We were swimming at the beach and she pulled her huge breasts out of her swimming suit. She let me play with them and suck on her large nipples. She also started playing with my cock. Later that day, after we were home, she let me look at her pussy and then introduced me to sexual intercourse. I do not think this hurt me, in fact in many ways I believe it actually helped me in getting experience and self-confidence.

At the age of seventeen, I joined the Air Force and I am still in the Air Force. I have been to three Air Force specialty schools and now I am in Computer Analysis.

My first marriage lasted for eleven wonderful years, during which we had two beautiful daughters.

During my adolescence, I was always told I had an extremely large penis; actually, my penis grew before the rest of me. Now, I am only average. Because I have always heard that women got turned on by large cocks, I was an exhibitionist for a short period of time. Then one day I discovered I was more turned on by men looking at my wife instead of women looking at me. My fantasy grew and grew. I envisioned a salesman coming by and my wife wearing a see-through blouse, miniskirt, minus all undergarments. He sits across from her and she sits so he has a good shot at her beautiful dark-haired pussy. They eventually wind up on the couch or floor fucking like hell. I am hiding, watching his cock slide in and out of her pussy and the expression of pleasure on her face.

I eventually got around to telling my wife my fantasy. She thought I was sick and should see a shrink. Gradually, I talked her into flashing a service station attendant in a gas station, then a salesman and a few repairmen. She never did enjoy it, but it led to really great sexual encounters between the two of us. She gradually started to like flashing younger boys and finally seduced a sixteen-year-old who had a cock like a horse. I watched the whole thing, and as soon as he got off, I was in her. Her cunt was steaming hot and as wet as Niagara Falls. It was fantastic. Still, it was all done to please me. She wasn't doing it because she enjoyed it. Gradually it led to the destruction of our marriage. I remarried too soon, and my present wife and I are extremely incompatible sexually. My dreams and fantasies are now of a beautiful dark-haired woman who shares my interests sexually, and otherwise. Together, we seduce men, women and boys, through her exhibitionism.

Still it's a fantasy, for I have come to realize that I shall never find a woman as sexual as I am, especially one with exhibitionist tendencies, as they simply do not exist.

Incidentally, although I loved your books, I find it hard to believe that even a minority of women are as sexual as your books depict. I rather feel that the majority of letters you have received are from men, describing how they wish their wives would think and dream or be.

CHRISTOPHER

Here's a fantasy of mine that came to life last spring. I've never told anyone about this experience until now. I'm a twenty-two-year-old guy, born and bred in Washington, D.C.

I've had this fantasy for a few years. It basically includes having a girl serve me sexually, and spanking her from time to time.

Well, last April I was walking with Carol, a close friend with whom I've never had sex. We shared intimate secrets—including me telling her that I'd love to fuck her—and her declining. Carol mentioned a movie (X-rated) that we passed in the street. I don't remember the movie's title but it was about a teen-age girl being kidnapped, tied up, and raped, according to the description that the theater ran. She commented on how exciting that sounded. Later, we stopped by her apartment for some food. We got pretty high after dinner, and I steered the conversation back to the subject of the movie.

Carol (she was nineteen then) seemed pretty excited about the film's subject matter. She told me she'd always fantasized about being raped and treated roughly by her attacker. Maybe if we weren't so high what followed wouldn't have happened.

I grabbed Carol by the shirt and ripped it open, literally. She started to put up a struggle but I could tell it was just a mock effort. I kissed her hard, on the lips, and forced her to kneel on the floor before me. I told her to take out my cock and "kiss it," in those words, till I came in her mouth. The sight of her fulfilling an old-time fantasy of mine, along with the view I had of my hard-on going in and out of Carol's beautiful face, quickened my orgasm. Carol couldn't keep my come in her mouth, and pulled her mouth away. I kept shooting on her cheeks.

I made her undress me and then I took off the rest of her clothes. Again playing the part, she began to struggle. So I grabbed some twine from the kitchen and tied her by the wrists to the bedposts. I decided to be fair and fulfill a fantasy *she* had mentioned earlier, namely eating her pussy as she lay on her back, totally helpless. It didn't take long for her to come. Now I was hard again.

I turned Carol over so that she lay on her stomach. This time I tied her arms together over her head. One thing I'd always wanted to see was a chick masturbating—for real, not like in *Penthouse*, et al. I ordered her to play with herself, and told her to get up on her knees to do it.

With Carol's ass sticking out as she kneeled on the bed, I gave her a hard smack on the tush. She didn't say anything, but stopped playing with herself for a moment. I pushed her hands, which were still roped together at the wrist, back to her pussy. Then I gave her a half-dozen more hard spanks on her bottom. Carol's ass was pink from the treatment I was giving it. I untied her hands, then retied them behind her back. She collapsed onto her stomach, but I wasn't through with her yet.

For a finale, I was going to fuck her hard, with her arms and legs spread-eagled on the bed. But as Carol lay on the bed, face down with her hands still bound behind her, she yelled, "Fuck me from behind!" I was happy to oblige, and after dipping my hard-on into her cunt for lubrication, I jammed it (much too hard, I regret) into her asshole. Unfortunately for her, Carol was asking me to fuck her cunt from behind. But I misunderstood and slid up her ass. Carol moved her butt back and forth trying to dodge the thrusts of my prick. The more she wiggled her ass, the better it felt for me, and I had the orgasm of my life when I came between the cheeks of her derrière.

Some fantasies should be lived out. For instance, the timid man who dreams of asking a beautiful girl for a date might well put fears of rejection aside and act on his wish. Even if she says no—even if the worst happens and she laughs at him—something will be gained: confirmation that being put down by a beautiful girl is not death. Courage is often a matter of learning that you can survive doing things that frighten you. Do it often enough and the fear is tamed.

Being rejected by a beautiful girl you don't know doesn't cost much. You didn't have anything to begin with. Deciding to act out a fantasy with someone you love risks forever scarring a relationship that means a great deal.

You may think it would be thrilling to make love to your wife in a secluded corner of the beach; the remote possibility of discovery only adds spice. If she does not agree, it does not mean she is inhibited; it merely means that your fantasy is not her fantasy. For you to demand it in the name of love does not prove you are freer than she— only bossier, or more frightening. While Penrod (above) tells us he was able to "coerce" his wife into fulfilling one of his fantasies, he doesn't connect the fear she must have of him with what he describes as their "deficient" marital sex life. Penrod's solution is to find women who are thrilled to help him put into practice those fantasies too "dirty" for his wife. Evidence of his masculine conflict can be seen in the statement that despite his wife's puritanism he'd rather be married to her than to any of the more permissive women he meets. "I would never consider having such a deep commitment [as with Mrs. Penrod] with any other person." For all her no saying, something in her must satisfy him very strongly.

Let's say the fantasy you want to act out is not as problematic as any of those mentioned by Penrod, but one as idyllic as the aforementioned lovemaking on a beach. It still may not turn out happily.

The fantasy is thrilling because while it is still in your mind, you are running the whole show: lights, camera, action. Not only have you made the sky blue and brought sweet music to play in the air and caused the sand not to rasp in embarrassing places, you have also choreographed the emotions for any people who might stumble upon you. You have written that they can only show amazement, admiration, and the desire to imitate you by joining in. But if the scene ever happened in real life, the emotion you might feel before strangers could well be such burning shame that you (and she) might never forget it. Les (above) started to put his homosexual fantasies into practice, but in the end decided not to. "I guess my reluctance . . . relates back to my strong Catholic upbringing." Whatever the reason for reluctance, if it is there, think again.

None of us is merely the product of our adult minds. The values by which you were raised are probably more firmly embedded in your conscience—your sense of right and wrong—than you realize. Reading a book or magazine article is not enough to free you to do everything you previously felt was forbidden. Behind the façade of enjoying the group sex her husband has talked her into, Mrs. Warren (above) seems really to have been getting off on fantasies of submission to her husband's wishes. If she loved what he was making her do, why was there so much anger? Warren found that persuading his wife to act out his sexual fantasies was the end of a marriage he experienced as "eleven wonderful years."

Christopher's letter (above) raises an important point: even after talking about your mutual fantasies, there may not be a true meeting of minds. Once passions are aroused by putting fantasies into action, unexpected and possibly dangerous energies may be released, if only because even in the wildest of sexual scenes something in us resists saying exactly what we mean. *Fuck me from behind,* Carol says to Christopher. She means vaginal penetration. In the heat of the moment, Christopher isn't going to slow down and parse out her euphemism. He acts in the way his enflamed senses most want to understand the words. He fucks her in the ass, inflicting great pain. Of all fantasies to choose to live out, S&M scenarios are the ones to be approached with the most caution, the most careful setting out of safeguards first.

In a sense, there is a measure of magical thinking in Christopher's conduct, a kind of wish fulfillment imposed on reality, allowing him to do as he wishes. "If I like it, she will, too." This is usually called projection, an extremely narcissistic way of dealing with the world. Other people aren't seen as entities in themselves, with their own wishes and fears. Instead, they are seen as mirrors of the narcissist. Says a psychoanalyst colleague of mine: "Half my work involves people who do not correctly perceive signals they get from other people. They can only see what they want to see, and that is usually in their favor. It leads to them bungling what goes on between themselves and others." Warren (above) says he doesn't think the women who sent me their fantasies are typical. In fact, he suspects they are really men. He has never met this kind of woman (or did not recognize her if he did). Therefore, she does not exist.

MURRAY

Not until a few years ago did I have any idea that my wife's fantasies were the center of her sexual fulfillment. I discovered this one night after we had attended a movie starring Paul Newman and Robert Redford.

Even in the darkness of the movie house, I became aware that my wife would go into a kind of trance whenever Mr. Newman was dominating the action or was the center of attention. When we got home, we had a few drinks, and we talked. My wife could not stop discussing how well Mr. Newman played his role.

Seeing her excitement and how stimulated she was becoming just remembering the film, I took it upon myself to pretend to be Paul Newman in our bedroom. I tried to stand the way he did in the movie; and I spoke to my wife, using some of the phrases we had just heard him use. I even encouraged her to call me "Paul." Between my (amateur) acting ability and my wife's (very strong) fantasies, I was a box office smash hit. The night ended early the next morning—sunrise, as a matter of act—with two of the world's most sexually satisfied people. My wife has told me about some of her other fantasy men, and I have told her my fantasies about women. Our reward has been each other's love.

PATRICK

First of all, I am thirty-four years old, married and a schoolteacher. My home sex life is rather dull, which accounts for the vivid imagination that I've managed to develop over the years, especially as I work with many gorgeous young women.

My fantasies always revolve around some of my students, who are aged from sixteen to eighteen. Being a confirmed "ass man" I am constantly distracted by the luscious curves all around me at school.

While masturbating I imagine that the girls are all ready and just waiting for me to make the first move. I never get turned down in my dreams (who does?).

I pick out one girl, and during the class, while the rest of the students are working, I move over casually to this student and start talking with her about her work. While talking I will absentmindedly stroke her hair, and she will respond by resting her head against my hand, carefully so that nobody will notice. We are both quickly becoming excited. She knows what I want, and she wants it too.

By this time I am becoming hard, and she will notice and push her chair back a little so that her shoulder is pressing against my erection, where she rubs it with little movements. In turn I point to her work in front of her and manage to brush against her breast "accidentally." The risk of somebody noticing what we are doing makes it all the more exciting to us. By this time we are both so horny that it must become noticeable, so I back off and suggest that she come with me to a storeroom to get some materials. The rest of the class continues working.

When we get to the storeroom I lock the door and then turn to her. She is waiting, roused, but not knowing what to do as I am the first man that has affected her this way. We kiss delicately, and then I turn her back to me and pull her to me. At first she doesn't understand why, but when I start touching and fondling her breasts and nipples she sees the advantages of this position and presses back against me. Then I slowly work down to her clitoris and the tension builds up in her until I finally reach under her jeans and panties and rub my finger between her slit. It is wet now and juicy with anticipation. She is frantically pushing and rubbing her ass against my cock by this time, and I'm almost bursting. I undo her jeans button and unzip her fly (for some reason it's always jeans in this fantasy), while at the same time she has reached behind her and is undoing my zipper and stroking my erect cock.

Its size scares her for a little while, and I have to gently persuade her that she can take it in. By this time she is really "hot," so she pushes it between her legs and guides it so that I can shove it into her quickly. (Right now I'm hard just thinking about it.)

We fuck quickly and excitedly, standing up, with her back still to me, with an added thrill from the fact that anybody may come into the storeroom at any time. She reaches down and fondles my balls while I excite her nipples and clitoris simultaneously. We both come together, and it's like the end of the world. When we walk out of the storeroom later, both of us are flushed and yet trying to appear normal.

While this may appear to be a quite ordinary fantasy, for me it became a fact about six months ago, and the student and I became lovers (and are still lovers). We fucked whenever we could, and there are a surprisingly large number of places around a school where one can meet and fuck.

I was her first lover, but she became a very willing pupil, and learned all that she could about fucking, anal and oral sex. We've tried just about everything, and she loves it all, as I do.

We both particularly prefer oral sex, as there is something really relaxing about just laying back receiving pleasure from a person who is really devoted to you (just as it is equally relaxing to give pleasure to another whom you love, without violent movements to distract).

So I think that I'm extremely fortunate in being able to live out my fantasies in real life. How many others can say that?

MIGUEL

My profession is the law. I am thirty-four, six-one, one hundred eighty pounds, dark complexion (I'm half Mexican), enjoy women—their touch, their taste, their smell, and ultimately their sexuality.

I have the usual male response ego-wise to seeing a woman I am making love to experiencing a particularly satisfying orgasm or series of orgasms. But I really get off when my partner totally loses her control while I'm keeping mine (at least for the moment). When I can feel my woman raising her hips to get more of my tongue in her cunt or to press her clit harder against my mouth, I get unbelievably turned on. Even if we've been fucking all night, that kind of response gets me hard again almost all the time.

I also get turned on by a proper woman's use of bedroom language particularly under sexual tension. "Please fuck me—*now*," "I want your cock," "Give it to me," "Don't make me beg you," are enormous turn-ons. The ultimate, of course, is that inarticulate scream or cry at orgasm, when her legs go rigid and her face becomes red and contorted. Afterwards, I like to lick the perspiration off her back, neck, breasts and chest, while she's coming down.

The foregoing has been to give you some kind of feel for my own sense of sexuality, however inadequate. This may help in seeing why or how the fantasies I have impact on me.

Fantasy One: Samantha was a receptionist for another law firm in the building. She was my type—slim hipped with well shaped legs and ass, with small breasts and supersensitive nipples. I used to love to slowly tongue-stroke her clit while touching her hardened nipples as lightly as possible—the climaxes she felt were shattering. One night, after an unusually long session of this type, Sam turned the tables and rolled me on my back. At first, she simply tongued my cock and balls, but after a few minutes she got astride, facing me. She had super muscle control and was able to squeeze my cock with her cunt as if it were a hand. I can still picture her—smiling confidently at the effect she was producing on me and by her own incredibly sexy appearance. A couple of times she bent over so that I could lick her nipples. My hands roamed between her breasts and her incredibly smooth thighs. Suddenly she came—and almost as suddenly recovered and continued milking my cock in her cunt. I was going out of my mind. I started to moan and then just at the moment of climax, she jumped off, took my cock deeply in her mouth, sucking and swallowing my come—I nearly had a heart attack! In fact, I experienced aftershocks of sensitivity at the tip of my cock as many women do. I think the thing that reached me was the incredible intimacy and closeness of wanting to better feel and taste my climax. And, while this was a true event, it is an old favorite if I need to masturbate.

Fantasy Two: A client had an interest in a court case in another city, where he was expecting to testify. Although I was not trying the case, my client wanted me to sit in and evaluate the developments as they pertained to him.

I noticed the court reporter right away—she was not beautiful but attractive and appealing. Long slim legs and very lithe figure. She was wearing a see-through blouse through which her bra was visible. As luck would have it, we ate at the same lunch counter and were able to make some small talk. After the afternoon recess, I wanted to ask the reporter out, but was expecting to brief my client at 8:00 P.M. I compromised by asking her to have a drink after work—she accepted and we went to the cocktail lounge at my hotel, which was on her way home.

We got on fabulously and in no time at all, it was seven thirty—time for me to go to meet my client. The only alternative seemed to be a "late date" for whenever I finished. She came with me to my room and while I picked up my briefcase, she went to the john. When she came out, she had a gleam in her eye—and no bra under her see-through blouse. I took her breasts into my hands—rubbing the sheer fabric of her blouse against her nipples. She pressed her mound up hard against my cock, telling me at the same time that she knew I had to go, but that her cunt had been dripping hot for the last hour. How (or why) I had the control to leave there, I don't know, but I wanted more than a wham/bam/thank you ma'am from that woman. In any event we agreed that I would see her immediately after I finished with the client. We went out into the hallway and while we were waiting for the elevator, she whispered in my ear, "I just want you to know where I'm going to start when I see you later." With that she unzipped my pants and took my cock in her mouth. The elevator came and left (fortunately empty) before she stopped. She looked up (she was kneeling in front of me) and said, "I just won't be satisfied until I have your cock—

I want you to come in my mouth and then I want you to fuck me and fuck me." Then she zipped up my pants, dusted herself off, and another elevator came.

To make a long story short—it never worked out. The client was unusually nervous, and by the time I finished the court reporter had been asleep for hours—and probably felt put down. The next day I left. I tried again the next time I was there, and discovered a boyfriend in the picture, and so I gave it up—but I often fantasize about that incredibly sexy court reporter and what might have been.

In thinking about it, the *most* incredible fantasy might well be that my letter would be included in your next book and that a woman reading it would intuitively and correctly know that she was "my type" and I hers. And, in her mind's eye, she might even picture a blue-eyed, dark-haired, half-Mexican lawyer. He would be a man who would undress with his eyes a woman for whom he felt an instant appeal. His crotch would bulge but not unusually, because his circumcised cock would be an average length, although perhaps a little thicker in girth. His dress might be conservative lawyer's clothes, or jeans and a T-shirt.

In the end, the only thing to do would be for the woman to approach and ask, "Pardon me, aren't you . . . ? To which he would instantly reply, "Yes—I'm the man from the book. I've been waiting for you to ask me!"

I am aware that perhaps the pitfalls of sharing and/or living out fantasies has been belabored to the near exclusion of describing the excitement—even exaltation—that comes from asking one's lover into the secret confines of the erotic imagination.

If you decide to go ahead, note that in the most happily played-out fantasies in this chapter, coercion plays no part. The ideas are discussed, and agreement is voluntary, with no threats of "Well, if you won't, I'll leave you and find someone who will."

A step-by-step approach is always safest. When you talk about the new blonde at the office, does your lover get edgy? That's a warning signal. If you do decide to go ahead, describe one of your fantasies with *her* at the center. No matter how outrageous, she is still the star. Questions of possessiveness or desertion do not enter.

Perhaps you can find a description of your fantasy in a book or film. Let her read the pages in the book, take her to see the movie. If the idea intrigues her, you might safely go on to say it's not too far from one of your own favorite thoughts. But if descriptions of unusual sex acts cause anxiety, maybe you'd better keep your fantasies to yourself.

Finally, be sure you know which of you really thinks some idea is "terrible." Are you certain she would be outraged to learn that one of your dearest wishes—which you've been afraid to ask because you *know* she'd find it dirty—is, for instance, to have her lovingly take your cock in her mouth and bring you to orgasm? If you haven't found some loving way at least to mention the idea to her, you might ask yourself this: Am I projecting my own prudish fears onto her?

4

Oral Sex

DAN

I am in my late thirties, hold several degrees and am happily married to a woman who fills all my dreams except those sexual.

I've had mild sexual fantasies since mid-teens, when I was still a virgin and much in love with a girl a year older than I, who hardly knew I existed—except at dancing class, where she needed me as a partner, the only one there tall enough for her. We used to ride occasionally with other schoolmates on group horseback picnics. My early fantasies visualized riding along with her (we never did), and then coming to a secluded glade, where she would lie on the grass (or often, for some reason I didn't understand, on a wooden picnic table which happened to be there in the glen), and I would caress her, kiss her, slowly remove her boots and riding breeches, stroke her tummy and bush, then climb up on the table and make love to her. (With my own repressed upbringing, I'm sure that even if I had ever succeeded in getting her to go riding alone with me, I would have been far too shy to have taken the first step to get that scenario moving, although God knows I rehearsed it often enough in my mind!)

In common with most males, I have always had a consuming interest in female genitalia. I am an inveterate crotch watcher and always have been, even on occasion to the point of inadvertently embarrassing the object of my scrutiny. Also an inveterate and confirmed bottom watcher. The current styles of tight jeans which so closely embrace callipygian beauty, moulding it to its most rounded and graspable form, are a delight to this ole roving-eyed male. Ditto the jeans cutting deeply into the pubic area, demarcating so clearly the full lips of the vulva for all to see, and showing the location of that lovely "gateway to heaven."

I have come to know, with absolute certainty, that if I had been a child of more primitive times, I would have been—literally (as I am now figuratively)—a worshiper of the Glorious Female Cunt. If a painter or sculptor, I am sure I would be spending all my time painting or sculpting heroic-sized copies of that most beautiful and most awe-inspiring creation of a benevolent deity. I have an orchid fixation, too; some years ago, one of the large format women's magazines had a series of half a dozen or so full page color photos, extreme close-ups, of orchids. Those were the most sensuous pictures of flowers I have ever seen, and they reminded me (and the illusion still holds to this day) of fantastically beautiful and colorful cunts of exotic design, full of promise of pure pleasures beyond any formal sexual experience. And ever since, I think of female organs as orchids, as being in every way as beautiful and seductive and full of promise as orchids.

My fantasies revolve about that most delightful of creations, the Glorious Female Cunt. I love to look at my partner's body, and to tell her what a beautiful cunt she has and how much I want to kiss it and taste and caress it with my tongue, and how much I want to tease and caress her clit, and bring it to a thunderous, star-bursting exploding release. So my fantasies are often replays of the actual image of a recent session of lovemaking, with much embellishing and lingering delight in rerunning all the foreplay of fellatio and cunnilingus. The climax of my masturbatory fantasy is when I enter my partner, but the most exquisite and enjoyable part is my adoration of the Glorious Female Cunt.

DONALD

I am a young-looking forty-eight year old, five-ten, one hundred eighty pounds, divorced, and have acquired an advanced degree. Women seem to be attracted to me, and I have on occasion taken advantage of this, but much prefer a close and meaningful relationship with one person. My youngest partner was twenty-six years my junior.

My erotic specialty, which I enjoy very much, is eating cunt. It is very pleasing to me to have my partner pump her crotch against my face as she nears climax and hear her squeals of pleasure as she comes. I also find it comforting in the sixty-nine position to "nurse" on each other, not try to stimulate her, or she me, just gently caress with our tongues, and hold and softly suck on each other with our mouths. It is very pleasant to go to sleep this way. Quite naturally I think, my desire to please my partner with my lips and tongue created a desire for her to reciprocate.

I have gone down on about ten women since I began lapping cunt about thirty years ago. The only one who did not like it was my wife, who thought I was queer, although on those rare occasions when she let me go down on her she did come.

Since my divorce I've enjoyed only five women. I know there could have been more if I had been interested. Two of these five have been deep commitments. The first commitment was with Peg and lasted three years, and quite naturally she is one facet of my fantasy. The other fantasy partner, Ann, is my current partner. Neither of these two have enjoyed the pleasure of making love to a woman. They are both excellent lovers, and I am sure they would enjoy caressing the smooth soft texture of a cunt's inner lips with their tongues. We, myself and each partner, have fantasized about it—and both have expressed their willingness to try. Perhaps some day we will. I think of the pleasure of Ann and me kissing and caressing with our tongues Peg's inner thighs. . . .

Gradually we near her cunt, and I reach it first. I gently caress the outer lips and then carefully probe with my tongue—and slowly penetrate the inner lips as Ann watches with her face only inches from mine. Then I slowly withdraw as she for the first time duplicates with her tongue the probing and caressing I have just done. I watch as she becomes more and more involved in licking, sucking and lapping. She is aware of how close my face is to hers as she laps, and she occasionally stops and smiles at me, and I lean in and briefly kiss her mouth before she returns to her newfound pleasure of lapping cunt. She becomes totally involved in bringing Peg to climax, and Peg, with considerable pleasure, achieves a fantastic orgasm as she pumps her cunt in Ann's face.

Then, and only then, does Ann look at me with an inquisitive smile on her face, in effect asking if I had enjoyed watching as much as she had enjoyed eating it. I smile back and gently kiss her to let her know I thought she was beautiful.

Later Peg and I repeat this same fantasy on Ann. Of course still later they suck on me, and I come. Then we form a daisy chain, nursing on each other until we drift off to sleep.

Both Peg and Ann enjoy sucking my cock, and I get considerable pleasure from watching it disappear in their mouth. I sometimes wonder what a cock would feel like in my mouth—and how exciting it would be to have it suddenly explode and my mouth fill with come. Sometimes after Ann sucks me off she kisses me, and shares my load of come with me. So the taste and texture of it would not be new to me. When I do think about sucking cock I can't relate it to anyone I know. I did suck cock as a kid of twelve or fourteen, and as I recall I enjoyed it then, though I never sucked until my partner came. Perhaps if Ann and I become involved in a four-way I will try it.

My sexual pleasure comes more from giving pleasure than receiving it, and I'm sure I would feel the same about sucking cock as I do about lapping cunt. Perhaps this is why I cannot fantasize an owner for the cock I'd like to suck. I'd want him to be at the same place I was mentally.

Obviously I'm very oral in my lovemaking—haven't mentioned fucking at all—though I do come faster fucking. Perhaps my oral preference is because thirty years ago when I started lapping, the pill hadn't been invented—and my partners couldn't get pregnant using their mouths.

Or, perhaps, it's because I live in my head. I love to look at a cunt up close; to smell the warm, faintly musky odor it emits during an unplanned lovemaking session; to feel the soft smooth walls of the cunt with my tongue—especially when the cunt's moisture is providing the lubricant for my tongue; to savor the faint sweet taste as I lap; and even the sound is a turn-on—both the sound of my lapping and her moans of pleasure. I love the soft warmth of her cunt hair against my mouth, and the feeling of her whole cunt in my mouth when I am sucking hard. All of these things happen in my head where I live—it's not like fucking which happens "down there."

I love these fantasies. They fill me with hope. It has long been my conviction that oral sex is the key: If women could be made to feel heart and soul that what is between their legs is lovable, it would be an enormous step toward feminine self-esteem.

And yet, how many times have I titled and retitled this chapter? Warmed by the extravagant ardor of such men as Dan (above), I forgave all past disparaging remarks from men about women's anatomy, and called these pages "Cunt Crazy."

"Nancy, if you use that word," warned a male psychiatrist friend, one I know is sympathetic to women, "women readers will just hear the outrageous syllable and turn off. From then on, they will discredit anything further you have to say, no matter how positive."

He was right. I was never comfortable with that title. It was an effort at false bravado, to use men's language instead of my own. While I warm and glow when Dan euphemistically speaks of women's "gateway to heaven," when Donald (above) describes the same activity as "lapping cunt," I feel deeply offended and turn off. I retitled the chapter "I Could Eat You Up."

"Nancy, you are losing the cool voice of authority by treating this subject with humor," warned my female editor.

The verbs men use are *eating, slurping, lapping;* their nouns are *cunt* and *pussy.* If I have sedately chosen in the end to title this chapter "Oral Sex," it is because my own semantic irresolution illustrates the ambivalence women feel about the content of these fantasies.

How can a woman be proud of what she has been taught to call "down there"? How can she take men's talk of "ambrosial female fluids" as heartfelt, if in the next breath the whole business is called sucking twat? Even as her lover moves to put his head down between her legs, she searches his face for a frown, looks for stiffness in his shoulders; she is certain he dislikes what he is doing. Praying that he will not resist, she makes a show of pushing him away. "No," she says, giving him another chance to withdraw. When he does, she takes it as confirmation. "I always knew he hated it."

During my years of research on women's sexuality, one complaint has come up more than any other: "All he wants is to get off himself. Once he comes, it's finished. What about *me*? And the "me" in female orgasm is the clitoris. Arguments about clitoral vs. vaginal orgasm go on and on; what is known beyond debate is that stimulation of the clitoris by the tongue is an almost can't-miss proposition.

This chapter would seem to solve the dilemma. Isn't it telling each sex that they both want the same thing? Far from taking the old macho stance that there is something essentially low, trivial, foolish, or base about the vagina— use it like a Kleenex and forget it—these men adore it. Judging from these pages, men want nothing more than to worship women with their tongues. Nothing has surprised me more—not even the discovery that men more often turn the sword of S&M against themselves than against women—than the joy with which so many men fantasize going down on women.

The question is: Where are these men in reality? How many sexually adventurous women have told me that after a night's total abandon—when they allowed their consuming pleasure in sex to be seen—they never heard from the man again. The answer, of course, is that this is a book about what men want *in fantasy*. To say they would be wholeheartedly ready for the same thing if they got it in real life is naive.

Note how often they happen to have chosen to marry women who will not permit oral sex. If they met a real woman, in real life, who pushed her pussy in their face, would they be overjoyed? Would they take her home to meet mother?

And yet, and yet . . . let's give credit where it is due. While some men may not be willing to put their mouths where their fantasies are, it is also true that among the several thousand from whom I heard, only a handful ever used the vagina as the focus of humiliation or degradation. When men speak disparagingly about genitals, it is almost always their own.

If many men put their wives on a pedestal and then complain that she is too pure to be thought of in connection with oral delights, isn't even this a sign of change? Twenty years ago they would not have complained—they'd have been proud of it.

Part of making something come true is to believe in it yourself. I have long felt that women's fear that men hated cunnilingus was in part, at least, simple projection. I would encourage every woman to try to take in the fervor with which these men fantasize about kissing, loving, nibbling, sucking, licking, and fondling the vagina. Part of the reason men may not be ready for it yet is that women aren't either.

FRED

I am a "cunt man," but though I have spoken to a number of my friends, quite frankly I find that the intensity of my interest—and fantasies—entirely outmatches any of their feelings on that score. Not all cunts fascinate me; but as soon as mental rapport with a woman develops, and some emotional involvement, I think first of adoring her cunt with kisses and loving long licks, and then examining it with a childlike adoration, noting in great detail the very minute anatomical differences in each sweet pussy (perhaps far more clinically than a doctor would). It seems to bring me great joy, which has always been shared by the excited lady herself, as the examination is always interspersed with loving long licks and nibbles on the clit. In my fantasies, too, I think of those lovely flowerlike cunts and lovingly fondle my circumcised penis till I reach a spine-chilling orgasm. But it is not only the sight of them, but *more importantly, their individual smells that transport me.* I wish Chanel or Avon could bottle a cunt-aroma/scent for bedtime sniffing!!!

I should add that I am twenty-four.

My favorite *cunt smell* is one that I perceive as clean but *a little "stale"*—which means that *the lass should not have washed soon before I lick her* and has been engaged in shopping, tennis, or any activity that makes it perspire. I love sniffing a cunt in the dog-bitch position, or failing that, kneeling between her thighs, sniffing and licking at the same time. In my fantasies, I sometimes imagine what the smell of Liz Taylor, Loren, or Lollobrigida would be.

RUSSELL

I am a prominent, successful, respected, middle-aged pillar of the community in a conservative town in middle America. My wife and I have been married for thirty-five years, and we have grown children and grandchildren. We both came from a background which considered anything other than missionary style intercourse to be perverted, dirty or sinful. My wife still has that attitude, and she will have nothing to do with fellatio, cunnilingus, or any other variation. She even feels uncomfortable having her breasts touched. We dutifully have intercourse two or three times a week; and she enjoys her orgasms regularly.

My fantasies involve cunnilingus. I love women's bodies, and I love to kiss them, fondle them, smell them, taste them, lick them and suck them. Over the years, I have had a number of discreet extramarital affairs, and I have always taken advantage of the situation to perform cunnilingus on the woman. I love the fragrance of a woman's genitals, the softness of the vulva, the slightly sweet, salty taste of her vaginal secretions; and I get an enormous thrill from feeling her come while I am licking her. I also like to lick a woman's anus. In fact, there is no part of a woman's body which I wouldn't gladly kiss and lick. My favorite fantasy is to have an affair with a woman who enjoys cunnilingus, and who would permit me to serve her in that way while she would come repeatedly until she is sated. Or, better still, to have two or three women who would permit me to go down on them in rotation, until they had all come as many times as they wanted to. Afterward, I would like to lick clean their groins, thighs, the cleft between their buttocks, and their anuses. I adore women's bodies and I think that all women are beautiful—stout or thin, young or middle-aged, tall or short, light or dark, or any race. I would perform cunnilingus on any woman who enjoyed it. My only requirement is that she be clean and fresh, not perfumed. I enjoy a woman's natural fragrance.

LOU

I'm almost fifty years old. The magazines of today weren't published twenty or thirty years ago. I had a well-built body then. I was a wrestler. The girls would admire me, but only straight sex was considered. Everything else was a disgrace according to people of that age (except me). When I was at ringside and waiting to go in, often there was a girl wrestling match going on. Boy how I would imagine me being in there with the girls being naked. I would've loved to eat their pussies. Something I've always craved, but never had the pleasure of satisfying. If they would've had porno movies then, I would've starred in them free, just to get to eat pussy. I love it, and have a stiff erection on as I'm writing this.

I was married once to a beautiful girl. But she wasn't the type to enjoy all the variety of sex, although now and then she would let me eat her, and boy did she have a sweet delicious tasting pussy. We spit up after twelve years of marriage. When I married her she was eighteen. I was thirty-five. Since our breakup about two years ago, all I do is fantasize. I keep imagining I have a number of girls to eat 'til I've had my fill. I also would like to eat one, while fucking another. I would also like to try anal sex with a willing girl. Since I'm from a small town, and shy, I guess my dreams'll never come true. If only those girls out there would know how good I can eat pussy they'd be standing at my door now waiting their turn.

I also fantasize sucking my own cock, and often try it. But I just can't reach it. Hope some day to lose enough weight to do so.

Getting back to wrestling, every time I was in a mixed tag team (and that wasn't often) I always managed to tangle with the girl on the opposing team. My main idea was to try to get her to put a scissor lock on me (wrapping her legs around my head). Working myself free from this hold, I'd always turn my face so it was right in her crotch. I know some of the girls enjoyed it, but would never say a word about it. But I had an idea when they'd squeeze my head with their legs, they were liking it. Some girls resented this and refused to wrestle with me. Once I saw a chance and slipped my tongue inside the rim of one girl's wrestling trunks. I touched her pubic hair with my tongue (My, I wish I'd had a longer tongue!). She rolled me once on the mat, and stopped momentarily. I was afraid the spectators would notice so I pulled out, naturally hoping nobody would notice the erection I had.

AL

My favorite fantasy these days is of eating cunt. I do it as often as I can and really love it. The first time I ever ate a pussy was when I was in college in the summer of 1947. I had always been afraid to do it before then as I thought that cunts smelled bad. I didn't know if they did or not, I just thought they did. Then one night, I was trying to fuck my new girl friend out on a bridge over a creek at the edge of the college athletic field; but I was too big for her (not that I am that well endowed—only about seven inches long and two and three-quarters in diameter when erect). Anyhow, I couldn't get it into her so I just naturally turned around and started licking her cunt and she reciprocated immediately taking my stiff cock into her mouth with no trouble at all. We sixty-nined until we both came and after that we used to do it regularly. I was quite pleasantly surprised to find that she smelled *good* down there. Since then, I have sucked off every woman I have fucked and there have been quite a few who would not fuck because of fear of pregnancy but would let me suck their cunts. I just adore it. I fantasize licking the clit, very lightly and gently (unless the woman asks for greater pressure) as many women are too sensitive there to stand hard licking, and work my way down her lips and across the perineum to her asshole and back again. There are many variations, of course; but

this is a basic pattern. I just cannot be happy unless I can
bring complete pleasure to the women too. I can't understand these guys who just grab a woman, climb on, fuck
her, come quickly, and climb off without any thought of
whether it is good for her or not. They don't know what
they are missing.

JERRY

I am twenty-six and single. I dream of sucking off an entire
women's sports team. For instance, the Immaculata College basketball (former national champions) team. To begin with, I go down on the women who are sitting on the
bench during a game. The spectators go wild because this
is spurring the first team on to greater and greater efforts
because they know their turn will come next. Naturally,
they win handily and set all kinds of scoring records.

Better yet, I'd like to suck off an entire women's rowing
team. They all seem to have such luscious thighs (and everything else). Winners would be first in line and I hope it
would be the "eights." I can't bear women who use feminine hygiene sprays and a sweaty, well-worked-out crew of
women would guarantee me the essence of their femininity.

My tamer dreams are of sucking off a woman's bridge
club, a bridal shower, or a Tupperware party. I'd love to
watch their shocked expressions turn to envy and interest
as they see how I am turning on the first, most adventurous and eager of their friends.

BRADLEY

I am a twenty-four-year-old male, single, with a B.A. in
psychology. Women tell me that I look a lot like Robert
Redford. I am heavier built, inclined to overweight if I do
not regularly exercise. I was an honor student in high
school and am considered athletic by my friends, although
not outstandingly talented.

Many female fantasies seemed to hinge on large penises

and lesbianism and most of mine do, too. People tell me
that I am as strong as a bull. Unfortunately, I am not endowed as such. Like the average man, I have had opportunities for sex frequently enough, but have only had intercourse with one girl, my love. I am very romantic, but also
very defensive. I hate to disappoint girls who think that I
am very handsome and very well built by letting them discover that I am not genitally exceptional. When I am hard
as a rock, I am only six inches long and one and seven-
eighths inches in diameter. Consequently, I frequently fantasize that I am about nine inches long and two and a half
inches wide, which I assume to be a nice size to be deeply
intimate with a woman and not hurt her.

I have fantasized making love with hundreds of girls:
those I see on TV, in college, in magazines, on the street. I
am turned on by well-rounded bosoms and beautiful faces,
but I am super turned on by cunts. I am not accustomed to
vulgarity but I find "cunt" a good word to express the to-
tality of pubic hair, vagina, and vulva. I think it nice that
women have such clean organs for I am repelled by anal
intercourse. I suppose that I am not sensual enough for
some women. I am much more a lover than a stud. Of
course I am well endowed in all my fantasies, my ego hoping I feel as good to females as they do to me.

I am very turned on by cunnilingus although my girl
friend finds it dirty and impersonal. From a picture in
Playboy, I have fantasized a woman with her legs open and
a scarlet rose representing the myriad petals of her labia
and I lick them all as well as her stamen (clitoris) which
doesn't smell like a rose but tastes bitter like the sexual
secretions of clean women but is nevertheless an overwhelming turn-on. Much of the excitement of females is
their vaginal odor.

I find fantasies of two gentle women kissing each other
an excruciating turn-on. I have also fantasized two women
sitting so that their cunts touched and from the recesses of
one came gliding out a very slick and appropriately large
penis. The penis was the color of a horse's and stroked in
and out of the recipient woman without the fucking woman
making any pelvic motions. I read so often of women dissatisfied with men that lesbian fantasies more appropriately
conjure visions of honestly ecstatic women.

High on a woman's list of sadly learned anxieties is that her odor will put her lover off. She douses herself with vaginal sprays or simply pushes him away when his mouth moves downward from her breasts. She is afraid he will discover what she has always known: She is not clean. Sensing her anxiety, the man responds with an ambivalence of his own. The woman's inhibitions are confirmed. No amount of washing has ever gotten it clean enough for her. How can it be dainty enough for him?

Thus do we contrive our own unhappiness.

Women, myself included, listen with barely suspended suspicion as men like Fred (above) describe their "childlike adoration" of the vagina. Page after admiring page of praise for oral pleasures are quickly discounted, devalued by just a few words: "My only requirement," says Russell (above), "is that she be clean." How quickly my own back went up. Aha, *that* is what men really think!

But Russell never said women were dirty. He merely asked that they be clean. Is that any different from what women ask of men? There is a world of difference between someone in a restaurant who wants his favorite dish appetizingly presented, and someone else who says the food smells bad, but since the cook's feelings would be hurt if he didn't eat it, couldn't the smell and taste somehow be camouflaged?

If you find armpit odor unpleasant, that is because it is not a natural product. It is caused by bacteria. On the other hand, vaginal odor is innate to the body. Positive reaction to it has been genetically built into male biology by millions of years of evolution. Men often mention their dislike of "feminine hygiene" sprays; any woman who thinks the smell of synthetic strawberries is "nicer" than her own is tampering with one of the most profound triggers of male sexuality. Even taste is scientifically reckoned to be more smell than anything else. Taste buds merely differentiate four qualities: salt, sweet, sour, and bitter. The look of food enters into the psychology of taste. Odor alters its very physiology. The subtle over- and undertones that make us rhapsodize about this wine or that are added by the sense of smell.

While this is not the place to explore women's conditioned ambivalence about their vaginas/pussies/cunts, the fact is that most women give themselves little chance to discover that the scent of the heated female is the most powerful aphrodisiac in the animal kingdom.

BEN

I'm twenty-eight, black and an inmate in prison. I have always fantasized about being with two women, preferably white, who would make me eat their pussy until I suck them dry and they pass out from pleasure. I have never eaten any pussy, but I've always wanted to and I believe I could be very good at it. The fantasy goes like this: I'm lying down asleep, and I am suddenly awakened by a strong but very sexy odor. When my eyes open I see a thick bush of black hair with pink pouting lips protruding through it. I look up at the body very slowly and see a beautiful woman of about thirty-eight. That age because women seem to be so much more sexy then.

She then tells me, panting very softly, "Suck, lick it good. I'm going to come all in your mouth. Lick me hard and slow." As I lick, suck and bite, she grinds her pussy all over my face. Now she's screaming, "Oh, please suck me harder and faster, it feels so sucking good." She makes me suck her for hours, screaming, "Suck me dry!" She holds my head and pulls my hair deeper and deeper into her pussy. I suck, kiss, lick and bite her pussy, paying special attention to her clit. When I think that I'm through she calls her eighteen-year-old daughter in and has me do the same to her. She lays on her back and grinds her pussy in my face furiously. What turns me on is that she's rubbing it in my face with wild abandon, lust. I love the smell and taste of pussy. It's not important that I come as long as I totally satisfy my partner. My dick is only seven inches long but very thick, about five and a half inches in diameter. Then they both proceed to lick and suck me as if I'm an ice cream cone that is beginning to melt.

Eating pussy is a natural, just like breathing. Anyone

who loves it as much as I do knows this. Even though I've never eaten any.

WAYNE

You are the only person in the world that I will tell my secret thoughts to. I thought I was the only person that had fantasies about sex. I'm sixty-one years old and my wife is fifty-one. We were both brought up with the old rule, sex is taboo. I have performed oral sex with my wife one time and she loved it. But my wife don't turn me on anymore since she bought twin beds. She just don't appeal to me anymore. We both go down to the mall and sit on a bench and watch the beautiful people go by. She watches the men and I watch the women and lust. I know this sounds strange to you coming from a man who lives on the southern tip of Alabama, talking about Black People. But Honey, you will never know how these black women down here turn me on. With the new hairdo and pretty clothes, they are beautiful. Sometimes I sneak off downtown (Mobile) and watch those beautiful black asses in slacks and bare midriffs and nearly go crazy.

I have this daydream about being in a motel naked in bed and this Big Black woman comes out of the shower and gets on top of me and we fuck all night. She lets me eat her to my heart's desire. Another one is where the woman is sitting at the dining table, the long tablecloth reaching to the floor and the man under the table is me, eating the woman's crotch. I've never written to anyone like this before. I hope you will let me know if you think I'm losing my mind at my age. Give these old fogies hell, sugar.

It would be simpleminded to classify Ben's fantasy (above) of eating white women, and Wayne's yearnings for a black woman, as racist. Sexual fantasies deal in extremes; a woman of the opposite color can easily be seen as the height of eroticism.

Notions of sex between black and white people are

sprinkled throughout this book, like salt and pepper—erotic spice for the mind. The fact that one man is in prison and the other is married to a woman no longer interested in sex heightens their need for fantasy. As long as you have to do without, why not dream up something really special? A man starving on a desert island doesn't think of boiled eggs; he imagines lobster mayonnaise. whole sides of beef, gourmet meals. Compared with straightforward fucking, going down on a partner is a wonderful extra, the cherry on top of the whipped cream. What strikes me most about the abundance and gusto of male fantasies is how cunnilingus is used as a quickly understood symbol for desiring the most intense pleasure possible. The desire for transcendence is in us all.

OLIVER

My fantasy involves eating out a very fat girl. Not infrequently I've been asked during sex to eat out my partner (cunnilingus). So far, I've come pretty close and then chickened out. Now, I'd love it. Here is the fantasy:

This really obese girl and I are naked in the shower. She loves to have her cunt eaten, by the way. First she douches herself, and then I give her a soapy fucking. This leaves her genitals sweet and clean. Then we hit the bed. (I should mention here that the idea of a girl climaxing in my mouth drives me wild!) I begin rubbing my chin and face into her enormous, wet, hot crotch; and she loves this. She pulls my head with her hands firmly into that juicy vulva and humps my face, slowly at first and gradually picking up the pace. Her fat pelvis is starting to swallow *me*! It feels great. Deeper and deeper I go. Her cunt is dripping wet and tastes delicious. I shove my finger up her asshole causing her vagina to contract in mild spasms. This massages my tongue and mouth, while I suck and lick her. (Hope I'm not getting too grotesque here.) That swollen twat and my stretched open jaws fit like a hand and glove. My tongue fully extends up her vagina and is deep in her awesome belly. Soon she is writhing in climax and I gulp mouthful after mouthful of that luscious fluid. Her cunt quivers slightly as I lick her out repeatedly and she is completely spent. What bliss. I lay my face on her pubic mound and tenderly kiss her cunt. It's one of those long, wet kisses as if I were kissing her mouth. She is spent and we rest. With my head on her vulva and her fat legs cradling me, we fall asleep for the evening. (The fantasy takes place just before bedtime, incidentally.)

In case you are interested in my age, I am twenty-two.

STEVE

I have been happily married for twenty years to a fine woman three years my senior. I am certain there is very little we haven't tried other than group sex and the torture, humiliation bit. As is natural, our sex life has slowed now to an average of three times a week (sometimes four). However these sex sessions are not dull routine as we still really dig each other. Her most dazzling and earthshaking orgasms result from my going down on her. Her whole pelvic area convulsed and shook at those times and she would cry out and drench the sheets with her lubricant and perspiration. Once she cried out that she thought she was going to die from the experience. After that, she was reluctant to allow me to eat her because she sincerely thought she might have a stroke or heart attack. So, as the years went by we indulged less and less in my eating her and she progressed more and more into sucking me. I have a point in describing this sequence in our life as I believe it explains (at least to me) the extremely erotic fantasies I now have regarding oral sex. The following is my great one:

I am in a large darkened room and there are dozens of succulent and sex starved females lying with their legs spread—exposing their round little bottoms and tantalizing patches of hair of many shapes and hues. Just as varied are the provoking little lips which protrude through the various bushes—just waiting—waiting for something that they know is coming—my lips, my tongue, my gentle, nibbling teeth. Also within this endless circle of quivering bodies I see something else that drives me up the wall in anticipation—clean shaven mounds with stark, beautiful features—

features not unlike a young maiden before growing pubic hair—pussies that I try to engulf completely in my mad passion.

Gently and tenderly I touch, trying not to hurry, caressing each in turn long enough for them to start getting aroused and restless with desire. As I progress from one to another, they let me know there is no end to the things they want me to do to them. They plead and moan and cry—none wants me to leave them but I must try to please them all. I can feel that they are getting delirious in their passion—their fingers are straying to their moist little cunts and are doing all manner of rubbing, stroking, stretching and pulling of the whole area around their pussies. As I have only one mouth and tongue, I must help them along, so my hands and fingers go to work on wet pussies—in and out, around, up and down and sideways with an intentional slipping of a wet finger into their little puckered rear end holes. This drives one beauty so gloriously crazy that she grabs my head and pulls my face hard against her crotch crying, "Eat me, eat me, lick me, I'm gonna come—oh . . ." and her voice trails off as her body shakes and I can feel the muscles contract and relax many times on my finger up her ass.

Now all of my hot little bitches are screaming for my tongue, lips and fingers and I love it! I am circling the clit of a precious redhead on my left while I lick my favorite shaved slit like a huge dog and the blond doll on my right is squirming with my fingers massaging her little valley and suddenly all three come at the same time and singing the same song! It is wonderful!

The whole room is reeking with sex and the beautiful smell of hot females. All of my little horny dolls have somewhat the same characteristic aroma but I delight in tasting and smelling little differences in each. By now those who haven't come are practically over the edge with their frantic fingering so I must work like a dog literally—licking the full length of their pussies, slipping my tongue in and out, around the clit, up and down, around and in, and suddenly that gasp and delighted moan of pleasure tells me what I did for her. I seem to know each one's desires because there are those who are so sensitive I must pull away quickly, others want me to linger ever so gently on their pulsing cunt but not move, others want me to lick up and down gently and there are those who want my tongue to slip up their little asses. I even have a few who must let go with a stream of pee and I do not care if they do as I love anything that they do.

At long last they are all completely satisfied and as I pass along from one to another I see in their eyes an expression of soul gratitude and admiration for what I have done for them. Arms are outstretched to me and I must hold them for a moment as their quivering bodies and moaning lips subside. End of fantasy.

In my great fantasy I do not fuck my girls. My analysis of my own fantasy is that since I get plenty of fucking in my life-style but am somewhat starved in eating my wife's pussy, I compensate for this lack by fantasy (daydream). I have also read so much material about women stating and complaining that men never want to go down on them either from ignorance or that they (men) find the female smell objectionable. I love and adore that smell to the extent that if my wife is horny and wants to trick me into the bedroom, all she has to do is run her finger through the lips of her pussy and put it under my nose. So, it is this failing in men that my fantasy tries to compensate.

By the way it probably would be of interest to add that I am sixty years old.

EDDIE

I am a male between fifty and sixty years old and since I can remember, I have jacked off thinking about some erotic woman or instance. When I was a child my sisters played doctor with me and they always examined my cock and balls. I used to jack off while thinking about feeling my mother's cunt and titties. She helped my fantasies by being lovable and adorable as all mothers are. I am married and have sired a number of children.

I wish I could be provided with enough sex so I would not have to jack off. Every morning I have an enormous erection and am ready for sucking, fucking, and eating and loving a cunt. I love cunt and most of all I love to eat cunt. There is no other sweet taste and smell as the aroma of a clean cunt. I love to put my cock in my wife's hot cunt and then have it sucked off while I put my tongue into the cunt that enclosed the cock. I jack off at least three or four times a week while thinking of my wife sucking my asshole. She hasn't done this yet, but I am hoping. I would love to see her in bed with another woman sucking each other off. I get her to jack off once in a while and always try to arrange it so that I can watch without her knowing it. This gives me a hard cock and tongue. I enjoy sixtynining but like it better when she and I suck each other for awhile and then stop to kiss and tongue each other's mouths. I would love to have her suck my cock and take the load, then come up and kiss my mouth which is full of pussy juice. This I call uninhibited love. I wish there was some way I could persuade her into my sexual world of fantasies and do them all filled with love and tenderness. I love her, her cunt, her ass, her mouth, her tits, her armpits and everything about her. If she would love me the same way in return, my sex life would be fulfilled and I would never look at another woman.

Every day of my life I yearn for my wife to do me like I do her. I fantasize her being a willing partner. Are there any other men like me? Women if your husband shows love like I have described, please for heaven's sake return his love ardently and do to him whatever he does to you. You'll never lose a husband if you comply and yours and his life will be complete.

My earlier books on women's sexuality were filled with rapturous fantasies (from both lesbian women and straight) of one women going down on another. This book makes it obvious men love cunnilingus too. Fellatio seems to be more of an acquired taste. Many men regret that so few women acquire it.

Perhaps there is an undying, unconscious memory of the pleasure baby boys and girls once found in a woman's body that accounts for this universal and almost guilt-free desire. There is something about the female shape, muscle tone, skin sensation, odor, and feel that speaks to the primitive memories of both sexes. It is also relevant, I think, to remember that some of the first pleasures we found in mother's body were taken through the mouth.

Oliver (above) says, "Her fat pelvis [which he is eating] is starting to swallow *me*." Ideas associated with the most impressionable time of life are being played with; the association with the mother of infancy could not be clearer. Other men tell of being taken in, pulled in, by the woman.

Right along with these regained joys of infancy, equal and opposite grown-up pleasure of power and control arise. For a man who has never seen his wife "out of control," how thrilling it must be to see her lose her inhibitions and become abandoned, an animal, just like him. Cunnilingus gives him this power. Ideas like these appeal to men like Steve (above), who say they like cunnilingus not only for the satisfaction it gives them, but even more for their pleasure in seeing the woman reach orgasm.

A man may have chosen his wife because she was a nice girl, like mom; but the almost never-fail magic of oral sex cracks through this unerotic façade and reveals his wife to be the sexy bad girl he has dreamed of all along. Steve says his wife's orgasms were so intense when he went down on her that she cried out that she was going to die from the experience.

The thrill of oral sex for men is that it resolves the masculine conflict, fusing both the good girl and the bad girl into one figure. And she is in bed with him!

A further idea grows out of Mrs. Steve's taboo on oral sex after her one intense experience; never again, she said, because it might cause her a stroke or heart attack. The reader may feel this is largely a rationalization; the ancient taboo that nice girls don't do it is at work once again. The question to be asked is this: Why would a woman reclothe herself in this antisexual role once she has tasted the pleasures of breaking it? What does she gain? I'm afraid the best answer I can give is that this is another form of power.

Traditionally, women have used sex for reward or punishment. To the degree that a woman denies a man her climax, she keeps him off balance. A Victorian idea, one totally out of joint with our times, but this is to talk about conscious attitudes. Many women do not believe in their newly won rights so much as they still *feel* their old insecurities. She wants sex, she wants to let go, but some vestige of the old training still holds her back: If he thinks he has failed her in the bedroom, he will guiltily give in to her demands in the rest of the house. A bitter victory.

"Why doesn't he enjoy going down on me?" women wail.

"Why won't she let me?" he agonizes.

The dialogue is reminiscent of people who complain that there are no suitable partners available of the opposite sex. "Why can't I find a man to take care of me?" the woman patient cries to her therapist. There are plenty of men who would love to take care of her. The problem is that such men have a price: The woman must do things his way. That is what makes them "unsuitable."

One of the myths with which we live is that orgasm and sexual satisfaction are the two halves of an invariable formula; one always means the other. But there are people who, while multiorgasmic, still don't enjoy sex. Many others who never or rarely climax love the closeness and excitement of sex anyway. The cry of many women is familiar: that once a man has reached orgasm, he doesn't care if she does or not. This is just the opposite of a wide body of research that stresses how often men measure themselves by their ability to bring their partners to orgasm. On a more positive note, William Blake, in his "Gnomic Verses," observes that what we all want, men and women alike, is to see "the lineaments of gratified desire" in the face of a beloved.

It is nice to give to someone you love; it is also nice to feel you have the power to do so.

5

Semen

THEO

I am now forty-nine years old, and I was forty before I found out how to turn women on! I met a twenty-two-year-old blonde who was aggressive because she was splitting with her old man. We met in an airport waiting room and made arrangements for our first get-together during a short flight when we'd both have a couple of hours in a distant town before changing planes to fly off in different places. It was the first great fuck for either of us! She had never gone down on a man before, and I taught her. It gave her such a feeling of power to be able to make me come that way, that she was more aroused than she could have believed! My wife never showed any aggressiveness, but this blonde was after my cock as soon as I climaxed. She wanted to drink every drop. We would stop along the road and go down on each other in the daylight and she always screamed when she climaxed, which really turned me on!

Having had some experience with professionals, I discovered that high-quality, expensive call girls were very gifted in sex. My fantasy is to be in charge of several girls; my duty is to break each one into the art of fellatio. I discovered that most call girls are amateurish at fellating a man and have some undesirable tricks they use to conceal their feelings about the client's semen from him. But if they are taught correctly, they grow to love it! And I would train them to do it the way my French girl friend did it. I fantasize having a training session with redheads, blondes, brunettes, blacks, orientals, and Latin girls—all beautiful and lusty, with the types of bodies I like. First the girl

should have her hair done up in a tight bun or be able to
toss it charmingly from side to side as she worked over my
throbbing cock! She would be instructed to face my feet so
that I could play with her ass and cunt as she played with
me! I would have a pillow under my ass to raise me about
six inches so she could have access to all the sensuous zones
and explore them! She would start out by testing my re-
flexes with a light kiss on my tummy to see if my cock
would rise, then progress down lightly kissing my pubic
hair and then to the inside of my thighs (this is the reason
for having the pillow) and finally to the perineum area
with light darting flicks of the tongue! I would instruct the
girls in exercising their tongues so that they could vibrate
like a tuning fork. Mostly, I would teach them the joy of
drinking men's semen.

When a girl was finished with her training, she would be
able to fully arouse a man and then start to work on his
cock (using mine as a training device) by flicking the head
of the cock with her tongue, then taking it up to where it
was comfortable, slowly withdrawing on the upstroke and
fast on the stroke down! Encircling the rim of the head
with her tongue and vibrating her tongue against the draw
string (the most sensitive area), never once touching the
cock with her teeth. This she would do by curling her lips
over her teeth to form an oval with her mouth! As she
progressed, her mouth would become quite wet with saliva
(a necessary art for the great fellator) and her cheeks
would pull in simulating as closely as possible fucking naturally! Finally, if the man had trouble coming, she would
use her index finger and gently massage his prostate gland
by inserting the finger gently but quite deeply into the
man's ass! This always makes them come (and is another
reason for the pillow), and she would come with him (he
has been playing with her delicious ass which has been
turned toward him all the while). She either waits until the
spurts stop (three or four) and swallows the sacred fluid or
lets it spurt on her face as a beauty treatment! Never,
never refuse it by spitting it out or letting him come in a
towel or tissue! Then she cuddles up quietly alongside him
while the passions subside! Then she refreshens his genital
area with a damp cloth and soft towel!

I would also instruct the girls in the art of developing

and using a snappy pussy! This is delightful to a man and a treasured possession of all women! First I would instruct the girls in how to develop their inner vaginal muscles and give them exercises to make them strong! Next, they would practice their exercises on my cock in various positions until they could squeeze at least sixty times a minute and could expel a cock from their pussy they would be so strong! However, the real purpose is to do the opposite. That is, to actually keep the cock inside and so milk it during the final strokes before climax. None of that wonderful fluid is wasted. By making you know she loves your semen, you can tell she has given you everything!

HAMILTON

I am thirty-three years old, married with two children, and have an active sexual relationship with my wife. Being an army officer, we have traveled and lived in Europe for a total of almost five and one-half years. Much of our present attitude toward sex has been positively influenced by the European acceptance of male and female sexuality.

We have been married for ten years. We met in college and lived together for nearly two years before we were married. My wife is three years younger than I and both of us are from the East Coast. We have experimented with many sexual techniques and enjoy oral and occasionally anal sex. We've tried group sex only once, with a girl we both knew and liked. None of us were really mature enough to handle the feelings that emerged.

Men often get a very incomplete picture of women because they are always told to "keep your hands to yourself" and "good girls don't do that sort of thing" by women (from mother to girl friend to wife) who seem to be programmed to deny female sexuality. Personally, I was very happy to discover women to be "just like us" (when it comes to sexual enjoyment) when I read your first book and got enough courage to ask my wife about it.

The following fantasy is long but I have tried to be as descriptive as possible in an effort to present my feelings accurately. In my own way, I would like to contribute to a better understanding of that much maligned human experience—sex.

I take an archaeological vacation to the site of Pompeii and Herculaneum. After a week of work, excavators uncover a crypt. I take it upon myself to explore the new discovery and find the crypt leads to an enormous cavern filled with statues, mausoleums, and, in the very heart of the cavern, a great marble temple! The entire cavern is lit by a ghostly luminescence. I soon discover the source of the eerie light, phosphorescent lichen.

My curiosity soon leads me to the temple steps. I know little of archaeology, but I know enough to realize I gaze upon an archaeologist's dream come true, a perfectly preserved section of the outlying district of an ancient city. I advance along a large hallway. Suddenly the passageway opens into a great hall. I stare in awe at the ancient wonder before me, the stone seems to move. I touch it to reassure myself, then it does move! I quickly look up, the columns are moving slightly too. Earthquake!

"Oh, my God," I think, "it can't be, it can't be!" As if in answer, the floor shifts and I know it's true. I am trapped deep within a mountain, this ancient tomb will soon be my modern tomb.

The giant columns sway sickeningly. With a sharp crack and a deafening roar the wall directly in front of me is splintered. For an instant I see a burning multi-faceted crystal, then I see no more. Blinded, I hold on to the altar and pull myself onto its flat top. I pass into unconsciousness.

After the quake has subsided, those in the outside world assume me dead. Two days later, excavators at the site of the previously discovered crypt entrance find the passageway still intact. Workmen located the great hall and in its center amid the remains of what appears to be a large altar, and discover a severely burned, but still living man.

Taken to a hospital, I am given little chance for survival. I can overhear my wife talking with the doctors. The doctors tell her I am dying, it's only a matter of time, a few hours, a day, soon. My skin is hardened, a crust; in some places only blackened cinder remains, but I feel no pain.

A week passes, yet I still live! It is a dark, cool night. I feel cramped and yearn to stretch. I move. First one arm, then the other. All the movements are accompanied by soft popping sounds. Last I open my eyes; I see!

I lay in a white hospital bed, the moonlight pours through French windows placed just beyond the foot of my bed. Among the show-white sheets lie black ashes and hard, discolored bits of what can only be skin. I look at my legs, my hands, and my arms. Bathed in the moon's silver glow, my body seems the color of polished copper. Weakly I raise myself, I must look in a mirror. Am I scarred, disfigured, mutilated?

With great effort I reach the bathroom and switch on the light. I stare down at my copper-colored hands as they grip the edge of the white porcelain sink. Steeling myself, I quickly raise my head. "Oh, my God!" bursts from my lips. "What has happened to me?" I stare at the reflection before me. I see myself, but not me at all. The face is the same, but subtle changes have occurred. The face is broader, cheekbones slightly higher, jaw squarer, and the eyes, the eyes! Where my eyes, once brown, looked out, now eyes of green, jade green, look back at me.

Needless to say, the attending physicians are overwhelmed by my metamorphosis, but none as much as I. Within a month I have regained my strength. I am taller and broader than previously and my hair, a glowing blue-black, is almost completely grown in. I long to return home, especially to see my wife and children again.

After a short time, my life returns to its normal pace. I return to my old job and home. My family, friends, and co-workers adapt to my new appearance. One of the most pleasant changes resulting from my alteration is a markedly improved love life. My urge for intercourse has increased and responses have heightened; this, in turn, has made my wife more responsive. Strangest of all is the amount and composition of my semen. I discovered this the first time my wife and I made love after my transformation.

We were both somewhat hesitant, but after a long session of foreplay, slowly getting used to each other again, the passion rapidly begins building. I caress each part of her body, kissing, licking, sucking-lingering on her throat, nipples (a long time there), small of the back, inside of the thighs, and cunt. She tastes wonderful and comes a couple of times as I lick her cunt and tease her clit with my tongue and lips. I then mount her (missionary position) and slowly start moving in and out. In a short time I can no longer control the motion of my hips and I'm fucking like a wild stallion, slamming into her. She meets me thrust for thrust, her head periodically thrashing from side to side. She noans, begs me to keep it up.

"Harder, deeper!" she cries. "Fuck me, fuck me, fuck me!" Then WHAM! I come like gangbusters! I've never come like this in my life, it's a gusher. My wife's eyes are wide with amazement, surprise, and excitement.

"Oh, God! Fill me up with that hot come. Fill me up!" she gasps.

Later, as I slide from her cunt, she's still gasping and panting. I look down and see her legs wide open, her cunt and ass soaked with come. I stare; I can't take my eyes off that delicious cunt, for covering it is my come, not the white, milky substance I'm accustomed to seeing, but thick, golden fluid. It looks almost like honey!

Lying there, my wife is a picture of beauty. Her face and chest are flushed with passion.

"Oh," she says, "I never felt that way before; you've never come like that before. So warm and wet and soft, I can't move it feels so good."

Later that night she wakes me, wants me.

"Just lie there," she whispers, "I want to touch you; love you all over."

As I lie there, I feel her lips and tongue moving over me, sucking, kissing, licking—it's marvelous! After teasing my nipples, she slowly kisses her way down my chest and stomach to my crotch. She kisses my thighs. My prick is rock hard, the head full and pulsating, but she ignores it. She licks and kisses around my prick and finally takes each of my balls in her mouth and begins softly caressing the head of my prick. Moving from my balls, she licks her way the entire length of my rigid shaft, teasingly licks the rim of the head and then slowly envelops it with her lips. With one hand holding and slowly kneading my balls, she wraps the other firmly around my prick and slowly begins to move it up and down. As she sucks, she caresses the head and rim of my prick with her tongue. She removes her hands and slowly begins to deep throat, taking as much of

my prick as she can, finally reaching the base. My hands
are gripping the sheets by this time. I want to grab her hair
and move her head up and down. Instead my hips begin
lifting off the bed to thrust deep into her sucking mouth.

She takes her mouth away, rises to her knees. Bending
down, she lays her tits on either side of my aching balls
and envelops my cock with her mouth. Her come-slick fingers go to my nipples and touch and squeeze them as I
pump in and out of her mouth. Faster and faster moves her
head and my hips. I can bear it no longer. I arch my back
and pour my hot come into her eager, slurping mouth. The
golden come runs out the sides of her mouth and down her
chin; she tries to catch every drop. There's so much she
can't possibly swallow it all.

"Oh, my God," she cries, "you taste so good! Sweet,
warm, and delicious!"

After many days and nights of loving, my wife tells me
that when she swallows my come it creates a fantastic urge
to fuck or suck me about a day later. She says the urge
peaks at about twenty-four hours and just about drives her
crazy for an hour or so, then fades.

I decide to test this theory and one night fill a medicine
bottle that has an eye-dropper top with my golden come.
There is a very lovely young girl at work and I have
dreamed of making love to her. She is the target of my test.

One day I see this lovely girl make a cup of tea. She is
called out for a moment and I take the opportunity to
sweeten her tea with some of the contents of my medicine
bottle. Observing her habits, I make it a point to be close
by when she takes her morning cup of tea. I do this for
three days.

By the fourth day I am beginning to feel foolish, nothing
has happened, and I make up my mind that the whole experiment is a bust. However, at eleven thirty, in walks the
girl and asks to speak with me about a problem she's having. I'm very busy at that moment and ask her to return in
about twenty minutes (I'm pressing my luck here). At
eleven fifty she's back and appears very agitated. She sits
next to my desk and we begin talking. I ask why she
wishes to speak with me (I'm not her boss) and she says
she's having problems with her job, can't talk to her boss,
and wants my advice. We go on this way and by five after

twelve the office is deserted except for us. She says she really needs my help and begins to cry. I stand, get a Kleenex, and take it to her. She stands, accepts the tissue, and says, "The problem isn't work. The problem is . . . well, really it's . . . (she begins to cry again) oh, hold me, just hold me!"

I immediately put my arms around her. I'm not sure, has my experiment worked or is she really in some kind of trouble? She lifts her face from my shoulder and looks into my eyes. The look is long and slowly our faces move toward each other and we kiss, long and deep. As I kiss her, I stroke her hair, it's soft as silk, and pull her body to me. She responds by arching her back and pushing her pelvis into me. After more kisses, I kiss my way down her throat and onto her soft, firm breasts. I unbutton her blouse and begin to kiss and suck her nipples. Her response is to stand and softly moan.

From here the fantasy may take a number of directions. Some of the common themes are as follows:

1. I make love to the girl and end up fucking her on the floor, next to my desk.
2. After kissing and sucking her tits, I eat her cunt till she comes. She then sucks me and swallows all my come.
3. After kissing her tits, she drops to her knees and pulls out my prick and makes love to it till I come all over her face and tits.
4. After eating her cunt, I turn her over my desk and fuck her from behind as I knead her tits and she rubs her clit.
5. I fuck her on my desk till we come together. After a short rest, she sucks me to a full erection and begs me to fuck her in the ass.

I now know that I possess the greatest aphrodisiac in the world: my own come!

Why a man's unambivalent love of her vagina opens a woman's heart was the subject of the last chapter. This one explores a parallel emotion. Why are men equally won by women who accept and love their semen? Someone who lets him taste it on her lips; who shows she feels some of the secret pride he has always had for "the sacred fluid"—as Theo (above) puts it—with none of the repugnance he has simultaneously come to fear on the part of women. In fact, Hamilton's fantasy (above) turns his semen into such "thick, golden fluid" that his wife becomes a love slave when she drinks it. He has discovered he possesses "the greatest aphrodisiac in the world."

Am I overemphatic in my belief that oral love, oral sex, reinforces self-love, which, in turn, is the necessary base on which to build belief that we are lovable to someone else, too? Isn't our very first experience of love oral? Isn't mother's withdrawal of the breast from our lips among the earliest signs that love can be lost? One of the first blows to self-respect was learning that various emissions from the body are unacceptable.

Psychoanalysts have long noted the unconscious mingling together in many men's minds of semen, urine, and feces—all three are emissions from the body. Toilet training taught the young boy what mother thought about the last two. A few years later, whatever he himself might feel at the sight of his first nocturnal emission, he knew what she would think if she found stains on his bedsheets.

Fortunately, there is one area of his body mother doesn't know about. She doesn't have a penis. To her, this is a warning that here are mysteries she had better not tamper with. To the boy, it is a visible sign that he is different from mother. If she does try to inhibit him, from what authority does she speak?

What can she know about semen? It is the sign of manhood, of sexuality and shared male experience—an arrow pointing him away from home. The boy and his friends once played elaborate pissing and shitting games together. When he is old enough to ejaculate, his semen becomes another door closed on mother and her rules. All these activities—which once almost lost him mother—have been rebelliously turned into secret male rituals, naughty but fun.

Ideas like these are abhorrent to little girls who are iden-

tified with mother's body for life. Think of the parallel between the boy's approach to semen and the young girl's view
of menstruation: Women's problems of shame and humiliation at bleeding stem from a lifelong association with
mother in which everything that emanates from the body is
suspect. A male critic reviewing a recent book on menstruation commented that if men bled once a month, they'd
probably have turned it into a triumphant assertion of
manhood. Which is what they've done, instead, with semen.

I do not wish to promote the idea that boys make their
assertion of independence from mother without guilt.
These differences between the sexes are shades of gray, not
black and white. Among themselves, men are proud of
their semen. In porn feature films, it is customary for the
male star to withdraw just before the climax. In real life,
men hate coitus interruptus. But in these movies, they want
to see something that speaks powerfully to their emotions—even more powerfully than sex brought to orgasm·
the camera zooms in just as the hero comes, and the screen
is filled with gallons of spurting semen. It is not a homosexual desire that the audience is expressing so much as
identification with the hero; they are proud of this sign of
potency as if it were their own.

On the other hand, their resentment that women may
not feel the same is shown in the popularity of those
twenty-five-cent movie machines in Times Square where
women are forced to drink semen from champagne gob-
lets—and love it.

From this difference in perception, this anxiety that
women do not value semen as highly as they do, men fall
from certainty. Just as a woman may feel most deeply accepted to be loved during her menstrual period, so does a
man feel most loved when a woman drinks every drop of
his orgasmic "sacred fluid."

As far back as I can remember, I've resented the idea
that sexuality is determined by our first years of life. How
could anything as infantile as toilet training have to do
with what goes on between adults in the bedroom? Years
of research have shown me that when I quarrel with
Freud, he is often right.

Without resort to psychoanalytic theory, how can we begin to explain men like Theo? All we would be able to say is that he sounds freaky, dirty. Adjectives that express our hostility to his ideas, but explain nothing about the mysteries of human nature.

To the Freudian, this eagerness to dismiss Theo with just an unthinking cliché or two is evidence of our own strong repression of toilet training humiliations. Theo is in fact a vivid reminder of the frustrations that live on in all of us, no matter how many years have passed since we learned continence. To the two-year-old mind— unconscious remnants of which are still evident in Theo's fantasy—anything that comes out of his body *is* him. He wants the woman in his present grown-up life to make up for the insults inflicted on him by another woman in his distant past. What better way than by teaching dozens of women the joys of drinking his sperm?

JOHN

I am thirty-five years old and a lawyer by profession. I have been married fifteen years and have had a fairly active sexual life. Fantasies have always played an important role in my sex life.

I still remember many sexual incidents that occurred in my youth. One, in particular, has played an important role in shaping my fantasies. It happened when I was about eleven. I went swimming one day at the municipal pool. The pool contained a locker room for changing, and there were small enclosed rooms available for an additional fee which afforded privacy. In the locker room, a man about thirty years old struck up a conversation with me and offered me the use of his locker room. When I went in, he followed me, closing and locking the door behind us. I was a little alarmed by this but I went ahead and undressed in his presence. As soon as I was naked, he began to fondle my cock and balls. I was frightened and submitted without protest. Then he had me lie down on a small bench while he sucked me to an immature climax. When he was finished, he removed his swimming suit and stood in front of me, legs slightly apart (I was now sitting on the bench).

Taking hold of my hand, he directed it to his cock and had me "feel" him until he became stiff. Then he made me suck him until he shot his load into my mouth. When he came, he held my head to prevent my pulling away, and I was forced to swallow most of his cum.

I kept this incident to myself, but took it in stride. In fact, over the years I have fantasized about it while masturbating, and have enjoyed it in retrospect. I think, though, that it planted the seed which has ripened into my later fantasies. These usually involve a dominant/submissive relationship with me generally assuming the submissive role. This is exactly opposite to my outward personality, which is aggressive and competitive.

Aside from some isolated experiences with mutual masturbation during my early adolescence, I have engaged in homosexual sex only one other time since the experience described above. That experience involved a youth with whom I had engaged in mutual masturbation, and took place a few years after my marriage. (Thinking back, I must have been about twenty-seven at the time). My friend visited us one evening after a long absence from town, and I took him home. I knew he was a homosexual, and on the way home he described some of his experiences. After a while, he suggested that we stop somewhere along the way. We were both a little high, and I pulled over on a dark side street. For a few seconds we continued to talk, before I seized the initiative and reached over and grasped his cock. Without wasting time on preliminaries, I unfastened his pants and pulled them down. I ran my hand over his cock and balls for a minute or two before taking it in my mouth. I think I gave him a pretty good blow job and I enjoyed the feel of his smooth cock filling my mouth. When he came after about five minutes I didn't think twice about swallowing his cum. After I finished, he sucked me off. I've seen him only twice since then and we didn't have an opportunity on either occasion to repeat this experience.

My fantasies fall roughly into four categories. In the first category, I am once again forced to perform homosexual sex. In one fantasy, for example, I am alone in a movie theatre when two young men come in and sit on either side of me. I am alarmed and try to leave, but they won't let me pass. They threaten me unless I do what they want. First, I

am forced to pull my pants down around my ankles while
they take turns feeling my cock and balls. I feel vulnerable
and humiliated sitting there half naked, but my prick becomes very hard nevertheless. Just when I am on the brink
of orgasm, they make me kneel on the floor and suck their
cocks. They both shoot huge amounts of sperm into my
mouth, some of which dribbles out the sides and streams
down my face. As a final humiliation, they jack me off,
directing my cum into my pants. I must then leave the
theater with wet, white globs of sperm dotting my pants,
and with dried cum streaking my face.

In my second group of fantasies I am dominated by an
attractive woman. Sometimes she is alone; sometimes there
is more than one woman present; and sometimes there is
either a male or female "slave" present; and sometimes the
woman is accompanied by a dominant male.

In a typical fantasy, I go to the house of a very beautiful
but cruel woman. As soon as I enter she slaps my face
several times and orders me to strip. I notice that several
other women are present and hesitate, but comply when
she slaps me again. It is very humiliating to take off my
clothes in the presence of so many women, and they watch
me intently and with amusement. When I am naked, the
woman ties my hands behind my back and puts a dog collar and leash around my neck. Then she leads me around
the room, letting the other women "examine" me. I am
forbidden to have an erection, but one of the women takes
my cock in her mouth and I immediately become hard.
This infuriates my mistress, who forces me to lie across her
lap while she spanks me with a hairbrush until I cry and
beg her to stop. I promise to do anything she says. She
then releases my hands and makes me "play" with myself.
When she has tired of this, she produces a large dildo,
which I am forced to suck so that the other women can see
what a good cocksucker I am. Then she makes me bend
over while she pushes the dildo roughly up my ass. When I
protest, she says that I will have to have my mouth washed
out with "something bad." While I watch her, she pisses
into a glass and makes me drink it. She then removes her
clothes, bends over in front of me, and makes me stick my
tongue in and out of her ass. Finally, I am made to eat all
of their cunts. Before letting me go, they make me mastur-

bate to orgasm while they watch and then swallow my own cum.

Another group of fantasies involves my wife having sex with other men and women. In one of these, I bring a good-looking black man home for dinner. Somehow, I have convinced her beforehand to have sex with him, and after dinner we go into the living room where she sits next to him on the couch. They kiss passionately, and her hand goes to his crotch. She fumbles with his pants, finally getting them unfastened and unzipped. They continue to kiss while she feels his cock beneath his underpants. Then she kneels in front of him and pulls his pants off, freeing his large black prick for the first time. When she sees it she moans passionately and buries her face in his crotch, kissing and licking his cock and balls. She becomes terrifically excited now and starts to suck on it greedily, forcing it deep into her mouth. He stops her before he comes and has her take off her clothes. When she is naked, he feels her breasts and cunt. She becomes wildly excited and begs him to fuck her. He has her kneel on all fours while he enters her cunt from the rear, fucking her dog style until she climaxes. Then he stands in front of her while she finishes him with her mouth. When he shoots his sperm into her mouth she swallows it hungrily, but the deluge of cum is so great that much of it escapes and streams down her face. She rubs this into her skin, licking her fingers clean.

In another group of fantasies, I am dominant. In one of my favorites, I take a woman (submissive) to the movies. Before we go I supervise her dressing. Her wardrobe for the evening is simple, consisting of garter belt, stockings and a silky dress which buttons down the front and clings to the contours of her body. I do not allow her to fasten the top button and several of the bottom buttons, so that fleeting glimpses of her nudity are possible. She wears a choker around her neck as a symbol of submission. At the theater, we sit in an uncrowded section. After the show is in progress, I have her unbutton the dress and open her legs. The dress falls open exposing her nudity. She is ordered to caress herself, which she does. At length, I produce a large dildo and tell her to stick it up her cunt. Just before the show is over I make her lick the dildo clean. She is permitted to fasten her dress before we leave.

When we get to my place, I tell her to remove her dress while I take off my clothes. After she has removed the dress, I make her lie across my lap while I spank her until she cries and begs me to stop. I go and get my dog then, a large German shepherd (I don't actually own a dog) and tell her to play with its cock. Reluctantly, she goes over to it and begins to fondle its penis, which becomes hugely erect. Then she is forced to her knees on all fours while the dog mounts and fucks her, bringing her to several orgasms. When the dog comes, I make her clean its cock with her mouth.

Next I tie her spread-eagled to the bed and use a vibrator on her, bringing her to the brink of climax repeatedly. When I sense that she has had enough, I untie her and push her roughly onto her stomach. At the same time I pull her hands behind her back and pin them there painfully. Then I force my cock into her ass and fuck her. When I am about to come, I pull out and shoot my sperm onto her face and into her open mouth.

I have never experienced any of my fantasies, but I would like to one of these days. In my opinion fantasies play an important role in sex, and sex games are healthy when engaged in by consenting partners. Unfortunately, though, for most of us our fantasies must remain locked away in "our secret gardens."

John's fantasies (above) are filled with ideas of domination and humiliation. If I have put them here rather than in the chapter on S&M, it is because they so clearly explore certain ultimate ambivalences about semen.

In John's one adult homosexual experience, he had no feeling of repugnance about semen; he didn't "think twice" about swallowing it. But his fantasies show his unconscious still holds notions that semen is disgusting and degrading. No woman could ever accept it. And if women won't, how can he? He is in a fury because he must see part of himself as vile.

This anger seeks an outlet. The symbol of shame—semen—becomes an expression of rage. Many men who carry enormous infantile angers into their grown-up relationships to women, have a hard time expressing aggression outward. Any such confrontation might cause the final break in love. Hostility gets turned around, against the self. Painful, but safer.

The black man's semen may be "hungrily" swallowed by John's wife. This is the traditional view of the power position between men and women, and as such, appropriate for a woman to do. When cruel females force John to swallow his own, it is an expression of his loss of power and masculinity.

BRUCE

I am in my mid-twenties, college educated, and enjoy sex a lot.

I have sex regularly with my girl friend. Usually, I don't fantasize when we fuck, it's mostly when I masturbate (which is quite frequently, sometimes twice a day).

I love to get sucked off, and many times will envision some lips sliding gently up and down my throbbing dick taking it all in, over and over, until I'm unable to withstand any more of this extreme pleasure and come into this hot, wonderful mouth.

Eventually this evolved to the point where I imagined it was my mouth. I can lay down with my cock limp and dream of curling my lips around it and sucking it all into my mouth and feeling it grow and as I think this, it will (in reality) grow very hard. At this time, I begin to masturbate (as I am compelled to do as I write this) and lick the first drops of cum from a fingertip, while in fantasy, my tongue is gently licking the tip of my hard hot cock. As my hand strokes my dick faster and faster, I feel as though I am sucking myself off passionately. I engulf my slippery erect prick in my mouth and pump and suck it until the precise moment when I shoot my hot cum into my mouth. At this time in reality, I come.

HERB

I'm forty-eight years old, married, the father of two boys still at home. My wife works, and I'm a composer and teacher of music theory. Our home life is good with probably no more problems than anyone raising children. Our sex life is great, but by that I mean that sex is the one thing in our lives where there has never been a problem, the one big thing we have in common. Our sex together began over thirty years ago, before we married, and it just goes on and gets better.

In my line of work, I've spent a lot of my life living in hotels and motels, and it is sometimes a really lonesome life. Far from a lot of wives' fears, it is not a life of sexual joy with new women all the time. In the first place, in the hours when most people are socializing, as an entertainer I'm working, and as a serious musician this requires all my concentration. In the second place, I've seldom found the results worth all the effort involved in picking up a stranger. I've never even understood the existence of prostitution. If I had to pay a woman for sex, she couldn't possibly give me what I was paying her for. To me, one of the most important aspects of sex is the knowledge that you are giving the other person as much pleasure as they are giving you, and a lot of this is knowing that they desire sex, not just as sex, per se, but sex with Me because they like Me as a person enough to want to be that intimate, and share this wonderful feeling with me. I don't mean to imply that my life on the road has been monastic, but the sexual experiences I have had were in the above category, and simply don't happen very often. Consequently, the natural result is frequent and skillful masturbation, and the development of a never-ending supply of wonderful fantasies.

For several years I've been staying close to home, but my work is naturally mostly at night, and as my wife works days, I find myself in the role of "househusband." Weekdays I must get up and get our little boy off to school, much of the time after having had only three to five hours sleep. I found that I had a hell of a time getting back to sleep until it dawned on me what a wonderful sedative a good climax is. Now, after everyone is gone for the day, I get out some pornography and go back to bed. Anything sexy to get quickly into the mood is useful before getting into a good sexual fantasy.

My fantasies fall into two categories, those based on reality, things that have actually happened or could conceivably happen, and those that I wouldn't want to really happen, but are at times exciting as fantasy. (Sound familiar?)

When I was five, the little girl next door, also five, and I played together, and when alone, played sexually a lot. Her big thing, aside from looking at and touching each other, was watching each other pee. From that, at her suggestion, we progressed to peeing on each other. We had several good private places where we could take off our clothes and play without ever being caught at it. We would sit naked' with her legs up over mine and our crotches up against each other, and watch and feel the piss come out of her little pee hole and my little peter all over both of us. She would then rub my hard little cock against her pussy, many times long enough that all the piss would be evaporated before we got dressed. At five years old, I knew nothing about a climax, but I have a sneaking hunch she did, and you can bet your boots that in my present fantasies, I did too. As I get into this fantasy, we progress to her standing up and peeing all over me, then squatting down over my mouth and me swallowing her pee as it comes out. Then she moves down and takes my hard little prick in her mouth and eagerly swallows my pee as I force myself to pee with a hard-on. Then she turns around and puts her pussy over my mouth and continues to suck my prick until we both come and she swallows my juice. Actually, her little cunt produced a lot of juice when excited, and I can still remember the smell and taste of it (much different from a female after puberty).

In the first grade I met a kid who introduced me to the old "Let's Play Doctor" game. I was all for it, and we spent many a happy hour examining ourselves and "curing" our "sore" little peters with hot saliva. As a matter of fact, we stayed close friends right on through school, and were frequent overnight visitors at each other's homes. As we grew older, the addition of a climax and ejaculation only added to the fun. But, of my fantasies about him, the most exciting are based on the first time, when we were six years old. Again, smell and taste play an important part in this. Neither of us are circumcised, and the excitement I remember as I played the doctor and skinned back his foreskin to examine him the first time is fantastic. The smell of his smegma (he called it cheese) was so sexy to me, I could hardly wait to get to the part where I "cured" him by sucking on his peter. Although we are both very clean people, in my fantasies now I ask him to go several days without skinning back his foreskin and washing his prick, so I can recapture the thrill of the smell and taste of it that first time. Ah, I have a lovely hard-on and can feel my lubricating juice coming out of my prick just from writing about this. I may have to (have to, hell, want to) stop and take advantage of this feeling for a good jackoff. (Incidentally, to me, the smegma under the foreskin of the clitoris has the same smell and taste as male smegma.) In our teens, I couldn't bring myself to swallow his come, but now in my fantasy (and probably in reality too, if given the chance) I swallow gallons of it as it squirts into my mouth.

WALTER

I am twenty-one, white, single and reasonably sexually liberated. I will be a senior at Syracuse University in the fall, and my major is pre-law. I have been dating the same woman for two years, and recently we moved in together. June is twenty-five, and is a social worker. She is sexually okay, but not passionate. We realize that our relationship won't last forever, because we both want different things in life.

I have not been able to share my sexual fantasies with anybody, because I don't think they would understand, because I don't understand all of them myself. I am glad that I have the chance to share one with somebody, even if it is indirectly.

Fantasy: There is this beautiful sexy girl sitting next to me in my family room, the lights are low, music playing. We are sitting on the couch, just got back from the theater and we have a drink in our hands. She sets her drink down and becomes the aggressive one. She slowly unbuttons my shirt and runs her fingers through my hair on my chest, and slowly goes down further and unzips my pants, and sucks my cock. Pulling my pants down further, she then inserts two fingers up my ass, and is moving them like she is fucking me there. By this time I've got my fingers up her. She then moves in front of me and takes my pants off completely and stands in front of me nude. She then starts kissing and licking me all over, starting with my feet, going up, avoiding my cock. She sucks my nipples, and licks my armpit; by this time, I am shoving her head down to my cock. She sucks my cock and balls till I come. She takes my cum in her mouth, and then we are kissing and I am tasting my own cum. Then we just lay there together holding each other.

SETH

I imagine a fat girl going down on me. She loves to suck cock and swallow my sperm, especially because of her voracious appetite. She sucks all of me at once; simultaneously devouring both dick and balls. (This would be feasible in reality since I'm merely six inches with an erection.) I imagine that she loves the taste and feel of my come in her throat and stomach I imagine having sperm all over her. She can't seem to get enough semen. After ejaculation, she tenderly sucks until my penis is drained and limp. Then my slippery dick recedes from her soft, saliva-soaked mouth. We embrace and kiss. It is a long, drawn-out kiss and we are satisfied.

Being hung up on fat, it isn't surprising that I love titties, especially large ones. The larger the better. I met a slightly heavy set girl named Deirdre who stayed at my place for a week or so. She was nicely stacked and loved fucking. She liked masturbating me or watching me masturbate and enjoyed seeing me come. Once she wanted me to see just how much tit I could devour. Of course, I gratefully obliged. This incident has become a source of fantasy for me when masturbating. I think of Deirdre and her love of our "breast feeding." This fantasy undoubtedly goes back to my early childhood or infancy days.

ALVIN

I fantasize that my wife is sucking my cock and, just before I come, I pull out and come all over her face or her tits. Then I kiss her and lick up my own come. We recently tried something very similar. I came in her mouth and, instead of swallowing, she held it, then kissed me so that I could taste my come.

I also imagine my wife and I watching each other masturbate to orgasm (she is shy about masturbating, and I have not yet been able to persuade her to do this).

I have another fantasy where my payload of sperm, and other fluids, is constantly at one hundred gallons. Whenever I get irritated at anyone, I imagine whipping out my cock, giving it a few shakes, and then giving someone (the irritant) a bath of one hundred gallons of come. (This one is great for my mind when I get "no" from ladies that are snotty, or also when driving amongst the idiot drivers.)

SALTY

The following is one of my favorite fantasies:

A very horny cunt is alone with me and three or four other men. We gather around her as she sits on the floor on a low stool. We all have our cocks in our hands and are stiff and hard. The vision of four other cocks interests me and arouses me. The girl turns herself on the stool until she sucks one cock for about thirty seconds and turns to get the next one. As we are all being sucked in turn for about five or six full circles, we are coming close to orgasm. I look down and my cock is nearly bursting with anticipation and the head gets that purplish look it gets when I have been aroused for a long time; the girl is fingering her cunt with two fingers, and with her other hand is fingerfucking her asshole. She is whining with desire for our semen. She tilts her head backwards until her face is pointing up near the level of our cocks, as we lean toward her and each of us is jerking very slowly to time the orgasm. As she opens her mouth and frantically licks the undersurfaces of all our cocks, we come almost simultaneously, filling her mouth and covering her face with five copious loads of semen, and she licks wildly to get as much on her tongue as she can.

When there isn't some other "hot, wonderful mouth" around to fellate him, Bruce (above) calls on fantasy to transcend reality. He dreams of going down on himself—a wish a number of men in this book mention, bemoaning the few inches by which they fail.

It is the dilemma of Tantalus: so near and yet so far. It is a temptation women do not have—though I have often wondered why little girls try to kiss their elbows, another bit of anatomy just barely out of reach. Whatever unconscious parallels there may be, it is typical of the difference between the sexes that the little girl's elbow is a much "nicer" goal than the little boy's penis.

What pure creatures girls must seem to young boys. So fresh, clean, and sweet smelling. It is difficult to believe they even have to go to the toilet. Men love them for their oppositeness, and in the song "The Girl That I Marry," the adjectives used to describe the ideal woman are pink and soft, very like a nursery. A certain antisexual purity in thought, word, and deed seems to be the feminine principle; and so the price to be paid for winning a girl's dainty heart is to be clean oneself.

As intuitively as salmon know to swim upstream, the boy who has resisted mother's efforts to clean him up all his life knows that when girls enter, it is time to change. Being "one of the boys" used to mean going around with a torn shirt and a dirty face, making it clear you don't care how you look. Now the definition of being one of the boys means being popular with the girls. Not only must he wash his face and check the fit of his jeans, but certain other, inner proclivities have to be checked, too. His sexual desires go underground, into fantasy.

Do we ever forget our first sexual longings? Is it possible

to put out of our mind the first, strongest, and most grati-
fying feelings of identity and sexuality? Years later, when
he is married and has children of his own, Herb (above)
still dreams about the little girl of long ago who once peed
on him while he peed on her. As if to reinforce the notion
that in the young boy's mind piss and semen are very
closely allied, Herb's fantasy now incorporates an additional element expressing what he has long wanted from a
woman: The little girl takes his cock in her mouth and
drinks his semen.

In a similar vein, Walter's fantasy girl signals her total
acceptance by licking him all over—armpits, nipples,
feet—until at the peak, she takes his semen in her mouth
and transfers it to his. This is oral ecstasy of a very high
order. Walter is getting the thrill of self-acceptance from
the very sex that taught him ambivalence in the first place.
Not only does the woman love it herself, she feeds it to
him from her own mouth.

Though I wince when men like Salty (above) fantasize
about shooting sperm all over the woman's face and
breasts, is this really a notion of aggression? He isn't covering her with acid. It is the essence of himself, the stuff he
loves most. Yes, there is the kick in soiling the sex that has
always been held out as the model of cleanliness; but what
does Alvin (above) do when he comes all over his wife?
He kisses her and licks it all up.

How exhilarating if, when a woman who stands at least
in part for that no-saying figure of long ago drinks the
man's semen, it turns out that she loves it! Approval of his
hidden self—his dirty, male, secret, sexual self—at last!
One of the varied shapes taken by men's lifelong masculine
conflict is fear that women love only half of him—the part
that is clean and nice as they are. In the fantasies in this
chapter the conflict is resolved: Not only do women love
all of him, but they don't want to be so disapprovingly
clean and antisexual themselves.

Both sexes were once equally "dirty" in their desires, but
our culture uses the notion of cleanliness as a physical metaphor to restrain female sexuality. A well-known price is
paid by women for this questionable distinction. This
chapter tells us that men pay a price for it, too.

HUGH

I am six feet tall, twenty-seven years old, white, one hundred ninety pounds, blond hair and blue eyes. I am married to a wonderful girl except that her sex drive isn't as active as mine. We've been married for eight years. We have one child, a boy four years old. My wife is five-five, blue eyes, brunette, one hundred five pounds and petite.

I have different kinds of fantasies depending on how I feel. Sometimes I feel rough and like to use dirty language.

The first fantasy is that I meet this girl with blond hair who likes to suck me off. I meet her at her apartment where we start kissing and then she starts undressing me all the time playing with me. I slide off her panties and bra and we go into the bedroom where we crawl in bed fondling each other and kissing. Then she starts running her hands all over my body till she reaches my penis. Then she runs her tongue up and down the shaft till I can't stand it anymore. Then she takes my whole penis in her mouth and starts sucking till I shoot my whole load in her mouth and she swallows it all and licks my penis clean. Wow! I've got a hard-on writing this.

My second fantasy is that I pick up a beautiful girl hitchhiking and after she's ridden for a while and we've been talking I ask her if she will do me a favor, since I'm doing her one giving her a ride. I ask her if she will bring me off with her hand. She says okay, so she unzips my jeans and takes out my penis and plays with it till I shoot off in her hand. Then I give her a handkerchief to clean her hand and by that time it's time to let her out.

It's time to masturbate.

Once again, it is important to distinguish what excites men in fantasy, and what they have chosen to be their reality. Hugh (above) daydreams of having a woman go down on him; but he doesn't want to put his wonderful wife in these scenarios, nor does he mention asking her to perform fellatio in real life. It may be that he doesn't associate her with such wildly erotic (and dirty?) notions: "Her sex drive isn't as active as mine." It may be that Hugh prefers to keep such sexually powerful ideas safely in fantasy. Many men are totally enthusiastic about having a woman suck them off. To others, the notion is just too scary.

In *Totem and Taboo,* Freud gives us a mythic history of the human race. The Father/King is murdered by his sons, who eat his flesh to take in his strength. Do men fear a symbolic passing of power to the woman when she takes their flesh in her mouth? (Connoisseurs specify that the woman must be careful always to curl her lips over her teeth.) The scenarios in this chapter gain intensity, I believe, because they *are* fantasies, freeing the man of any real castration anxiety. The vagina turns out not to be *dentata* after all.

Fellatio rarely dominates women's fantasies, but for one who has developed such a taste in reality, few sexual acts offer such unexpected rewards: to bring the man to intense sexual pleasure at her will. To feel the power of giving him total and complete acceptance.

I have always resented the psychoanalytic notion that going down on a man is symbolically similar to breast-feeding; that it is a regressive form of sexuality. From my own experience and research, the notion that a woman who likes to perform fellatio is "really" in search of maternal succor is naive.

Perhaps a Freudian case might be made for the unconscious wish on some women's part to drink a man's semen in order to take into themselves the status the male is given in our society. But the women I've heard call semen "the power drink" or "a vitamin shot," have a smile of satisfaction of a different sort. For the woman who has learned the excitement of taking the penis in her mouth, lovingly working it to full erection with lips, tongue, and saliva, and then bringing it off—feeling the pulse in her mouth as the semen spurts and she swallows it all—for her, this is neither mother's milk nor a symbolic taking in of status. This is power of a different kind, the power of the pleasure bringer.

6

Anal Sex

JACKIE

A little background on myself. I'm six-two and weigh two hundred pounds. I'm a musician who is pretty famous, so I'm writing you under a pseudonym. I hope your readers won't think of me as jive for putting this shade on my identity; but a moment's thought should make them understand the somewhat sensitive position of somebody like myself, who is more or less in the limelight. The image is part of my bread and butter, baby.

I have no set repertoire of fantasies because my fantasies grow and change like my music. Actually, there are basic ideas though, like fucking a woman with myself on top of her. I really dig the male superior fuck. Square business, I dig it. I can go through a day where I'd normally have a lot of trouble, but let me get off a good load the night before or that morning, and I'm ready to knock down brick buildings. I love a woman to turn me on by *patiently* sucking my dick, prick, cock, penis—whatever you want to call it. I like her to tell me she likes sucking me and I like her to say she likes it.

Other basic themes of my fantasies concern a woman sucking me off and swallowing my come. I hate when she wastes my come by spitting it out. I lived with a girl for about six years, and she used to like to suck and play with my nipples so that now they're somewhat larger than usual and very sensitive. I think a lot more men than will admit it, freak off with girls sucking their nipples. I know my woman did, and I dug it.

Here's one of my fantasies; and as stated earlier, it is largely based on actual experience. I'm with the girl I went

with for six years and who sucked my nipples. Her name is
Louise. Louise and I first tongue kiss, then I get on top of
her after holding her hands; kissing her face, forehead, lips,
neck; breathing on her; licking her ears; etc. I begin sucking her titties and she takes my prick in her hand and jacks
me off, asking me all along the way if I want certain things
done. Ouch! This woman! She jacks me slowly, up, up, up,
till my cock is like a flagpole waiting for her tongue-flag to
wrap around it. Jacking me slowly, now and then licking
my cock, massaging and jacking, now and then sucking my
nipples. After some moments of this, I can't stand it and I
go down on her, licking and sucking her pussy. I turn her
over on her stomach; and she obeys my every gesture, sup-
ple and willing, loving. I lick and tongue kiss her big glorious, juicy ass, rubbing my face and nose in the lovely
crack, doing analingus. (That's why a beautiful ass on a
woman automatically turns the heads of we men who can
kiss a woman's ass in our minds forty times a day!) I kneel
behind her next and stick my cock up her cunt. I would
like to fuck her in the ass, to be honest with you; but I
think ass fucking may hurt her. I fuck Louise's pussy dog-
style, then pull out and lay her on her back, her legs high
in the air. She looks so beautiful and nasty. I love her for
revealing her sex nature to me. As I fuck her this way,
she's turning around, twisting around to look at me and let
me see the naked lust in her eyes, the truth of her nature
expressing itself in her act of love with me. Finally, before
we come, I pull out and lick her from head to toe; we
slobber over each other. She says, "Jackie, you want me to
suck your dick? Tell me what you want me to do. I want
to be your very own whore. My pussy belongs to you alone
and it always will." "Get on your knees and suck my dick
and look up at me. Then I'm going to lay you on your
back and fuck you while you beg me to fuck you." I stand
up. She kneels on the floor in front of me and sucks me off.
I'm hard, hard, hard. I pull her up and lay her on the bed
and start fucking her madly but sensitively. She starts
crying out, "Fuck me, fuck me, oh fuck me, Jackie!" God
how I love the woman and all women because of loving
women like this! Then she screams and tells me how good
I am. I then wet my finger and stick it up her sweet asshole
gently. She can't take it, and she takes off, screaming and

sobbing and demanding: "Fuck me, fuck me, oh fuck me!"
Meanwhile, she gives me the finger in return up the ass.
We both see stars together.

How casually men include anal play in their erotic reveries. Their dream woman intuitively know to pay close attention to their anus.

Women today wear men's clothes; men may swap some of their aggression for women's more "feeling" qualities. Down deep where it counts, though, certain gender lines still rigidly hold. The most bizarre fantasies of oral and group sex, homosexual and animal sex, even varieties of S&M, may come to a woman easily and (if I may use a loaded word) naturally, but in neither of my books on women's fantasies was it necessary to include a chapter on anal sex.

My own disinterest, even aversion to it, speaks of my particular lifelong unevaluated fears and prejudices. As children, boys and girls alike are fascinated with all orifices of the body, but in our pattern of culture, an early taboo is imposed on girls against taking anything into the body. "Stanley Jones!" says the horrified little girl, "you're not going to put that in your mouth?" A further branching off from male development takes place as the girl slowly introjects what is called "the cloacal concept." The urethra, vagina, and anus—all three come to be sensed as one undifferentiated hole she has "down there." It is her secret, smelly shame, as the perfume industry is all too aware.

When Stanley Jones is a few years older and takes Betty Anne to the drive-in movie, he tries to touch her vagina. While it is not an automatic move on his part—as easy as it was for him to kiss her—it isn't altogether depraved in his eyes either. After all, he has been touching himself all his life—casually when he pees, with a thrill when he masturbates. To him, her vagina is the most magical thing on earth, the mysterious, glamorous opposite to his own familiar penis. *He thinks of it in far nicer terms than she does!*

In her mind, he might as well have tried to put his finger up her ass. How can he want to try (touch) something so vile? "You're a beast, Stanley Jones!" she cries.

His conflict is reinforced. Maybe, after all, there is something wrong even with touching himself. There must be some bestial side to him, foreign to lovely girls. The unsolvable paradox women present is this: They are so wonderful to be near, they do everything to encourage you to come closer, but when you do, they make you feel dirty. What men love is what women hate.

Years later still, when Stanley is in bed with his wife, he tells her he loves her. "Yes," she says, "but will you love me forever?" Why can't women believe in his love? He reaches for her, kisses her mouth, her breast; when his hands move tentatively for the seductive crack between her cheeks, she freezes. "See, I knew you didn't love me." He *is* a beast, to try something so disgusting on his own wife.

Can women—can anyone—be totally surprised if men sometimes want to live up to what appears to be everyone's idea of them?

Again and again I hear from a man dreaming of finding someone who would love his asshole right along with his penis. *Love me, love my ass,* men seem to be saying in these fantasies—and in all fairness, they are avid to return the compliment. "I love the surprise and heat," one man says, "when a woman suddenly realizes what you want to do is put your tongue right up her rosy asshole as far as it will go." In the mind of a man who loves oral sex, anus, penis, breast, vagina—they're all lovely to lick, tongue, eat, slurp, enjoy, revel in. Why should anything be left off the menu?

In recent years, Plato's Retreat opened in New York City. The place is a sociological phenomenon, open to the public. No liquor is sold, so it comes under the legal defini-tion of a club, and what members do is unregulated by the usual alcohol licensing laws.

In effect, it is a place for swingers, for orgies, for con-senting adults in any number (though men cannot come alone) to play out their mutual sexual fantasies. Sexual freedom is total but noncompulsive: You can watch or you can participate. You can take your clothes off or not as you like. *The Village Voice* sent a reporter, who found the club's principal furniture was made up of beds, thick rugs, and couches. Having entered of your own free and desirous will, anything goes. Amid scenes in which all permutations and combinations of sex were being explored between people who may have met only thirty seconds ago, the *Voice* reporter told me he had questioned a habituée who said she liked to come to the club several nights a week. "If a girl wants to be popular," she said to him, "she'll let it be known that she likes anal sex. That's what all the guys are looking for."*

Given two equally endowed women, what makes one preferable to another in a man's eyes except that something she says, something she does, *some idea the man has formed of her*, exerts an attraction perhaps invisible to the eye? Why, in fact, do so many men with eager and loving wives at home plead they have to work late at the office and go to a prostitute instead—often one who is not half as beautiful as the neglected woman waiting beside the telephone? Why will a man who barely looks up from his newspaper when his wife undresses for a bath feel a secret glow if his neighbor's wife happens to cross her legs carelessly? In the state of nature, physiology is dominant: The aroused stallion will not pass up the first female in heat for the most beautiful mare in the world if she is ten feet further away. The answer is that for human beings, the most powerful sexual organ does not lie between the legs. It is between the ears. Human erotic psychology finds forbidden sex is sexier sex. That's why we call it "dirty." The name speaks of shame—but that is its charge, too.

In real life, men often shy away from the sexually voracious woman. In fantasy, she is one of the great turn-ons. One frequent fantasy symbol for this erotic fervor is the woman so eager for sex she'll masturbate with a dildo, or call her dog to bed. Jackie (above) speaks of his sexual passion for a woman who falls into poses both "beautiful and nasty." For many men, the ultimate degree of sexual abandon is signaled by the woman who revels in anal intercourse. It is the most forbidden, "dirtiest" sex of all.

VITO

I am fifty-one years old, married and have two children, now away from home. I am a businessman in a small town. A sporadic sex life with my wife led me to have an affair with a younger woman, a divorcee. We would meet a few times per year. The hassle of avoiding prying gossips in a small town made us break off and she is now married to another.

I have fantasized all my life, on a variety of sexual themes. My current favorite puzzles me since it is full of paradoxes. First, I am a rather strongwilled person while my former mistress was not, yet in the fantasy we play the opposite roles. Second, I do not like pain in any form, but in the fantasy it is the pain and sexual domination of my partner that gets me off. I use this fantasy quite often during masturbation.

The fantasy begins as my mistress and I are together in a motel room. She is angry with me and will not let me kiss her. She makes me take off my clothes. After I am nude, she ties my hands behind my back. She then lifts her skirt and removes her panties and makes me step into them. As she pulls them up to my crotch she tells me not to get a hard-on or I'll get a spanking. All the while she is fondling my penis and balls. Naturally I get an erection. She slaps my hard penis and says, "You disobeyed me . . . now you are going to get your fanny warmed." She sits on the edge of the bed and forces me across her legs. She pulls down the panties and caresses my buttocks, running her finger down the crack. Then she begins to spank me with her open hand. The spanking lasts a long time and my buttocks get hotter and hotter, the pain gets stronger until I plead with her to stop . . . promising to do anything she wants.

After another swat or two she pushes me off her legs to the floor and commands, "Now eat me. Lick my pussy till I come." She spreads her legs exposing her warm moist cunt. She has been turned on by the spanking. I crawl between her legs and begin to kiss and lick her pussy. She starts to moan and grind her pussy hard against my lips. She locks her thighs around my head so I can't pull away. As she writhes against me she beats on my head and shoulders with her fists. At last she has her orgasm and slumps back on the bed. I fall to the floor, my tongue and jaws aching.

In a few moments she has recovered and says, "Now I'm going to rape you, but first you need to be cleaned out." She grabs me by the penis and drags me to the bathroom. She forces me to bend over the edge of the tub, parts my buttocks cheeks and stuffs a large nozzled douche syringe into my anus. It has not been lubricated and I cry out in pain. The water is hot as it courses into my rectum and I whimper and moan. She then rams the douche in and out of my rectum. As I cry out, she crams the panties I had been wearing into my mouth as a gag.

In spite of the pain, I am more aroused than ever. My penis is hard and throbbing. Finally my mistress withdraws the syringe from my rectum and allows me to evacuate. While I am sitting on the toilet, she sees my penis standing straight and tall. "I told you not to get a hard-on," she rages, "and now you get another spanking." This time she throws me face down on the bed and proceeds to whip me with the belt from her skirt. I am still gagged so all I can do is moan in pain. At last her arms tire and she tosses the belt aside. She rolls me over on my back and proceeds to mount me. "Now I'm going to fuck you," she says, and she slides her cunt up and down on my penis. She is careful not to let me climax. My balls begin to hurt, but still she will not allow me to come. As she works up and down, she reaches behind my body and down between my legs. She grabs my balls and just as I am about to explode, she gives them a hard squeeze. The pain causes me to lurch and squirm. A few fast thrusts of her ass and she hits her climax. Then she rolls off me and collapses on the bed.

When at last she has recovered, she rises from the bed and gets a large double dildo from her suitcase. She inserts one end into her pussy and fastens the straps around her waist and thighs. She laughs and says, "If you thought the enema was bad just wait till I rape your ass with this."

She ignores my silent pleas and forces me over on my face. "Pull your knees up," she orders, giving me hard slaps on the buttocks. I bring my knees up under my body. My hands are tied behind me and my face is buried in a pillow. My ass is raised in the air making a most inviting target for her big rod.

My mistress takes her finger, moistened by rubbing her wet cunt, and slips it into my asshole. Then she mounts me from the rear. I can feel the head of the massive dildo pressing against my anus. It is beginning to force its way in. The pain begins and I writhe in agony. I feel that I am being torn apart. Tears come to my eyes. At last the dildo is in my rectum to the hilt and I groan as she makes the final thrust. Before I can recover she begins to push it in and pull it out, fucking my ass with hard thrusts. There is pain. I can feel the dildo filling me completely.

As the movements continue, the other end of the dildo begins to do its job inside her cunt. The pace quickens and I know she is nearing another climax. She is breathing hard and thrusting faster and faster. Her reaction begins to trigger a response deep down inside of me. I feel myself building to a climax too. Finally the pace is too much and with a squeal of delight she has her orgasm. And that final quivering thrust as she goes over the top sends me up to a blinding orgasm too. My throbbing penis squirts its juice and I collapse in a trembling heap.

Usually by this time, I have masturbated to a climax, so the fantasy ends.

De Sade took sexual fantasies perhaps to their most formal development, erecting immense edifices of philosophy and literature on the base of his erotic musings. And yet in his writings, the vagina is rarely the focus of obsession. It is the anus that is the target of his most ardent desires.

For reasons to be discussed in a later chapter on sadomasochism, de Sade did not see sex as sensuous pleasure, but as a battlefield for erotic mastery. In Vito's fantasy (above), we see this conjunction of sex, pain, and power in classical, almost de Sadian form.

At the risk of fatuity, I'd say that even though Vito reverses the usual de Sadian roles—it is he who suffers, not his cruel mistress—it would be a very rare woman who would have invented this fantasy for her own pleasure. Women are capable of cruelty, of course—but almost

never the specific kind in which Vito (and de Sade) re-
veled. When introduced to anal notions, women may come
to enjoy them; they can grow as eager as any man, but it
seems to take a process of initiation. It is something to be
learned, like a grown-up taste for martinis or oysters.

If women flinch when their anus is touched, the inhibition is not so much that the experience might be painful
(though that is a factor), but that it might be dirty,
smelly—everything opposite to what a woman is supposed
to be.

Men show little such hesitancy; they would include the
asshole in sexual play almost from the start. Only because
most women instinctively draw away do they desist.

At the moment, I'm not talking about homosexual men,
to whom anus and mouth must be prime vehicles for receiving the penis. Nor am I thinking of the adventurous
male who thinks of anal intercourse as just another interesting position, a tighter and snugger fit perhaps than the
vagina, and this more conducive to stimulating friction.
The issue I'm discussing right now is this: What attraction
does anality have for men that it does not hold for women?

Long before sexual feeling becomes focused in the penis
or vagina, we go through what Freud calls "the pregenital
phase." The baby's first great source of pleasure is the
mouth, through which comes food, warmth, love, and
milk. Toilet training brings other parts of the body to the
fore. The ambivalences surrounding elimination move
into the spotlight. When we do well, we are rewarded with
kisses and caresses—which to the baby are forms of erotic
gratification. But sometimes, just when we have done what
we think is wanted, we get frowned upon and even
spanked. We are like a puppy being housetrained: We
don't understand the complexities of time and place. What
is wanted from us? Slowly we begin to learn; certain distinctions come to be made. Degrees of displeasure are perceived: Mother may not like her little boy to pee in his
pants, but to shit is even "dirtier."

The anus becomes the most forbidden part of the body,
thus invested with its own secret glamour.

As one psychoanalyst said to me, "Considering that both
sexes begin by taking pleasure in anal activities early in
life, and that our earliest experiences cut the deepest, you

might say that to *stop* being interested is more unnatural, more repressed, than the reverse. The love affair on the part of both sexes with the breast never ends, but women turn off all their interest in the anus."

Why?

Because mother passes on her own repressions to her daughter far more successfully than to her son.

Mother was raised to believe girls must be "ladies," fastidiously clean, fragrant as roses. She has no serious doubt that this commandment is practically divine in origin. *She knows.* Isn't she female herself? But she is not so sure of her son. He resists all her efforts to keep him neat and clean. In the end, she gives up, resigning herself—"Boys will be boys," she sighs. All his friends seem to be messy, too. It becomes familiar, another way to tell boys and girls apart.

Being dirty may not be nice, the boy learns; but it does not force on him the terrific coefficient of anxiety it has for his sister, who has had standards of personal hygiene drummed into her as one of the surest signs of her femininity.

Let me add here once again that I am talking in generalities, in terms of tendencies. All men are not totally comfortable in sweat-soaked T-shirts, nor do they all desire anal sex. What I am saying is that *being dirty does not threaten male gender identity*.

MITCH

I am, I'm sure, a typical sex-preoccupied, fifty-year-old married salesman. My wife is attractive and sexy enough so that most of my fantasies have been experienced with her in one form or another, physically that is.

But, as you know, so much of sex is mental. The buildup and preliminary action has become more important to me as I grow older. I love to talk about the coming events, to make little ceremonies out of them. My wife finds this embarrassing and tedious, beyond a few brief words or actions.

Lately, my fantasies have involved the beauty of the

female ass. I imagine being with someone very refined and
dignified—Claire Bloom or Eva Marie Saint are two of my
favorite celebrity partners. We are acquainted for some
reason and at a party. I know that I'm going to have her
eventually, but am shocked to hear her make dates with
other men during the party.

"Dahling," says Claire Bloom to one man in that wonderful refined British way, "you do have a load for me,
don't you? I'm dying for a little snack. I know a room
that's empty, dahling. Come, I'm famished. Excuse us,
won't you, dahling." And she leaves me to go off and fellate this man.

"Richard, dearest! I'm standing here feeling so empty!
Can you fill me? Please, dear, I know what depths you can
plumb. I remember that monster of yours—let's dash upstairs now. Excuse us please" (to me).

The thought of such an intelligent woman of class being
so forward and raunchy excites me greatly. As the party
goes on, I observe that she has had oral sex and intercourse in various combinations, never losing her cool dig-
nity between these acts. I'm dejected and disappointed and
very excited.

She notices this and starts to make little promises.

"Dahling, I know I've shocked you. But that's me, don't
you see. Anyway, my dearest treasure is for you."

"Oh, dear, you're angry with me." (After returning from
a quick lay.) "Please, dear, you know I'm saving my most
secret place for you."

And later as we dance, the thrilling promise, "Oh, lover,
I'm ever so ready! You'll love it. My greatest mystery, all
yours."

Finally alone with her, she wears only high heels. Bending forward from the waist, her beautifully manicured fingers stroke her ass which is soft and so white and gorgeous.
Slowly her fingers part the cheeks, slowly, as she croons
her invitation.

"You see, dahling, no one else has touched me here.
You may kneel and look, dearest. Oh, how I need to be
kissed now. This is really the secret me, dahling. Here, just
a little wider. There, sweetheart, my secret lips, yours only.
Kiss me gently there—oooh—I'm in heaven."

And I'm in heaven too. This mental picture of myself

making love to the ass of this well-bred beautiful woman. Slowly kissing at first, then daring to tongue those mysterious hidden lips—so well bathed, so sweet and clean. And her words of encouragement. Her sighs. And at last I stick my tongue up into her asshole and suck. I'm erect and full of come—my heart pounds as I suck and lick and kiss Claire Bloom's ass—or Diana Rigg's—or Joan Kennedy's ass. Then after many minutes of sucking, "Oh, darling, what you're doing to me, I'm dripping. I'm so happy." And at last the refinement is gone—"Suck it, you ass licker. Eat my asshole, you bastard! Serve me, you prick. I want my lovely ass served! You are licking the asshole of Joan Kennedy"—the names flash through my mind—"ooh—lover—now feed me!" We fall into sixty-nine and I come gallons as she drinks and I lap and we both try to drown each other in cream!

Your name and face and beautiful ass now predominate my fantasy. Has this now become an obscene letter? Please forgive me if it has, Nancy. But now my fantasy is:

Nancy Friday reads my letter. She finds it more intriguing than most. She knows how lovely she is in the place I long for most. When her research brings her into my area, she drops by to visit me at my work. I'm not handsome, but a nice guy, safe and discreet. She senses this.

I am honored by her visit. When she tells me that she's at the nearby Holiday Inn, she knows that my visit to her room would be like visiting a shrine. Could it possibly come true that I could kneel behind Nancy Friday and see and taste her mysteries? And hear that beautiful voice croon to me—"They're all yours!" I can only fantasize.

Please don't be angered by my final fantasy. It is as honest as those that I had before I saw you on TV. I have never written an obscene letter. I don't make obscene phone calls. I'm really concerned that you might think of my frankness about your effect on me as other than part of my desire to participate in your research.

I'm five-eight, high-school educated, with night courses at college in public speaking, salesmanship, psychology. I sell appliances. I talk to women of various ages all day. Maybe that's why I'm able to fantasize so readily.

LAWRENCE

I hope I am wrong, but I think that men are more psychologically rigid than women and are therefore less tolerant of sexual images that are not compatible with the image of being male.

When I was ten and eleven, a neighbor boy, five years older than I, would visit me and persuade me to have sex with him. Frequently he would penetrate me anally, which was painful at first but soon became surprisingly pleasurable and I found myself anxiously waiting for his next visit.

This submissive-anal erotic tendency is still with me, although I have left behind the homosexual inclination. Not surprisingly, this sexual desire finds gratification in fantasy.

I meet a woman in a bar who is committed to the feminist movement and against the rigid role playing we have all been conditioned to. She declares that men should submit to sexual dominance by a woman to experience the vulnerability of the passive role. She calls this "asshole liberation." I act quite naive and tell her that I agree with her. I say, "Maybe my asshole needs liberating." She suggests that we go to her place and I agree.

Her roommate happens to be home and I am told that if I am sincere in what I've said, I won't object to her watching. I make no objection. The three of us go into the bedroom and I am told to strip naked; the women remain clothed. My excitement heightens when they tell me to get on the bed on all fours, my ass towards them. One woman applies lubricant and the other inserts a vibrator in my ass. It is all I can do to conceal my pleasure.

The formality of the "liberation" ends quite abruptly when one of them straps on a dildo and tells me to lie on my back, and raise my legs high and wide. There I am, unbeknownst to them, relishing their domination, peering up at them from the bed, my legs high and spread. The woman with the dildo mounts me and penetrates me with no pretense of being gentle. I wince in pain but soon the pain is gone, replaced by the tactile rushes of her pelvic thrusts. I am no longer able to conceal my passion. I moan and groan in ecstasy, mumbling, "Fuck me, oh fuck me," and beg her not to stop. My enthusiasm encourages her and we fuck with abandon, finally stopping when I've reached the climax of my life.

Frequently it *is* the climax of my life. Orgasms from masturbating are some of the best.

The contrast of ideas in the two fantasies above is instructive. Mitch has followed the usual path of male development. He has taken in the injunction that playing around with the anus is dirty—but he is not going to surrender like a mama's boy. He wants it anyway! In his fantasy, Mitch meets a famous woman (the center of the world's attention, as mother once was to him). She is also very refined—once again, the way mother was. But instead of acting passively about anal play, she demands it of him! Mitch gladly complies. The supreme excitement is that *he is thus corrupting authority*—getting things his way, not women's. What a kick, what a sense of power, to find that these very pure and exalted ladies, the ultimate extension and epitome of the mother who first forbade him his dirty desires, love asshole play themselves!

What is more, by suddenly using all the forbidden words in the books, by asking of him what is the most taboo of all, these haughty mother-surrogates suddenly change into that image of male delight: the woman who is sexually abandoned as a teen-age dream. The real mother said, "No, never!" The fantasy woman says, *"Yes!"* to the most forbidden way of all! By making his fantasy women lose their cool and reduce themselves to his animal level, Mitch's sexuality is reinforced by a terrific sense of power, his masculine conflict resolved.

Lawrence (above) shows a different path of anal/genital development. Here we see the classic psychoanalytic idea that erotic patterns of submission, domination, passivity, and aggression often grow out of the war of wills that takes place between mother and child during toilet training. Lawrence himself makes the connection, calling his sexual attitudes "anal-submissive." Mitch was aware that his anal desires were forbidden, but he battled to fulfill them anyway. Lawrence is more obedient, learning to accept and enjoy the anal intercourse forced on him during childhood.

His story shows that he continued to look for the same pleasures even in heterosexual life. He wants anal play, but it must be "forced" on him, this time by a powerful woman. This is akin to female fantasies of rape—a way of guiltlessly gaining desired sexual satisfaction by saying it is the other person's fault.

At one time a dominant woman forbade Lawrence to take any pleasure in his anus. In his fantasy, another powerful female insists that he *does*. In submitting to her will, Lawrence gets what he wants.

As little boys grow older and the psychosexual development continues through puberty, the penis comes into its dominant own. But the old, more primitive sources of bodily pleasure do not entirely vanish from the unconscious.

When a man wants to include the woman's anus (or his own) in loveplay, he is first of all responding to his physiology, to nerve endings and sensitivities that have as natural an erotic response as any other part of the body; but he is responding to psychological excitement, too: He is breaking mother's old taboos, a perfectly acceptable, even lauded, male role in our culture. When he asks his wife to kiss his anus, he is not necessarily trying to humiliate her, as she may think. He'd do it for *her*, wouldn't he?

LEWIS

I'm male, twenty-one years old, single, and not very good-looking. I attend college full time and work almost full time as a print shop apprentice. I am quite horny and have indulged in masturbation almost every day for over fifteen years.

In my fantasy, I am with this very horny girl. I start by giving her a nice warm bath (she loves receiving enemas, or so I imagine). Next we go to bed. She lays down on her stomach with her legs spread apart, and I begin licking all over her corpulent buttocks and up the deep slit between them. Then I give her a "ream job" with my tongue (analingus). Continuing, I massage her massive bottom and proceed to kiss, suck, and rub my face all over it. Next I mount her fat ass which feels overwhelming to my thin body. (I am built like a rail—six feet, three inches; 160 pounds.) Her entire body against mine is like heaven. Anyway, using lubricant, I slide my cock up her anus which is good and snug. I shove it all the way in, and we're ready to go. By the way, simultaneously as I'm humping, she is frigging herself. We both approach climax together as I hump harder and harder. Soon, I'm shooting a huge wad of semen up that tremendous fanny. I get even more excited knowing that she loved the feel of my hard penis—shooting syrupy sperm into those hot and receptive bowels. Immediately she goes off and we lay together in rapture.

Occasionally during this fantasy, I'll finger my anus while rubbing a *lot* of hand cream on my cock and balls. The hand cream produces a kind of airless suction on my genitals which simulates the sensation of a great fuck.

HENRY

I am a man in his sixties; a widower after thirty-six years of marriage; father of two sons and two daughters. All are married and performing well in their jobs.

I was an only child of a very strict and rigid upbringing; my mother got a divorce; I am deeply convinced she did her best. However, there were missing links in my education. I did not get any sexual instruction at all; that field was severely taboo, and I had to pioneer my own way.

My wife was a university student as well; during studies we were very good comrades, and we took painstaking care for the education of our children. But sexually, our marriage suffered from continuous incompatibility. Being taught in early youth that women did not aspire to sexual activity and sex was a mere exertion of men, I now was confronted with other prejudices about sex. Sex in itself was absolutely superfluous, according to my wife, and only a means to bear children.

My most favorite fantasy is: women, of their own initiative and freedom, exposing their bare buttocks. I do not mean young women or girls. No: I think of full-grown, mature women of forty, fifty years or older, endowed with bulging, fleshy bottoms, showing flowering cheeks. They

must have a vital, robust, square-built bum with massive,
weighty buttocks, fully and roundly developed. I hate
formless, plump, or baggy buttocks or drooping members.
I am a very artistic and over-sensitive man. Visualizing naked beauty is the very root of my existence. I like those
cushionlike bottoms the Greek sculptors achieved for us,
like the "Venus of Syracuse." And the modern artists: Mail-
lol and Rodin. I see my fantasy woman greedily bending
over, pushing out her asshole in full relief, pushing forward, lifting her ass up to me to be licked, or fingered deep
inside. She is intensely desirous for analingus and presses
backward to meet my mouth. I love it when my face is
taken within her cuddling buttocks in a firm grip: Analingus means the culmination of sexual intimacy; and being
long engaged in that anal intertwining. I leave it to the
woman to choose later to be fucked in her cunt.

For me, however, the crucial point is: *The woman herself must be covetous of displaying her bottom,* of challeng-
ing my watchful eyes to her ass, of raising her spreaded
buttocks in heat. My sensitive tongue slips all over or into
her for true release in analingus.

Sometimes I fiction that there are three or four women,
with massive bums and large buttocks, boldly pushing forward and openly showing their assholes. They compete together as to who has the most magnificent bottom or the
most lascivious, lusty ass; and they join in provocative
movements to display their anal graces, eagerly awaiting
my choice. I'll never try to watch a woman surreptitiously
or to look at her bottom when she is afraid or ashamed.
The very emphasis lies in the utmost pleasure the woman
herself takes in offering me her behind.

7

Starry-Eyed
Oedipus

TIM

I am married to a lovely woman and we have two beautiful
children, a boy and a girl. We both teach music, and our
income is twenty-five thousand dollars per year.

My fantasies are about my beautiful mother and me. In
them, my mother is thirty-six but looks much younger. I
am a sixteen-year-old boy with a perpetual hard-on. On a
Sunday morning in summer, we go for a walk in the country. It is peaceful, sunny, and warm. My mother has a
white simple dress on. Since the path is narrow, I walk
behind her. I cannot help but notice her beautiful legs. Her
calves are shapely, like upside-down bowling pins. As she
walks, her dress flaps; and her beautiful milk-white thighs
flash before me. She has tied her long blond hair in a pony-
tail, which goes so beautifully with her round face and
makes her look much younger. She sways her wide hips
unintentionally and rolls her round, ample ass. When my
mother stoops along the way to pick a flower, her dress
rises, exposing her thighs and her snow-white panties that
hide her big and delicious ass.

When we come to a secluded spot, Mom wants to pee. I
pretend I too want to pee and turn away from her. Then I
turn around, fumbling with my fly and letting my mother
see my huge hard-on, while I take a good look at her
pussy. My mother seems embarrassed, but she steals a glance
at my erect cock. Whether my mother is pleased or annoyed
at my boldness, I don't know. Women are too clever for us
men.

We continue to walk. We come to a farm where they are
raising race horses by inbreeding. We see people trying to

get a stallion to mount a mare. My mother suggests we stop and watch. She tells me that of all animals, only horses fuck in a similar way like people. She tells me that mating horses closely related makes them a better stock. The stallion that is about to mount the mare is her very own offspring. We are both fascinated by the huge size of the stallion's cock. As we watch in awe, the stallion, with the help of men, finally finds his way and sinks his cock slowly into the mare's belly. My mother seems very excited and is rubbing her thighs together. I ask her if inbreeding is desirable among horses, why not between people? She does not know the right answer and only tells me that society frowns at such matings.

Then my mother tells me that this is more of a sociological than biological problem. The rivalry between siblings. But I have no brothers or sisters. My father no longer cares about my mother and has left her. "Where there is a will, there is a way." If this rule has any truth in it at all, then it should apply to my mother and me as well. Would sexual union between two close relatives who love each other deeply make their relationship more beautiful? Of course it would. My mother agrees with me and feels that many things do not make sense. Being a practical woman, my mother feels that it is all right for me to fuck her as long as nobody knows about it. I mount my mother from behind, as we observe the stallion fuck the mare. My cock throbs and expands in my mother's sweet, receptive cunt. I dare not move in and out lest I come too soon. It was so simple and so natural. I wonder what the fuss is all about. Fucking my mother was the most beautiful and rewarding experience in my whole life.

Here is fantasy number two.

My mother and I have been lovers for four years. We are celebrating the anniversary of four years of bliss. At dinner we have filet mignon and caviar and the best champagne. My mother is dressed in an evening gown which is black and strapless. Her white, smooth skin shines blemishless. She wears no panties or bra. Just black nylon stockings and garter belt. We sit opposite each other at the table with candlelight and eat to music of Mantovani. We eyeball each other across the table like in the *Tom Jones* movie. Then I dance with my mother. She puts her arms around my neck, and I take her big ass-cheeks in my hands and caress them lovingly. My mother rubs her belly against my throbbing hard-on. Then we sit on the sofa and watch television. She sits in my lap, lifts her dress over her hips, and impales herself on my huge prick. We sit like that for a long time while I caress her beautiful breasts. Then my mother turns around and straddles me face to face. Then she puts her arms around me; and so coupled, I lift her and carry her to bed. My mother is a big woman, but I am bigger, and it is easy for me to carry her like this. I put her lovely legs on my shoulders and she doubles up until they touch her breasts. In this position, we can achieve the deepest and most satisfying penetration. I fuck her lovingly for a long time.

Why do I love to fuck my own mother? Why do people climb mountains? Why do they cross oceans in small rafts? Why do men go to the moon? Because it is a challenge. I want to be different. I want to prove to myself that one does not have to be an imbecile to enjoy incest. I want to prove to myself I can do it and survive. What young, healthy man did not have wet dreams about his mother?

Since I grew up without a father, it was my mother who had to tell me about the birds and the bees, and teach me all about sex. It was a blessing to know that the solution for our sexual needs was within us. It was so convenient. We were both very busy. My mother painting pictures, and I practicing music six hours a day and working besides. We had no time for the outside world. Of course I would want to meet a nice girl and marry some day, but how about right now?

My mother watched her little boy grow into a young man with satisfaction. I was her ideal man. I could do everything to her my dad could not. She would teach me how beautiful sex is. To abandon myself to the sweet joy of copulation without a trace of guilt. To feel that sex is as normal and as natural as breathing.

I was about thirteen when I started fucking my mother regularly. To have fucked my mother gave me self-confidence, and I was elated that I had become a man.

Women today take better care of themselves and look years younger. They are very appealing to their young and horny sons. Watching young girls on the beach clad in string bikinis that only cover their nipples and the triangle between their legs, one wonders how their fathers can possibly resist them.

There are more fathers fucking their daughters than there are brothers fucking their sisters. Motherfucking is considered rare and that makes me much happier. I am different. I am unique. I am daring. I have done something most young men wish they could do if they had the guts. How many young men know what their mother's cunt looks like? Are their mothers frigid, or do they love to fuck? How does it feel to penetrate the womb you came out of with your cock? To revisit the place that nourished you for nine months?

Most people are revulsed by the notion of an adult having sex with a minor. The moral and/or religious arguments against it are well enough known; I would base my own aversion on the possibility of danger or damage it holds for the younger partner. There are plenty of adults who cannot handle the physical and emotional intensities of sex; putting this kind of overload onto the immature nervous system of a child may be more than he/she can bear. That is why in cases of statutory rape, the fact that Lolita does or does not invite Humbert Humbert into bed is legally irrelevant. The law wisely says no consent is valid before someone is old enough to understand the perils and consequences of his/her agreement.

How much more strongly we feel when the older person is a mother or father, and the younger a son or daughter. Adults have difficulty even in thinking about the idea, and yet almost every week brings us another TV documentary on the subject, another novel, drama, or film that explores erotic ties between family members. I don't think the whole explanation is that we live in a sensation-hungry world and incest is the last taboo still not commercially overexploited. The subject is so fraught with anxiety that mere shock value alone would not be enough to keep people from turning the dial. On the surface, show-biz explorations handle this anxiety by viewing incest with alarm, but wily producers know that their real message lies underneath, in the audience's unconscious: At one time of life, these ideas were not shocking at all. Incest is a lively topic today, not because it is strange and alien, but because it is an expression of emotions loose in the air we breathe: This is the age of the single-parent family.

"Oedipus, shmedipus, who cares?" goes the old joke. "Just as long as you love your mother." The oedipal phase of development is so familiar, the notion so accepted, that even uneducated people laugh. Okay, so all boys go through a childhood triangle in which they love their mothers and resent their fathers. What else is new?

This is new: Medical opinion now puts less emphasis on the old Freudian fear of the castrating father who will punish the little boy if he becomes a rival. Instead, one of the everyday facts of family life is seen as more important in determining why boys give up on mom and look for love in girls their own age: Dad is already there, always around. He is just too big, too powerfully implanted in place for the son to hope to substitute for him. When it finally sinks into the little boy's heart and soul that mother is not going to give up this grown man for him, he sighs and turns his attention elsewhere.

This is the reality principle working at its best, teaching us to give up dreams that can never come true.

Or can they?

This dynamic is a description of psychological events in what is fast becoming an old-fashioned, almost storybook family, in which there was indeed a father who came home every night, talked or played with the children, handled his share of discipline, and dealt with problems that faced the family as a whole; at the end of the evening, he took mother into the bedroom and closed the door. Why would a boy give up the security of having a father like this by trying to become his rival; how could he hope to succeed if he did? Needless to say, it is *not* a description of the growing number of American families where dad often has to work late at the office, returning only after the children are asleep—if indeed he isn't out of town on a sales trip, run off, or married to someone else.

Even in those families where father is physically home every night, he may be emotionally absent, too worn out by the competitive world to have anything left over for his kids. *Or for his wife either.* Tim (above) tells us that his father "no longer cares about my mother and has left her." The nuclear family is splitting, perhaps never to be mended again in any foreseeable future.

The New York Times Magazine (July 10, 1977) called the number of pregnant, unmarried teen-age girls who are determined to keep and raise their babies on their own a crisis of "epidemic" proportions. For people of all ages, divorce grows ever more familiar, one of the routine hazards of life, like having a flat tire or getting fired from a job. Consider some other figures from the Bureau of the Census:

> The divorce rate had doubled (from 2.5 to 5.0 per 1,000 population) in the decade 1966–1976. By 1978 it rose to 5.2. One out of every five (5.4 in 1977) children of school age today lives in one-parent families.
> The number of households headed by women has increased by 55% in the past ten years. An estimated 45% of children born this year will live in single-parent homes for at least part of their youth.*

Figures like these are usually considered only in terms of the psychological damage done to the children concerned. What is ignored is that the single parent too often suffers emotional—and sexual—deprivation. Can we be surprised, in this permissive age when everyone seems to be in favor of doing everything, if a lonely young mother decides she will not be the only one starving at the feast of life, and slides over the border between a son's affectionate kisses and a young man's embrace?

Indeed, in a house where a sexually developing boy lives with a sexually forlorn woman, can it be said that incestuous wishes are entirely the grown-up's idea? Please note how often men in this chapter write that they grew up in a family in which the father was either dead, absent, or disinterested. This is one of the characteristic emotional plagues of our time, so prevalent that the Mormons have begun to

---

* Paul C. Glick, Senior Demographer, Population Division, Bureau of the Census. Personal communication June 12, 1979.

run TV commercials to fight it. The screen shows a man picking up a set of golf clubs. A voice asks him, "Remember when you promised yourself to spend more time with your kids next week? It's next week."

Every time dad storms out of the house during a quarrel or goes off on a jaunt of his own, the son's hopes that this time mother will be his alone are nourished. If the oedipal rival has left for good, if there is no longer night-after-night proof in mother's bed in the shape of a man twice as big as you that mother can never be yours, what desires may not be reborn? To a child, whatever the parent does is a lesson about how the world works. It feels right, it's natural, "how things are." "Go to school and you'll learn to be a smart boy," mother says, and her son goes. "Come to bed and kiss Mommie," she says, and the boy comes.

DYSON

I'm twenty years old and have enjoyed many times the company of a female as well as fun with a few of the guys whom I have known since school days.

Let's go back to the time I was about eight years old. It was when I was jerking off my cock in the storage room in our home. Guess the room was to have been a bedroom but our parents never finished it and it became the back room where we kept everything from camping gear, Christmas ornaments, clothes, to a bed which was my play bench. When I wished to jerk off I would go to this room, strip my clothes off and lay on a mattress which was stretched out on the top of a bed frame and play with my cock. I tried to roll up into a ball and suck my cock but could only get the tip to my mouth. So it was just fun to play with my cock and to imagine I had a girl or boy with me. Guess I must have been noticed by my two older sisters because I got caught stark ass naked by both of them. Scared boy I was as they told me they were going to tell Mom what I was doing. My older sister, who was sixteen, laid down by me and kissed me and told me that neither one would tell Mom so to relax. Then my other sister laid down on the other side of me and both of them kissed me

like I was a lost friend. In a very short time both of them
had me locked in their legs and were running their hands
all over my belly, neck, sides and the big surprise came
when my oldest sister got my cock in her hands and asked
me if this is the way I was playing with my cock. She was
pumping my cock real fast. My other sister was kissing me,
giving me a suck mark on my neck, and when she got her
lips up to my mouth she forced her tongue into my mouth
and that was all I needed. Then I felt a funny feeling at my
cock. My older sister got completely undressed and was
taking my other sister's clothes off. We were all naked.
Both of them went down on my cock, sucking until I
started to squirm. The more I squirmed the bigger the hug
I was getting. I told them my cock was getting sore so they
quit. We laid there for a long time and both told me that if
I would not tell Mom we could all do this a lot. We got
dressed and after that day when either one was alone I let
them suck my cock.

Both are now married, and while we sometimes try to
get together for more sessions, my sex life with my sisters
has been mostly reduced to thinking about how it would
be. The big turn-on in my daydreams is that if my
brothers-in-law knew, we would be in a hell of a mess, but
since they don't know, it just adds more to the fun. My
favorite fantasy is to imagine one of my sisters lying naked
in bed with her legs spread apart, and my other sister, she
is naked too, she holds the cunt lips open with one hand,
while with the other, she is guiding my cock in. Then while
I'm pumping away on the one, the other gets on the bed,
ass backwards to me, so that while I'm fucking one, I have
the other's juicy cunt facing me to suck out.

BENNET

I am twenty-five, single, and a salesman. Income about
$20,000 gross.

My sister, who is two years younger, lives in a town I
am visiting. She is an artist, free-lancing. Tomorrow I am
going to look her up. I have not seen Sis for a long time,
and I am very fond of her. Tonight I am going to find me

a girl and have a good time. A taxi driver gives me a number to call. The lady on the phone tells me she has just the girl I want. She will send the girl to my hotel room at 7 P.M. The fee will be a hundred dollars. I shave, shower, dress, and wait. At seven, I hear a knock on the door. I wonder what the girl looks like. When I opened it, whom do I find there? My own sister.

She seems confused, and wonders whether to run away or come in. Sis knows that if she tells me this was a mistake, I would wonder where my date was. I tell Sis I am delighted to see her and that I was going to look her up tomorrow. I propose to take Sis out on the town. I take my sister to a beautiful restaurant. There we have a few drinks and a beautiful dinner. Sis asks me how are Mom and Dad. I tell her they are fine. I ask Sis why she stopped writing. Well, she did not want to disappoint Mom and Dad, but she did not like office work. One of her girl friends had suggested since Sis was already dating men, to do it for money. The work was easy and pleasant. A certain lady would get her clients and keep her out of trouble because she had friends at City Hall.

When the time came for us to leave, Sis wanted to come to my hotel room so we could talk some more. Once in my room, we had a few more drinks; and Sis begged me not to tell Mom and Dad what happened. I tell my sister I love her and will not utter a word. My sister feels since I was willing to pay $100.00 for a girl, I must be very lonely; and she would stay with me all night. I tell Sis that if she does not want it, I don't want it; and Sis tells me if I want it, she also wants it. We come to the conclusion that we both want it. So, I will sleep with my little sister.

I call her my little sister out of habit. Like me, my sister is tall and hefty. Since she left home, she has filled out in the right places. Sis would make a beautiful cushion beneath any man. As I look at my beautiful sister, I ask myself: Is there any valid reason why I should not fuck her? Being a call girl, my sister must have fucked a least a hundred different men. Was my beautiful sister not good enough for a horny bastard like me who would fuck a rattlesnake? All my life long I have been fighting for women's rights. To see women degraded and oppressed by men always made me sick. Hell yes, I would love to fuck my sister; but I have to make it right, I want to enjoy every minute of it. Now I am afraid if I don't fuck my sister right away, I will never get another chance. I undress Sis and kiss her from head to toe, including her beautiful cunt that looks exactly like Linda Lovelace's.

As I fuck my sister, I try to feel the difference between her and other women. Is it different fucking one's own sister? Yes, but not in a physical way. Because of our affinity, it is more beautiful in a spiritual way. Fucking my sister was much more emotionally satisfying. It was more love than sex. I could easily fuck another woman without loving her. I don't think I could have fucked Sis if I did not love her.

SAILOR

I am in the United States Navy, on board a ship which is presently deployed in the eastern Mediterranean. I am nineteen years of age. I will turn twenty in September this year. I am white, blond haired, blue eyed, five-nine. So much for an introduction.

When I am in bed with a lover, my ultimate goal is to please her as much as I can. I do this with an extreme amount of foreplay. I love to eat pussy. Well, when my lover and I are fucking, naturally, I start to feel myself starting to come. Yet it feels so deliciously fine, fucking her, that I want to go on as long as I can. So what I do is I try not to think of things like how good it feels, how soft her skin is, and all the other wonderful sensations and feelings. Instead of coming, which means an end for a while anyway, I have trained my mind to switch to rather complicated math problems. I manage to get to a level where I am still rock hard, but not as near to climax as I was. Then I build up to it again, switch back to math in my head, and I just seem to go on and on, until I want to come. I can last anywhere from thirty minutes to two hours, depending on how long I want to last, and how responsive my lover is. This might sound sort of weird, but it's always worked for me.

I find that my sex life is very active. I can go many

times. However, I do have sexual fantasies. They are
mainly about my sisters. One is twenty-nine, the other is
twenty-four. I feel that it stems from the fact that I can't
seem to distinguish between memory and fantasies. My
oldest sister and I were very close. I used to spend hours
watching her make her face up. I used to love to brush her
hair. She always like to get me to massage her back for
her. This was when I was a little older, just getting into my
teens. She still does, whenever I take the time and effort
involved to visit with her. Whenever I would massage her
back, I would get very horny. I never did once say anything about it. I remember when I was very young, she was
laying on her bed and I was laying beside her playing with
her pussy. However, I don't know whether this is a true
memory or a fantasy that my head has made up. I had to
have been around seven or eight at the time this might
have happened. I also remember around that age a dream I
had that I married my sister. Just recently, within the last
year, did I realize how much I would like to fuck her, and
I intend to do so. My sister and I have planned a long trip
together, when I get back to the United States. We will be
with each other on the road for about five days, and I
intend to let her know that I have feelings for her that go
beyond brother love.

DAN

I am thirty-eight years old, married; and we have five children. I am the middle child; I have an older sister and a
younger sister. Growing up in our home was not especially
happy because my father was a real domineering
bastard; and all of us, including my mother, had to toe the
line at all times.

As soon as I could, I went into the service. Not long
after I got out, I married. It really bothered my younger
sister that I had to get married because my wife was pregnant. This sister, Sally, and I had always been close. In a
way, she idolized me; and I must have really disappointed
her. Anyway, she went away to nursing school, got married, had two kids, and we seldom see each other.

I tell you all this because for the past three years I have had a consistent fantasy about Sally. My wife and I don't have a very good sex life anymore. She puts out for me, and that is about all. The only way I can come with my wife is when I fantasize. Almost all of my fantasies when I screw my wife are about Sally. I've never told my wife about this because she is very jealous of Sally. Always has been.

Here is my fantasy about my sister: There is a party at my house. A lot of people are there, including Sally. At some point, she and I are dancing. (She and I both love to dance.) The music is slow, a 1950's song. She snuggles up to me and rubs the back of my neck. Her pelvis tilts gently, but firmly against my crotch. I try to ignore this, but there is no denying that my cock has become hard. Sally looks up at me and quietly smiles. It's a magic moment. I think, God she knows what she is doing. My hand around her waist slips down to cup her firm, rounded ass. The fingers of my other hand gently stroke her breast. I feel happy and excited at the same time. But I'm also afraid the record will stop and the spell will be broken.

Sally whispers in my ear, "Dan, Dan, Dan." I kiss her on the cheek. She looks up at me and kisses me on the mouth, a full, wet, sexy kiss. I say to her, "Oh, Sally, I want you so much. I've wanted you for such a very long time." She says, "I'm yours."

I take her by the hand, and we go into one of the kids' rooms. At first we kiss gently, as if discovering each other's lips and faces for the first time. Then our kissing becomes more passionate. A full moon is coming through the window. I say to her, "You are the most beautiful, the most enchanting woman I have ever known; and I mean every word of that." Slowly, almost delicately, I unbutton her blouse, and what a delight to discover that she isn't wearing a bra. I kiss each of her breasts. I unzip her skirt and it falls to the floor. Slowly, my hands descend with me as I pull down her panties, over her firm tummy, exposing her bush, and down her legs. Quickly, she steps out of her panties and kicks them aside. I pull her to me; and my hands run over her shoulders, her back, her ass.

Sally pushes me back and unfastens my pants and pulls

them down with my briefs in one sweep. She is on her knees and takes my cock in her hand, holds, caresses it, looks up at me, smiles, and says, "Is this delicious thing for Sally?" God, I'm shaking, but I manage to nod and whisper, "Only for you." She takes my cock, now throbbing, into her beautiful, moist mouth. I have never been sucked like Sally can suck. I cannot stand it. I pull her up to me and throw my arms around her tight. Then I pick her up and lay her down on the bed. She lays there, smiling at me. I look down at her and say, "You are gorgeous." She lifts her arms toward me and says, "Come to me. Come to me now." I lay down over her, and she gently guides my hungry cock into her wet cunt. We move slowly together, savoring the wonder and the beauty of splendid screwing. Together the tempo of our fucking rises. Her hands go back down to my ass and grasp it, pulling me into her with deeper intensity. I feel such ecstasy, such joy, as we come together. She holds me, and I hold her. Tenderly we kiss each other.

We help each other dress. We rejoin the party. My wife comes up to us and asks, "Where have you two been?" Sally answers, "Oh, we were just looking at the moon."

When I read Fitzgerald's *Tender Is the Night*, in my teens, I felt he'd gone too far even for fiction. Who could believe a father would do that to a daughter? Is it surprising that when I read the material in this chapter my reaction was sheer disbelief?

Oh, perhaps I could give some credence to men like Dyson, Bennet, Sailor, and Dan (all above); even people who shudder at the thought of a sexual relationship between a mother and son might be able to believe in slightly less primal forms of incest. One of the aspects of Lord Byron that thrilled fluttering Victorian hearts was suspicion of a love affair with his sister. In fact, brother-sister attraction is one of the sure-fire ingredients in modern gothic novels, books which sell in the millions.

But given my own upbringing, sex between a father and daughter, or a mother and son, was as remote as having three heads. I could believe that men like Tim, with whom this chapter began, had *fantasies* about their mothers; but as for basing these notions on actual events?

Perhaps I was influenced in my disbelief by a well-known story about Freud. Early in his career, he was astonished to hear from a great number of female patients about damaging sexual advances they had received from their fathers. Was Vienna a secretly raging cauldron of incestuous vice? Further investigation convinced him that his patients were mostly telling him fantasies—ideas so dreaded, but also so fervently wished for, that the line between the real and the imaginary had blurred.

As I read and reread the material in this chapter, I could not but think about that. These fantasies are so ambiguous; as each man tells his story, he seems to slip from the present tense to the past, jumps to the future and then back. Bennet just launches into his fantasy/memory with no clue as to whether he wants me to take it as fact or not. Sailor asserts, "I don't know whether this is a true memory or a fantasy that my head has made up." In the end, I decided it was all wishful thinking; the man was trying to persuade himself it was reality; if he could convince me it had happened, maybe he could believe it himself.

As a check, I showed this chapter to several psychiatrist colleagues. To my surprise, they told me they had no trouble accepting as fact what these men say. Yes, they were fantasies, imaginary reconstructions of past events—but that did not mean the autobiographical material was not true. Most of these men, my consultants believed, had had real incest experiences. These doctors said that they often came across similar situations in their practices.

To my contributors—in this chapter more than in any other—I offer apologies for having doubted your veracity. To readers who are shocked by this material, or would accuse me of encouraging incest, my reply is that to have excluded this theme would have been to condemn those people candid enough to write me about these ideas as being too awful to discuss.

In the last analysis, if I do not want to condemn, neither do I want to condone. The mothers in this chapter who seduced their sons do not seem to me to be rapists. But what about the sons who did not write me? The emotions aroused by these fantasies are too contradictory for me to easily resolve. If I am naive and bewildered, I can only say I am not alone in my confusion. Most people find it so impossible to contemplate incest that in old-fashioned religious debates, the atheist had one question that notoriously left believers speechless and gasping. "Who," he would ask, "did the children of Adam and Eve marry?"

JAKE

I am sixteen and my mom is forty-eight.

It all started one night when I came home from a date. I went right upstairs to bed, and I was laying there jacking off, about ready to come, and my mom walked in and turned the light on. We just both stood still for a while. She said she had come up to put my sheet on my bed. She sat on the bed and I got up and put my underwear on, and sat next to her. She asked me if I jacked off very often, and I told her about twice a week. I noticed that she started staring at my dick, and I could see under her nightgown that her tits were erect. Then she asked me if I wanted to make love. The next thing I knew, we were sitting there frenching with her tongue deep inside my mouth. We must have frenched for ten minutes. Then I started kneading her tits, and we started rolling around in bed, still frenching deeply with our tongues, and then she started whispering in my ear, "Fuck me, fuck me. I gotta have that dick." So I took off my underwear and was ready to fuck and she had her nightgown off, and I was on top of her fucking away. I came three times that night and she must have come a dozen times.

My father does a lot of traveling, and is gone sometimes for three or four days. My fantasy now is that I will sleep in my mom's bedroom. When I get up in the morning and take a shower, she will get in the shower with me and give me the best blow job I've ever had. I'll shoot half a gallon of cum in her mouth, and she will swallow it all. After that, we will fuck standing up. Later that day, when I come home from school, we will fuck in the kitchen. Whenever my father is home, we will go for walks in the

woods and make love or go to a drive-in and get in the
back seat of the car and fuck.

BUTCH

My sex life began at an average age with my cousin, who
was a year younger than I. My father left Mother when I
was a young child, so I did not have any idea as to the
feelings of having a father around. Mother has worked
since she was deserted, having been hired by her former
boss because she was very well educated in his particular
field, patent attorney. During that time, after school, I
would stop off at my aunt's home until Mother finished
work. My cousin was very talented with a baton and did
fancy dancing while she was performing. She would always ask me to be with her when she was practicing in the
yard or the large room in the lower level of the house.
While she was doing head turns, cartwheels, head standing,
etc., she wore a very skimpy outfit. The pants were loose
and it was while she was doing cartwheels that her little
cunt was exposed to my view. It excited me to be able to
see her cunt so plainly. During the warm weather, she
would wear an even skimpier outfit; and the shoulder
straps always dropped down, which would get her irritated.
Her breasts were not yet showing, but just the sight of her
nipples gave me a thrill. As often as her straps dropped, I
would kiss her nipples and she wanted me to do that often.
She asked if I would suck them like a baby, and I did.
Well, soon I was exploring her bottom; and she never
made an effort to stop me. It soon was a regular event with
us, each time leading to more and more types of sex fun.

At night when I was in bed, I dreamed about what I
would do. Jacking off became a regular event.

Whenever my cousin and I could get in a hidden place,
we would take our clothes off and play with each other.
While I was up close to her cunt, my cousin asked me to
kiss her cunt. That did it. Soon I was sucking her cunt, and
she returned the pleasure by sucking my cock. Well, as
time went on, my fantasies became a lot more elaborate,

dreaming about girls who I saw at the pool, on the street, or met at a show.

One time when I was about twelve years old, I was in my room and really beating my meat. I had a mirror between my legs and was watching the hand jacking off my cock. The event happened I was so afraid of: My mother came into my room to wake me up for school and found me beating my meat. All she said was to get dressed when I was finished. Well, a guy hates to face his mother after he gets caught red-handed, so I did not leave my room to come down for breakfast. Soon Mother was back in my room and wanted to know what the matter was that I had not come to the breakfast table. She hugged me, kissed me, and told me to hurry as though she never saw what I had been doing. After we ate, she stood up, came over to where I was, took my arm, and had me stand up. She gave me a kiss like I had never had from her and whispered to me that she loved me very much and to have a good day.

That evening after we had finished the dishes, Mom spent a bit of time helping me with my lessons. She kept kissing me more than she ever had before. When it came bedtime, she told me to be sure to give her a kiss before I went to bed. That was a complete surprise to me. I did go to her room. She was in bed. She opened the bed sheets and told me to lay down by her as she wanted to have a talk with me. I knew then what she had on her mind. She started off by saying, "What you were doing this morning is a natural thing for all boys to do, so do not think you are alone." She told me that girls and boys all over the world are doing the same thing. She made me feel so relieved about playing with my cock.

The next night when she called me to bed with her, I was surprised to find her without a bit of clothing on. She told me to remove my p.j.'s. She liked to have me lay up against her body with my back to her, and she reached down and held my cock while we were talking. That soon led her to jacking my cock, and she asked if I enjoyed what she was doing. Sure I did. Then she asked if I would suck her nipples, and she placed herself in a position so I was underneath her breasts. I was sucking her tits like a baby would. That led to other sex acts. She asked if I would be willing to suck her cunt, if she showed me how.

That was nothing new for me. All during the time I was having sex with Mother, I often imagined that it was Donna (my cousin) I was sucking or fucking.

Today I am very happily married. Can you be surprised to hear that it is my beautiful mother I often think about, dream about, while masturbating? Who could ever forget such a mother?

PHIL

I am an out-of-state pharmacy student, attending the school here in Oklahoma. I enjoy dating many women, so I don't really have any sexual hang-ups, just fantasies.

I imagine myself back in the Victorian period. I am at a private dining club, with fine hanging chandeliers and silver and crystal on the tables. The only other people at the club are sitting across from me: my mother, sister and an acquaintance of my mother.

I gaze at their voluptuous breasts, which have very suggestive cleavage, and which are semi-covered by fine glistening silk.

Then there is soft music in the background, so I ask my mother to dance. While dancing, I move my chest slightly, but subtly against her breasts. I then dance her through a door to a room which is quietly lit and secure. I unzip the back of her dress and begin placing kisses from the top of her smooth-skinned back, moving across and down. I then come to her hips. With her back still facing me, I move my head up from her hips and around past her arm and tilt my head to kiss the side of her tit.

At this point, I feel she's agreeable to my overtures, so I turn her around facing me, and with my hands on her shoulders, I look into her eyes and kiss her on the lips. She then takes my tongue into her mouth and begins sucking on it.

Like a lion who bites his prey on the neck, I put my lips on her neck, just below her ear, and gently bite into her skin. I have just made a fresh kill.

I then put her down gently on a low-lying padded table

and completely undress her. I place a wet kiss in the soft area between her tits. The palms of my hands are soft, and slightly sweaty, when I feel her buttocks. I then go down towards her legs. I part my lips, and suck in the skin of her thighs, while feeling it with my tongue. I lick her soft skin on her inner thighs, and smell it with my nose. Again, I part my lips sucking her skin in while feeling it with my tongue and wetting it.

I next go to her vagina and kiss it as I would kiss her lips. I push my nose into the skin of her thighs and finally my nose moves into her cunt and I inhale lightly. I move up to her ear and whisper, "I like the musk smell of your cunt."

Her feet are slender, skin smooth, with high arches. My hands clasp her ankles, as in bondage, and while raising them, I kiss the arches of her feet.

I then move up to her face, give a slight kiss to her lips, and tell her that her cunt imparted a musk odor to her tight-fitting panties, and that I want them so I could commemorate this occasion.

I then seduce my sister and my mother's acquaintance and likewise collect their panties. Later, in my own privacy, I sniff each of the panties and find that each one has its very own, distinct and delightful shade of musk. However, the loveliest is my mother's.

CHET

I'm thirty years old, was widowed a few years ago, and I am a rock star. I'm good-looking, I guess, since I'm supposed to be somewhat of a sex symbol; but I don't think I am all that attractive to women. My wife died seven years ago, and I haven't remarried; don't know if I will, because I think she was the one true love of my life.

I am a bastard—literally—because my mother and father were only fifteen and sixteen when I was born, and they were not married. My mother died in childbirth or shortly thereafter, and I think my father held it against me. At least I remember my childhood as being mostly a time when he slapped me around or tormented me and picked on me. We lived in the country for a while; but when I was about nine years old, we moved to St. Louis; and that's where I got really screwed up about sex. My father was wild when it came to women; there were whores in our apartment all the time, different ones, in and out. I could hear them in his bed; and I had an idea of what they were doing; but since it was dark, I never exactly saw them fucking. But one day, one of his girls started on me—I guess as a game, really. I came into the apartment and saw her sitting on the couch; and she told me my father was in the shower. I was about ten then and not really grown, but starting to look less like a kid and more like a young man. She started kinda flirting with me and reached out for my hand. She rubbed it a minute and then reached out for my pants and started to rub. I got hot pretty fast, which just amused her. I remember she unzipped my pants and took out my penis and started to rub it. Then she leaned over and put her tongue all over my cock, and about the time I went crazy, my father came back into the room. The girl told him I had made advances toward her and had asked her to suck me, and he backed me into a corner and threatened to cut off my cock if I so much as even looked at his girls again. WAS THAT CLEAR?? He scared the shit out of me, and for weeks afterwards I would look over my shoulder while I was peeing because I was afraid he might cut off my penis. This same girl sucked me another time, again just a game for herself probably, but it stirred up feelings in me that I didn't know what to do with. She'd wait until my father was somewhere else and then she would start in on me. This time she had my pants open again and was sucking me in the closet, when he came up the hallway. She just went out and shut the door on me and I had to stay there until she and my father left. She got me all hot and excited and then quit before I ever got to where I was going. I can see now that she was using me like a toy to amuse herself, but at the time I didn't understand what she was doing to me or why. It left me very frustrated, and it made me a little afraid of women. I never actually went all the way with a girl until I married my wife. At school I petted with girls, and I let a few suck me, but it almost always made me a little anxious and insecure. If I had a fantasy then, I guess it was that I could capture some girl's affections and really make it all the way with her, that she wouldn't laugh at me or use me just for her own pleasure.

The odd thing is that I find I'm often a toy now, in my adult life. I do know women who treat me like a person, and for that I'm thankful, but an entertainer also has lots of women who just want to screw him and all I am to them is one big penis, I guess. I've had women write me notes asking if I'll take them to bed, and one woman said it right to my face. "Fuck me!" If that's liberation, I don't want it. Maybe that's a reaction to what happened to me as a kid, I don't know, but it is probably true that I would like to place my woman at least a little bit on a pedestal. My wife was very sexy, but also very much a lady, and I was faithful to her during our marriage because I felt a very deep love for her. I've slept with other women since her death, but not just for a fuck if I can help it.

But I have realized that sometimes when a woman is sucking my penis, if I close my eyes I can see all the way back to my father's girl friend, and it churns up something inside of me when I remember what it felt like to have her tongue over me when nobody else had ever touched me there before. The thing about it is that a kid being sucked by an older woman is very vulnerable, both physically and emotionally. The American ideal of a man is somebody strong and tough, completely self-assured, and all that bull. So naturally men try to live up to this and nobody wants to admit they are weak or insecure or vulnerable. But when you don't know too much to start with, and you have an experienced woman sucking the part of your body that defines you most definitely as a man, she is really in control of your maleness. If she bites you, you'll have physical pain, if she makes fun of your penis or teases you and torments you the way I was tormented, you have an emotional pain that can hamper sexual relations throughout your life. I know that women are very sensitive and I try to protect their feelings, but a lot of women don't realize that I'm also very sensitive about my manhood. The fact that I, and most men, don't feel all that free to admit it doesn't mean the insecurity isn't there. Locker room bull is one thing, but to really be honest about your deep fears and fantasies, that's another thing altogether.

Freud was one of those rare scientific minds able to think about the unthinkable. He based his oedipal theory on findings that the desire for incestuous relations with the parent was biological, inborn, and unavoidable, but that guilt would inevitably follow. However, the men in this chapter often show no more guilt than a Thoroughbred mare being mated with her son to "improve the breed" (Tim)—or father and daughter rabbits doing what comes naturally in the woods. The salient point about men like Butch and Jake (above) is that they are not crying out against the seduction of the innocent; no accusations are being made that sex with a mother, older sister, or aunt had broken a life. *These men are rapturous.* Wouldn't any wife be envious of the language they use to describe their love for their mothers, hers for them? In earlier chapters we spoke of one of the forms men's basic conflict takes: the split of love vs. lust, and the consequent division of women into "good" and "bad" figures. For these men, there is no such division. One woman is both love and lust.

"When I was in psychoanalytic school in the fifties," psychoanalyst Dr. Richard Roberitello said to me, "the big idea was still that most neuroses stemmed from unresolved oedipal feelings. And having sex with your mother—what could be more guilt producing than that? But psychoanalytic theory has now advanced to placing the seminal disturbances much earlier in life. My own clinical experience has also worked to change my mind."

Dr. Robertiello went on: "Of course, if sex within the family is sneaky, guilty, manipulative, charged with fear, shame, and so on, it can be shattering. Since these adjectives precisely describe character traits in most people, incestuous behavior is still likely to lead to devastating results. What I am saying is that it need not be that way. This is especially true in the single-parent family where ideas of jealousy, or being found out, need not invariably arise. Patients who have been introduced to sex by a young

widowed mother or a divorced father—they may have
problems, character neurosis, whatever. But I know people
who had strong incestuous relations with a parent when
little. Today, they do not seem to me to have any greater
sexual problems than anyone else. I am a classically
trained, Freudian analyst; for me to say this is an enormous and radical change in thinking." Here is the most
important clue: *It is not the physical fact of sex that matters so much as the psychological message the parent im-
parts along with the erotic experience.*

I hesitate in writing this. Fashionably with-it parents
may read what I have said and decide they are single-
minded about how beautiful sex is, and therefore can give
their child a loving introduction to the erotic life. This is
dangerous ground.

For all her astounding candor and sexual acceptance,
even Tim's mother taught him their relations must be kept
secret. In his letter he says he wanted to make love to his
mother "to prove I could do it and survive." Survive what?
Punishment at the hands of his absent father? Society's
rage? We don't know, but the fervor of Tim's defense of
incest hints he may not have come through the experience
as guiltlessly as he believes.

While I believe that Freud was right and that all of us
have repressed oedipal wishes, I think it is mindless to mis-
interpret him and decide that all repressions are "bad."
Would you like to be liberated from the iron, unconscious
barrier that keeps you from wetting your bed at night? My
own feeling, as a matter of fact, is that the people who
wrote me so happily about real incest are probably the rare
exceptions. I am convinced that the incest taboo has strong
survival value, not only for the individual but for the race.

A child's first years are better spent, for instance, on
socialization and education than in coping with the intensities of lived out sexual relationships with people to whom
he is so vulnerable. Chet (above) still carries the scars of a
semioedipal relationship in which one of his father's girl
friends took sexual advantage of him.

But these are social values; they are not biological im-
peratives. What can be objectively stated is that we are
born with a desire to have sex but with no bias about having it this or that way. We are paper. In our first years our

parents hold the pen. If what they write is done with love and without ulterior motive or guilt, we will probably not be hurt by anything they do. My only warning is to echo that of Dr. Robertiello: This kind of parent is rare. Many a wife will try to use sex to hold a husband, thus tearing him with guilt. It is much worse if a mother tries to do the same with a son.

JEFFERSON

I am fifty years old, married, with two children.

My wife and I for some time were made more passionate during our fucking sessions by the recounting of the follow ing by me—

When I was about eleven, I sucked my father's penis. He was a good man, but drank heavily. Many times when he was sleeping heavily, after much drinking, I saw his stiff brown prick. Dad had the biggest pair of balls I have ever seen. A few times I would stand by his bed and pull the covers down so I could gaze at his beautiful organ. I would masturbate right there.

The summers in New York were very hot. He would sleep on the couch in the front room, and I, because of the shattering heat, curled up on the floor on a blanket near the couch.

On one very hot night, he was asleep on the couch after drinking. I woke up and saw the sheet he was covered with standing up like a tent around his stiff organ. I crept closer and pulled the sheet down and looked closer at his wonderful prick. I lightly took his balls out of his shorts and stroked them. A few times I had seen my mother suck his organ, and I thought it would be wonderful to try the same. Now I was on my knees on the floor, my head resting on his thigh. Getting up my nerve, I held his thick penis and kissed the crown. My mouth sucked half of his cock into it. He moaned, but continued to snore. His penis now was almost all in my hot young mouth, and I sucked hard, and moved my head up and down slowly. It was heaven. Many minutes passed and I continued to suck my Dad's cock. He moved a little and moaned again.

I felt he was near his climax and sucked harder, and moved my head up and down faster. Then his cock began to pulsate and he started to spurt his semen into my mouth. I sucked on and on, taking all of his juice into my mouth and swallowing. Father came and came, and I held his organ in my mouth until no more semen came. I covered him again and jerked off into my undershirt. (When I would tell my wife this, she came and so did I.)

Next day, Dad gave me no sign that he knew what had happened. Some nights later, I did the same. He woke up as he was about to shoot, and held my head tight as he flooded my throat. He called me a "cocksucker" as he finished in my mouth. Father then pulled me on the couch, and sucked my mouth taking some of his own semen in his mouth. He took my hand and put it on his prick. Making me get on my knees, he sucked my anus, it was wonderful. His penis was stiff again, and he made me get in the "sixty-nine" position and he sucked my penis into his mouth and his prick sank into my throat. We came together strongly.

My wife and I talk about these past events. In fantasy we think: my father on his back, his cock deep in my wife's vagina. She is pumping hungrily on it, I am sucking and licking her asshole, and his balls. Or: My wife sucking Dad's penis and he sucking her cunt while I am fucking my wife in her asshole. (She loves this fantasy and goes wild.)

I feel some comment is necessary on Jefferson's communication (above), which seems to be rooted in real experience he had as a child with his father. Since it is the only such expression I received, I showed it to several therapists for comment. The three I happened to interview said that in their clinical practice, it was new to them too.

If I had mentioned this fantasy/experience to three other psychiatrists, would I have gotten the same answer? Perhaps not. Jefferson's ideas may be rare, but I find it impossible to believe that any sexual notion can be unique to one person. The most consistent thing years of studying sexuality has taught me is that there are untold numbers of troubled people walking the earth, feeling they are the only

ones so "strange" and "unnatural" to have done or thought
whatever it is that is on their minds. "The more years I
spend in practicing analysis," a doctor once told me, "the
more I realize we are more alike than different."

8

Fetishism

Much as my present thinking may owe to Freud, something in me still resists his iron determinism. The child is father to the man, yes—but where do the mysteries of temperament, personality, and individual genius enter? How about the randomness of genetic inheritance? During the second draft of this book, I asked my typist what she thought of the material. She said she was "shocked to see how much of what we do and feel can be traced back to infancy."

She had my sympathy. Isn't the full human being something more than a toy train running on tracks laid down in childhood? I had based my life on a boast that I'd "made myself up." In retrospect, it seems my refusal to give Freud's teachings any credence was evidence of determination to ignore, forget, repress—choose the word you like—my first years and their inevitable humiliations and traumas. The books I've written were a painful education. But I chose to write them; on subjects whose genesis lies in our earliest years. Something in me wanted to understand puzzling facets of my own behavior, patterns of my life that no amount of intellectual rationalization about my adult years could explain.

In sex we especially resist the notion that our fears and desires are conditioned by developmental events that occurred long before we even thought about our present lovers. Freud's theories of infantile sexuality were the scandal of Vienna; even the medical profession turned their backs on him. Today, we still don't want to think of children as feeling anything in that sweet talcumed area between their legs.

Who wants to surrender the flattery implicit in the notion that our characters have been carved by ourselves alone, out of life's granite? This self-administered pat on the back may superficially feel good; the price is high. If everything we do is conscious volition, why do we get into so many unhappy relationships for reasons we cannot name? How do we explain sexual anxieties and guilts, those patterns of repetitious failures, *over and over of the same kind?* Is it bad luck that is our enemy—or is the fault in ourselves?

For all my desire to believe in human choice and spontaneity, and in the remedial efficacy of life itself—only the penetrating insights of psychoanalytic theory are any help in unraveling the mysteries of fetishism.

ROY

I am a foot fetishist. I love bare feet, shoes, high-heel boots and anything pertaining to the female foot. The story starts this way. From the time I can remember, my mother, a beautiful woman then in her early forties, would give me horsy rides on her foot. At that age it didn't bother me sexually, but it always felt good. By the age of thirteen or fourteen, she still allowed me the horsy rides, but now I am sure she realized that I wasn't just playing. I was coming in my p.j.'s. The reason I know this now is because when the "ride" was finished, she would give me a complete going over with both feet, usually with her beautiful high-heel and pointed toe shoes on, kicking me between the buttocks, under my balls, and wind up rubbing her foot on my cock and bringing on another come. Then to bed. Needless to say, my fantasy is to have four girls or women in my room, then I strip naked and roll all around the floor while they take turns kicking me in all the vulnerable spots until they have brought me to as many comes as I can possibly take. Sound kinky?

True.

KIP

As far back as I can remember, I was indulging in frequent
masturbation and fantasies. I remember wearing diapers
and rubber pants and I am sure I was lying on my tummy
and masturbating against the diaper toweling before I can
remember. I enjoyed my mother's attention when she held
me to make "weewee." I can remember this and that the
feeling of doing a "weewee" was pleasant. I also remember
taking a diaper to bed because I sucked the corner to go to
sleep. The real secret reason, however, was that as soon
as I was left alone, I would lay on my tummy with the
toweling under my penis and wriggle my legs.

Back to infancy; I must explain that my mother had a
wardrobe of pretty feminine clothes but also a range of
rubber aprons. She wore a rubber apron for all wet jobs,
and attending to me. I was therefore well aware of its delicate touch and I regarded it as special. No doubt because of
the wet connection I associated it with the "weewee" feeling
and also because it was while wearing this that my mother
carried out hygiene attentions on my penis, pulling back
the skin and washing below the glans and working the skin
back to stretch it so that there was no need for circumci-
sion. I always became erect during this performance and I
am sure she enjoyed virtually masturbating me, although
her conscience caused her some trouble here, and I was
not allowed to wriggle my legs because that was naughty.
When I asked why, she gave me some answer which I remember as having something to do with girls and ladies,
but I did not understand.

I fell in love at five, when I went to infant school, with a
pretty little girl whom I admired from a distance, and
when I asked my mother as she attended to me at bath
time, if little girls had to have their skins pulled back, she
explained that girls and ladies did not have a penis—only a
hole. I was deeply shocked.

My father caught me masturbating in bed brooding on
this problem, and I had a long lecture about it being bad
for me. I would hurt myself and it was not for little boys to
do I misunderstood him to mean that it was for little girls

to do, an idea which made me want to masturbate even more.

About this time I had my first dry orgasm. I decided that girls and ladies felt nice like this all the time and could reach a seventh heaven of delight, which was when they wore a rubber apron. But if I continued to do this thing which felt so nice and was reserved for girls, I would be taken to a hospital where a beautiful fairy type of nurse wearing a beautiful rubber dress and apron and would make me wear rubber as well, and force me somehow to masturbate on and on to some extreme orgasm (I could not put that into words then). Then my penis would disappear and I would turn into a girl. This idea I both feared and wished for.

I masturbated to this fantasy for years after wearing my mother's rubber apron at the same time. She did not seem to notice if I sneaked one out of her cupboard.

On rare occasions. I had a bed-wetting accident. This made my mother very cross. She would start a cleaning up and changing operation. I was washed and laid across her rubber-aproned lap for a spanking. My penis in contact with her cold wet rubber apron was beautiful; the smacking tended to make my penis rub against the apron as well.

Rubber aprons disappeared during the war and I masturbated with a rubber hot-water bottle filled with cold water, the neck folded back to tickle between the scrotum and the anus.

I met my wife when I was twenty-one and she seventeen. We were both shy. It took me much effort to find the courage to ask her out, yet in a few months, we were masturbating each other at every opportunity, and she was the first, the last and only. I am pleased to say that at forty-seven, she still has a face and figure (no corseting) which is the envy of many girls half her age.

My wife has never taken to the rubber idea, although she accepted it willingly enough at first—when I bought her the first rubber apron. I tried very hard to give her special attention.when she wore it for me, but slowly a jealousy of it developed; recently, I have had some success with cunnilingus as the prize and I enjoy doing this for her just under the bottom edge of the apron. Rubber and her juices have a certain affinity and similarity. (I was even instinctively aware of this as a child.)

Rubber fantasies are still with me and when my wife masturbates me I fantasize that nude rubber-apron girls are doing it or that she is wearing a fantastic rubber night dress or that I am watching Miss World in rubber and seeing rubber-aproned girls masturbating themselves and each other.

In another fantasy, I am required to visit a house somewhere, and I am surprised to be received by a beautiful woman wearing a rubber apron night dress. She soon makes it clear that she is going to seduce me. I am very virile and achieve multiple dry orgasms, as when I was a child. I use fantasies like this when I am having sex with my wife, and it has the effect of actually making me last longer and hover on the brink a fair part of the time. Even after coming, I can remain semihard and carry on gently a little longer.

How could anyone decide to make a shoe or a diaper into the sexual be-all and end-all of his life? Where do these tastes come from? When the four women enter Roy's fantasy (above) we can see why he might want to dress them in sexy shoes or stockings as a form of imaginary fore-play—but why does he come to orgasm, not when in contact with their vaginas, but with their feet? What is the sexual power of the fetish?

There are two main schools of psychiatric thought on this subject; I must warn my readers that if both sound bizarre, how could they be any simpler than the subject they set out to explain?

The classical theory of the fetish centers its explanation around the Oedipus complex. To Freud, the most important determinant in male behavior is the degree to which the boy succeeds in overcoming problems due to rivalry with the father for the mother's love. Behind this is fear that the father, being bigger and stronger, will punish his young rival by castrating him. To this way of thinking, the fetish object somehow becomes linked in the child's unconscious mind with his own penis.

We can see this process at work in Kip (above). As far back as he can remember he has had masturbatory memories of "wearing diapers and rubber pants." These ideas are immediately linked with mother's attention "when she held me up to make weewee," and also with her handling his penis. She "[pulled] back the skin and washed below the glans." He would become erect during these ministrations. At night he would take a diaper to bed with him in order to masturbate.

The connection between penis, diapers, rubber pants, and sexuality that involved mother could not be more clear.

In this kind of associative thinking, the sight of the fetish makes one immediately think of the penis. Here lies a magical escape from fear that daddy will perform his dread punishment on the boy who wants mama. The fetish *is* the penis; when the boy sees it, when he touches it, his unconscious is relieved. He has not lost his penis—*here* it is! The enormous relief from anxiety is expressed as a rush of sexual energy. Confirmation that this kind of activity is connected more with joy at retaining the penis than with winning the woman is in the often-observed fact that it is the fetish itself that excites the man's principal attention. The vagina is there, but it has only secondary glamour.

NEIL

About half of the time, my fantasies are really *recollections* of previous sexual encounters, slightly embellished by "clothing" the girl involved in garments that are sexually attractive to me. I have been turned on by women's shoes since childhood. One of my earliest sensual memories is that of being in my older sister's closet, sitting on the floor among her shoes and smelling the exotic woman smells of perfume, powder and good leather. I don't recall doing anything, just being there in a dark, semiforbidden place and being stimulated. The attraction intensified during adolescence when I discovered masturbating over "girly" books as an exciting, everyday outlet for my growing sex drives. As you probably know, the models in those magazines were almost always dressed in provocative lingerie and inevitably wore garter belts, dark nylons and high heels. The footwear in vogue during my teen-age years was pointy-toed, stiletto-heeled plain pumps and as I've discovered from extensive reading on the subject of fetishism, this is the type of shoe that still attracts most fetishists. I differ somewhat, as my preference has changed as fashion has changed. In high school and college, I could be tremendously turned on by a girl wearing knee socks and brown penny loafers or saddle shoes. Again, unlike most fetishists I've read about, the shoe *itself* has no intrinsic attraction; I'm turned on by the *lady,* but it greatly intensifies my desire if she is fashionably shod.

I am thirty-one, divorced and a reasonably successful securities salesman living in a singles apartment complex. My sex life is quite active and I prefer "serial monogamy" rather than dating several girls at once. I like to get into my girl's fantasies and act them out with her if she is liberated enough to do it. Consequently, I have been into about everything a man and woman can do together—everything but *my* particular fantasy. I feel that shoe fetishism is *very* common, as witness the aforementioned "girly" books, but it's one of those things that men are ashamed to discuss with each other. I have asked girls, on occasion, to leave their shoes on when we go to bed and their reactions have all been the same—passive compliance without excitement and, I'm sure, a degree of distaste. Like "Can I take my shoes off *now*?" immediately after climax.

My main fantasy, with variations, occurs about half the time I masturbate or make love. To save space, I'll put all of it together, but really I never have the whole fantasy at one time, just parts of it:

A man is tied to a chair in a woman's frilly, feminine bedroom. Sometimes I am the man, sometimes an observer. He is naked or wearing women's underclothes and stockings. A beautiful woman, sometimes black, is seated before him on a divan trying on shoes of all kinds: classic styles like Gucci loafers and I. Miller pumps; funky, whorish shoes with platform soles and sky-high heels; teenybopper shoes like penny loafers and clogs. While she does this, she is continuously teasing the man verbally: Do you like this pair? Would you like to lick this shoe? How would you like this heel rammed up your ass? The man writhes in his chair and she occasionally rubs a shoe against her open vagina. Finally, she releases him and he falls at her feet, scattering the huge pile of shoes and licking and kissing her shod feet passionately.

On one occasion I did discuss this fantasy with a woman. We had dated and made love on several occasions. She was a graduate student, working on her master's in psychology, and lived in the complex. She was leaving the city and transferring to another school and we went out for beer and pizza on her last night in town. We returned to my apartment, smoked a joint and started to make love. I asked her to leave her shoes on, something I'd done with limited results with other girls, and she willingly complied. We fucked, it was great and we lay and smoked another jay. Maybe it was the dope or the beer or the fact that I'd never see her again, but when she asked me, smilingly curious, why I had wanted her to leave her shoes on, I spilled my guts and laid the whole fantasy on her. Perhaps it was because of her psych background, but she wasn't revolted or disgusted with my revelations, but seemed genuinely interested, and almost aroused. She asked me if I would like to do it with her and I was so excited I couldn't stop shaking. She asked me if I wanted her to go to her apartment so she could get some high heels, but I was afraid she would change her mind if I let her go, so I told her what she was wearing was perfect. She had on a pair of Bass Weejun loafers, the new, clunky style with higher, chunkier heels than the old penny loafers. She told me to kneel on the floor and she teased me verbally, almost like my fantasy woman. She lay back on the bed and rubbed herself with one shoe then slipped it back on and ordered me to lick the "stuff" off. While I licked and kissed her shoes, she masturbated and when she was about to come, asked me to finish her with my mouth. I did this eagerly and masturbated myself to orgasm at the same time. We talked for a while afterward, almost as if nothing unusual had happened, and she finally left to return to her own apartment. I never saw her again, although I think of her a lot. I would be almost afraid to see her.

Later that week, I bought a pair of identical loafers in the women's shoe department of a local department store. I was both nervous and highly sexed up waiting for the clerk to return with the shoes. Nervous because I was sure the clerk would know they were for me, rather than my wife as I had told him, and excited at the prospect of having a pair of her shoes. I hurried back to my apartment, stopping only to buy a pair of L'eggs panty hose at a drugstore, ripped off my suit and donned the stockings and slipped into my lady's shoes. I must have masturbated three or four times that night and for a week or so continued to isolate myself behind locked doors and do the same.

I guess my point, if I'm trying to make a point, is that I have a good sex life and my fantasy helps embellish it. I have to finish now as my date for tonight is due shortly. I am grilling steaks for us on the patio, and I'm already wondering what kind of shoes she'll be wearing. See?

There are men who say that the fetish—the shoe, diaper or whatever—merely adds spice to the sexual broth. Essentially, they declare, it is the woman they want. That she may be wearing high heels only heightens the arousal. Neil (above) states the idea flatly: " . . . unlike most fetishists . . . the shoe *itself* has no intrinsic attraction; I'm turned on by the *lady*, but it greatly intensifies my desire if she is fashionably shod." Nevertheless, he finishes his letter with an anecdote about feeling "highly sexed" while buying a pair of women's shoes in a department store and then using them to masturbate "three or four times that night" though no woman was present.

The Freudian fetishist is defined by the fact that his desire is not primarily for the woman. Like Neil, he'll often just go home and curl up with a pair of galoshes instead. *He has his penis.* Relieved of his anxiety that he might have lost it, he feels safe, snug, sexy, satisfied. He doesn't need anything (anyone) else.

So much for Freud. To me, the theory has a certain logic; but it doesn't carry that *click* of inner certainty when a psychoanalytic insight hits home. But then, since I am not a fetishist, why should I expect it to? A more recent explanation for fetishism comes from the English school of psychiatry in which Dr. D.W. Winnicott is a

leading theorist. Here, the feeling is that the fetish cannot
be merely reassurance that the penis has not been damaged. Instead, it is seen as a defense against an earlier, pre-oedipal anxiety. The object of fear is not the punitive father, but loss of the life sustaining mother. To Winnicott,
fetishism stems from a time when separation from mother
is death itself. Just as Linus hangs on to his security blanket
when alone and worried, so does the fetishist arm himself
against infantile fears of losing mama by grasping the fetish
in a tight, loving embrace.

Support for Winnicott's idea comes from those fantasies
in which the fetishist's object is a diaper or a rubberized
item like the apron worn by mother when she bathed baby;
these are totems from the pre-oedipal age. Even the astonishing frequency with which the woman's foot or shoe is
chosen as the fetish may be seen as evidence for Winnicott's theory. From the infant's floor-level point of view,
when he becomes frightened and comes crawling back to
mother as fast as he can, isn't the shoe the first item of her
person he can grasp and hold on to for safety?

In the language of this theory, the fetish is a "transitional object"—helping the toddler bridge his fear and loneliness. Having this unconsciously remembered evidence
of mother's warmth and reassurance with him, he is encouraged to go forward into sexual pleasures.

Both theories have much to recommend them, and perhaps a synthesis could be made: A thoughtful reader will
no doubt already have noticed that while Kip's diapers
(above) could have become his fetishistic object, because
they were easily associated with his penis, so were diapers
also early linked with mother's safety and love. In the absence of consensus among psychoanalysts themselves, we
may feel free to choose either explanation that feels right.

There is, however, an additional piece of evidence to
consider: Girl babies have the same unconscious fear of
losing mother as little boys do, *but instances of fetishism
among women are so rare as to be practically unknown.*
(Incidentally, kleptomania is a problem exclusive to
women.)

As women take on many of men's responsibilities in an
"equal" world, we have already seen increase of incidence
in the female sex of traditionally male complaints like heart

disease, and even baldness. It is interesting to speculate, as
women become more independent—if, like boys, they increasingly become trained to separate from mother as early
as possible—will we also see women fetishists? This
would say a lot for the Winnicott school of thought over
the Freudian.

However, that time is not yet. While it is true that the
fetish seems always to be overdetermined—analysis shows
it can be both a transitional object (as Winnicott uses the
term) and an item that has somehow come to be imprinted
with associations of love and excitement—*it is also used as
a form of penis displacement.* On this evidence, we must
say that fetishism is strongly sex-linked to the male. In this
light, Freud's argument becomes very persuasive.

TUCKER

I have as far back as I can remember always been greatly
fascinated by ladies' dainty and elegant footwear when
worn by women who have nice shapely legs and well-
formed feet so the shoe or boot hugs and fits the contours
of feet and legs, often to such perfection that gives the
viewer the concept of being a part of her own personal
charms, or one might say fitting almost like a second skin.
And so whenever and wherever I feast my eyes on such
ladies wearing shiny black high-heeled patent leather shoes
or boots, I become sexually stimulated and very horny.

It can happen at work in the department store where I
am employed or at staff parties and house parties and anywhere in public; yes, even in church or at funeral parlors.

It is obvious most women are ignorant of how their
beautiful glossy black leather footwear affects the senses of
some men, but undoubtedly lots of women are very much
aware of what their shoes and boots can do for them. They
carefully select styles and the finest softest shiny leathers
which can be so very instrumental for seduction purposes.

When I become infatuated with the lady's sexy shoes or
boots, I make a real study of admiring the high curved
arch of her instep which the high slim heel serves to emphasize and I get the urge to kneel down and fervently lick

and kiss the shiny sexy shoe leather in humble homage and become the lady's personal boot slave. Those are my secret thoughts when I masturbate or when I screw my wife. She has ridiculed me so often for this special "thing" of mine in regard to ladies' footwear.

And so to punish her for it, I always visualize myself as being some other woman's sex slave and I have pretended to engage in those pain and pleasure games even with some of her own girl friends. I am bound helplessly hand and foot by them and whipped with a riding crop on my behind for their own amusement, then made to lick their glistening black patent leather boots as preliminary homage tribute before performing cunnilingus for them.

I have never performed cunnilingus as my wife says nice people do not do such vulgar things, but it has always been my urgent wish to some day become acquainted with some domineering lady who derives personal sexy pleasures from having another woman's husband honor her in this humble fashion.

I have been masturbating ever since I was twelve years old. It was a fourteen-year-old girl who initiated me into this pastime. My mother had her come in to stay with me when she went out; she liked to spank me with a flat household yardstick on my buttocks when we played games. She usually wore pretty black patent leather ankle-strap shoes which I just adored and she let me kiss and lick them on my bended knees which she herself found most amusing.

In school the sight of my lady teachers' high-heeled shiny shoes always served to give me unbearable erections and I just simply had to masturbate.

JACK

I am thirty-three years old and divorced. My ex-wife was the first person with whom I had a serious sexual relationship, more before marriage than after. Ours was fairly conventional, possibly owing to my lack of experience at that time. Limited oral sex and standard man-above and man-behind positions. Since our separation, I have been fortunate in meeting a number of ladies of different nationalities, and I have enjoyed a much more varied and interesting sex life.

Masturbation has been a regular part of my life as long as I can remember. The first orgasms that I can remember came from rope climbing. I must have been eleven or twelve years old at the time. As I remember it, there was no erection and no ejaculation; but it was very intense and lasted much longer than it seems to today. Almost like a female orgasm, I have imagined.

One common factor of all my dreams, both in my teens and today, is high-heel shoes. I can be aroused by shoes in a shop window, in pictures, and by seeing women wearing them. I am very excited if my partner agrees to wear them when we are having sex, and in particular if she touches my penis with the heels during foreplay. My favorite shoes are those with a large open toe and sling-back at the heel. Five inches is the perfect height. If higher, they become unnatural and affected. I had a very happy relationship with a lady who helped me enact a fantasy which I had had for a long time. After sucking my penis until it was completely wet, she took off one of her shoes (my favorite type) and slipped my penis inside so that the head of my penis protruded through the open toe. Then, by sucking the head of my penis and working the shoe up and down the shaft, she brought me to a wonderful orgasm in her mouth. This gave me both a physical and mental pleasure. An extension of this fantasy is that instead of sucking my penis, she lays back and guides her shoe, with my penis inside, to the lips of her vagina and very slowly and gently allows me to push the heel inside her. We are then joined only by the shoe. I can then bring her to orgasm by fucking her with the heel, while the upward thrust pushing my penis through the open toe brings me to an orgasm over her breasts and face. This fantasy, I think, will never be enacted as I am afraid that it would be too painful for the woman, even using very slim heels and as I cannot tolerate the idea of giving pain.

I should mention that I don't think my love of high heels is a true fetish as, although they give me great and harmless pleasure, they are not necessary for me to achieve an erection or ejaculation. They are cream on the cake; a sexual bonus.

My latest and most constant fantasy is that of being a woman. I would love to wear women's clothes, in particular high-heeled shoes; and I am fascinated by stories and articles of transsexual operations. I try to imagine what it would be like to be reborn again as a woman, at thirty-three years of age, and all the problems—legal, physical, and mental—that would be involved. However, I have no interest in having sexual relationships with a man. I have tried hard to imagine what it would be like to suck a man's penis. To be homosexual would be the obvious answer to all my fantasies; but consciously, I don't want that at all. Possibly my subconscious has other ideas; but as it is keeping a very low profile at the moment, I cannot assume anything. My own feeling is that I am a lesbian with a penis; and in my fantasy of changing sex, that is what I become— a lesbian—but with a man's knowledge!

I have come to accept what I am and this makes life much easier. It probably also explains the failure of my marriage and my inability to date, of having a long-term relationship with any of my women friends. I believe they have an instinct about these matters; and although I behave and look like a male, I believe that they can sense something which doesn't quite fit. I trust and hope that I will find a female partner who can accept a gentle male, rather feminine in thought; possibly a homosexual with a vagina!

KEITH

My real thrills usually start while I am at work, which is a rather large chain store. I really get turned on by women who wear short dresses or the long ones with the slits in front to expose a little thigh. Although I am only seventeen, I get turned on by women who are at least twenty or twenty-five years old, and up to about fifty or fifty-five years old. If they are not too ugly at about fifty. I wonder what kind of legs Doris Day has. Mitzi Gaynor has what I think are the best.

On with the fantasy. At work I pretend some lady with excellent legs and a good body comes up and asks where the bathroom is. After we are in the back room, but not yet to the john, she says she would like me to eat her pussy and fuck her. We go over to a corner and kiss. Then she lifts up her dress which uncovers a pussy with panty hose covering the bush. I start to lick her cunt through her panty hose (brown or suntan). After she starts to have her first orgasm, I pull her panty hose off and lick her come and then we fuck for a while. Then she leaves.

Another turn-on is when something has to be put into a lady customer's car. She has a short dress on and when she sits down, the dress goes up even further to expose a couple of excellent thighs. She insists that I take a tip. I refuse and tell her that with her nice looks and nice legs, that anything she needs is free. This is where the fantasy starts: She says that she is divorced and would like someone to talk to, so we make arrangements to meet at her house that night. When I arrive at her house, she answers the door in a short black dress, brown panty hose and boots. She has me go into her bedroom and put on what she has laid out on the bed. A dress which comes to about my knees, dark brown panty hose and nothing else except for these two garments. I go back into the living room. She is sitting in a low chair exposing a lot of beautiful legs. She says I can do anything I want. I kneel down in front of her and start kissing her legs from toes to knees. She asks if that is the only part of her body I like. I now slide my hands up under her dress on the outside of her legs to her pussy, which feels great with super soft panty hose covering it. I then take off her dress and she only has panty hose on. She has nice tits with nice nipples to go with her slim figure. Her pussy is hot as I rub it, still covered by panty hose, until she yells for me to fuck her. I lower my panty hose. She does the same and we fuck for what seems like hours. We both then put on our panty hose and roll around in a sixty-nine on the floor. Her nyloned pussy and thighs cover my face and my balls and cock covered in nylon cover her face. We meet at her apartment every week for our little sessions.

(A turn-on is taking a shower in panty hose and remem-

bering all the legs I have seen that day, which makes me
come.)

Time for a shower.

In some of the above fantasies, the man imagines himself
wearing the fetishistic bit of feminine apparel. This raises
the vexed question of transvestism and homosexuality.
Please note that one does not necessarily mean the other—a
confusion often found among even sophisticated people.
The great majority of homosexuals never wear women's
clothes. On the other hand, there are men who love to put
on women's clothes, but who have never had a homosexual
experience in their lives.

In their sex play, lovers try out all sorts of positions, but
rarely does a man suspect himself of being "secretly" homosexual because he enjoys having the woman on top. Jack
(above) is so in love with his fetish that he, too, endlessly
dreams up variations of erotic play that center on the high-
heeled shoes, including putting them on himself. But then,
instead of taking this as a simple instance of the erotic imagination looking for new paths of excitement, he decides
he must be homosexual. He likes to put on women's
clothes, doesn't he?

I find something courageous in the way he follows this
naive confusion to the end, inventing homosexual fantasies
for himself. But they "arouse no excitement in me," and
judging from the internal evidence of his letter, he never
had a homosexual affair in his life. Why do so many people
rush to label themself as exactly what they fear most?

Jack's lack of genuine interest in his homosexual fantasies illustrates a way of exploring several important ideas.
First, fantasies are a way of playing out private whimsies
and speculations about yourself. Second, fantasies can be
an end in themselves. They are not necessarily desires that
you secretly wish you could act out if you were braver.

Incidentally, not all fetishists act out transvestite ideas. If
it is not the woman's high-heeled shoe but her foot that
becomes eroticized, the idea is hopeless. You can wear a
shoe, but can you take off a woman's foot and put it on?

Another fascinating aspect of fetishistic thinking is the

extraordinary amount of detail connected to the object. The fetish is lovingly described, lingeringly examined. The exact height of the heel, the brand name of the panty hose, the color, the shapes, the feel, and the smell. Nobody is exactly clear why fetish objects become so particularized, but we can make a beginning if we remember that the fetish stands for something important as life itself.

If a man says he is in love with his wife, are we surprised that he pays enormous attention to how she looks? He prefers her hair swept back because he likes to see her forehead; he likes Arpège and is unhappy when she experiments with Chanel No. 5. "Why do you wear black," he laments, "when blue makes you look like an angel?" If you love someone, there is no detail about her that is unimportant. Why should we be surprised if the fetishist brings the same attention to his beloved object?

Finally, I'd like to speculate on an idea mentioned by Tucker (above) who wonders if women are aware of the seductive powers of their shoes. His own reply is ambivalent, but he has put his finger on something that has always mystified me: Both sexes are much more turned on by women's shoes than men's.

Think of the disproportionate amount of money women pay for their shoes; the huge amount of space given shoes in their closets and suitcases; the pain they will endure to wear a size too small, a heel too high. A woman comes home with a new dress. "You must imagine it with these shoes," she says, holding them out. "You must be crazy," her husband replies. "A hundred dollars for those shoes? It's a floor-length dress and nobody will ever see them!" The woman smiles to herself. *She* knows the importance of shoes.

If, strictly speaking, women aren't fetishists, why *are* they so crazy about shoes? Are they intuitively aware that men are more turned on by shoes than they admit? Can it be that Winnicott is right after all—that long before daddy's cordovans entered her adolescent life, the little girl, crawling on the kitchen floor, became entranced just like her brother with the glamour and safety of a nearby woman's (mother's) foot?

9

Water Sports

One of the great principles of nature is economy of design—illustrated, for instance, by the human hand with its startling evolutionary triumph, the apposed thumb. Here is the ultimate in multifunction adaptability—one tool enabling us to pick up food, arouse a lover, soothe a baby, hold a weapon, or type a book—or indeed, make a more specialized tool for a more specialized use. But in designing our genitalia so that they, too, can serve more than one function, perhaps Nature overreached herself: one piece of machinery used both in sex and urination. What's more, both penis and vagina in such close proximity to the anus that you can't blame a kid for getting mixed up.

Many people never get the confusion entirely straightened out. Of course they know the difference in grown-up, cold blood; but in the dark, roiling hotbed of untamed and infantile emotions we call the unconscious, the glamour and mystery of one rubs off and gives erotic meaning to the other.

None of the above is to be understood as saying the men in this chapter are children. Their psychology is more complex. They have mature physiological drives, but their erotic signals are somehow channeled through avenues developed in their first years of life.

One of the ever-popular themes in porn-palace movie machines is what devotees call "water sports" or "golden showers." You put a coin in the slot, pull the curtain, and nobody knows that you are getting your charge from someone wetting her pants, someone else being urinated on, or even drinking it.

We might easily dismiss this as just a marginal attraction, of interest only to the dirty raincoat crowd; but a few years

ago, the climactic scene of a national best-seller struck a
similar note: a famous film producer lying in a bathtub
with several young women sitting on the edge. They peed
on him while he masturbated. What gave this book its
enormous appeal was the whisper that it was based on real
people in Hollywood and was an accurate picture of life in
those plush precincts.

"Nothing human is alien to me." "The proper study of
man is man." I nod assent to these tag ends of philosophy
right along with the best of you. But the eroticization of
pissing and shitting? How can that be? Is it as hard for you
as it is for me to understand why loss of sphincter control
can get people horny? The men in these fantasies are as
difficult for most of us to identify with as if they were Martians. Our distance from their ideas, our alienation from
these people, even the tolerance with which we may smile
at them, are functions of how well we have repressed—
"forgotten"—that at one time in our lives, every one of us
went through the humiliating toilet training experiences
that these fantasies symbolically reenact. In this chapter, I
ask you to remember again. Tough work.

BERNARD

I hope you include fantasies from urinology devotees, especially diaper fetishists. I suspect interest in wearing diapers
is very common; many fetishists probably think they are
alone, as I did at one time. This fetish seems more
shrouded in shame than others; and despite your assurance
of anonymity, I cannot bring myself to sign this letter.

The feel of a thick mass of diaper, held tight by waterproof pants, is *wonderful*. I use bath towels for diapers,
under plastic incontinence pants mail ordered (to preserve
anonymity). I suspect a large number of the incontinence
pants sold by Sears and Ward's are used by diaper fetishists.

I fantasize being a child . . . most commonly a four-or
five-year-old little girl who still wets at night. After drinking liquids profusely, I lie in bed and wet myself. Often I
wear the wet diaper all evening, wetting it again and again.

I collect accounts of the toilet training of children as published in child care books and magazine articles.

More recently, realizing that I am not the only diaper
fetishist, I fantasize meeting a female who enjoys diapers. I
imagine a slender, neat, small-breasted woman, naked except for her taut plastic pants over a bulging diaper. She
would come to me, pretending to be a child, whimpering
about her wet diaper. It would be interesting if she had
continued to be a bed wetter since childhood and really
needed to sleep in diapers and waterproof pants. I suspect
many diaper fetishists were bed wetters in their childhoods.

DENNIS

There are two or maybe three main desires of mine. I say
desires even though I use them as fantasies while I masturbate. I am working on making them come true.

I dream of meeting a bisexual divorcée who is horny,
and will try anything as long as she doesn't get caught, and
her having a very horny daughter. I talk the mother into
letting me have sex with her young willing daughter with
the idea of talking the daughter into having sex with her
mom. So she leaves me alone with her daughter and as we
have sex, I ask her if she ever thought of having sex with a
grown woman. She says that she thinks it might be nice to
try. I tell her that her mom might be game.

I tell each one separately that when we are all together,
and if everyone is hot for what I have suggested, they
would know when I would take out my peter in front of
both of them and start masturbating. Of course, you can
see where my dream goes from there.

My second fantasy is a very raunchy one, as it concerns
defecation. I dream of a woman who is also into golden
showers and defecation. I will write it as I dream it when I
beat the meat, because it is easier for me. You can clean it
up if you so desire. But maybe you can feel in my words
how strong I desire this.

I have a woman squat over my mouth and let go with a
very hot strong-smelling stream of piss into my mouth. (I
have had this done! It is very delightful!) Then hold a

mouthful and make motions to indicate a question. "Do you want me to spit some of your piss into your mouth?" To have her grin and put her mouth over mine and suck her own piss from my mouth and to swallow it. Then to have her stand up and straddle my chest and stay standing and then to proceed to shit upon me! To watch the turds ooze out of her asshole and fall from her while she is standing and to hear and feel her shit go splat on my chest! To smell it. Then to lick her asshole clean, and ask her if she wants another kiss, and to hear her say, "My, your kisses taste and smell good!" Then to have her lay on top of me with her shit still on my chest squeezing between us while we fuck with her on top!

I told you this would be raunchy. Please forgive me. I don't believe that there is a woman that digs shit as much as I do. It is very frustrating!

I am a white single male, aged thirty-three. I have lost fifty-five pounds and am now 168 pounds.

My folks divorced when I was thirteen. My mom was an alcoholic. I remember one night when I was awake late at night, she came home with her girl friend and her girl friend's boyfriend and all three of them got in bed with each other. I felt hurt and guilty and turned on all at the same time.

I also remember one time she was lying in bed and I was talking to her. I was about seventeen then. I thought of making it with her then, but didn't. But had a strong feeling that I could have.

Remember one thing, all of the desires I have said are true. Too damned true. And I dig using dirty language with a woman while I get turned on telling her about myself.

HANK

My first and foremost fantasy is to be a baby again. I am twenty-eight years old and have been wearing diapers and rubber pants all of my life. I have never used them for their intended purpose, except of course when I really was a baby, but I just love the feeling of wearing them. While masturbating in them, I imagine myself being diapered by a beautiful woman. She takes off all my clothes and lays me down on the diaper that she has laid out on the bed, and brings it up between my legs, and pins it at the sides. Then she pulls my rubber pants up around my diaper. She then prepares a baby bottle of milk and feeds it to me, all the while she's talking baby talk to me.

My second fantasy is to lay down naked in a bathtub and have three girls take turns each stripping in front of me and then wrapping their panties around my cock, then squatting down over me and peeing all over me. Then they take their panties from around my cock and wipe their pussies clean, then stuff them in my mouth.

Any mother knows that an infant will often pick up its feces and hold it out to her as a love offering—a piece of himself, something he has produced. Why isn't she as proud of it as he? Left to his own devices, a baby feels no repugnance in putting anything in his mouth. Only when we leave the animal state—or if you prefer, the state of innocence—do we become more fastidious.

But it was a struggle—"the Battle of the Chamber Pot" in psychoanalytic parlance. We all lost, but the men in this chapter never completely surrendered: They are going to get their own back when mother is not looking.

Children often get into trouble as a way of holding mother's attention. A similar element may enter to explain why processes of elimination can sometimes be invested with erotic glamour. In the day-after-day struggle to teach her son continence, mother focused totally on him, neglecting sister, interrupting conversations with dad, watching and waiting beside her son for the first sign he had to go. And more specifically, what area of his body got her most intense attention? His penis and anus.

Breaking mother's rules about cleanliness renders the unconscious at least three pleasures: (1) It is revenge on mother for forcing the boy to learn clean habits against his will. (2) It establishes his independence; he is not "listening" to her, but to his own desires. (3) It focuses life back on that part of the body which she had once made the center of the universe. When a little boy pisses behind a tree, he's not just relieving himself. It is a symbolic act. There's a kick in it. It's freedom!

Choosing water sports as the ultimate way of defying authority carries a certain irony. On the surface it signifies rebellion, being grown-up, tough, unbound by dainty, sissy notions. But underneath, wanting to handle excrement shows a yearning to live once more in the freedom that only babies are granted. Properly understood, water sports fantasies are not so much about wanting to break away from mother and her rules as they are about wanting to live once again in the Edenic anarchy before she made rules for us at all.

Another confusion about water sports: They are often mistaken for fetishistic activity. For instance, Bernard (above) calls himself a "diaper fetishist," but it is apparent from his own letter that it is not the diaper that turns him on. If that were so, he would just go out and buy a diaper and play with it, and that would be enough. For Bernard to get his full enjoyment, however, he must lie in bed and wet himself. The diaper may have become eroticized because it happened to be what he was wearing as a child, but it is the act of wetting that carries his special excitement.

There may be an overlap of emotions here; but as a rule we can say that the fetishist is someone who finds his principal excitement in an inanimate *object;* the person who goes in for water sports or other forms of humiliation gets his kicks from an *activity,* performed either by himself or another person.

MELVIN

I am turned on by the fantasy of a woman wetting herself accidentally. I guess this comes from an actual happening. We had been out drinking one night last year, and my wife had to piss. I kept riding around looking for a place to stop and she was almost hysterical before I finally stopped at a service station. I will never forget my excitement as she ran to the restroom and found it taken. She ran back to the car

and stood there nearly crying as she asked me to help her.
I looked at her face and she was biting her lower lip and
whimpering helplessly. I looked down at her crotch just in
time to see the stream of gold flow out from under the legs
of her cut-off jeans. She just stood there until she was finished, then she got in the car. I took her home and screwed
her in the driveway without even caring if someone looked.
Now every once in a while she will dress up and wait as
long as possible before letting me watch her wet herself.
It's a great turn-on.

FITZ

I am a twenty-five-year-old married male medical student.
I have decided to send you information about my sexual
fantasy (I have only one) because I feel it is held by few
other men. My sexual fantasy deals exclusively with wom-
en's urination.

My fantasies are an outgrowth of two incidents that occurred during my adolescence. The first occurred when I
was fifteen. I was standing close to a young woman who
peed in her jeans while waiting in line to use a ladies room
at a county fair. The other incident occurred two years
later. I was in the midst of a heavy petting session with a
girl in a secluded wooded area when she suddenly said, "I
gotta pee." She then yanked down her panties and peed
right there in front of me. I was fascinated, watching her
thick, copious, yellow stream rush to the ground. I was
sexually aroused by both of these incidents.

My sexual fantasies thus always revolve around a
woman who desperately needs to relieve herself, but for
some reason is unable to find a toilet or reach a toilet in
time and is forced to relieve herself in an unorthodox manner. The unorthodox manners include squatting in semi-
public areas, wetting her clothes, or using receptacles other
than a toilet to deposit her pee (i.e., trash cans, kitchen
sinks, swimming pools, telephone booths, tissue boxes).
Sometimes the woman in my fantasies is able to accomplish her task without anyone finding out about her mis-
deed. I come to climax when they pee. This has been my

sole masturbatory fantasy for several years now. I enjoy normal, ordinary, but quite satisfactory coitus with my wife. Our intercourse does not involve any aspect of my fantasy. In fact, my wife does not even know of my fantasy.

CYRUS

I am a reasonable-looking guy, fit, healthy, mature (forties), active and fairly intelligent—I think. I live in a most staid, stolid and quiet town. Now to my story. I am into w/s and this was started several years ago by accident as I shall relate. This first part then is factual and gives birth to my fantasies.

I was courting a pretty nurse called (not real name) Pat. One early morning, we were returning from a party driving down what was then a brand-new highway. In those days, there was no speed limit, but stopping on the road was a very big no-no, unless an absolute emergency, such as a mechanical failure or heart attack or some such problem.

Pat suddenly announced her need for a toilet and I confessed a similar requirement. We both, however, knew that the next turnoff was near Pat's apartment and there was no way off the road until then. It was not much longer before Pat looked at me and stated the situation to be desperate for her; was it for me? To which the answer was obvious. Reminding me that doctors do not recommend holding ourself to the point of pain, Pat suggested letting go just a little to relieve pressure. Since I was already beginning to overflow, driving with one hand clutching my groin, I didn't object. I glanced at Pat and said, "We're nearly there now." "Good," she said, "once inside the door we're safe."

Outside her door we both stood clutching ourselves and jiggering about like a couple of Indians on the warpath (or was it a rain dance?). Finally we are in and the door bangs shut. As I turn towards the bathroom and enter, Pat pushes against me and clutches my groin. Despite everything I rise and clutch at the crotch of her shorts. Amazingly we masturbate each other to a thundering climax and then urinate where we stand, in our pants. I should have felt ashamed, but didn't.

A week later, Pat was pretty drunk and when I helped her out of the car amongst some bushes, she simply spread her legs and bent her knees until I could see her green panties, and pissed right there. This time I am fascinated watching urine spurt out of her panties and onto the grass. I become fiercely aroused and we made love.

Thus was I introduced to water sports. Our sex was always shattering. I did not marry Pat and my regrets are of no importance now. I know now that I am highly aroused regardless of who is peeing. However, for the same reason pictures of nude women leave me cold, so a girl emptying herself must be wearing panties in my fantasies.

My fantasies take several forms but usually consist of a young lady still dressed for tennis being taken short in her sports car in the middle of a traffic jam. She hangs on desperately. (I should state here that I myself dress in tight underwear and very tight pants for these fantasies.) Back to my girl friend in her car. She is in trouble and she pees just a little, enough to soak her crotch. She is forced to do a little every few minutes now. Suddenly the traffic starts to move and our lady must now drive. (I am getting quite wet myself now.) Our girl gives up and urine spurts in an enormous stream between her long legs, off the seat and onto the floor of the car.

To get to her apartment in daylight, she dons a tight pair of track suit pants in red, and makes it into her apartment where she does not even attempt to be normal, but stands in front of a mirror and watches the darkening patch as she pisses noisily yet again. I myself am soaked by this time and have to masturbate furiously to get rid of the sexual need.

On odd occasions, in my flights of fantasy, the poor woman is forced to sit in her own shit as well.

Always after these fantasies and after masturbation, I am both amazed and sometimes disgusted with myself. I do not like being kinky (and in all honesty that is what it is). However, I cannot stop. I am sure that if ever I am fortunate again to meet a girl interested in w/s, I will eventually lose interest after trying it "for real" again. I am convinced

it is the only cure for me, since I could never openly discuss my hang-up with anyone other than someone else into
this weird business.

It seems to me that it is not the urine which excites, but
the act. In short, "being very naughty." Whether it is a
childhood hangover, or an act of rebellion together with
sharing that act, which is the "come on" for such flights of
weird fancy, or another deep-rooted need to rebel against
our normal everyday restraints, there are very obviously
many people who, "normal" in all other respects, need an
escape which is *different*.

I wish I knew.

────────────────────────

It is no coincidence that in this superconglomerate age,
when people feel so powerless that 50 percent of the electo-
rate doesn't even bother to vote in presidential elections,
increasing emphasis has come to be put on what is called
the "human potential movement." If you can't change your
outer environment, work to change the inner.

People in desperate circumstances do something similar.
It is called "identifying with the aggressor." This usually
entails taking on some of the qualities that most oppress us.
People who have fears and anxieties about being victims
dress up in Nazi Party uniforms. "If you can't lick 'em,
join 'em."

In Melvin's fantasy (above), the woman's need to pee is
urgent, but there is no relief in sight. Is it very difficult to
imagine the scene reversed—when Melvin was a little boy,
desperate to pee but sternly forbidden by a woman
(mother) to do it until he could find a toilet? The harsh
treatment that once was Melvin's lot to bear is now turned
around. It is exciting because he identifies not with the person in pain but the oppressor—the stern disciplinarian he
once perceived mother to be.

However, Melvin's fantasy rewrites history. When Melvin could not hold himsef in and wet his pants, his mother
most likely scolded him, perhaps spanked him, too. But
now, having put himself in his mother's place, he can treat
the woman the way he once wished mother would have
treated him. When she wets herself, *he gets so excited that*

he cannot wait to make love to her. His fantasy is a rebuke to the cruel mother of long ago and a sexual turn-on at the same time.

Melvin's psychology has certain similarities to Fitz's. Both men are inflamed by notions of women so outrageous, so out of control that they will do anything, women so on fire to satisfy their natural body functions that modesty and social inhibitions are forgotten. We will meet this woman again and again throughout this book. In various guises, the totally abandoned woman is the queen of male fantasy.

It is unfortunate that given the way we are all brought up, mother is the one who is going to be remembered as everyone's first great puritan. So much of men's rage against women stems from the second year, when mom had the necessary but thankless job of teaching continence.

One of my hopes for the future is that as mothers have to go out of the home to work, fathers will have to play a larger role in their children's earliest years. We may never feel grateful to the person who toilet trains us, but I see it as a great advantage to men and women alike if this thankless job is divided up between two people, mother and father, a man as well as a woman. Mother has had to bear the tantrums and ingratitudes of socialization alone too long.

Until father takes some of the brunt of the infant's anger, it is all too easy for men to see every woman as naturally stepping into mother's shoes, singing her old song: "No, no, no!" In the heady excitement with which the woman in Fitz's fantasy pees in "trash cans, kitchen sinks, swimming pools, telephone booths," he finds license to break the rules himself. Why not? The woman herself has broken the First Female Commandment: She has said *yes.*

10

Voyeurs and Exhibitionists

We speak of "feasting the eyes," a metaphor that tells us there is a primitive, even somatic pleasure to be derived from something supposedly so intangible as looking. Satisfying food is being offered, a basic hunger is being fed. A walk through a rose garden shows these needs are felt equally by both sexes.

There is a need complementary to looking: the equally primitive and satisfying desire to be seen and admired. "Let me take you in," men say to women; rarely is it heard the other way around. A woman may adore a child with her eyes. By the time she's adolescent, society has made it clear she must not ogle men. Nor do "real" men seek attention for their physical qualities. Equal and reciprocal hungers in both sexes are not being met.

The situation is complicated because there is no socially acceptable way to say "Feast your eyes on me." Even though women are allowed—*encouraged*—to exhibit themselves as the source of physical beauty for both sexes, they must pretend to do it unawares. To attract attention is unladylike; to solicit compliments is bad manners. If, despite all these strictures, she succeeds in catching a man's eye, there are further rules. *Why, the way that nasty beast stares! He just undresses you with his eyes!*

Is it surprising that when a woman is admired, she only half enjoys the flattering glance? The other half is wondering if it is flattering at all. Am I being a fool, a show-off? Have I gone too far?

I have heard supposedly evolutionary arguments used to explain that natural selection demands that men be the lookers, women the exhibitors. This sounds to me like another version of the refrain that men are active, women

passive. Before they are culturally inhibited, children of
both sexes shout "Hey, look at me!" and have to be taught
not to parade naked into the living room when there are
guests. It is testimony that the desire to be seen and liked/
loved for what one shows is, once again, innate.

If the situation is difficult for women, I think it is even
more so for men. Their desire to be seen and admired can
only be expressed through the woman on their arm. No
wonder these inhibited desires go underground and emerge
in fantasies. The forms the masculine conflict take in this
chapter are love of women for what they show, anger at
women that they either do not show enough or do not wish
to see what the man himself would like to reveal.

Voyeurism and exhibitionism bear a kind of inverse relation. Each speaks to opposite faces of the coin. There are
men who feel complete satisfaction in just looking at a naked woman. This is the pure voyeuristic act.

Others will see a naked woman—in magazines for instance—and masturbate with fantasies of fucking her. For
other men, this one-sided relationship is not enough: They
want the woman to become aware of *them*. Their frustration is expressed with catcalls, shouts of praise, whistles,
obscenities on the telephone, sexual invitations—attention-
getting devices in which desire/admiration and hostility are
mixed in various degrees. When men transfer their own
need for attention onto the woman with whom they identify, getting other people to look at "their" woman may
bring feelings of pride and pleasure; it may also earn the
woman the man's irritation or anger—he begins to resent
his secondary role in all the looking that is going on. Perhaps the most hostile attention-getter of all is the man who
exposes himself.

The men in this chapter express these ideas in different
ways, sometimes singly, sometimes in interwoven patterns.
One theme will often predominate while the others remain
hidden. The dynamics of men looking at women and wanting to be looked at themselves are complex and, to me at
least, very new. Therefore, let's begin with the simplest
case: the pure voyeur, a man for whom the act of just
looking at a woman is enough.

JAMES

While I love to fuck and have an active sex life, I also enjoy just looking. Simple, unadulterated staring at beautiful female bodies and cunts. To me, there's no such thing as ugliness when it comes to women's bodies.

In the last five years, women's cunts have come out of the closet. When I was a kid, bathroom iconography portrayed the "female parts" as a little hairless V. As a result, I concluded that girls/women were virtually genital-less; and I'm sure this suggested that they were sexless. It is now possible to walk into a supermarket and walk out with color pictures of women's cunts. These cunts are arrogant, intricate, moist, hairy, labial, honest-to-god genitals as important as any penis.

My many feminist and lesbian acquaintances say these pictures objectify and exploit women, but I find little difference between Betty Dodson's advocacy of being Cunt-Positive and the latest Penthouse Pet who's languidly fingering her cunt. I personally don't think of fucking the women in magazines, or have them beg me to do this or that. When I masturbate while looking at pictures, I basically just respond to the woman, naked; and I'm thankful that she exposed herself to me.

One recent fantasy involves sitting somewhere where I can't be seen and having a parade of purposeful women walking by in braless tube tops, halters, thin dresses, etc., and feeling very alive, safe, and sensual on the street. I would be inside, celebrating their sensualness. (In a street-safe society, I'd be willing to wear revealing clothes for the enjoyment of others.) Unfortunately, women with flowing hair and rippling nipples are now said to be asking for rape, our streets are dangerous, and bras seem to be regaining favor.

It seems as though many women in your books would like to be able to reveal and expose themselves; perhaps in a to-be-hoped-for rapeless and insultless society, sensuality would be like "good grooming" is today—part of the everyday experience for most people. Turn-ons and sexual anecdotes could become like small snacks throughout the day rather than big heavy meals with HUNGER in the middle. Seems healthier.

The ogler, the peeper, the voyeur—they have always been figures of fun, fear, or contempt to women. But sexuality and aesthetics are so intertwined that any discussion of the subject would be incomplete if it did not include the power of beauty—as a positive and satisfying end in itself—to command attention. Almost every system of aesthetics begins by taking the human figure as a universal standard. "To me, there is no such thing as ugliness when it comes to women's bodies," says James (above).

Voyeurism is a general term for people who get sensual satisfaction from looking, often with the knowledge, consent, and even full participation of the sexual object. What would you call the Miss America contest or the afternoon *passeggiata* on the Via Veneto? The man who peeps into a woman's bedroom is performing a reprehensible and illegal act; he is raping someone's privacy. As I understand the term, a Peeping Tom is one who does it on the sly, with no permission given, and often with feelings of hostility in his breast. He may be an unsavory creep, hot to catch a secret glimpse of the sexual and forbidden; but let's be clear: Morality and legality aside, it is beauty that lures him, too. We name the man who goes to museums to look at Rubens's nudes an aesthete. Maurice Chavalier, who loved to look at beautiful young women, was called a *boulevardier*. Yet we sneer at the man who goes to strip shows. For all of them, the eye is one of the organs of love.

Of course, there is no hard and fast line of distinction; but only when peeping is the sole sexual outlet, only when it is so complusive that the man is driven to find his satisfaction in ways that get him into trouble with his family, the neighbors, and/or the law, are we justified in calling it pathological. To my mind, until that boundary is crossed, it is a matter of taste and manners. Bad taste, bad manners if you like; but nothing more.

James (above) gives us no evidence that his voyeurism is compulsive. Looking is not his only sexual outlet, nor does a stolen glimpse drive him to want more. "I basically respond to the image of the woman, naked; and I'm thankful that she exposed herself to me," he says. These are the words of the true voyeur: His connection with the woman is through the eye alone.

The use of the word "thankful" is instructive. James sounds like a polite little boy who has just been given something he has long wanted. Once in every little boy's life, mother's naked breast, flesh, and body were a feast of life. Then, just as he reached the age when he stopped taking it for granted—and really began to *look*—it all stopped. Mother began to cover herself up. If James is "thankful," and at times wants nothing more than a glimpse of the woman, it is because the sight of her body has reopened the door to that time when that was all he needed to feel all right with the world. The feeling is sensual but pregenital.

None of this will make women love the voyeur more, but it may be a measure of comfort against fear. I myself had always assumed that when men maneuvered to catch a glimpse of naked women or leafed through a girlie magazine, what they saw triggered scenarios of what they'd like to do next: Peeping is the beginning; doing something to the girl is the end. But I was wrong. This is not to say that men who look at *Penthouse* don't like to imagine having sex with the woman. Some do; but also, some do not. In either case, masturbatory fantasies are a long way from rape.

The voyeur likes sex. He likes looking. Sometimes the two are combined. Sometimes they are not. James's fantasies are in line with, and evidence for, contemporary psychiatric thinking, which classifies voyeurism not as a "perversion," but as a complete satisfaction in itself.

GREG

My age is twenty-seven years. Happily married, have one child. When I'm in bed making love with my wife sometimes I imagine that I am screwing another woman, someone I know and whom I've been to bed with in the past. I never express these thoughts to my wife, not because she may feel offended, but because I feel guilty.

One fantasy is that I've bought an antique mirror. To my surprise, I find that when you look in it, you see whoever you want, but with no clothes on. I take the glass out of the mirror and make dark goggles out of it. By wearing them, when I walk in the street, everyone I see, fathers, mothers, children, men and women—they are all naked. I enjoy the idea of traveling in buses this way, especially when the bus passes a certain insurance company office I know which employs hundreds of young girls. This gives me a strong sense of power, and a vague feeling of guilt, which I enjoy. The feeling of guilt adds to my erotic sense that if they only knew what I was doing. . . .

Here goes my other fantasy: A friend of mine works at a large scientific research place. He discovers a pill. If you take it, you become invisible. I remove all my clothes and go through a lot of houses where I know beautiful women live. I observe many people, dancing, singing, walking, all naked. Some will press their own firm, rounded breasts, others wash themselves between the legs with soap. One will be sitting on a large chair, lolling back very comfortably as she shaves her pubic area. I like to imagine what their response would be if they knew that some invisible person was watching them. This excites me very much. In one of these fantasies that takes place in the bathroom, when a naked girl lathers her body with soap, I pour water on it for her. She is startled, surprised. She looks wildly all around to see what is happening. She wants to put some clothes on. She suspects someone is there, but I have hidden her clothes. After enjoying this scene to my heart's content, I leave for another destination.

I go to a hotel. To my astonishment, all the guests here are women, and they are playing dirty games in the bathrooms. Two women are making love with each other. This is very exciting to me, because I cannot think what is more exciting than lesbian love. Here is a seventeen-year-old girl. She is masturbating with her fingers moving in and out very fast. She closes her eyes and moans. In the meantime, she is shouting, "Fuck me, bastard!" Probably she is imagining that her favorite movie star is screwing her. Another woman is using a candle, another has a banana, and one has a slide rule to sate her lust. Just at this moment, my invisible pill begins to wear off. My body has begun to appear for anyone to see. The girls look at me with surprise and fearful eyes. But one of them is so much in heat that she welcomes me very gladly. Another end to this fantasy is that the women gang up to punish me for looking at them. They beat me up and throw me into a garbage heap. Maybe they even call the police.

JOSH

I have often fantasized about making love to women who model in magazines, nude and seminude. I see one in a magazine and I fantasize seeing her walking down the street and I tell her, "I have a magazine with you in it nude. You are a model," and she says, "Don't talk so loud, someone will hear us," and then she says, "Let me see it." I say, "It's at my apartment." So we go there, and I show it to her. I say, "It's hard to believe that your breasts are size forty-four, you being five-three," and she takes her blouse and bra off and out pop two big breasts. I stare at them, and I touch lick, kiss, and suck them.

Then she says, "Have you got a camera?" and I say, "Yes." So she strips nude and says, "Take your own picture," and I do. She sees I have an erection, and she says, "I would like to have my lips on that." I strip nude and say, "Let me give you a tongue bath and suck your sweet delicious cunt." Then we sixty-nine. We fuck and fuck, and later when she leaves she says. "I enjoyed my day." As I look at her pictures, I look on the back and they are autographed and her name and address is on them and a short note which reads, Call me any time.

I fantasize about making love to a call girl I meet while walking down the street. As I bump into her, I rape her with my eyes. She senses what I want. So she says, "You know, I make a hundred dollars every time I make love to a man." I say, "I know." Then she says, "But yours is free."

The boy's older sister is getting dressed. Shyly, silently, he watches through the door unconsciously left ajar, enraptured by the mystery he sees. Suddenly she catches him. In a mixture of embarrassment and anger, she slams the door in his face. She has taught him that his adoration is dirty.

A few years later, these emotions become formalized, perhaps best exemplified in a kind of ballet found at any beach. Here are all the young girls, wearing their new bikinis for the young men's adoration. They are proud of how they look in their near-nakedness; but they are uneasy, too, always adjusting a strap, tugging at an elastic pant leg. The young man looks, sees, and adores; but he knows he must turn away from staring too directly. He and the other guys make up a name for what they are doing and even call it a male sport: *girl watching*. Behind this socially acceptable façade, he can avenge himself on women who will not show him what he wants to see. He can stare all he wants, mobilizing the women's guilt against themselves. *What kind of prude could object?* It's healthy, as all-American as the old song "Standing on the Corner," a kind of national anthem for girl-watchers. The wink in the lyrics was that you would stare all you wanted, but nobody could send you to jail for the fantasies thus summoned to mind.

The boy standing on the corner alone feels pathetic. Standing on the corner as one of the gang whose pleasure it is to look at the girls is a male rite of puberty. Group reinforcement is needed, because this is a time in men's lives when it seems girls hold all the aces. Sexually ripe, and yet symbols of a culture at least verbally dedicated to virginity, the girls have a dread power. They can reject. By giving themselves the rights of connoisseurs, looking, grading, passing, and even rejecting in their own turn, boys strive to keep themselves in countenance.

Voyeuristic fantasies reverse the woman's power; it passes from her to the eye of the man. By keeping himself hidden or invisible, the voyeur imposes his will on the woman. She has lost her ability to say no; has been unknowingly frozen into the position of an indulgent mother who allows the boy everything he wants.

Greg's invisibile, disembodied floating (above) gives him the voyeur's sexual satisfaction without emotional or even physical involvement. Sometimes even fantasy is not enough to ease old, infantile guilts; and Greg is discovered by angry women who put him in the garbage can. But other times they take him to bed. This is the direction of Josh's fantasies too. He may "rape" the prostitute with his eyes; but instead of getting mad at him, she takes him to bed *free*.

Wanting to see, but afraid to look, men invent voyeuristic fantasies to heal a paradox, the conflict in themselves.

JESS

I am a forty-four-year-old man (a fat forty-four-year-old man!) with a speech impediment. I have very little formal education. I am not retarded. I have been on public welfare for much of my life.

The only women I have ever had sex with are professionals. I don't do this as much as I should like. I don't like to give a woman less than fifty dollars. And there are so many times when I just don't have fifty dollars. Now they say that men have for a long time had a buyer's market. In one sense this may be true. But I have a feeling that a fat forty-four-year-old woman with a speech problem, who was willing to do all the things for a man that I fantasize doing for a woman, could be able to get sex without paying money.

I once saw a fat woman and a skinny woman, in an exhibitionist act in a carnival sideshow. The women made jokes about their figures, to which the men in the audience made such encouraging remarks as (to the fat woman) "You can't get too much of a good thing, baby!" Or to the thin woman, "It's not what you've got, it's what you do with what you've got." The thing I remember most, and think of when I masturbate, is the fat woman squatting facing me and saying, "Look, mister, look! Look at that big hole! How'd you like to stick it in there?"

It is true in one sense that the situation in our society which makes it possible for such a show to exist is very unfair to women. But look—me and the other men paid to see the show. We let the women know that we liked what we saw. Suppose a fat man and a skinny man wanted to exhibit themselves in front of a group of women. Where would they find women who would pay to see them?

I used to measure my fondness for a certain admirable male friend by my ability to forgive his one character flaw: he is a stripshow afiçionado.

"How can you go to those dreadful places?" I would ask.

"You should come with me sometimes," he would reasonably reply. "You'd be surprised at what goes on."

I was. Curiosity, this book in general, this chapter in particular, drove me there. I expected to see a nasty spectacle of mutual contempt—men who sneered, female performers who returned the disdain. Instead, I saw a mutual love feast. Customers cheered their favorites like fans at a hometown baseball game. The dancers responded by trying even harder to please. The audience's warmth and admiration were tangible, and there was no denying the obvious pleasure the strippers took in being adored by so many men.

One of women's most popular fantasies is exhibiting themselves to the cheers and adulation of thousands of men. That is exactly what goes on at strip shows. Why was I so prepared to find it an ugly scene? A woman has to ask herself: Do we dislike men who go to burlesque because we feel they will hold what they see in low esteem? Or is it projection and defense—projecting ourselves into the dancers' place, and angrily defending against the contempt we feel our female bodies must arouse in these men? Is the low value placed on the naked female body put there by men, or by us women ourselves?

A very proper friend recently told me of a secret midnight frolic in a Caribbean nightclub. She got up on stage in pasties borrowed from a stripper and proceeded to outdo the star. Even though my friend had acted out her desire in an almost fantasy setting—a half-drunk nightclub two thousand miles from home—among people gathered for the sole purpose of expressing love for the naked female body, I was awash in admiration(and envy). Most women wouldn't have taken the risk. Exhibitionism may be a great female desire, but in reality it is usually kept well within safe limits. Only in fantasy can the woman safely control the audience's response, and guarantee herself beforehand that the men will love what she breaks all the rules to show.

There are women who enjoy watching burlesque. Now I know why. They are not afraid for the reception the strippers will get. Instead, they identify with the way famous G-string stars love their bodies, their breasts, their vaginas. They are confident that men adore them, too. The audience's applause confirms that love.

In the show I attended, only one man shouted something awful to the dancers on the stage. The men around him turned to glare disapprovingly. When he kept up the jeering, the manager was called. The man was asked to leave, like an unruly outsider disturbing a family picnic.

Was he maddened that he could not touch what was so temptingly revealed? Was his fury increased by memories of other exhibitionistic women who had similarly seemed to lure him on, only to reject him in the end? Maybe. But it is my feeling that he could be justifiably—if inappropriately—venting his anger against a culture that gives men no audience, no applause, no socially acceptable outlet for their own exhibitionism.

When a young boy is taught his naked penis is offensive to women, he learns shame. A few years later, he would gladly adore every corner and crevice of his girl friend's body if only she would let him; when he asks for the same response from her, and shyly leads her hand to touch his fly, she slaps him down. That's when he learns anger.

Not all strip shows are mutual love feasts, and both men and women play games of show-and-look powered as much by anger as by love. For instance, it is usually said that exhibitionism is a purely masculine deviation, but don't men encounter it every day of their lives?

Take the braless young woman in the wet-look T-shirt, the secretary who wears no underwear beneath her short skirt. Grateful for any whisper of yes behind the deafening female no, men just can't believe such women can be making a sexually aggressive move. She may be wearing jeans so tight that her labia are defined like two halves of a peach, but the average man on the corner thinks she must be unaware of how much she is showing. He takes the encounter not as a form of female exhibitionism, but as a sly event in which he "steals" a glimpse of the luscious forbidden.

The woman, of course, who has spent an hour in front of her mirror, both knows how much she is revealing and doesn't want to know. She floats in a rosy glow of enhanced sexuality, nervous all the while at how she will be perceived. Her training as a Nice Girl says she would be bad to seek attention or praise for her body too directly. Hence, the fingers that anxiously button, unbutton, and then rebutton the top of her neckline, all evening long.

A psychoanalyst told me this story: When he asks female patients if they are aware of how provocatively they dress, almost invariably he is met with denial. "She can be standing there in a see-through blouse with a skintight skirt that reveals the line of her panties," he says, "and she'll say, 'Who, me? I'd never be that obvious.' "

It is not that she minds a man who looks, goes the female refrain, it is *how* he looks that is offensive. This denies the self-accusation of exhibitionism by raising counternotions of ugly male manners. What is often the point here, I feel, is control. Calculated, sometimes hostile control. The woman wants the right to send out a mixed signal: Admire me, but don't touch. As for the man, how is he to know that the way he reacts to her is so important to her notion of herself as either a femme fatale or a hooker? Behind this confusing presentation she makes of herself as naughty but nice, she is just waiting for him to make a wrong move. A slight, approving smile from him and she is affirmed, walking past him with all the reassurance in the world. A catcall or snigger and she is humiliated, angry at herself and furious with him. Little wonder that men feel so frustrated, so much in awe, even threatened and resentful of the power of women's beauty.

This is not to say that any woman deserves the rude remarks she gets from men working on the street. There are hostile people everywhere who need little excuse to vent their rage at vulnerable targets. The shouted insults may even be seen as competitive anger directed not so much at the woman as at the imaginary (fantasy) man she is on her way to meet.

Seen in this light, bringing the women down a peg is

comparable to Mickey Mouse cartoons of knocking the banker's top hat off with a snowball. None of this may salve the woman's feelings, but the hurt may be lessened if she could understand the cause: His rage is not directed at me, but at the strictness by which he feels tied and thinks I am free. "If I were in her position," these men might be understood to be feeling, "I wouldn't be so snooty, so unresponsive. But goddamn it, I never am in her position. Look at her. My eyes tell her I think she's a knockout, but her eyes tell me that to her I don't exist! *She's making me invisible!*"

Jess (above) talks, too, of the one-sidedness of voyeurism. In the show he attended, even though the strippers were not attractive, "We let the women know we liked what we saw." What if two equally unattractive men wanted to exhibit themselves? he asks. "Where would they find women who would pay to see them?"

This has a certain pathos. The undressed male is not presented to the little girl as a seductive figure, but as a scary one. Consequently, in the long presexual years she has no chance to develop the association between a naked man and the erotic. Her masturbatory fantasies do not intimately link the two so that forever after they form a Pavlovian chain: See the one, feel the other.

Certainly it is true that many women like to look at men, dressed or not; but the desire dates from a comparatively grown-up stage of life. As such, it is easily kept within the bounds of social control. The new women's magazines are teaching their audience to delight in the sight of penis, V-shaped torso, and narrow hips. Does this mean that, as women give themselves more and more permission to express their desires, we eventually will find "Peeping Janes" lurking outside football camps and boys' gymnasiums? I doubt it. Women's looking is not powered by the voyeur's kind of infantile and irresistible longing. From the time when mother's breasts were all the beauty the world could offer, both sexes have had feelings of enlarged, enhanced life from seeing a gloriously naked woman. The male body holds no such primitive magic. It is one of the dissymmetries of our biological life.

KENNETH

I cannot conceive of American women having such fantasies as exist in your books. In fact, all the American women I have known are real prudes and have as much sexual imagination as a six-month-old baby. Notice I said American women and not another race of women such as Oriental.

I am thirty-two years old, white, twice married and have two beautiful daughters. I have also been in the military for fifteen years.

Now to my fantasies and my sexual life as a whole. As a young teenager, I enjoyed running around the house nude whenever I was alone. I was much larger developed at this time than the other kids I went to school with. Each time I went to the john and the other guys were there, I was always teased about the size of my cock. This all went to my head and I became an exhibitionist. This period lasted five or six years. In my high school years I developed acne, and it was near impossible for me to obtain a date with kids my own age. Therefore, I went out with younger girls. Quite often in these cases, the girl's younger brother or sister had to accompany us. On many occasions, the younger brother would watch as his sister and I screwed on the back seat. This was a turn-on for me. After high school, I joined the service and have been in the service ever since. I was still a bit of an exhibitionist.

While stationed overseas, I married a beautiful Oriental. Her skin was luscious, she had nice breasts and an extremely beautiful and hairy pussy. After a couple of years of marriage, I started fantasizing her exhibiting herself to other men, and even fucking someone else as I watched. My own exhibitionist tendencies ceased to exist. Gradually, I talked my wife into exposing her breasts very discreetly to someone. From there she finally agreed to expose her beautiful pussy. Our main places were freeway service stations, out of town mobile home parks; the men were salesmen, repairmen. She became quite good at it and even started to become excited if the person she was showing it to become excited, and because she knew I was getting excited. I then tried to get her to seduce someone all the way. As she was really interested in exciting the younger set, we eventually found a boy of fifteen or sixteen. She seduced him as I watched from a closet. As soon as he left, we had the best bout of sex we had ever had. From there we tried swapping, but it was a total flop. Back we went to exhibitionism.

Then one day she said she wanted to watch me make it with a young chick. I agreed and since I already had some-one in mind, it was rather easily accomplished. What we didn't expect was her inability to cope with it and this in-ability drove me to become emotionally involved with this girl; solution—*divorce*.

Now all I have is my fantasies and past memories. Straight sex doesn't turn me on. My present wife is a prude from the word go, so I cannot fantasize about her.

MEL

My wife did not fantasize before she read *Secret Garden*. Now she asks me to tell her wild stories while I masturbate her.

First let me tell you a little about us. I am twenty-six years old, and my wife Brenda is twenty-five. We have been married for six years and have one child age three. I have a high school education with a little college (two months).

Brenda's body is perfect except for a couple of small stretch marks on her stomach from the baby. Her breasts are beautiful with large brown nipples. She is really a knockout. The reason for such a description of her will be clearer after you hear my fantasies.

My experiences with sex didn't start until I was about thirteen, although I started masturbating at about eight. When I was thirteen this couple moved in next door to my family. She was about thirty and a beautiful brunette. Her husband traveled a lot, and she was home alone a lot. She never closed the curtains in her bedroom and I used to watch her undress from my bedroom window. However it was only from the waist up that I could see without getting closer, so finally one night, I sneaked over and looked in the window. Finally she came into the bedroom, and started to undress. My heart was beating wildly as she pulled off her bra and panties and lay down on the bed. She started to caress her breasts and then her fingers found her cunt. As she started to masturbate, I felt my dick strain to get free. I quickly unzipped my pants and tried to pull it out, but as I did, she climaxed, raising her hips off the bed, and I came in my pants.

They lived there for two years, and I saw her on many occasions after that, and even though she went out of her way to let me see her naked or partially dressed, nothing ever happened between us. Probably because of my shyness. (I think she was willing.)

She was my fantasy girl and I dreamed of her until I met Brenda. We only dated for five months before getting married. Brenda was a virgin and I really had a time trying to teach her about sex. Our sex life is really good and it was several months after we got married before I masturbated again. I fantasized about this little doll who lived next door in the trailer park where we lived. I admit to peeking through the windows at her undressing two or three times.

After Brenda became pregnant, we had a lot of time to talk about sex, and not so much time to do it. We used to lay in bed at night and talk about screwing while we masturbated each other. As she got bigger and more out of shape, she also got sicker and we couldn't screw at all after the sixth month. That's when my present fantasies started. I would get out the nude pictures of Brenda that we had taken after we got married, and we would lay there and I would look at her picture, while she beat me off or ate me, and then I would stroke her clit and tell her how beautiful she was, and how exciting it would be if someone saw one of her pictures. She used to go wild when I would talk to her about undressing in front of someone or getting caught naked or wearing a short dress and showing off her lace panties or some other sexy kind.

After the baby was born, she exercised and worked hard until she had her figure back in perfect shape. Then she went out and bought all kinds of sexy panties and bras. As soon as she was back to normal, I started to talk to her about it more and more. But she is very shy, and I could not get her to go through with it. I was anxious and rushed her a little, but she never got upset. She just told me I would have to wait until she could get her nerve up. In the next two years I fantasized constantly of her undressing in a motel with the curtains partially open, so that someone could walk by and see her. Then last summer, while on vacation in Florida, I waited one night until she went to sleep and then I opened the curtains and uncovered her. She was only wearing a pair of yellow bikini panties, and they were sheer. She was lying on her back with her legs spread and her breasts sticking straight up. I hid in the bathroom and watched as five different men and one boy about fifteen stopped and stared at her. (I left the lights on.) The next night I told her what I had done, and she made me tell her every detail, as she masturbated herself to three climaxes before we screwed each other. She loved it, but still could not do it when she knew what was happening. However, I did do it one more time before we left, and she knew I was going to, but again she would not knowingly participate.

Since then she has slowly worked up to wearing short dresses and sitting carelessly and getting out of the car with her dress up to her hips in front of men. We do all of this in nearby towns or places where we are not known.

SANDY

I am a twenty-six-year-old grad student currently finishing my Ph.D. dissertation. I spend my days writing and typing at home while my wife works, so I have ample time for sexual fantasies.

I have far more kinky impulses than does my wife. She greatly enjoys "normal sex," but has little interest in the exotic. She encourages my fantasizing since it gives me satisfaction without requiring that she herself engage in weird sexual practices.

I often find myself fantasizing that something (hypnosis, a birth control pill with erotic side effects) has made my wife as horny and desirous of sexual adventure as myself. A typical fantasy follows.

It's our anniversary and Patsy (my wife) has agreed to

do anything I want her to do. I suggest that we go to a nearby restaurant which caters to the "swinging singles" crowd. I wear very tight-fitting pants, through which my bikini-style underwear shows (the pants are white and the briefs black). I also wear a ruffled shirt with a deep V neck (I *never* wear anything like this in reality). After dressing I lay out Patsy's clothes. She emerges from the shower and is shocked, for I have chosen many of the items which in real life she lets me buy her only on the condition that she never has to wear them in public. (I at first thought this was simply a highly developed sense of modesty, but Patsy has explained how deeply she resented being whistled at or approached by strange men when she is walking to work and doesn't want to give them any encouragement. This makes sense to me and I have come to understand that women often have good reason for not acting out fantasies). The apparel included an orange acetate nylon mini, by far the shortest she owns, brown stockings which look like ordinary seamed stockings but mysteriously stay up without garters or panty girdles (as Patsy says, one of the virtues of fantasies is that such problems take care of themselves). Her shoes are very high-heeled sandals with a strap around the ankle, like women wore in the 1940's. Her only undergarment is a pair of crotchless panties—bright orange with brown lace trim. She actually does have a pair of these which turn me on in the strongest way, but only wears them in bed. When Patsy sees the panties she protests, but I remind her of her promise and being very horny herself she agrees.

After she has dressed I put my finger in her vagina—already covered with a viscous (even the word sounds dirty!) liquid. I then use my fingers to rub the secretions behind her ears and between her breasts, treating it as perfume. I love the smell of her juices when I go down on her and this lets me get a whiff just by leaning close to her.

We walk to the restaurant, both of us aware that every man on the street is staring at her. The sky is dark—it's just before one of those big Midwestern thunderstorms—and the wind is fierce. Patsy's dress keeps blowing up, exposing her thighs and offering a glimpse of the panties. The contrast between the orange panty and the white cleft of my [sic] bottom reminds me of a giant multicolored Oreo cookie (besides sex I like food a lot). She whispers to me that the wind is ruffling her pubic hair.

The restaurant is packed. It doesn't take reservations so we get in line. People are pressed in all around us, waiting for a table. Patsy gives a little gasp of alarm and a sharp "Oh." I'm too busy keeping people from trampling me so I fail to notice that she is squirming and giggling a bit.

We finally get a table and as we sit down Patsy says, "You're incorrigible! What were you thinking of, putting your finger right up my you-know-where and rubbing me like that!" I looked at her and swear that I didn't touch her, but I now understood her squirming. She realizes that a complete stranger has given her an orgasm and that somebody's hands are impregnated with her goo. I suggest she kiss every man's hand to find out who her admirer was, but she doesn't think that is a good idea.

At my insistence she agrees to give him a better chance to see her. She walks across the room toward the bar and then drops her purse. A zillion things fall out and Patsy bends slowly, from the waist and keeping her knees straight. She must stay bent over for a count of one hundred as her entire rump is bared for any who wish to look. Finally she straightens up, and, blushing, walks back to her table.

Patsy and I enjoy a delicious meal and when I ask for the check the waitress tells us that Patsy's exhibition was so exciting that the manager has given us a meal on the house.

I am now so horny I can't wait. We go over to the men's john and I make sure it's empty. We go in one of the stalls and make love standing up. Patsy comes quickly, but I'm still going strong when we hear the door open. Patsy gives me a look of panic, but I lift her onto the toilet seat, so only my legs appear beneath the stall. Two men enter and begin discussing what Patsy had done by the bar. They express in gutter language their admiration for her body and speculate on whether she was a "pro" putting on a show to drum up business or just brazen. As Patsy listens she grasps my penis and sticks it in her mouth (she doesn't do this "in real life"). She sucks and licks, acutely aware, as I am, that the slurping sound might be heard. I have a tremendous orgasm, letting out an involuntary groan of relief. One of the men asks, "Hey, you okay in there?" I recover and have the sense to tell them that I just had a hair stuck in my zipper. They chuckle and exit, still talking about Patsy's performance. We then sneak out and go home—to bed and less dangerous but perhaps more affectionate sex.

When I have fantasies I sometimes imagine that I am Patsy (or a Victorian spinster kidnapped, bound and forced into ecstasy by diabolically skillful lovemaking). I rarely identify directly with the male aggressor in the fantasy, being half the victim and half the avid but invisible voyeur. Costuming is very important. There is no single item of clothing—but I find incongruous attire exciting (e.g., a prim hat, umbrella, buttoned shoes and nothing else). Most women in my fantasies are either my own age or sometimes older (I sometimes imagine a fifty-five-year-old grandmother who has been given a miracle drug so that her body is that of a Vargas pinup girl—from the neck down). I also worry a little about their sadistic (or masochistic—since I identify with the girl being humiliated?) content.

I have no idea why the humiliation theme is so prominent. My parents never punished me for masturbation or other sexual activities (they never even discussed such things).

In the animal kingdom, it is usually the male who is the flashier of the two sexes. Among humans, there is only one time in life when males feel free to exhibit themselves. Boys like Kenneth (above) want to see each other. They admire someone with a penis larger than theirs. This is the age of athletic heroes, when boys go for pinup pictures of big muscular men, football players, etc.

There are homoerotic components here, of course, but what is really at issue is the youngster's need for a model he can identify with. He already has unfavorably compared himself with his father, and is anxious that he may never match the old man. If a friend has a large penis, the boy may take it as a competitive threat, but it gives him hope he will soon have one himself. The attention Kenneth's big size got him "went to (his) head."

This happy state of affairs stopped for Kenneth—as it does for most men—when young girls entered the scene. Girls not only don't applaud the male genital, they don't want to see or touch it. How unfair! The young girl is allowed to show her burgeoning breasts by wearing tight sweaters—the tighter the better. But if his erection shows beneath his trousers, the boy becomes the joke of the dance floor. From here, it is only a step to Kenneth, who angrily transfers all his exhibitionistic desires onto his wife.

First he talks her into exhibiting herself, then persuades her to watch while he makes love to a younger woman. The result is divorce. Is there some evidence here of a feeling that men are punished for making their sex a public matter? Kenneth says his second wife is so antisexual that he can't even fantasize about her. But since he is the one who chose to marry her, is it too big a stretch of the imagination to say he may be using her to curb what he feels are his sexual excesses?

Kenneth's fantasy is characteristic of a complex process: Men who fear disapproval or punishment for giving their own exhibitionistic desires free rein often transfer these desires onto the sex to whom it *is* allowed—women. A lot of hostility often accompanies this switch, since it means giving up a primary satisfaction for one taken secondhand. The woman may have all the fun, but the fantasist sees to it that she is also degraded by the process. Mel insists that his wife exhibit herself to strange men. When she says she doesn't have the nerve, he waits for her to fall asleep and then raises the curtain and turns on the lights.

Ideas like these are further developed in Sandy's letter (above). He wants to wear to exhibitionistic clothes—he wants to be seen. As a man, he cannot. Therefore he dresses his wife in the daring outfit he would like to wear himself. (Note the mistake in identification Sandy makes midway through his fantasy. "The contrast between the orange panty and the white cleft of my bottom . . ." says Sandy. But it is not *his* bottom that is wearing these revealing clothes; it is his wife's.)

Wealthy men wear their money in the form of diamonds

and minks carried by their women. Sandy has Mrs. Sandy wear the kind of clothes that will express his forbidden exhibitionism. By identifying with the attention his wife is getting, Sandy assuages and feeds his own need for attention.

The next step in Sandy's fantasy is important: He imagines he in fact *is* the woman. This gets him the attention he has always wanted, but at the price of being humiliated. I do not feel Sandy's fantasy reveals evidence of homosexuality so much as it shows strong needs to be punished for the kind of show-off sex mother forbade so long ago. Sandy may say that his parents were not punitive about sex, but in his next sentence he tells us "they never even discussed these things." They may not have been overtly punitive. They certainly were repressive. And breaking repressive rules carries punishment.

The urge to transvestism is not necessarily homosexual; as mentioned ealier, many transvestites have never had a homosexual experience in their lives. In Sandy's case, wearing women's clothes is less homosexual than humiliating. When a woman dresses in trousers, she is taking on the attributes of a class more powerful than her own. For a man to put on a dress is to surrender his upper-class status, which is why so few men do it.

"In America," says Dr. Robertiello (to whom I'm indebted for many of the ideas in this chapter), "the strong, reserved man is set up as the ideal. Men are not allowed the splendid, unabashed exhibitionism of women like strippers and models. What some men do instead is unconsciously identify with the beautiful woman's direct and uninhibited demand for admiration." What is important is not so much that she's a woman as that she is getting the kind of worship and adoration the man has not received since he was a baby in his mother's arms. And so right along with his pride in having a beautiful wife comes the man's anger at her for putting him in the shade, seen only in her reflected light.

MAURICE

I can summarize myself in one brief sentence! I am a perfect exhibitionist in search of the perfect voyeur!! In my forty-two years, I have found a small handful of women who have been sufficiently liberated to derive real sexual pleasure from watching me perform. Throughout my life, I have never been able to accept as fact what psychiatrists and psychologists have attempted to foist on me, i.e., "women are not sexually stimulated by viewing a man's body and genitals." I am eminently qualified to *disqualify* that statement! Mainly because I have had the courage— yes, BALLS!—and the conviction to *test reality* in the public domain.

I am a professional fine arts painter of some twenty-three years' standing. My philosophy is based on what makes my cock hard, and my nuts tingle. A person who cannot stand naked before me is not self-accepting. I despise with my whole being American standards of physical beauty. The 40-26-38 female ideal and the twelve-inch cock, wide as an ax handle, are repressive weapons.

One of my greatest sexual fantasies is masturbation while several women watch. If women envy men at all, it is not for the penis per se, but rather for the biological capacity to ejaculate as proof of orgasm. I'd like to masturbate for you so you can "see" that lovely loss of control (orgasm) as my gyzym shoots and gushes out the head of my cock. I like to start out with my penis soft and shriveled up so a woman can watch the phallic metamorphosis: big, bigger, biggest!

In my fantasy I find the perfect voyeuse—a "peeping Jane." She is very authoritarian. She comes to my room where I am stretched out naked on my bed. She commands me to dress, but I decline. About an hour later, I hear her coming down the hallway with the medicine cart, so I just continue masturbating slowly with Johnson's Baby Oil. As she draws abreast of my door I make several more slow thrusts then glance up. Her eyes are glued onto my swollen, glistening cock. Like a person mesmerized, she walks in and hands me my pills. I begin to talk to her while I pick up my bottle of baby oil and anoint myself. I fondle myself with naughty abandon, stretching my scrotum, rolling my testicle about and tickling all around the glans. As I get harder, I squeeze my cock as the skin on the head gets as smooth and shiny as a patent leather plum. Then I begin an earnest demonstration of my technique, slowly fucking my fist, turning my erect cock this way and that, so she can view it from many angles.

As I am just about ready to come I take my hand away and she says, "You're a very lovely, beautiful person!" My cock jerks as come shoots out and the expression on her face is my most precious treasure. I squeeze the last of my come out and lick it off my hand and she grins and stands there watching.

After that, her whole pattern changes. She uses any excuse to come to my room, finally bringing me some art materials so I can do a portrait of her. I can't tell you how thrilling it is to perform uninhibitedly to an appreciative audience. Believe me, it blows my mind in my fantasy when she brings a girl friend who wants a "portrait."

No, I'm not well endowed. Just under seven inches and rather narrow, but I feel my cock is beautiful.

DANIEL

I'm fifty-one, married twenty-seven years, four children, two of them grown and gone now, a third nearly so; master's degree, professionally trained. I often think I must be one of the Dirty Old Men, but if so, I have been a D.O.M. for a long, long time.

I have had a long and fantastically active sex life, 85 percent fantasy! During actual sex, while masturbating, and at any other odd and frequent period, day or night. Considering the degree to which my mind runs to sex, and the wild dreams I have for sex, masturbating has probably saved my life, or, at least, kept me out of the police station, booked for rape, exposure, or peeping. I am not aggressive, and long before women's lib I firmly believed in the woman as an equal partner.

My masturbation probably developed in a normal fashion. "Sex" began with the girl next door, when we were curious enough about each other's bodies to show ourselves to each other in the nearest vacant lot. A later stage brought an energetic competition with a pal up in our attic to see who could come to orgasm first—long before either of us could, biologically. Then followed a period of daydreaming about girls I knew in school, and occasionally teachers. When I was in my early and middle teens, I worked out a game with coins. I would spread out ten or fifteen pennies on the bed in my room when no one was home, with each coin representing a different girl or teacher. Since I had never had a single thing to do with any of these girls or teachers sexually, this was entirely a figment of my imagination. Anyway, there they all were, lined up across the bedspread. Then I would begin to flip them, heads or tails, which would indicate yes or no to my question addressed to each one in turn. Would she remove a certain article of clothing, dress first, then slip, and so on, until she was, in my imagination, completely naked? Naturally, the first one to be naked won. I had to keep straight the state of dress or undress of each one as I went back and forth over that line of pennies.

I had never seen a nude female figure up to that time, so my imagination was forced to extraordinary feats of visualization. During this game, I erected quite fast, and the entire game was played with me slowly and deliciously handling my prick. As I recall now, I frequently failed to reach the end of the game, to see who had "won" before I came. To this day, through a long and often uneasy marriage, I recall some of those people, and fantasize about them, creating and recreating scenes where they all desire me. Strange to recall this to print, because this is a part of the me I have lived with all these years without ever telling a soul, nor would I willingly and openly to this day. I offer it as a kind of clinical evidence of what goes on in the mind of one man.

Needless to say, none of these fantasies has ever worked out in reality. Just one moved briefly but fleetingly onto the stage of reality, but I boffed it—and many, many more like it—and then it receded forever into the world of fantasy. For a time I found after-school work doing odd jobs for one of my teachers, an old maid. She never encouraged me in the slightest, of course, but she was very much on my mind, sexually. It added to the excitement that she was still a teacher in the school I went to. One morning finding myself in her bedroom to wash windows, I saw a pair of her panties lying on the floor. Urged on by a rising erection initiated by simply being in her bedroom, I picked them up and felt of their smooth silkiness. I thought of what they had touched on her. On an utterly spontaneous impulse, I ripped off my pants, and, with my hands shaking so violently that I could scarcely use them properly, I pulled her panties on. One look in the mirror, and the combined visual and physical experience induced an immediate ejaculation. Fortunately, I managed somehow to pull her panties far enough down so that I ejaculated into my hands rather than into them. I was scared of what I had done, perhaps the force that had been released in me; ashamed and thoroughly confused about my whole sexuality. The fantasy that I was trying to bring to a reality ended one hot day when I was stripped to the waist sawing wood down in her cellar. My fly had been left carelessly (so cool a youth was I, even then!) open to attract her attention. She saw clearly, but I became so excited having her there watching me that when I put my foot down on the floor from the sawhorse I was leaning against, out popped my shamelessly stiff prick. She hurried up the cellar stairs, with never a word, apparently too embarrassed to say or do anything. That was the closest I ever came to her, although I did continue to work for her for some time to come.

As I think of them, most of my fantasies have been about older women. The fact that I was brought up in a fatherless home by my grandmother and my working mother has undoubtedly provided the necessary ground for these fantasies to grow in. But in what inverse way I am not sure.

Much later, while on a furlough cavort in the army, I had a girl tell me that I was "not a man, but a horse!" That's all I needed to know to set my ego in motion. It ruined me for years. I had the crazy idea that all I had to do was show it to a woman and she would break her neck getting to me. Of course, it was not so. But I tried. If there is such a thing as discreet indecent exposure, then I did it. Not in public, ever, not ever in such a manner that would be construed overt or frightening. Always appearing quite accidental—in hotels, boarding houses, tourist homes . . . where the possibility was quite reasonable that it was, indeed, accidental. I'm sure I didn't carry it off as well as I thought. But on the few occasions when I received "interested" vibrations, I failed to follow up, through some ineptness on my part, and these experiences, in turn, became the subject of further fantasies.

When the sex instruction books began to hit the book stores, I read avidly, seeking confirmation that I was not perverted or abnormal or obsessed with sex. I don't remember when I learned that women masturbate, but whenever it was, I turned on *fast!* I have been looking ever since for the woman who will invite me to watch her masturbate. Nearly all my present-day fantasies include that aspect, and that is one dream that I would not hesitate to carry out! My wife and I recently had a beautiful opening out of our feelings and for a while, we were on top of the sexual world. During that period, I confessed my masturbation practices to her, and in doing so, felt that tremendous surge of relief from guilt that must provide the basis for all confession, spiritual or otherwise. In addition, during that dreamy period, I persuaded her to masturbate, after she told me she had done it a few times, alone. She managed to do it twice, but soon decided that she doesn't like the feel of her own finger.

There I am, my dream still hot and hopeful, but with no prospects of realization on the stage closest to me—my own bed! I suppose I am luckier than most people who harbor frustrating fantasies all their lives. I, at least, have had several of mine come true, and for that, like the old woman in Synge's *Riders to the Sea,* "I must be satisfied."

The pleasures of seeing a naked woman do not interest Maurice (above). Instead he wants her to look at him. "I am a perfect exhibitionist," he says, "in search of a perfect voyeur." It is his life's ambition to prove those psychiatrists wrong who say that women are not sexually stimulated by seeing a man's naked genitals.

Maurice gives us a chance to clear up a common misunderstanding. In our society, female exhibitionism is a form of seduction, but male exhibitionism is a hostile act. The man who flashes his penis at a woman who has not asked to see it is not trying to win her; his goal is to scare her to death. He is trying to overcome his feeling of powerlessness vis à vis the women whom he feels have rejected or restrained him. He is angrily reacting to civilization and its discontents. The prime fact that works against men like Maurice is that in our civilization, using the body to sexually attract is the role assigned women.

Looking good is a passive form of magnetism, and thus comes within our cultural definitions of femininity. The girl in the tight red dress need not say anything or make unmaidenly advances. She can even pretend to be aloof and disdainful. Men will flock around anyway. But women have not been trained to come forward merely because a man is handsome, let alone because his trousers are so tight you can see the veins in his penis.

Early in life, poor Daniel (above) felt that his enormous penis was the sign in which he would conquer the world. But the result was that he was "ruined" for years. Exhibitionism, revealing the aspect of himself he was proudest of, brought only rejection. This is not to say I am in favor of men being allowed to exhibit their penises. What I am trying to explain is the anger and guilt many men feel when they are caught up in social contradictions.

The man who preens, primps, or goes too much out of his way to attract attention to his physical self is putting himself in jeopardy; he could be considered effeminate. It was not always thus; the Greeks, for instance, used the male figure at least as often as the female as a standard of beauty in their sculpture.

A man's power and wealth get him attention, but your bank account is not you. It is a trite truth that nobody wants to be loved for his money alone. Long before wealth, long before you grew up and became president of this or owner of that, all of us—*both sexes*—had the desire to be praised, to be loved and applauded for ourselves, for what we physically are. It may be nice to be loved for your sterling character, for being a good father/husband, for your achievements, kindness, intelligence; but there is a lifelong

hunger to be loved for the self—incarnate in the body—
alone.

Yes, we live in a male-dominated culture, and ours is a
phallus-worshipping society, and men alone have a cock—
the culturally accepted symbol of superiority. But the fundamental, underlying contradiction to all the above is that
most women do not like to see it.

The Greek sculptures were products of a way of thinking that is now twenty-five hundred years old; as recently
as your mother's time, people were still putting fig leaves
on statues. Every day, I hear from saddened or angered
men about the averted feminine eye, the hand withdrawn
as if from a red-hot coal. I would like to ask women readers: How must it feel to be the gender that has a sexual
organ considered so nasty that nobody, not even the
woman who says she loves you, wants to look at it?

11

Women with Women

The previous chapter was about catching a glimpse of women naked. The fantasies here go a step further in sexual discovery: finding out that women have a powerful erotic life of their own, that they are secretly so lustful they will even seek satisfaction with their own hand or another woman. Far from making the man feel unnecessary or left out, this vision sharpens his appetite: Women may pretend to be no sayers to sex; underneath, they are just as horny as he is!

Patriarchal attitudes may reserve to men the right to make the opening moves. The price is guilt. "She's such a sweet, naive kid. I shouldn't have talked her into it. Now I'll have to take care of her." Another price is a kind of tedium and sameness—why is it the man who always has to take on the job of initiating sex, and therefore the responsibility for making sure the woman enjoys it, reaches orgasm?

The first two fantasies in this chapter firmly excuse men of all responsibilities: Men aren't even present. The scenes that are played feature women who are self-starters in sex, who enjoy sex, who themselves make sure that they reach orgasm. Worries left over from childhood about sexuality and aggression, wherein sex is seen as a violent or degrading act men impose on women, are eased: If women are really like this, sex is not the man's "fault." Women do it even if no men are around. What's more, they don't just lay there: They are so eager for orgasm they'll give it to themselves!

Crosby's and Trenton's fantasies (below) tell us that there are times when men enjoy the pleasure of being around sex, but without carrying any of the responsibility for it. Who hasn't felt this hesitation in himself/herself, at least for a moment, when some new amatory adventure seemed to loom: "Do I really want to get involved?" In real life, of course, the answer is usually yes. In fantasy, it needn't be. This doesn't say that men like Crosby or Trenton are especially fearful or impotent—just that once in a while they'd like to be free of the societal imperative that every man must be ever ready to sexually satisfy every willing woman who comes along.

In the end, the image of women making love to women grips the male imagination because it expresses one of the dominant themes of male fantasy: the sexually insatiable woman.

Women who masturbate, who make love to other women, who use dildos or animals for sex, who not only initiate sexual action but overpower the man and "rape" him—*women who would not dream of saying no*—release the man from his earliest inhibitions. He need no longer fear making his proposition, need not fear he may not perform well. The sexually enflamed woman in this myth is so close to orgasm right from the start that nothing is going to hold her back.

CROSBY

I am nineteen years old. This fantasy is my favorite. It probably originates from my reading because I have never seen anything like this (unfortunately). The people in it are real, but most of the events are only in my head:

Linda is a high school English teacher who is very popular with the students. She is very friendly with everybody; but best of all, she has a fantastic body with huge tits. Quite often her class has a party at someone's house. Everyone is invited, including Linda. One of these is a swim party at Ellen's house, and eventually most of the people go home. Linda and another girl, Laurie, help Ellen clean up. Quite exhausted when they finish, they plop down on the sofa; but Ellen suggests that they take a sauna to relax.

As the temperature rises and the sweat runs down their bodies, the suits feel uncomfortable; and at Laurie's suggestion, they remove them. Linda is almost asleep; but Ellen and Laurie can't help but stare at Linda's beautiful body, especially at her glistening cunt and large, firm breasts. Finally, Ellen asks Linda if she would like a massage. Turning on her stomach, Linda says yes; and the two girls jump beside her, starting their caresses at her back. They switch to her legs, one girl on each, moving upward toward her lovely ass. When they reach it, Linda turns over, revealing her moist tits and cunt. Unable to contain themselves, Laurie and Ellen move their fingers to her tits, squeezing and fondling them, finally rubbing the nipples. By now, Linda is fully awake and very excited, watching the two pretty girls massage her breasts. Putting her hands on the girls' heads, she pulls them down until their faces are at her breasts. Together, Laurie and Ellen begin sucking the very erect nipples, still squeezing the masses of flesh; but now each with one hand on her own cunt, working their fingers to a frenzy. Linda pushes Ellen's head to her own cunt, while also pulling Laurie's cunt toward her own mouth. Laurie sees Ellen's cunt unoccupied and awaiting a tongue. The three of them suck and lick each other, building to a fantastic climax, bathed in sweat and steam.

Later, as they shower together, the girls again suck on Linda's enormous tits, while at the same time fingering her cunt and ass. Finally, in the bedroom, Ellen produces a dildo and a vibrator, and once more the girls bring Linda to a series of unbelievable climaxes, fucking her in the ass with the dildo and rubbing the vibrator around her cunt lips and across her clitoris.

Three people or more in my fantasies are typical. The way I see it, two people can do much more for a third than one can.

TRENTON

I am twenty-seven and have a B.S. in business. I have been happily married for almost four years; and my wife and I have a great life together, especially our sex life. Before marriage, I was a virgin, not because the chance had not passed my way, but because I felt that for me the best thing was to wait for marriage. I had about six to eight partners during this time and we did all but go all the way.

I am truly turned on by women of all ages, sizes, and colors. To me it's not so much a woman's body that turns me on but a combination of personality and the physical. Women turn me on anywhere from age fourteen to fifty. I have never had any relationship with a woman other than my wife since we wed; however, I would like to. It's not that I'm not fulfilled, but variety is the spice of life.

The fantasy that I have most often concerns two women together. They are in a room and it is as if I am invisible. They cannot see me, nor do they know that I am watching. They start off talking and sipping on a cocktail. The conversation turns to sex. One woman is thirty-seven, about five-seven, slightly overweight but still very pleasing to the eye. The other is in her late twenties or early thirties, five-two with large tits and beautifully muscular legs. Both are married. They are talking about their own experiences as well as their friends. Dee, the older of the two, is telling Pat about how excited her husband was the first time she shaved off her pubic hairs. Pat said that she had wanted to do that but wasn't sure of the correct way or how she would look after. Dee said that she had just shaved yesterday and invited Pat to see. Pat was a bit shy but willing. Dee then raised her skirt. She had on a garter belt, nylons, and a pair of white panties. Pat unhooked the garters and proceeded to remove the nylons. All the time, Dee was telling her how her husband loved to nibble and suck her out when she shaved it. Pat was getting very excited by this and began to feel Dee's soft, smooth legs, caressing them softly. Pat now was on her knees, slowly pulling the white panties from around Dee's hips. Slowly the smooth soft mound appeared. Dee then moved her fingers to part the lips of her cunt which was now wet with anticipation. Pat moved closer and watched Dee finger herself and began to move her fingers over the clit. The smell of sex was in the air and suddenly Pat's tongue was moving over that beautiful, warm, wet pussy. Dee remained motionless, just resting, laid back on the couch. What seemed like hours later their eyes met and Dee stood up and removed the rest of her clothes. From there, they went up to the bedroom where Dee undressed Pat and then shaved her pussy. The two then engaged in their new form of lovemaking until they heard Dee's husband drive up in the car and they both made a dash to get dressed and act as if nothing more than a cocktail get-together had occurred.

There is no counterpart to this chapter in either of my books on women's sexual fantasies. The image of two men making love often arouses not lust in women but anxiety—the enemy of sex. The reason lies not in biology but in women's training.

Women are raised to find their identity in partnership. Achievement is halved, without nourishment, if she does it alone. And so anything that even remotely threatens to take the man away from her arouses fear: his job, his friends, hobbies, Thursday night out with the bowling team. Trenton (above) makes himself invisible so he can watch two women making love, but the average woman would feel just too left out to invent such a scene for her own enjoyment: *These men don't need me!*

If a woman did have a fantasy about sharing her bed with more than one man, it would certainly not be a scenario of her watching two men perform with each other. On the contrary, the idea would be controlled in such a way that the men would be placed in rivalry for her. Extending this reasoning beyond fantasy, it is easy to see why women seldom initiate these trios. In real life, how could she control what might happen, what guarantees has she that the men might not form an alliance against her? The possibility of such pain far outweighs any potential pleasure. It's not worth the risk.

When I was in my early twenties and a man asked if I had ever had sex with another woman, I knew he would love it if I said yes; the implication was, wouldn't it be fun to repeat the scene with him present? This fitted right in with my understanding then that all men were sexually ravenous.

As I got older—perhaps as the men in my life got older—I wondered, still naively, How was he planning to satisfy two women? A more contemporary question might be—now that so much has been written about the expertise of lesbian love—Wouldn't a man resent having to compete with a woman? But that is a question that would only occur to women. The average man would shrug it aside. Watching two women making love satisfies a desire so primitive, so central to men, that all other considerations are secondary. The risk is worth it.

CLIVE

I am twenty-three and have been married for three years. I love my wife very much, and we share fantasies occasionally. I find that when I am fucking Jane (my wife), I can enjoy it much more if I know she is imagining being screwed by some other man. Sometimes she'll talk out loud in her fantasy and tell me that I am better than this other guy and that she would rather screw me. She will not, however, give the other man a specific identity. (He is not anybody we know.) I suspect that this is because she does not like me to fantasize about specific other women. She is particularly jealous of a former girl friend of mine; and once when I mentioned her in a fantasy, she became upset.

I would like to tell you this particular fantasy which I cannot share with my wife. I feel that maybe if I share it with you, I will feel better. I am getting horny thinking about it. Here it is:

My ex-girl friend, who lives in another town, has come to visit with Jane and me over a weekend. (She and Jane were friends long before I knew either of them.) I am constantly being excited at seeing Anne (old girl friend) in very skimpy clothing and once even walk into her room and see her with no top on. However, I know that if I make advances, she will tell Jane.

On Saturday, after seeing Anne's beautiful breasts, I have to go out for about an hour. When I return, Jane tells me that while I was out, she and Anne had started discussing sex and even got so horny that they played with each other a little bit. She says that she would like to have a threesome with Anne. She tells me that she will go to the store; and while she is gone, I am to try and seduce Anne. I am successful and am eating Anne's juicy pussy on Jane's return. Jane comes into the room and tells me that it's not

nice to screw without her. She undresses and starts kissing
Anne's breasts. It is not long before Anne comes. Anne
swings around and starts eating Jane's pussy while I am
screwing Anne from behind. We all have orgasms and I
hold both of these women whom I love while we rest.

I once asked a novelist friend for his description of heaven.
"To sit under a tree in summer, with all the women I have
ever loved; and none of them are jealous of each other."
Any man who has felt his wife bristle if he even mentions
running into an old girl friend on the street will recognize
in this a very masculine heaven indeed.

The idea of two women making love seems to many men
a step toward this blissful goal. A man may love his wife
but, like Clive (above), still have reservoirs of feeling for
another. Not to put too fine a point on it, let's leave out
love, and say he may have the hots for both. He wants to
go to bed with them at the same time. In reality, this is not
easily accomplished. Jealousy—the serpent in my novelist
friend's heaven—rarely sleeps. The man who dares suggest
the idea of multiple sex to his lover is usually met with
tears or anger. In these fantasies it is of the utmost importance to note that the women are described as not being
jealous of one another. Equally crucial to the emotional
tone is that no male rival ever enters. Only women's love is
in the air here, women's sex, women's kisses, women's
tenderness and affection . . . and all for him.

I don't think either sex is "naturally" more monogamous
than the other, but women accept fidelity more readily
than men. It is a form of magic talisman: If I don't stray,
neither will he. Once again, this can be traced back to
women's symbiotic training in fear and loss: Without him,
I'll die. Fantasies invented by men like Clive are a release
from the monotony of marriage, the fact that in the real
world, choosing one woman means giving up the other.

STEVEN

I am forty, married, with three boys ages ten to eighteen. I guess I'd be considered middle income class—over thirty thousand dollars. My fantasy is a little "far-out," but parts of it are real experience.

The fantasy always involves my cutting the hair of beautiful women, and I do that a lot. It's not my occupation, just a hobby, but I'm very good at it.

Anyway, this fantasy involves a beautiful brunette with very long hair. She wants "the works." First of all she has a glass of wine as I seat her in the chair and fasten the neck cloth around her and raise the chair to the proper level. I begin by piling all of her hair on top of her head and then cutting it in layers, till we end up with a very short wedge. I then use an older vibrator-type electric clipper to taper her neck and sideburns. She is thrilled with the haircut and has another glass of wine.

When she is finished, I tilt the chair all the way back so that she is nearly fully reclining. I lift the neck cloth so that she is uncovered from her breasts down. I lift her skirt as she helps me remove her panties. I then put a soft fresh towel under her seat. By leaving one foot on the foot rest and letting the other one dangle, she completely displays her entire pubic area, and is at an easy angle for me to proceed with her haircut. My electirc clipper is still warm from shaving her neck. I snap the clipper on and begin shaving her legs from the knees up. Her pubic hair is very thick and bushy. She comments on how long it's been since her last clipping. As I get to her beautiful mound, I use a flat comb to lift the hair. I then press down softly with the vibrating clipper, and she squeals with glee. Once she's entirely clipped from the knees to the navel, I brush her off with a soft brush and then cover the entire area with warm moist towels.

Next, with the old-fashioned shaving mug and brush, I lather her entire crotch and shave her till she's shiny and clean. Finally, with an electric hand vibrator, I massage her pubic area and legs with a soothing hand lotion. I now lower both of her legs, so that I can sit on the foot rest between her legs, and go deep inside of her with a lively tongue, till she nearly falls out of the chair, as she has a massive orgasm.

Next I help her to an awaiting whirlpool spa in the next room, where she relaxes while I prepare for my next customer. This time a beautiful blonde with thick hair to her waist. She, too, asks for "the works." My third customer is a very cute redhead with really thick hair. She wants an Italian "boy cut" and she gets it—everything. When I'm done, all four of us end up in the whirlpool spa and one at a time, we fuck till I can hardly move. I then simply pass out.

When I awaken, I find myself strapped into my own barber chair. My arms are tied to the arms of the chair and my legs to the outside of the foot rest. My only clothing is the cloth around my neck and the towel that I'm sitting on. All three girls are stark naked. I see the redhead giving the blonde a crew cut with my clippers. The blonde is saying that I left it a little too long. The brunette is right behind me and with a tongue in my ear says, "Now it's your turn, darling," and she begins to cut my hair, really doing a great job too. Next the brunette tilts the chair all the way back so that my head is just level with her cunny, all smooth and fresh. She slowly turns my head so that I face her. I feel the redhead go to work on my upper legs with the warm vibrating clipper, while the clipped little blonde goes down on me, moving up and down ever so slowly with her flicking tongue and warm mouth. I'm busy with the brunette who has to hold on to the chair to keep from falling down. After about three minutes, the girls trade places with each other. I feel the clipper close to my penis which is now being sucked softly by the brunette. The redhead straddles my head so that I can just barely get my tongue inside her to tickle her clit. Everyone has a great time.

Finally they lather me up and the brunette does a great job with the razor. Not a single nick and smooth as silk. The little blonde has to use a stool to stand on so that I can suck her clit. She holds on for dear life as I am vibrated with soothing lotion and sucked by the redhead. She does the most fantastic job I've ever had. My right hand has been loosened so that I can massage the cunny of the brunette as we all come together.

I've tried this with one, but I've only dreamed about three. Got two friends who need a haircut?

PRENTISS

In my fantasy I meet a gal who asks me—out of a clear blue sky—if I would come to her apartment. She says she needs help with something, but never says what and I do not press.

Once at her apartment she begins kissing me and I respond as I figure I know what she wants. Sex. As we're locked in a kiss, I feel her unbutton my shirt, undo my pants, drop my pants and shirt to the floor.

Then she calls out and three other gals run out and grab me. They're dressed and range in age from sixteen to thirty (which is my age). I'm half-carried into the bedroom where my hands are tied to the headboard and my legs are spread and tied. Before doing so, they remove my underpants so my cock is set free.

Pillows are stuffed under my hips to raise my ass off the bed and a pillow is set to raise my head up. Hands feel every inch of my body but they all converge on my half-raised penis and they intently feel it, exploring it, my balls and my groin.

They gather around my cock so I can't see what they're doing, but I can feel a hand pumping it. It's gentle at first, but it gets furious until I'm about to erupt. When I can feel them move in extremely close, that's when a hand massages the head. I'm lost now in ecstasy and I come. I can hear *oooo*s and *ah-h-hs* as I shoot white sperm out.

When I'm finished, the gal who brought me licks me clean.

They leave.

I'm left alone for a long while. Then the youngest returns. She strips to show a young body with small, developing breasts. She's as thin as I am, but very lovely with the promise of more beauty to come. She lays beside me and kisses me. I return her kiss. Her hand reaches down and massages my rod back into bloom. Her kissing grows more passionate as she rubs her tits over my chest. I lose track of how long this goes on, when she mounts me and starts riding my organ up and down. Up and down until I come. She collapses on top of me.

We rest and then she leaves.

Again the first gal returns to lick me clean.

After some time gal number three, the next oldest, enters. She's already nude with small firm breasts and as innocent looking as one of those bright-eyed portraits one sees at places selling pictures for the home walls. She's about twenty-two or so with short hair. She looks down at me for a long moment, runs a hand over my limp penis, and then climbs on so her pussy is over my mouth. Without saying a word, I begin licking her, tonguing her, probing her and sucking on her and continue to do so until she comes. She tastes sweet and can really moan and groan up a storm.

She, also, collapses atop of me and rests for a while before leaving.

Again there is this waiting period as if planned, so I can recuperate.

The last woman enters, all of twenty-eight—or thereabouts, with the face and figure of a plain, ordinary girl next door. Oh, she's lovely, but no fashion model. She climbs on me, face down, and starts sucking me. Playing little games at first, and continuing to a full-scale, first-class suck job. She drinks every drop of cum. Occasionally, I'm able to get at her pussy that moves past me, but she doesn't stay long for me to do much, as it's obvious sucking is her pleasure.

Once she leaves, the first gal I met returns. She unties me, bathes me, feeds me, then kisses me and drives me home.

Well, there you have it. That's my wildest fantasy, but it's by no means able to compete against others I'm sure. I'm not normally obsessed with sex, but would enjoy more on a regular basis. I'm just too shy.

GENE

I am fifty-five years old. I love my wife dearly and have always fantasized. I wanted nothing more than to please her sexually, to see and hear her fully aroused and satisfied.

I hope your readers, especially the older ones, find men's fantasies helpful to them in loosening up their hangups. I say, "Women, express yourselves. Encourage your lover and let him know what thrills you." I think most men's greatest pleasure in fucking is really pleasing the woman. And I can assure you that the pleasures you experience will be equally enjoyed by him. I can also say that the woman who refuses to "go down" on her lover is depriving her man of a terrific thrill. It isn't only the physical thrill that I enjoy, but knowing that my wife wants to do everything she can to please me is very important to me, and makes me love and want her even more, if that is possible.

My wife has a nurse she works with. Nancy is about thirty-five years old and divorced. She is pretty sexy looking, and a very nice person. My wife is very fond of her. In my fantasy, my wife and I have taken a motel room and are having a drink when our conversation drifts to talking about Nancy—what a sweet person she is and what a shame that her marriage has broken up. We both like her so much that we wish it were possible for Nancy to enjoy the thrills of private life as we do. My wife asks me if I have ever thought about Nancy sexually. I say, "Sure, you know I would be lying to you if I said no." My wife asks, "What would you do if someone knocked on the door and it was Nancy?" I say, "Ask her to come in and join our party." My wife and I assure each other that our real desires are for each other, but it would be the decent thing to do to try and arrange for a little excitement for her. I suggest to my wife she call Nancy on the phone and see if she would care to join us. Nancy accepts and my blood begins to run hot in my veins.

Before Nancy arrives, I give my wife's cunt a few licks with my tongue just so that she won't have any inhibitions when Nancy arrives. Nancy does arrive, looking sexier than ever. This is the first time for an experience like this—a threesome. My mind gets jumbled at this point. Those two gorgeous women's bodies and mine at the same time. We all three are very gentle and deliberate with our fucking and sucking. I visualize me being able to make Nancy come with my cock in her pussy, and making my wife come by licking her cunt. We all have to lie back and rest for a while after that thrilling experience.

My prick is completely limp! What a shame. My wife says, "Damn! What are we going to do? You've got to make me come with your cock in my pussy!" Then Nancy begins to fondle my limp prick. Stretching it up across my tummy, then kissing it, taking the head of it into her mouth and gently sucking it. It begins to grow. Nancy says, "Look, Doll, see it grow!" Doll says, "Oh, thank you! Make it real hard." Nancy doesn't have any trouble really getting my cock to throbbing again. Nancy says, "Okay, Doll, here is your hard throbbing cock!" With my cock in my wife's eager hot pussy, I am experiencing unimaginable thrills again. While I am fucking my wife, Nancy positions her own lovely cunt to where I can get to it with my tongue. I make both of those lovely women come at the same time!

LEONARD

I'm fifty years old and still very active sexually. Never really had much sex before I went to Europe in World War II. The women in Europe really turned me on to oral sex. They seemed to just love to suck cock. I would often get a "blow job" at a "cathouse" around noon, and go out in the evening and pick up a chick on the street and let her suck me off in a park or out in the country or in a hotel.

I didn't start eating pussy till after I returned to the States. Despite my late start, I think I am quite good and just love to eat a woman if she really enjoys it.

I really do enjoy a one-to-one relationship with women, but my favorite fantasy is to have four women make love to me. They all have good figures and long hair, but are quite different otherwise. One would be very blond for example, with very white creamy skin. Maybe another would be blond also, but with a nice tan where her bikini didn't cover. One would be perhaps part oriental and the other a lovely dark-skinned Mexican or Greek. At least two of them are very much into making love to each other, even though they all look very feminine.

I am laying on a big bed with my ass near the edge and my legs spread out on two chairs. The four girls get undressed very slowly, and help each other undress with lots of fondling and kissing. After getting nude, they start loving me. One sits down on the floor and starts tonguing my asshole. One starts kissing my neck and ears and the other two start licking my cock and kissing each other. I am very turned on watching two women kiss, especially open-mouthed kissing and tonguing each other.

The two that are "working" on my cock just lick all over it and meanwhile, the one on the floor is working around my asshole and getting her pointed little tongue right in it. The one kissing my ears and neck also has very lovely breasts with pink nipples, which she lets me kiss and fondle any time I like. I hold back as long as I can, but when I just can't stand it any longer, one of them takes my cock in her mouth and very gently sucks me off, while the other one continues to lick my ass. When I finally come it is really great, and the two kiss and share my come. They lick me clean and put me to bed and I go to sleep, knowing at least two of them will be there when I wake up.

My second favorite fantasy is to be with two very feminine bisexual women. They make love to each other for a very long time, while I watch. Again there is lots of open-mouthed kissing while I just watch and get really turned on. After they have loved each other thoroughly, they suck me off and we all go to sleep in a big bed.

My third favorite fantasy is one that I believe is shared by many men, even though I'm sure many of them would not admit it. In fact, I'm not sure you should print it. I surely would not want to encourage a potential rapist or anyone who might be unstable in any way.

Anyway, I'd like very much to make love to a very young girl. In my fantasy, it is someone who knows me very well, and trusts me, and someone whom I can trust. She is young enough to be without pubic hair, but old enough to have small firm breasts.

I don't know or really care if she is a virgin or not. But she knows about sex and enjoys it. We have lots of time and privacy and I undress her and give her a bath. (Or we take a bath together.) As I dry her off, I start caressing and kissing her body all over and very slowly work my way to that lovely hairless pussy, and open it up and lick and kiss it for hours and hours, until she is exhausted.

If she were not a virgin, I would then fuck her, but I would not hurt her in any way, not do anything she did not want me to do.

A typical fantasy in this chapter begins with a man watching a woman masturbate. Very often, she is his wife. The scenario then proceeds to the entrance of a second woman. The two of them make love. The climax is reached when the man reveals himself, and there is a sexual trio.

The progression is logical, and can be seen to follow a double curve. As the man's anxiety diminishes, his erotic desires grow. First, he is aroused by the idea that women (his wife!) actually do like sex. They masturbate, just like him. Next, seeing two women getting along together sexually so well, so lovingly, allows him to enter the fantasy, knowing the women will not be hostile toward one another, nor turn on him in jealous fury. Above all, since his wife has broken the rules, she cannot censure him for also wanting to. Instead, as we see again and again in other fantasies in this chapter, the women pool their energy and talent to take care of him.

The usual idea is that a man who wants to go to bed with two women is expressing himself as a sexual tiger. The fact is that in all these fantasies, strong elements of male passivity (or receptivity) are being expressed. *The women do to him.* In Steven's fantasy (above), they strap him to the barber chair and have their way with him. Force may have entered, but there is never pain; it's not masochism that is intended. These aren't women out to hurt men; they want to satisfy their own lusty appetites while sexually satisfying his, too.

Indeed, what strikes me about the fantasies in this chapter is the strong element of trust established in them. We say that trust is the basis of women's orgasm—she trusts herself and the man enough to let go of self-control. The

male orgasm may have a bigger element of the physiological, but the erection is dominated by the mind. How much
does the man trust his own body not to betray him?

Afraid that he may not be able to satisfy the women . . .
knowing that women are potentially multiorgasmic while
he cannot repeat with nearly the same frequency . . .
many a man refuses to play a game where he can't win: He
retreats into impotence. Though some men have told me
they have never in their lives worried that they might not
be able to get an erection, I don't see how the idea cannot
occasionally occur to any man past seventeen. Here, once
again, fantasy applies its balm. Far from not being able to
satisfy, Gene (above) is able to make two women come at
the same time. He is fifty-five years old. Little wonder it is
his favorite fantasy—but younger men, too, enjoy imagining scenarios which reassure them of their virility.

This idea is beautifully brought home in Prentiss's fantasy (above). There is the obvious problem of timing. How
is he going to get enough rest between climaxes so that he
will again get an erection? "There is this waiting period,"
he says, "as if planned, so I can recuperate." The four
women keep coming and going in his fantasy, giving him
all the time he needs.

How like ministering angels! These women aren't going
to shame or embarrass him; they aren't out to "drain his
precious bodily fluids." Gene (above) laments after sex
with his wife and another woman, "My prick is completely
limp! What a shame." But lo and behold, the other woman
brings him back to life again. "Oh, thank you," he says.
Then he makes both women come at the same time. Not
only do these women with their trusting ways and sexual
expertise make him virile, they help him reach the exalted
stage of Superman, satisfying one woman after another
without thought of failure. But isn't it the women who
really have these superpowers? It is only because of their
treatment of him that he can accomplish what he is afraid
he could not do alone.

Leonard's fantasy (above) perhaps most clearly expresses the passive wishes hidden in these superman fantasies. His four women are tender, take care of him—
sexually first, hygienically later. "They lick me clean and
put me to bed." The repeated reference, in these fantasies,

to being washed and cleaned up by the same person who has just encouraged you and participated in getting you "dirty" beautifully rewrites the role of the first woman in every man's life.

It is only after Leonard has gained strength and self-confidence from these four women that he feels free to act on their model: They have taught him to trust his sexual partners. Now, in turn, he teaches trust to a young girl, almost as a mother with a child.

Leonard suggests I not print this last fantasy for fear it might encourage a child molester. In similar fashion, some women were angry that I had printed so many force/rape fantasies in my earlier books on women's sexual fantasies. Ignorance feeds on itself, and ignoring the fact that women do fantasize about being sexually overpowered will not make the incidence of real rape disappear. A fantasy is not necessarily a real desire, the wish is not the deed, saying it doesn't make it so. Leonard's fantasy is not something he really wants to do.

In various places in this chapter, I have used the word *passive* as a kind of shorthand. It stands for an idea that is difficult to define exactly. The men in these fantasies are more done to than doing—in the sense we might say they are passive. But since they are the ones who are inventing the fantasy, aren't they activists, too? This is another example of the conflict in the male psyche: The overt content of these fantasies posits the man as a hell-for-leather riproaring, erotic fellow for whom one woman is not enough. The latent content is the supreme joy these multiple women furnish, ministering to and soothing male physical and psychological anxieties by taking the responsibility for sex.

Passivity has overtones of not caring, neutrality, almost of a defeated inertness. "Do with me what you will." These men know exactly what they want women to do with them. In their imaginations at least, they occasionally enjoy seeing themselves on the receiving end of sex, actively constructing scenarios to get what they want—*even if what they want is a "passive" experience*. They are men who dream of women in all shapes and sizes and color. They are in a rage against being expelled from a time they unconsciously remember as filled with feminine nurture, tenderness, sensuality, and comfort. They want to recreate Eden.

And with no other man there.

LUKE

I am in prison. But I would like to make it clear right now that I am not in here because of any kind of sex rap. I am a white male forty-two years of age. I have been married, but am now divorced. Everyone says I look to be about thirty-five years old, and believe me, I am really thankful for that. I am a fanatic for keeping myself in good physical condition.

I think the two main reasons I am such a fanatic about physical fitness are (1) I have always had a nagging fear of getting old, and (2) I have a fear of not being able to get it up when I do get out of here. I don't really know why I have this fear, because all my life I have had (and still do) a very powerful sex drive.

As for fantasies, whenever I was loving a woman, I never fantasized. I never had to. Of course during masturbation, I always think of women. But the women I think about are those I have been to bed with or women I have known and would have liked to go to bed with. But I can't recall having a fantasy about a complete stranger. That is, not until now. Here is my fantasy:

I really can't remember when it began, but I have always had a desire to spend one night making love with two good-looking women. When this fantasy first entered my head, it was with women I have known. But since I have been in prison, it has changed to women that are complete strangers. I fantasize that I have been released from prison. I go into this real nice bar, and I see these two foxy gals sitting together in a booth and they are talking. One is a lovely blonde and the other gal is a sexy brunette. Both of them have long hair. (I love long hair on a woman.) I offer to buy them a drink and they accept. I tell them I have a proposition I think will interest them, and they tell me to sit in the booth and explain. So point blank I lay it on the line. I tell them that I have always

wanted to spend one night loving two women. I tell them
that I would like to take them out to dinner, and that I will
also pay each of them one hundred bucks if they will spend
the night with me at a nice motel. I also tell them that I
have just been released from prison, and that I haven't had
a woman for several years.

This really turns them on and one of them says it will be
like getting a man virgin and they start laughing. And last
of all, I tell them that they must do whatever I ask them to
do (nothing kinky), but that I will want them to love each
other and that I will want to have anal sex with one of
them while they are eating each other. I also tell them that
I want them to demand that I perform cunnilingus on them
both, and they really like this part. I tell them that I have
always wanted to see two cute gals loving each other. When
I see pictures of women making love, it really turns me on.

Anyway, I take them out to dinner, and I buy them some
drinks. But I don't have anything to drink, because I don't
want anything in my system that will dull one minute of
this night. (I would like to say at this point that I am a
Virgo, and I guess I have always been a nut for small details and for being clean.) Anyway, we are in this nice
motel room and I have bought tooth brushes, mouth-
wash, douche bags, K-Y jelly, toothpaste and whatever else
we will need.

So after I have showered and shaved, we all end up on
the bed in the nude with me in the middle. Now during
this fantasy, every scent, each sound and detail are crystal
clear. I can smell the perfume the girls have on, I can smell
the sweet scent of each of the girl's hair. I notice how beautiful their bodies are, their terrific asses (I've always been
an ass man.) I don't seem to have to say anything to them
at all. From here on they seem to know what turns me on
and it is really great.

I am kissing their sweet mouths, sucking those beautiful
tits, my fingers are in their hot wet cunts. They are moaning and gasping in joy. Then I am pushed onto my back
and the lovely blonde straddles me, facing toward my feet,
and guides my throbbing cock deep into her warm sweet
cunt. At the same time, the sexy brunette straddles my
chest, facing me, and pushes her wet pussy against my

mouth, and I really begin to eat her out. Both women are moaning and crying out pretty loud now. They are really getting with it. (I hate quiet sex.) I can smell the lovely woman scent of the foxy brunette I am eating, and even though her knees are on each side of my head, I can still look up into her lovely passion-filled face, and notice each detail. Her eyes are closed and her head is twisting from side to side. Her pink tongue is licking her sexy lips, her breath is coming in short gasps. Her face is covered with sweat, which is running down between her beautiful tits that my hands are squeezing gently.

The blonde is really riding my cock now. She is moaning and crying out in joy, "Oh, God, I'm so close, so close, and I can't hold back any longer." Then both women scream out together as they climax, and at the same time I shoot my load in one of the most powerful orgasms I have ever had. Then we all collapse completely drained.

We try different positions, and come again and again throughout the night. But in this fantasy, I don't ask the gals to perform analingus on me or to go down on me. But whatever they ask me to do to them, I do it and love every minute of it. Especially if I am performing oral sex on them, be it analingus or cunnilingus. I would like to say a couple of things about this fantasy.

When I first began to have it, I had not read or heard too much about threesomes having sex together. But I guess nowadays, it is no big deal. But I really want this fantasy to come true. I am saving my money and if I live to get out of here, I will make it come true regardless of what the price will be. And I will work it out right down to the smallest detail. I guess it has almost become an obsession with me. Next to being free, I want that one night with two good-looking women more than anything in this world.

PERRY

I am thirty-one, white, college educated, and a civil servant. I am eight months a newlywed. Two years ago, I successfully completed three years of psychotherapy. I fell in love and got married. One consequence of my oppressive inferiority problem, prior to therapy, was that I was a virgin until I was twenty-eight years old.

With no women in my life during the years prior to therapy, I jacked off in concert with my fantasies. I still do two or three times a week, which is down from my pretherapy frequency of two or three times a day. Nowadays, I would rather make love to my wife when I get in the mood.

I had this first fantasy when I was nine years old. When going to sleep, I imagined myself standing between two beautiful women and being snugly embraced by their big breasts which extended out of their chests like soft, warm tentacles. This gave me an erection which felt good. End of fantasy. I had no idea what an erection was for and no knowledge of female anatomy below the waist.

My current favorite fantasy to jack off with has evolved from pornographic books I've read. Basically, two gorgeous, wealthy black women, mother and teen-age daughter, kidnap a pretty white woman and her virgin teen-age son and daughter. In the basement of a secluded manor house, the white people find themselves shackled to a wall. Black mother and daughter strip them and examine their bodies. Black mother chooses both white teenagers for sex and black daughter chooses white mother. I extend the fantasy in great detail as black mother, with a lush figure, introduces white blond daughter to sex beginning with her first orgasm during cunnilingus and ending with black mother strapping on dildo and fucking the white girl in her cute little ass. Black mother can't eat enough of the white girl's blond pussy. Black mother also loves to tangle her fingers in the girl's blond hair and bring the white girl's head to her nipples and pussy. The white girl's resistance changes to enthusiastic partnership.

When black mother leaves the white girl, she goes to another room where she easily seduces the teen-age white boy. She fucks him a lot. Sonny is put on top and black mother wraps her long legs around his back and squashes his face between her big breasts. When he comes, a fat, naked black maid enters and sucks on his prick until he has another erection. Then he is put on top of black mother for another fuck. Black mother has him practice screwing the black maid in the ass.

Black daughter has been initiating the white mother into lesbian sex. She starts by tying the white mother down on her back and sitting on her face. After that it's on to sixty-nine and later, fun-with-dildo-time. White mother continues to protest, but not much. (Boy, do I like lesbian sex!)

The white family, now sexually liberated, is sent home. I see incest in their future.

When my wife and I make love, I fantasize as I approach orgasm that I am a big black guy screwing my wife.

P.S. You know, it feels strange writing this down.

12

Animals

GERALD

I had my first orgasm when I was twelve. I was playing with my cock and it kept feeling better and better until that indescribable explosion of passion which I shall never forget, though I'm well past fifty.

Those were the days when premarital fucking was frowned upon and anyway, I was too bashful to ask girls for a date, much less fuck them. But I often wondered what a girl's sexual organs looked like and how it would feel to put my cock inside a girl. There were no picture magazines then so I could only fantasize. I was in my twenties before I finally got a good look at a girl's bottom! I lived alone with my hand on my cock for years, not realizing how beautiful the world of sexual experience there was to enjoy outside of myself.

Since we lived on a farm I discovered a unique way of getting my sexual needs satisfied. I began to experiment with cows. First I tried it on the calves about a year old but they were a bit too tight and would not stand still. So I took to fucking older cows, some of which seemed to enjoy it as much as I did. I figured this is what it must be like to fuck a real girl and would fantasize I was doing just that. I did worry, however, that it might be possible for the cows to get babies instead of calves, for then my secret would be discovered.

In my mid-twenties I finally got up enough courage to date girls and eventually became married. Sex has been my greatest pleasure and still is. Every time I fuck my wife I can't get over the thought that I am actually fucking a real woman and not a cow. I believe in monogamy and marital faithfulness but still find the naked body of a woman is the most beautiful sight on earth. Her genitals especially, surrounded by soft, silken or wiry hairs, and the lips parted showing that little center of pleasure, never cease to amaze me. If only women knew how desirable they are!

The boy who, like Gerald (above), fucks a four-legged friend in the barnyard does not enrage us. In fact, most people to whom I've shown his letter say they find it touching. When Kinsey reported in 1948 on the number of men who had had at least one sexual contact with an animal, nobody called him a pervert or even expressed great astonishment. Boys will be boys.

But twenty-five years later, when I wrote in one of my books on female sexual fantasies that women often invented scenarios of sex with animals, there were cries of outrage and disgust. And these were only daydreams—though it is my opinion that women have more real sex with animals than can be statistically determined (for obvious reasons).

I feel that erotic reveries about animals are not quite so compelling to men as they are to women. The appeals of these fantasies to the feminine imagination—secrecy, safety, the thrill of the forbidden, release at last from the need ever to combine sex with love—are simply less important to men. In fact and fantasy, men have a wider variety of alternatives.

When a man does imagine himself having sex with an animal, it is often to experiment with anal feelings and sensations most women will not—or could not—provide. However, in the end, men usually agree the effort isn't worth it. "I have considered the thought of a man being fucked by a dog, anally—maybe even myself," says Rick (below), "though something would be obviously lacking." *It is when the animal is partnered with a woman that these fantasies reach their fiercest peaks of pleasure.*

The usual explanation is that this kind of man gets off on notions of degrading women. Sometimes this is true: In North Africa and the Middle East, for instance, as in other feudally male-dominated cultures, the softest erotic joys are often reserved for homosexual love, while pain, torture,

and abasement—including sex with animals—are brought
into experiences with women. Perhaps we don't have to go
so far from home to find men who get an erotic thrill in
women's humiliation, *but I have not heard from one single
man who invented animal pleasures to express cruelty to
women.*

Nor is it any different in women's fantasies. Quite the
contrary: When a woman invents an animal fantasy her
thrill is not in abasement, but in her power and authority;
for once, she is in complete control. How, when, where—
everything that has to do with yes or no—is completely her
choice. The men in this chapter would have it no other
way. Their excitement is not that the woman is hurt, but
that she is so happily sated. Here is a woman totally outside their experience, so eager for sex she will take it any
way she can.

In real life, sex brings with it emotional responsibilities.
Animal fantasies are a vacation from all that. To a woman,
they represent the ultimate break from the rule that she
may only have sex in a "meaningful relationship." To the
man, the woman-with-an-animal is the dream: someone
who wants a nonpersonal, nonintimate, nonentangling
fuck. If she is reduced to "the animal level," well—what's
wrong with that? It is the level on which an important part
of himself has always operated (and about which he is secretly proud anyway).

It was the first woman in his life who made him feel
ashamed of this aspect of himself, an idea that has been
reinforced by every woman he has met since. The woman
who seduces her dog declares she is the same as he—wild
and out of control, no thought of guilt or delicacy. Just sex,
pure sex, animal sex—and let love, tenderness, commitment, and all the other rules come back tomorrow.

In the most primitive dreams of both sexes, we are all
seduced by ideas of being stripped down, relieved of the
burdens of civilization, operating on an unthinking, biological level at last. Society and our parents made us good
girls and boys; these fantasies are a trip away from all that.
They get behind the façade and let us enjoy a few safe
moments as the uninhibited animals we all were at the beginning of life.

BUCK

I have always envied dogs and their tremendous, long-lasting climax. I've never owned a male dog that I didn't jack off, or one that didn't love me for doing it for him. Sometimes just watching a dog's prick jerk and squirt for fifteen or twenty minutes or longer is enough to turn me on; and other times, all that doggie come puddling up on the floor seems an awful waste; and in my fantasy, it is all going down my throat or up my anus.

Dogs, I have found, are just as orally excitable with a male as with a female. Good old "Rover" gets just as horny licking on my cock as he does licking on my wife's pussy. Unfortunately, it doesn't have the same effect on me as it does on my wife (and a lot of other females, apparently). No matter how good it feels when he licks my cock, it is just not the same as having it engulfed inside a mouth, and doesn't even bring it close to a climax. So when he gets hot and starts hunching, it is time for my hands to go to work—one on him and one on me.

The dog we have now has a big prick, and masturbating him is kind of tricky. As I gently rub my highly excited prick and keep it just on the verge of coming, my fantasy takes over and I am on my hands and knees and that big prick is hung up in my asshole and squirting all that wonderful come up inside me. Or it is in my mouth and I am swallowing all of it, or it is in my wife's pussy and his come is running out down her legs, or it is in her mouth and she is swallowing it while I eat her pussy, and on and on.

I feel impelled to include here the reason why I doubt if I ever actually will try the dog cock in the ass bit. My friend from the six-year-old "doctor" days actually got this done a few years ago, with quite disastrous results. With careful planning, he got his big bird dog in the house when he was absolutely sure his wife was gone for the afternoon. After undressing, he let the dog lick his cock until he was seriously showing interest, then got on his hands and knees and presented the dog with his rear end. The dog thought this was a fine idea and entered into the game wholeheartedly, licking his ass with much gusto, and then mounting him, proceeded to hunch away. With a little guidance, he

got his cock right into the anus and forthwith shoved it all
the way in, big knob and all, and energetically fucked him.
My friend said it was very exciting and fulfilling, all that
he had thought it might be; and all went as expected for
a while. The dog stepped over his ass, turned around, and
settled down for a long come; my friend was almost coming with the excitement of the whole act. Here he was,
locked in the bedroom, actually fulfilling a wild fantasy in
complete privacy, when he heard the front door open and
his wife call his name. Rather than try to explain to his wife
what he was doing in the bedroom with the dog, that he
couldn't let her in, for as long as it would take that dog to
finish coming, he did the only thing he could do. When he
told me about it a week later, his anus was still sore. Of
course, in my fantasy, the dog and I both come until we
are soft, soft, soft; and his cock slips out of my come-wet
anus quite easily; and I can spend hours secretly enjoying
his come soothingly oozing as my anus relaxes.

RICK

I am fifty-five years old (dirty old man category!), a college graduate, and retired military officer. For the past
nine years, I have been teaching eighth graders in a public
school. I am three years into my second marriage, the first
having broken up following infidelity on my part which I
wasn't mature enough to keep quiet about. I have three
sons by that marriage, all grown and married. Both my
marriages I consider as highly satisfactory in matters sexual. I was raised in a relatively sheltered New England
atmosphere and in the Episcopal church.

Now as to my sexual fantasies. To start with, I have
masturbated since age eight or nine; and I will continue to
do so as long as I'm healthy. In my younger years I did it
many times while viewing pictures of naked women; and
occasionally, I do now, although with my years of experience, I have the capability of forming all the most sensual
and erotic pictures I need totally in my mind. More often
now, I will use the printed word if external stimulation is
needed. Hence, I am never at a loss for fantasy, and it is

always present during masturbation and often during actual intercourse. In the latter case, I never tell my wife about it; they usually involve some other woman I've had in the past who was particularly good in bed. So, if you haven't gathered it by now, fantasy plays an almost indispensable part in what I consider my very active sex life.

In recent years, there has been an area in matters sexual that I seem to have gotten hung up on; and I'm not sure why. That is the area of bestiality. The concept of the body of a human being sexually connected to the body of an animal, I find most intriguing. I think about as many aspects of the phenomenon as possible; but most often, it comes down to the human female welcoming—if not requiring—sexual penetration by a male animal. The idea of horses, donkeys, and bulls is most exotic, of course, due to their great dimensions. However, these matings don't appear as very practical for regular occurrence. Ultimately, my fantasies boil down to a woman being fucked by a dog, preferably a pet that she has access to on a daily basis, and preferably of the larger species such as the German shepherd or Great Dane. Further, it is a requirement that she take his "all" with his first mighty thrust; and as his "knot" swells to full size inside her, her relatively small vaginal sphincter muscles hold him fast (in other words, they are "hung up") until he is spent, which in most dogs is from twenty to thirty minutes. The knot at the base of the canine penis will grow up to five inches in diameter (a fact) in these larger species; and further, the dog does not come like a man but will maintain his erection for up to thirty minutes, pumping his semen all the while.

Hence, we have our lady on her hands and knees, for he has taken her typically dog fashion, writhing in a steady stream of orgasms as her sex is inextricably connected and meshed with his, which may be an interminable length of time by human standards. To date, I have only read about such a phenomenon but feel intrigued with the idea of actually witnessing it sometime.

Further, I have considered the thought of a man being fucked by a dog, anally—maybe even myself, though something would be obviously lacking here. As to why I am intrigued with the idea of an animal sexually possessing a human female, I cannot answer.

DALE

This fantasy has been with me for about four or five years; and when I do masturbate, this is always what I use. It goes as follows:

Our children are gone for the evening, and my wife and I are home alone. We get into some very heavy fucking and my wife becomes insatiable. She screws me into an exhausted mass of limp meat, and still wants more cock. She brings in our German shepherd and plays with his cock until he's as horny as she is. She then proceeds to fuck the German shepherd in every position possible, and loves every minute of it.

In real life, I would give almost anything if this fantasy could be acted out. My wife doesn't want to, so we have done nothing about it as yet. However, I have not given up on it happening; and I do bring the subject up occasionally. The dog fantasy really turns me on, although I don't understand why. A couple of facts go along with this fantasy and may very well have a bearing on it. As a boy, on the farm, I had sex on a regular basis with our sows and cows. My wife has confessed that her virginity was lost to a family pet, a large collie dog. I believe that my fantasy began about the same time that she told me about the collie. Neither she, nor I, feel any shame or guilt over our animal contacts as children.

KING

Read a book on sex long ago. It stated that man's desire was for the deepest possible penetration. As for the woman, her desire is to admit the penis into the very center of her being; and her many attempts to do this bring into play the most exquisite parts of her sexual anatomy. Finally, this brings her to the supreme quiver. I have but to think of some of these passages and I get a hard-on.

Sometimes while I was fucking my first wife, and my cock was in to the hilt, she would say that my cock touched that spot that drove her to ecstasy. She later told me that my cock was not long enough to reach that very sensitive place every time. She even told me that she wondered what a really huge penis would feel like. And if it could reach that spot every time. So size does make a difference at least in some women.

This fantasy of mine is based on a "stag" movie:

Scene opens: A young, dark-haired girl is seated on a couch. She is nude except for white, six-inch heels. Her legs are crossed. A large male boxer appears. She pats him for a moment. Then she opens her legs, and the dog sniffs her cunt. Soon the dog is lapping her cunt. She opens her legs wider and moves her ass to the edge of the sofa. When he tries to mount her leg, she pushes him down; and the dog makes eager, prancing movements as though he can't wait to fuck her. The girl pats her cunt, and the boxer licks her cunt again. Then she stands up. All the while, the boxer is licking the girl frantically. Next she drops to her hands and knees. The dog approaches her rear end and sniffs and starts to lick her again. Then he tries to mount her, but she teases him by rapidly moving her ass. The dog starts to lick her again which she seems to enjoy as she remains motionless. Now he mounts her with more determination and succeeds in grasping her about the waist with his front legs. He starts to make thrusting movements and the tip of his red cock can be seen searching for her cunt hole. The girl rotates her hips slightly, and the red tip enters her cunt.

Now he goes to work in earnest as more and more of his cock comes out of the sheath. The camera moves in close, a large red bulge appears at the base of his penis; he is thrusting madly now, at last the bulge goes into her cunt. The camera moves back and NOW appears the most erotic scene that I have ever witnessed in my life. The dog's feet have left the floor. Clinging to the girl's waist, he thrusts wildly. Faster and faster he drives his cock deeper into the girl's cunt. It continues until suddenly all movement stops except for spasms as the dog comes. He then collapses to the floor, panting rapidly. The camera now moves in for a close-up of the girl's cunt. It moves in so close, her cunt can be seen twitching. Then a thin stream of clear dog "come" pours from her cunt to the floor. She remains on her hands and knees for a few more minutes as she enjoys her orgasm. Next, she gets to her feet, approaches the dog, and lifts him by the front legs so the audience can see his huge penis still dripping. . . .

LUDWIG

I have never written anyone on a subject like this before but was so pleased to see so many of your female readers honestly expressing pleasure in expanding their sexual enjoyment, that I'm glad to see you explore the little-known subject of men's fantasies, and want to contribute my own experience to the search.

Since my wife and I have raised our children and seen them happily married, it has been our custom to take half of our vacation together and the other half separately. She usually goes visiting or shopping with friends or relatives, and I go deer hunting in the north woods. I usually do my hunting from a blind made of balsam boughs and I rarely see another hunter except when I come out of the blind at night to head for camp and pick up my companions on the trail back to camp.

In the blind I am truly alone for hours at a time except for the wild creatures of the forest and I have lots of time to think back and relive past experiences. It is a lonely but restful experience and after a few days of fresh pine-scented air and mild exercise, I find myself missing my mate and getting more and more horny! As I think back, I remember one occasion that I shall never forget. The following is what actually happened to me!

I was a boy of about eleven or twelve, living on a big farm, and as boys do at that restless age, I roamed the fields and the woods far and wide. On a very hot summer day, my faithful companion, a big male collie dog, and I came to a deep pool in a creek that flowed through the valley. We were hot and tired and it was far from other people and farm houses, so I didn't hesitate to strip to the buff and jump in with the dog joyously joining me. The running water was so cold that I soon became chilled and crawled out on a grassy bank with my dog, Ted, right behind me. I came up on the bank on my hands and knees and before I could even dry myself on my shirt (or in the sun), Ted mounted me like I was a female. I tried to move out from under him but he weighed almost as much as I and was now covering my whole back and gripping me with his forepaws—meanwhile pumping his stiffening weapon closer and closer. Suddenly after several sharp jabs that made me yelp, he found my rectum with his juicy prick and rammed it in full length. It hurt fiercely—*yet it felt good!* Suddenly he gripped my sides so hard with his forepaws, he drew blood and began spurting into my virgin passage. It was like an electric shock and triggered a new and unfamiliar reaction in me. My boyish penis suddenly began to swell like Ted's, which was still in me, and I too had an "electric shock" in my own weapon. I began to spurt like a pulsating lawn sprinkler for the first time ever, and must have shot semen at least three feet from me for what seemed like two or three of the most glorious moments of my life to date. It was like the Fourth of July. Finally after several minutes in which I began to wonder if he would ever be able to get his gigantic, swollen prick out of me (and didn't care much at that moment), we collapsed together on the grassy bank, and actually dozed off a while before another swim and the long walk home.

All of this came to me later in my deer hunting blind in northern Michigan, and I got so horny that I began to wonder how it would feel to be a female and get such a royal fucking. In my fantasy, I got to thinking of myself as a young widow who had lost her husband within the past few months and had as my only relief and comfort a young and virile German shepherd dog. I now set down her thoughts as in my imagination I was reliving her experience:

"I live in a small house on the edge of a little southern town in a sparsely settled suburb. My friends have insisted that I get myself a dog for both company and protection. Since I am only thirty years old, and don't want to remain a widow the rest of my life, I decided it would probably be a good idea if I could find the right kind of canine companion in the meantime. So about a month ago, I found a beautiful light-colored German shepherd about one and a half years old, owned by some people who were moving to Atlanta and couldn't take him with them. They sold him to

me and I was delighted to find him gentle, clean and house-
broken. In fact, he is cleaner than some people I know,
and loves to have me bathe him—expecially when I slide
his beautiful tool out of its sheath and splash warm water
on it! He sleeps in my bedroom at night and has his own
shaded yard to run in during the days, but is fenced in
(fortunately for me, I found out later!).

"One morning I had just finished my shower and had
come into my bedroom to towel off, when I heard the local
fire truck pull up across the street at the Browns'. I ran to
the window and, not wanting to stand in the window before all those men naked as a jaybird, I dropped down to
my hands and knees and was looking out to see where the
fire was when I found out! Suddenly Duke padded up behind me and began licking my cunt with his long rough
and wet tongue. No one had touched me there since my
husband died five months ago, and it felt so good my nipples stiffened till they stood out like spikes! My pussy began to contract and expand and I began trembling all over!

"But I knew I shouldn't let him do this so I wheeled
around from the window to get up. As I did so, Duke
mounted me doggie fashion, holding me down with his
ninety pounds of weight, covering my whole back and gripping me around the middle like a drowning man. I tried to
get up but my legs felt like rubber, so I tried to crawl over
to the bed to lie down. As I moved, Duke began jabbing
me with his dripping prick all along the inside of my
thighs—and occasionally hitting the lips of my cunt—
meanwhile, he was sliding further up my back and holding
me so tight he was scratching my stiffening tits with his
claws. But somehow now, I didn't care! I wanted to feel
more of that beautiful weapon! So I dropped down to my
elbows and spread my knees just a bit—and BINGO!! he
hit the slit and rammed his hot rod all the way in—deeper
than anything had ever been before—it must have been
buried in me at least eight inches! Suddenly he gave a little
extra jump and I felt a bigger bulge like a knot go inside
my cunt lips and then we were locked together and he began to cream! I came so many times that I fainted and
collapsed on the floor.

"When I came to, we had separated and Duke was lying
quietly licking a long, but very red—and much smaller—

tool. I knew I had had the best screwing any woman had ever had, and I made up my mind right then never to let Duke out of my sight again. I didn't want him to wear himself out fucking any neighbor bitch who might come around looking for servicing!"

I'm afraid the balsam screen in front of my deer blind got a liberal dosage of rich cream from the furious flogging I gave my throbbing member that afternoon. The next morning when I went back to the same blind, my screen of boughs was rudely trampled down and there were deer tracks all around the stump upon which I had sat. Do you suppose a suffering doe in heat might have come by in high hopes, and ended up frustrated?

I am saddened by an image of men all across America measuring, measuring, measuring, measuring. Even as I read King's words (above), my heart aches that his wife tells him his cock is "not long enough to reach that very sensitive place every time." Hasn't it occurred to either of them that it may not be his lack of inches but her inner controls that keep him from driving her to "ecstasy?" Never mind. The fact remains that men worry about their size, and that the large male dog in King's fantasy alleviated this anxiety by standing in for him—as any best friend would.

Men and women choreograph their animal fantasies to a different rhythm. For men, it is an engineer's approach, the mechanics of the job. Comparisons are made. There is much talk of the "knob" or "knot" that is part of the dog's erection. The length of the climax is timed, and the quarts of come all but weighed and measured.

A woman would be brought down by such graphic accounts. While the dog's size is exciting, the merest glimpse of the red tip leaving the hairy sheath closes her eyes to reality, and opens her up to the still greater thrill of the forbidden. For once in her life she need not worry, "What will he think of me tomorrow?"

In the end, we are left with the realization that men measure the animal's genitals and performance so closely *because they identify with him.* They do not see the animal as a sexual rival any more than spectators at a prizefight feel competition with their hero in the ring. "Go to it!" the audience screams at their favorite. When their man wins, they are as happy as if they had delivered the KO themselves. When it's over, the fan leaves the ringside feeling, not less a man, but more.

When in fantasy Dale's wife (above) has screwed him "into an exhausted mass of limp meat, and still wants more cock," who appears on the scene as an ally? The pet German shepherd. Does Dale feel humiliated, competitive? No. This is his favorite fantasy. He gets to watch the dog fuck his wife, finishing the job for him. The fantasy does not spring from his wife's insatiable appetite so much as his own: he hungers to be more virile than any man can ever be (but he suspects all other men are). The family pet, tonight at least, puts this male fear to rest.

CRAIG

I am twenty-four years old, a college graduate, and have a very sexy girl friend. She is still somewhat reluctant to discuss her fantasies with me; but after reading your books, she has become a little more open. I have admitted that I have had sexual fantasies, but have yet to tell her about a single one.

One fantasy goes like this:

The couple next door have been transferred to another section of the country. He has already left to start to work, and his wife is staying here to try to sell the house. She (I'll call her Betty) is about twenty-six years old, five-nine (slightly taller than I), 37-26-36, and sexy as hell. I receive some of their mail, so I go over there. It's about ten A.M. I go to the back door (as usual) and find it open. Looking in, I see Betty lying on her back completely naked, with her collie licking her cunt. Betty is wriggling around on the kitchen floor, moaning with pleasure, urging the collie on. She spreads her legs wider and pulls the collie's nose and tongue into her. I am watching silently, getting a tremendous hard-on. Suddenly, she pushes him away, and spinning around on the floor, she grabs his prick and begins to suck him off. She swallows practically all of the pink, fleshy cock. I begin to strip off my clothes as she shifts positions again. She rolls over and gets up on her knees. The collie knows what to do. He's up on his hind legs and over her ass. She reaches around and guides his cock into her dripping cunt. His cock plunges in and out as Betty pushes her ass back to him. Before I can finish stripping, Betty lets out a low, long moan. The collie shoots his prick into her harder and faster, and is ready to come. Betty lets out a scream as the collie shoots his wad into her pussy. After a few moments, she pulls away from him, leaving him whimpering. The collie licks her cunt when she rolls onto her back to rest.

Now, for the first time, she notices me. She smiles and tells the collie to go downstairs. Then she takes my cock and leads me to her bedroom. I lay on my back as she begins to suck my cock and stroke my thighs. She drives me crazy—licking, nibbling, stroking, sucking, pinching my cock and balls. She then mounts me, her boobs bouncing up and down as she rides me. When I near the point of no return, she hops off and kneels next to me on the bed. Her boobs surround my cock when she leans over and rubs her breasts together. In a few moments, she's back on her knees with her ass sticking up. I get behind her and drive my throbbing cock into her slippery cunt. Reaching around, I grab her boobs, stroking them and pulling on the nipples. She yells for the collie, and in runs the panting canine. "Let him fuck your ass," she moans, "he knows how." The collie jumps up behind me and begins to search for my asshole. I reach back and grab his cock, place it at the hole, and push it in slowly. He shoves it in quickly and begins humping. I'm going wild!! My cock is ready to explode as I feel Betty's cunt tighten around it. The collie's cock is filling my ass to the point of tearing it (and me) open. Heavy breathing is interrupted by Betty's loud moaning scream, followed by my orgasmic gasp and the collie's LOUD high-pitched yelping. We collapse on the bed, the collie pulling out and hopping to the floor—my cock still in Betty.

PAUL

I am thirty-five years old, happily married, and have two children.

My fantasies are usually in the form of daydreams prior to going to sleep or any time I'm alone and relaxed. They are not always accompanied by masturbation. A very exciting one goes this way:

I am in Africa, in charge of crating wild animals. I have a lioness drugged and secured with leather straps so she can't move to bite or claw. The big cat is in heat, her pussy is hot and inviting, and I am very hard but also very much afraid of her, aware that she is a dangerous animal. The shamefulness of the act and the fear of discovery add to my excitement. She growls and strains against the straps as I approach from the rear. The hair is up on the back of my neck as I touch my penis to her cunt lips. My body is tensed for a fast withdrawal. I penetrate her slowly and she responds by arching her back and moving her lips sensuously. The sensation is out of this world, very intense. Her cunt is very hot and fits me perfectly; my thrusting becomes faster and I come quickly and copiously.

I am immediately ashamed and look around to see if I am discovered, but all is well and I promise myself to do it again and be one of very few or perhaps the only one to have experienced it and lived to enjoy it.

I have had this one first as a night dream and since as a fantasy. A tigress, Saint Bernard, mare and heifer have all been fantasy partners even though in real life I have never had my penis in an animal.

One of the persistent legends of history is that the insatiable Catherine of Russia was killed while attempting sexual union with a horse. The sling broke; the weight of the animal crushed her.

Men need no proof of their own sexual desire; the bulge in their pants never lies. What becomes almost more important, therefore, is to find a woman who is equally aroused, who gives evidence of it—not in equivocal words, but in acts as indisputable as an erection. This is why animal/human sex has always had a vivid place in the erotic imagination. It is the logical culmination of ideas previously discussed: women in heat, women hungry for sex, the woman out of control, who masturbates, takes another woman to bed, or even seduces the male—all these notions about the wantonness of women find ultimate expression if she will turn to a dog or horse for sex. All their lives, men have dreamed of a woman who will match their "animal lust." Women like Catherine are the Queens of Fantasy.

All this having been said, let me hasten to add that the idea carries a certain ambivalence for men. One sex therapist tells me that his patients often talk of porno films about women and animals. "They can do this," the doctor said, "because the movie is not something they thought up. When I ask them, since these scenes held their interest so strongly, if they ever have such fantasies themselves, the answer I invariably get is 'no.' The emotions let loose in these fantasies are just too threatening to admit."

This leads me to risk repeating what must be a familiar litany by now: We must not confuse fantasy wishes with desires we hope will come true. Some people would like to act out their fantasies. Others would be repelled or frightened. Many a man finds a woman who is ready for a Great Dane sexually provocative—but only if she is safely locked up inside his head.

13

"She Made Me Do It!"

I am awed by the work of the unconscious. I awake in the morning, go to my typewriter, and find problems that defeated me yesterday have been solved in my sleep; new words, fresh ideas flow—at least for an hour or two, until repression sets in again. Fantasies perform similar work, offering alternatives to knotted, conscious, logical thought.

They are safe playgrounds in which the imagination can experiment with problem solving. "How would it feel if I did this, if she did that. . . ?" Time and space along with human events are being rewritten; roles and reversals one might not dare assume in life are tried on for size.

Many men describe their reality as a place where they must be "strong." (How I hate that word. Isn't it too simpleminded to explain anything so complex as human relations?) Only in fantasies can they relax their rigid definitions of masculinity—occasionally allow themselves to follow, for instance, instead of lead. The woman is assigned the sexual initiative, and God, doesn't it feel good!

It may seem lusty and dashing always to be the one who chooses the woman, who decides when, where, and how the bedroom scene will be played. But isn't her role safer? The man is like someone who has suggested a new restaurant to friends. What if it doesn't live up to expectations he has aroused? The macho stance makes the male the star performer. The hidden cost is that it puts the woman in the role of critic.

Having tasted the pleasures of abandoning sexual responsibility in their fantasies, some men wish they could carry over these attitudes to daily life. Younger men in particular seem to feel that this is little risk to their gender identity. More traditionally minded men do feel a threat; even if they found a woman who likes to lead, wouldn't she regard them as lacking in manliness? Wouldn't they themselves?

The preceding chapters dealt with women so hungry for sex that they masturbate, take other women or even animals to bed—scenes in which the man just watched or occasionally joined in. Here at the heart of this book, we come to the logical culmination of such notions: fantasies of sexually secure, dominant women who invite, take, or even force the man. *One of the major themes in male fantasy is the abdication of activity in favor of passivity.* Role reversal.

In these scenarios, it is not the man who is the seducer, but the woman. Only one idea is more popular among the men I've heard from: sadomasochism. And even in S&M, as we will soon see, more often than not *it is once again the woman who takes the commanding role*. What the two chapters have in common is the profound desire in men to be relieved of women's anger, sexual guilt, fear of rejection and/or poor performance. Men may put up a façade, broadcasting their eagerness for the role of ever-ready sexual stud. And in fact, they often do enjoy playing it out. But in their heart of hearts, right along with this active desire, is a passive one: let *her* do it for once.

These ideas may puzzle people who take the surface appearances of male sexuality for the whole. Once we are aware of the masculine conflict, the glamour of these ideas is overwhelming; the man's rage is eased, his love doubled. The beloved figure who once denied him sex is now making him do it, seducing him in ways that have always been beyond his wildest dreams.

Earlier in this book, I granted that my contributors were special; I don't think that if Mr. Gallup polled the male American population he would come up with the same results. (How can you poll the unconscious?) Nevertheless, I feel these ideas represent the yearnings of some buried part of every man even if, because they threaten conventional notions of masculinity, they become unconsciously disguised. The hypochondriac, for instance, may secretly enjoy surrendering responsibility to his wife, but his various "maladies" enable him to say he doesn't enjoy it at all. This is what I mean by an unconscious fantasy: one that denies itself, but happens anyway.

Let's take the woman who asks a man "What are you thinking about, sweetheart?" He might be lolling back in the dark, lost in a reverie of being seduced, having sex thrust on him, passive and inert while the dream partner does all sorts of unspeakable, pleasurable things to him. "Thinking?" he says. "Nothing. Only you." My point is that this man is not consciously lying. I have mentioned often enough that women's favorite fantasies are about rape/force/"He made me do it!" It turns out that men's favorite fantasies are not about raping/forcing/making women do it. In fantasy, men want exactly what women want: to be done to.

Is the average man going to admit that? Probably not even to himself.

Is what Michael (below) describes really rape? Is he hurt, humiliated? Fundamentally, is what happens to him really against his will? There is no more pain or reluctance on Michael's part than there is in similar fantasies, beloved by women, of the demanding male brute.

The force being used in both cases is an excuse, a psychic guilt-alleviator. Just as women's fantasy attackers "make them" open their legs so they can innocently get all the uninhibited fucking Nice Girls are otherwise not allowed, so men like Michael feel they must be "raped" in order to get the kind of lovely, sexually done-to pleasures they've always wanted but feared would show them to be unmanly. The simple taking in of love, passivity, is the common and universal ground from which both sexes start, a yearning none of us entirely outgrow.

MICHAEL

I am black, twenty-two, and boyishly cute (according to a lovely woman I work with, who is ten years older than me). I earned a B.A. in political science recently, and am using it well—as a junior high school English teacher. This is not bad except that I wanted to fly with the Air Force. (I'm a frustrated fighter jock.)

Okay, that out of the way, I have a fetish which forms the basis of my favorite fantasy.

I fantasize being raped—by a woman. I have heard of it, but don't know how the victims got it up and *kept* it up.

Anyway, my rapist is a young lady who works in the guidance office; she's my age, quiet, sweet looking, and she has one maddening quirk—we're the same height shoeless, but *she* wears platforms. (I spent some time as a cadet in a paramilitary search-and-rescue unit as a teenager, so I habitually wear black low-quarter shoes). I *hate* platforms!

We've never really done anything together; she's not a bit like what myself and my buddies find, feel, fuck and forget on the singles bar scene we usually prowl. I like her too much to think of her that way, which is a happy first for me. We are so busy in our separate jobs that we don't even see each other much.

One other thing; she is hard to talk to; this is because I'm a victim of the good old all-American male double standard; she's no pickup, so I get tongued-tied around her. To her, I must be the picture of studied indifference.

In the fantasy, we've been on our first date, a rather nice evening of quiet dinner, movie and conversation afterwards in a favorite cocktail lounge. Now, we're at her doorstep, and I kiss Evelyn (her name) good night. Her door is opened as I turn to walk away—and suddenly, I feel hands on my shoulders and a shoe kicking my knee. My balance is gone and I'm falling, victim of a perfect rear takedown. As I fall, I'm sorting things out; where'd he or they come from, and I better start fighting back; they'll hurt her!

In the split second before I respond, I see who did it—sweet pretty Evelyn! What the fuck is *this*!

She gets me in a full nelson, drags me inside, closes her door; we're in her hall. "Get up!" I do.

"Now," she says, smiling, eyes shining, "now I get my chance to see if what's in your pants is as good as what's in your head!" I'm too shocked to reply, and she grabs my shirt collar and takes me to her room, still a bit shocked but feeling old Lucky Seven growing in my pants.

She pushes me onto the bed, kicking her shoes off and removing mine, not quite so gently. The rest of my clothes come off, and soon I'm lying on my back, wearing a half-unbuttoned shirt as she skins out of dress, bra, and panty hose, never taking her eyes off the cock sticking out of the shirt, smiling, nipples erect, licking her lips as she slinks

onto the bed and unbuttons the shirt. I'm not so shocked
now that I don't like this more than a little! My cock feels
like it's going to burst, but she doesn't slide onto it—she
keeps moving up me and the last thing I see is her pussy
before it ends its move up my body—and lands on my
face. And she smells just the way I *like* a woman to
smell—*herself*! 100 percent natural soap-and-water
woman! Hey, this is fun!

I lick along the lips to her clit repeatedly, trying not to
touch it even though she's rocking her hips against my
face. Her thighs come off my ears and I hear her moaning,
breathing really hard. And I'm really *caring* about pleasing
her. I touch her clit with my tongue and she cries, "There,
there, lick it *there*!" And I do; she's not touching my cock
and it seems like it's going to explode, but it doesn't, she
does, and I get to watch! My tongue's working her like a
pencil eraser gone mad, and suddenly she comes, tears in
her eyes, hands behind my head pushing my head *hard*
between her legs repeatedly as she gasps, moans, screams
and finally, after a seeming hour of inhaling her, she lets
go, moves off my face, grinning a salacious, horny grin that
tells me it isn't over just *yet*. And I'm smiling, too.

She mounts me like a horse—not down on my cock
yet—but teasing. And I want her to, I don't want to move.
She puts it between her legs, the bottom resting between
the lips of her pussy, not moving, just sitting, arms out,
teasing my nipples until they're just as erect as hers. And
she talks to me, for the first time since we got into bed.

"Look, Michael. I've been working with you for four
months now. And I've wanted you to talk to me—beyond
simple hellos and line-of-duty dialogue. I wanted you to
take an interest in me, but you kept walking on by whenever we both had a chance. You know that I sat in my
office wishing you could stop by and talk, *wishing* that
you'd ask me out?" She rocks her hips and I grow stiffer as
I feel her clit moving along the big vein.

Then she lifts herself a little, moves me to the entrance
(oh, God, she's *so* wet!) and slides onto me, bending over
to rest full-length on me, lips nuzzling my neck as we
thrust at each other. And soon we're both on the verge of
coming, her lips leave my neck and cover my mouth. Her
nipples bore through my chest and I feel her pussy con-

tracting around my cock, *hard*, again and again, and I want to watch her come so I pull her lips away and see them curve into a smile as she opens her eyes, staring at me as I begin to come, nothing like the joyless singles-bar balling—it rumbles inside me and I feel it, it's so *hot*, spurting up and out of me, each new shot triggering another and oh, God, I feel so empty—it's as if I really have given myself to *her*!

At this point in the fantasy (which, strangely, is a recurring wet dream!) I have the orgasm I describe—in my sleep! Sometimes I lay in my room, stoned, reliving my fantasy and masturbating, sometimes I relive it when I'm balling a pickup, but never—NEVER—do I think of it in school! The results would be too embarrassing. Besides, I think that for me, the time has come to stop bar hopping, gather my courage and ask her out so we might work on making that fantasy reality!

CONRAD

I have always suffered from guilt feelings and even self-reproach because I knew, even as a small boy, that I had feelings which my parents and peers would not approve of. And thus I have shown one face to the world and concealed quite a different one.

There is nothing extraordinary about me: I'm in my forties, middle-class, reasonably attractive for my age . . . nothing about my physique or personality could be considered outstanding. I am married and have a good relationship with my wife. Our marriage is not perfect, but neither of us expects it to be. There have been times when I tried to share my fantasies with my wife and she tried to understand. The fact that I'm unable to really convey my needs to her is not her fault. She has done a better job accepting and adjusting to the role that society has told her she must accept. I have encouraged her to share her fantasies with me and had some success. Nothing of what she has told me could be considered bizarre, but I may have failed to really dissolve her inhibitions. My problem is that I had hoped her fantasies would be compatible to my own, but that isn't

very realistic or reasonable. I find it better to encourage
her to be what she wants to be in sexual imagery, and
allow my own little fixations to remain dormant.

As a boy I was not very athletic and was never competitive or aggressive. The idea that I had to "win" the affections of a girl and "sweep her off her feet" only seemed
awkward and foolish to me. I was a backward adolescent
and very slow to mature, and slower still to develop rapport with girls. I was always attracted to the more gregarious and outgoing types, but they never seemed interested
in me. I found myself waiting for the girls of my choice to
take the initiative . . . which, of course, they never did.
Obviously, I did eventually get to the point where I asked
girls out, but I found making sexual advances very difficult. I still do.

My earliest sexual desires or fantasies were always of
large healthy girls, who would aggressively make all the
advances. I didn't realize till years later that I wanted to be
mothered and even dominated by a woman. But, as I came
to realize it, I felt deeply ashamed of myself for having
such unmasculine thoughts. What would my male friends
think? What would they think even today? When I was in
my twenties I was convinced that I was a latent homosexual . . . even though I've always found men to be sexually repulsive. (In that respect, I've never understood how
you women can stand us . . . thank heaven you do!) I
suppose I've always attempted to overcompensate for what
I felt was my "deformed" or perverted sexuality by being a
shade macho in my everyday life and marrying a feminine,
"straight" girl with a nice "straight" marriage. Let me explain that I find her femininity very attractive. But I always
"wear the pants." I must fulfill the cultural role. In reality,
I've always dreamed of a woman who would be the final
authority over my very life . . . who would always be resourceful and responsible for us both and, most important,
who would always be the sexual aggressor.

Considering all the cultural taboos and mores which
brand such feelings as warped and maladjusted or unnatural, I never imagined that there could ever be a woman
who had instincts like this. Since reading your books, I'm
not so sure how many such women there may be.

Incredibly, my fantasy did indeed temporarily come true

several years ago. I met a woman a few years younger than myself when I was very nearly forty, and we had an affair. It lasted several years. I don't know why it ended unless she simply wearied of our fantasy game and wanted something more. But while it lasted, it was beautiful. After we met, I found I could communicate with her as I had never done with anyone before. It wasn't simply that she understood my dreams . . . she "dug" them. She became very aroused when I explained them to her and she did indeed become the aggressor.

She loved to be on top when we made love and could achieve orgasm in no other way . . . she had to be in control at all times and, to me, it was like being born again! I cannot describe the wild sort of abandonment to ecstasy I felt by just lying underneath her for hours at a time in completely helpless surrender to her ravenous cunt. She would thrust her hips so furiously when she climaxed it felt as though she was about to suck my entire body up into her big, beautiful hot mother hole! She would reach her shuddering orgasm and then remain on top of me with her lovely thighs locked around me while she'd recuperate. In the meantime, she would not allow me to come but would still be holding my throbbing little cock up inside the wet furnace of her vagina. Soon she'd start pumping again without ever releasing me. If I couldn't stand the sweet sensations anymore, I'd tell her before I came. Then she'd stop pumping for a short time, and begin what she called "slow fucking." She would fuck me very, very slowly . . . expertly easing my little stiff stander all the way out and all the way in and never increasing that maddeningly slow rhythm. In the meantime, she always held me down with one hand under my ass . . . sometimes with a finger up my rectum and would not allow me to move. She was fucking me and not the other way around . . . she wanted that understood. And I loved it and loved her too. I loved her big hot beautiful cunt. It was like a sacred altar to me . . . the place of creation. She would come many times and when she was finally finished using me, she'd let me come with her.

I don't know why she gave up on me. It all seems like a fantasy when I look back on those few years. But it really happened! Even if she never calls me again, I know I'll never forget her; never stop fantasizing about her.

NED

I have fantasized about sex almost every day since my teens, if not before. I repressed the fact that most of my fantasies involved female dominance; and it was only a few years ago, in my mid-twenties, that I finally acknowledged this unfulfilled need in myself. My wife's preferences were for traditional male dominance, so I always took the aggressive role; but I was often anxious about sex.

Recently, my wife has begun to take a more active and aggressive role; and we have sex more often as a result, since now either of us is likely to initiate sex. My wife is very responsive sexually, so I am pleased with our sex life; but I do realize that sometimes she would be more satisfied sexually by a more aggressive male.

I am a professional man. When I was young, my father was often away from home on business. While I did not have a strict upbringing, my parents did set a strong moral tone. I generally was a good little boy who followed the rules.

Fortunately, a woman friend loaned me a copy of *My Secret Garden*, which naturally aroused me at times; and now I regard my autoeroticism as a tribute to the women whose fantasies aroused me so! It was particularly exciting to me to know that somewhere a real woman existed whose idea of ecstasy was so close to mine, at least, my own fantasies. I could imagine meeting such a woman, but even just knowing she really existed was enough. I like to think that somewhere a woman will read the creation of my mind and find some satisfaction or pleasure in it.

Fantasy Number One: I am on a beach with a tall, blond girl. No one else is there. She is very muscular and athletic looking. She smiles and asks me to rub some tanning oil on her back. As I do, she unsnaps the back of her swimsuit top and takes it off. I am excited but a little put off by her aggressiveness. She turns around and has me rub oil on her large tan breasts. Then she rubs oil on my chest as I lie on my back.

Suddenly, she grabs my swim trunks and starts to pull them down; but I grab them and protest. She grabs one of my wrists and twists it behind my back. She is very strong and powerful, and wrestles me down on my back. As she holds the one arm behind my back, she is holding the other wrist down, her legs wrapped around one of mine so that I am pinned down, with her on top. Her oily breasts rub against my chest and she kisses me so hard she almost bruises my lips. When I resist, she twists my arm further until I stop fighting. She forces her tongue deep into my mouth; and I can feel her thigh pressing into my crotch, giving me an erection.

She pulls my suit down with one hand, twisting my arm as I try to resist. I try to push her off, but she is stronger, and it is no use. She mounts me as she holds both my hands down, and I can see her large oily breasts flopping as she moves up and down on me. She looks down at me in triumph and excitement, and breathes deeply with each stroke. I am willing now, and I feel the tightness of her cunt around my shaft as she works me up to a beautiful climax.

Fantasy Number Two: My wife and I have a male visitor, who is staying in a room in our house. He is very strong and handsome, and I can tell she is attracted to him. I ask her if she would like to have sex with him, and she is obviously excited at the idea. I tell her I will not object if she goes to him that night, if she just has a "quickie" and then comes to bed with me. That night I go to bed a little early, and later I hear them go into his room down the hallway from ours.

Later, there are sounds of bed springs and my wife's moaning. I hear the door of his room open, and my wife says she has to go now. He says he isn't satisfied yet; and though she protests loudly, I can hear them grappling in the hallway near my door. She pleads with him not to, but he insists that he will have her right there. I am excited but afraid to open my door. She shrieks, but there is sexual excitement in her cries. Her excited shrieks of pleasure gradually become moans, louder and more soulful than she has ever had with me.

Finally her moans are low and sobbing. I hear footsteps down the hall to his room. The door to my room opens; and she comes in, clutching her torn clothes. She gets into bed with me and complains that he was too rough, but I can tell she deeply enjoyed the experience. As I embrace her and enter her, she trembles all over, but her trembling is as much for him as it is for me.

Michael (above) gives us an example of someone gripped by the macho imperative society has dealt him, unhappy with it, but unable to move beyond it except in fantasy. The conflict can be heard in his own words. He is the kind of man who gets angry when a woman's high heels make her taller than he, but he "fantasizes being raped—by a woman." The dash in this sentence denotes his astonishment, but does the event arouse his male fury? No. "I'm really *caring* about pleasing her," he says. "It's as if I've really given myself to her"—something he has not been able to do with his real-life one-night stands. What bewilders and shocks him is that once he's relieved of the necessity for being ever dominant, his tenderness comes out.

If Michael were a masochist, he might pick a whore or a lady wrestler as his aggressive, conquering antagonist. Instead, he chooses "sweet looking" Evelyn, "not a bit like what myself and my buddies find, feel, fuck and forget on the singles bar scene." He dolefully admits he is a product of the "all-American male double standard"—an admission I doubt really embarrasses him. Conceding you're a male chauvinist may make you a pig to a feminist, but it certainly does not make you less of a man, at least in your own eyes. In fact, much as his fantasy turns him on, Michael will probably marry an Evelyn, whom he will put on a pedestal at home, while continuing on to find, fuck, and forget other, less sweet women . . . wondering all the while why he never found his dream girl.

If Michael is an example of how the new male attitudes toward tenderness have not yet been fully integrated into the contemporary male character, Conrad seems more all of a piece; his desire to be seduced in fantasy seems to be more closely meshed with what he is like in real life—he is gentle, less aggressive than Michael. Conrad's plight is equal and opposite to the position of those women—also victims of society's war against individual temperament—who are basically sexually aggressive, but who repress these desires for fear they are "unwomanly."

Then we have Ned. His two fantasies map his basic split. In the first, the woman takes the lead—as he has always wished. But the second fantasy shows identification with the man who brutally tears his wife's nightgown—an image of traditional, overpowering male sexuality.

It is notorious that in times of stress such as ours, when both sexes are trying to break out of limiting roles, people become anxious that they have gone too far, and fall back on older, more conventional forms first learned in childhood. The model for this is in childhood itself: The baby goes crawling away from mother to explore the fascinating new world in the next room, then becomes frightened at finding itself alone in new circumstances. It comes rushing back to mother's skirts.

Ned's first fantasy about women taking the lead is new and unexplored territory to him. It is exciting, but fearsome, too, stirring up anxieties of loss of masculinity. Ned hastens back to safety, dreaming up a second fantasy, one that posits old-fashioned notions about barbed-wire masculinity.

The ideas in the air today on gender identity and role reversal are so new, so untested, that neither sex feel they can completely trust the other to play their part wholeheartedly. No matter how a man may fantasize about sexually assertive, take-charge women, he often becomes inhibited when he meets one in real life.

There can be several reasons for this. First, while it feels good to be sexually done to in fantasy where you control everything—no pain or humiliation—it is not so easy to find the right woman or situation in reality. Second, while fantasies end in glorious climaxes, real relationships go on the next morning. It may feel good to give in to the woman the night before; but when she continues her assertive ways in front of your friends, it is less appealing.

A man meets an up-front woman who says, "Let's skip the movie and just go back to my place right now." She tells him what she wants. She likes her nipples sucked, she

likes her oral sex this way and not that. At one point she
may take over and command him to just lie there while she
does this and that wonderful thing to him. When they say
good-bye that night or the next morning, does he just feel
it, does he see it in her eyes, or does she actually say—all
hope and yearning dependence—"Will you call tonight?
When will I be seeing you again?" Last night's sex began
as shared responsibility; she even implied it was all her
idea; but intimacy has a way of regressing us, and the
morning sun shines now on a curious reversal. He has re-
treated back into his role as the man who takes care of the
woman. She has once again become someone who wants to
be taken care of, someone who ever needs to see sex in
terms of romance, growing intimacy, and a hold on him.

And so it goes. Men and women long to meet on some
new, common ground fertile to happiness; but the profound revolution of freedom for both sexes cannot be won
just by declaring you are different; we do not change
merely because we've read a few magazine articles or
books such as this. Attitudes and action can almost be said
to be functions of the will. We can decide that we like this,
or want to do that. What we feel in our gut moves to a
much slower rhythm, and in accordance with emotional
developments that have a life of their own. Our deepest
feelings—what we learned from our parents—change between generations, if they change at all.

We take one step backward for every step and a half
forward. Many women have found to their sorrow that
men sigh for up-front women, but once they are back in his
apartment, things are different. She excuses herself to go to
the bathroom and emerges stark naked—only to find he is
put off by her cool, in-control manner.

This is one of the characteristic sexual impasses of our
time. The man may turn angry or impotent; the woman
feels she could kill herself for shame. To confuse what we
want in fantasy with what we can handle in reality is naive.

GILBERT

I had a relatively uneventful life until puberty. Early puberty was a wrestling match between God and the Devil. Finally, I gave in to sexual fantasies (with guilt for a while) and during one of these I came for the first time at age fourteen. Since then until now (age thirty-eight) I have only come about once or twice without a fantasy. The range of these fantasies has covered almost everything. The greatest variety occurred during my young years while masturbating.

The Sexy Female is the most powerful theme. She takes many forms but the basis for her existence is related to a "human female in heat" who will do almost anything to get the sex "she *needs*"! She has to have it—and some male(s) have to give it to her any and all ways. She needs her pussy licked and I or someone else has to do it. She needs to be fucked and I or someone else has to give it to her. It is her strong powerful desire that triggers my desires. She is sometimes sophisticated, sometimes a floozie, sometimes a straight woman trying to be "good" (but her sexual desires are too strong). We do it her way and I'm glad. I can love her like a male would and I can love her like a lesbian would.

My current fantasy involves my wife and allowing her sexual identity to go as far as it can go. Fantasy and reality get mixed together. I come to her pleasure, her excitement, her thrills, her "jumping for joy," her emotions—and I come often. I have fucked numerous women, but can never come except with a fantasy. My wife is too fucking sexy and I love every minute of it!

MORT

I'm only sixteen, but have an okay sex life. I'm an artist (love to paint girls). I'm fairly tall (6'1") and get an erection the second someone says *girl*(s).

They say guys don't fantasize but I fantasize quite a bit. It goes something like this:

It's a heat-wave type of day at a sandy beach. I'm walking down the beach looking at the girls. They get up one by one and follow me. Then I go back toward some woods beyond the beach. (By now I am calmly masturbating.) All of a sudden the girls all jump on me. I start eating out one, but there are so many I never get a chance to finish on one of them. They are kissing and licking me like crazy! One is sucking on my cock and another licking my balls. I come, and then tell them that they all can suck on me. By now I really come, and this one ends. For some reason I don't lose my erection.

I usually read or look at books and magazines when masturbating. I go to the bathroom and sit on the "pot." I like to look at hot cunts in magazines. They turn me on past no return. Sometimes if I am feeling guilty, my fantasy answers by having the girls bite off or stomp on my dick.

CLEMENT

I am 27, and my only sexual experience has been with prostitutes since I am quite shy and socially introverted. However, I do masturbate frequently and have fantasies while doing so. In most all cases they involve sexually aggressive women.

For example, in fantasy number one a woman in a leather jumpsuit holds me on the bed and essentially rapes me, holding me tight and giving me deep soul kisses. Sometimes she straps on a dildo and shoves it up my ass.

In fantasy number two it is a female vampire who while sucking my neck is sucking on my dick with her pussy. This really brings me off.

And in fantasy number three I am a beautiful lesbian and can feel what my lover feels when we make love. I've even had a dream about such an experience and did I ever hate to wake up.

The women in these and other fantasies actively work at making love to me. I suppose it is society's requirement that men always be the aggressor; and yet, I do wish that I someday could find a woman who will take some of the pressure to perform onto herself. Hopefully I am not the only man to feel this way.

DEKE

I have gone to a strange apartment to deliver a package. A beautiful girl answers the door and lets me in. She has long honey-blond hair, a sexy face and a superb set of high, firm tits. She has on a pair of red "hot pants," a tight white silklike blouse, and a pair of eight-inch high heels with small black straps that have tiny padlocks on them instead of regular straps. As I hand her the package, she "accidently" pushes her breasts against my arm and I feel her erect nipples through the taut cloth. I notice her eyes giving me the "once over," but they linger on my crotch. I notice also that there are several pairs of panties laying around and a bunch of brassieres with locks on the couch.

Then her roommate walks in; and I can feel my eyes bulge. She is a luscious redhead with a tiny waist, big green eyes and she is wearing only a pair of black lace bikini panties and the eight-inch high-heel shoes with the tiny locks. Her bare breasts are firm, round globes of bouncing flesh, each crested with a hard pink nipple on a tan, quarter-size aureola. She comes right up to me and puts her arms around me and gives me such a long, warm, lingering kiss—I can feel my cock "come to attention" as she presses against my body. My hands find her breasts and I'm squeezing them as she pushes her tongue into my mouth. They offer me a "Whiskey Sour" and turn on the hi-fi. I take turns dancing with them and they tell me their names. The blond one is Mona and the redhead is Laura. While I dance with Mona, my hands slip down on her buttocks and find their way under her tight blouse. Her boobs are superb also, with erect nipples that I can feel as I thrust my hand inside her 38D bra.

Then with Laura helping hold Mona, I suddenly unbutton the blouse and unhook the bra, and peel off the tight red hot pants. She is laughing and gasping as we hold her down on the rug and we wrestle around. I kiss her big breasts and flat belly as Laura works Mona's panties down her squirming bottom, and pulls them off her long legs. I have Mona's nipples in my mouth, sucking them eagerly, as I feel Laura's hand grab my stiffening cock; her hand pushes between my legs and she proceeds to stroke me into a full erection. Having unzipped my pants, opened my belt and pulled off my pants and slipped off my Jockey shorts, Laura then brings out a black leather "harness" with all kinds of belts and velvet ropes, which she straps onto Mona's body. As I watch, the young woman is bound with the thing. It is like a corset with a full zipper on the back, but straps on the sides, allowing a person's arms to be secured in place. Mona's full breasts are thrust up and bulge seductively as the cups grip her snugly and velvet ropes bind her ankles and wrists. A leather gag with a rubber ball fixed to it is inserted into her open mouth and she is "finished."

We lift Mona and place her on a large queen-sized bed in the girls' bedroom, and Laura puts a record on the stereo. It is Ravel's *Bolero*, and at Laura's urging, I place myself at her service and follow her suggestions. The music begins slow, and I guide my stiff cock slowly into Mona's parted thighs and thrust into her damp cleft. The music gradually gets louder and my hip action tries to match the tempo of the music as I plunge deep into her. Mona's eyes are wide and she is moaning deep in her throat; her hands opening and closing and her hips moving up to meet me with each stroke. As the classical piece nears the end, I can feel her body tense and a pressure building up in my loins, and I speed up. Then the climax and I erupt in a series of tremendous pulsations, as the record comes to an end.

Out of what notion of human nature comes the widespread feeling that men are terrifically nonmonogamous fellows who feel no sexual guilt at all? In reality, no boy goes through the oedipal stages of life without learning inhibition; but the role playing goes on—men must at least pretend to feel no shyness or guilt. Women are the ones who usually resort to erotic imaginings for encouragement to let go. Gilbert is one of the few men I've heard from who cannot climax—during masturbation or intercourse—without the guilt-melting heat of fantasy.

His anxiety about approaching a woman is so strong that he must imagine that it is not his idea; she will do almost anything to get the sex *she* needs. It is the woman's idea. She is in heat; Gilbert carries none of the blame.

The fantasy of the sexually ravenous woman handles almost any amount of male inhibition. The mythical woman is so enraged with lust, *so fevered*, that it might be said the man is closer to giving her medical treatment than seducing her. "Yes, yes, YES!" she signals him. "If you take me to bed, you are not hurting me, not doing anything wrong. You are saving my life!"

Mort (above) gives us a message from the Freudian unconscious, furnishing evidence of how close to aggression and violence many men feel sex to be. When Mort looks at nudie magazines, he feels anxious because he imagines women will seek revenge: "If I am feeling guilty . . . the girls bite off or stomp on my dick."

But the notion of castration gets no more than five or ten words from Mort—very little for an idea that, if truly feared, would be of the first magnitude. The rest of what he tells us is how lovely imaginary, sexually aggressive women are to him. The emotions at issue in this chapter are not so much sadistic as redolent of *Tea and Sympathy*.

DAYTON

I am married, twenty-eight; and for a long time, my sexual fantasies were centered around two subjects.

I am always aroused by the thought of making love, or engaging in any sexual activity, with a thirty-five- or forty-five-year-old married woman, or just seeing a nude picture of such a woman. I always like the look and the feel of a mature naked female body and an experienced cunt. I imagine a married forty-year-old housewife who was our neighbor when I was young. She is alone at home; her husband is at work. She invites me to her house, the reason being to help her move some heavy objects. It is just a half-hour job. After we are done, she invites me to stay for a soft drink and cake. Then she tells me to sit around because she has to change her clothes.

After I have been sitting for over fifteen minutes and she hasn't returned, I kind of wonder what has happened to her. I walk toward the bedroom, and the door is slightly open. To my surprise, she is lying on the bed and has taken off her top and slid her pants off her hips. She kicks them away with her foot. Now she is in her bra and panties. She has a full body and very good curves for her age, and she is very nice looking. Now she runs her hands down from her neck to her bra and reaches back and unfastens it. She starts to fondle her thirty-six-inch breasts. She is very aroused. Then she moves her hands downward over her belly and reaches inside her panties and starts to play with her cunt. She then takes them off and her beautiful cunt is in full view. To my surprise, she has a shaved cunt with just a slight trace of hair. By this time, my heart is beating rapidly. I am concentrating so hard I accidentally push the door open. I am very frightened and do not know what to do. She walks toward me and pats my shoulder and whispers, "It's okay." She guides me to her bed and begins to take off all my clothes. She bends down and starts to suck my penis, a feeling that I never experienced in my life. She then guides my hand all over her body. When I touch her shaven cunt, it's very wet. She reaches down and clues me to finger fuck her. It feels warm and wet. She reaches over with her hand and lowers my head toward her cunt. She wants me to suck her cunt. That is one of my greatest sexual fantasies.

RUDY

The first time I saw her, I wasn't prepared for that kind of a happening.

I had been thumbing my way west, hoping to reach the Pacific coast before I ran out of money, and doing all right. I had been on the road for two days, and had covered a thousand miles.

The red convertible came over the hilltop like a rocket.

Its pipes were screaming and the chrome glistening in the sun. I could tell by the speed it was coming that there was no room for me in there, so I didn't even put out my thumb. Then to my amazement that big red monster fish-tailed to a halt a dozen yards up the road. I was so surprised, I just stood there gawking. The tires screeched in protest as she gunned the motor and reversed back down the road to where I stood.

"Want a lift or don'cha?" she asked in a husky southern drawl.

"Yes, ma'am!" I replied, getting my head together.

"Well, plant your butt and let's git it on the road." She was smiling, and the twinkle in her eye told me this was going to be one good ride. I dumped my stuff in the back and slid into the bucket next to hers. She drifted into low and come off the clutch like a teenybopper. She went through the gears like Parnelli Jones and when she was finished we were sizzling along at eighty miles per. Then she looked at me and winked.

"Hold on, honey, I cain't drive but I sure do aim this thing," she said. Then she laughed. It was a deep throaty laugh, rich and full like she was. She was tall, maybe six foot, with long legs and big beautiful feet. She was clad only in the briefest of summer frocks, that crept up those long legs almost into her lap. She drove barefoot with her legs and arms stretched out straight in front of her. Her ample bosom bounced freely as the car hurtled over the uneven road. I just watched her, fascinated, as she drove. She was almost a part of that big red machine, coaxing every last ounce of power and performance out of it, her long slender fingers wrapped loosely around the wheel. I had ridden with fast drivers before and had even felt safe with one or two of them, but she drove with such ease and self-confidence that in no time I was completely comfortable at her side. The phrase "she drove like a man" comes to mind but I can hardly remember any man who drove that well.

Her skin was like black velvet, smooth and soft; it almost glowed with life. Her bold Afro features were like an ebony carving. Her mouth was full with sensuous lips and big white teeth that flashed at me as she talked. Her nose was large but perfectly formed with a little upturn at the end. Her neck was long and graceful, tapering to good square shoulders that rippled with her almost masculine strength. Her ribcage was big and her breasts sat high and handsome on it, full and firm with a glorious valley between them. The skimpiness of her dress revealed large firm nipples that strained eagerly against it. It was obvious that this girl was turned on with her driving and the power she controlled. Her body tapered beneath her breasts to a small waist and immediately flared again, flowing into large firm hips and a flat plane of a stomach and round soft buttocks. My inner eye ate her up like a big piece of chocolate cake.

To make matters worse for my warming loins, that dress, as she drove, crept ever upward into the luscious lap. Soon I was able to glimpse the stark white of her panties and the glorious arch of her mons jutting against the thin material. I couldn't help but stare. She carelessly let her left leg slip sideways as she pushed her pelvis slightly forward in the seat. The effect was electrifying. The taut material of her panties dug into her pussy, outlining the firm pouting lips.

"You sure look hungry, boy," she said, coyly grinning. "If you don't talk to me I'll have to cover it up."

I felt the blood rush to my cheeks as she laughed that deep throaty laugh. My cock was twitching like crazy, trying to make an erection in my tight jeans. I felt like a schoolboy who had just been caught jerking off in the john. I wanted to apologize but her freedom about the matter stopped me cold. She knew what she was doing to me with her body and just plain didn't give a damn.

Her left hand lay in her lap and her index finger was idly stroking the indentation in the crotch of her panties. I wanted to reach out but I was paralyzed. Then, pushing up the hem of her dress, her hand slipped beneath the elastic of her panties. I watched, spellbound, as her fingers slid over her abdomen, and down between those waiting lips. I saw her middle finger arch and bury itself within her. She was masturbating, right there in front of me! I raised my hand to reach for her but she stopped me cold with a word.

"Don't." Her voice had picked up a bit of an edge. "We are going eighty miles an hour and I am running this thing.

You seemed to want a show, well, I'm giving you one, but don't reach for me, it could kill us both." I couldn't help myself. My eyes were riveted to her crotch. Then as if it weren't enough she lifted her ass off the seat and pushed down on her panties. There it was, in all its voluptuous glory. A huge puff of curly black hair, the crimson head of her clit just barely peeking out. The full inner lips gleamed with a coating of her sweet juices.

"Isn't it pretty?" she asked softly. "It tastes even better than it looks. I may even let you have some later, but right now I just want you to see me. Now I'm going to ask you to do something for me, but I don't want you to get carried away. I want you to take these damn pants off, but that's all. Don't try to touch me or we may both wind up dead."

I was ready to do anything, so I reached forward slowly and hooked my thumbs beneath the elastic of her panties and pushed them down toward her feet. She pulled her left foot free and spread her legs. From where I was positioned I could look right into her sweet little honey pot, and I could almost taste the sweet moistness of it. I sat back and watched as she thrust two fingers into herself. She sighed, and her finger came out wet. Then she reached out slowly with her hand and ran her glistening fingertips across my lips. She dipped them again and repeated the move. This time I opened my mouth and sucked the sweetness from her fingers.

Then when I thought I couldn't take another second of just sitting there watching that beautiful pussy, her foot came off the accelerator and slid onto the brakes. A side road was coming up fast on the right. The tires screamed as she brought the big car to a halt just past the turn. She jammed it into reverse and backed around out of sight of the main road. Then she reached forward and killed the motor; flopping back in her seat, she puffed like a steam engine.

Then she opened the door and slid out of the car, flopping on her back in the tall grass at the side of the road. I needed no invitation, I was out of the car and around to her side in two seconds flat.

She closed her eyes and smilingly held out her hand to me. I dropped to my knees beside her and slid my hand softly up her thigh. My fingers felt numb as I touched the crinkly curls on her mons. She reached down with her hands and scooped up her dress, drawing it off over her head. She was magnificent, lying there with the sun bathing her in her naked beauty. I moaned with joy as I lurched forward and buried my face in her. Her velvety thighs closed around my head and I could feel the soft skin against my ears as I stretched out my tongue into her tunnel of love.

I ran my tongue back and forth across her throbbing clit; then, pursing my lips, I drew it into my mouth, sucking as hard as I could. I thrust my chin against her buttocks and drove my face into the very depths of her. I felt her fingers in my hair pulling me even tighter to her. My face was smeared with her juices and I could barely breathe. Her legs were locked so tightly around my head that the muscles in the back of my neck ached, but I was oblivious to the pain. That hot sweet cunt was on fire in my mouth, and she was like a wild thing, thrusting and bucking as she came again and again. Finally I could stand no more. I tore my head from between her legs, clawing at my clothing in my frenzy to be free of it. Then I was nude and my cock found its own way, piercing the lips of her cunt and sinking deep inside. I could feel her throbbing pussy practically eating me alive. I wanted to just stay there and savor it, but there was no controlling her. She arched wildly, thrusting her pelvis up to me in her panic to have more of me. As we came closer and closer I could feel nothing but that hot cunt sucking the very life from me. Then like bolts of lightning from deep within my guts came the hot cum coursing through my aching cock and filling her. Her legs wrapped around my hips like a vise and she screamed and sank her teeth into my shoulder.

After a long time I rolled off of her and she came to me and pressed her warm wet body against me and we slept.

LOWRY

A constant fantasy is myself with an older woman. I would love to have an affair with a more mature, refined, enthusiastic and horny woman. The age to which I refer is thirty-five to possibly fifty, but my fantasies usually end at forty-five. You would be surprised at the number of men my age that are dying to make it with a more mature lover.

I fantasize about meeting this woman at a bar, restaurant, or grocery store. She is a cashier, a secretary, the woman down the street, a teacher; but usually it is an Avon lady and I am the only one home. She enters. I sit on one side of the room, and she begins to tell me of the products she has. I start to think of her sucking my cock or of her cunt with her legs spread apart. She asks if I would like to move closer and see what she is selling. I get up to move closer and she notices that I have a big hard-on, and I notice that she notices. She looks at me, smiles, and licks her lips. I ask her not to be offended but that I would like to show her my cock. She says that she would like that, and I pull my pants down to my knees. As I do this, my cock spring out and bounces up and down. She touches it and comments about how pretty it is. I ask her if there is anything I can do for her, and she tells me to get totally nude. I do this, and she asks me to walk around the room as she looks at me. I walk over to her, and she tells me to bend over. She then looks at my asshole and tells me to lie down on the coffee table on my back. She then begins to jerk me off and lightly tongues the head of my cock. She stops, stands up, and instructs me to pull her panties down as she pulls up her skirt. I do this and she asks me to kiss and lick her all over her legs and butt. She then stands with her legs very wide apart, and I bury my head and tongue as far up her cunt as I can. Her whole body trembles as she reaches orgasm. She then sits down and tells me to come close to her. I do and she puts my cock in her mouth and sucks me until I come and she swallows my sperm. She then dresses, kisses me, and leaves.

I love to please my lover, and I have never forced any of my sex mates to do anything that they didn't want to do. To use force for sex repulses me.

LENNIE

I am twenty-four years old and single. My fantasies almost always happen when I am masturbating.

Fantasy Number One: This fantasy concerns a make-believe happening between myself and two real people that I know. I am alone at my cousin's house when the doorbell rings. I answer the door and it is his mother-in-law, Marge (fictitious name). She wants to know if John or Debi (also fictitious) are there. I tell her they aren't. She says she'll wait for them if it's okay. I don't see any reason why not and let her in. She is not overly beautiful but is quite attractive for forty-five years old.

There is a book on the table that I've been reading. It is what we used to call a "dirty book" or "fuck book." Marge looks at the book, looks up at me, and then she picks it up and starts to page through it. While she is reading it I am getting a terrific erection just reliving some parts of it in my head. She then says to me that some parts of it are very erotic. I agree with her and to my surprise, because I am very shy, I ask her which part she is reading. She turns toward me on the couch, which makes her skirt ride up on her thighs and I can see her panties. She says she is reading about the man and woman having oral sex with each other.

She then begins to read out loud from the book. Finally I can't control myself any longer and reached over and kiss her violently. She comes alive immediately. Her hands unzip my trousers and she gives me the best blow job I've ever had. Pretty soon we are both naked on the living room floor fucking like mad. Suddenly, we are joined by Debi who is twenty-one and Marge's daughter. She has returned unknown to either of us. She has taken off all of her clothes and is masturbating while Marge is on top of me sliding up and down my hard-on. I have Debi squat above my mouth and I begin to tongue her madly. We are all in this most pleasant state of being for a while until Debi climaxes, which makes me explode, and this causes Marge to have a tremendous orgasm. I also come in real life at this time too.

If this fantasy ever came true I would love it. But as I say, I am quite shy and could never make it happen by myself.

Fantasy Number Two: I am at home alone when the Avon lady comes to the door. She says she is new and would like to get to know her customers. I invite her in and we look at her samples of men's products. She is forty to forty-five, quite attractive, and has on a rather short skirt which shows off her shapely legs. I have an aching hard-on after a few minutes from wondering what she would look like naked (I often imagine this about women I see). I sort of shift positions to be more comfortable because of my erection. She then looks at the bulge in my pants and says, "Here, let me help you." She reaches over, unzips my trousers and takes out my cock. She plays with it and then we have oral sex and intercourse with each other all afternoon until she must go.

KENT

I have never revealed this fantasy to anyone for the same reason that prompts me to keep this letter anonymous. I am a professor of psychology at a fairly large university; neither age (I'm fifty-six) nor my own sessions in therapy, however, have rid me of my "fear of being found out," a deep-seated guilt complex of a sort. Both my fantasy and the reason I'd never act it out involve this fear. It's a classic situation: having sex with a student.

The student in my fantasy is a real person, a young woman who was in an advanced seminar of mine several years ago. She is dark, Italian looking, and almost scarecrow thin except for large breasts. I imagine that she has come to my on-campus apartment one evening ostensibly to discuss her applications to graduate school programs in clinical psychology. Competition for these programs is fierce, and she wants my advice and recommendations. Her gestures, looks, and attention reveal nonacademic interest in me, however. (My wife, age forty and also a psychologist, is away for the week; I have no children from this marriage.) I offer her refreshments and she accompanies me into the kitchen, brushing against me now and then. We are having rather a comfortable discussion as she is very bright and asks provoking questions; but although I am very attracted to her and am feeling relaxed (we've had some wine), I cannot make a pass at her for fear I'm reading too much into her behavior and that she will tell others. She turns the subject to sex, though, asking me about the effects of drugs on sex (I'd implied in class that I have used heroin, which I have), and moves closer. She touches me cautiously and casually as we talk about this, then becomes bolder and slides her hand toward my crotch. She sees and feels my response, and moves closer, unbuttoning her blouse at the same time. Now I can respond more actively, and we go to my bedroom. She undoes my pants and undresses herself as she sucks me, then comes up underneath me on the bed, telling me as we fuck how she nearly goes crazy just watching me in class. Then she comes, several times, holding me tighter as she does and moving her hands up and down my back and sides and rear, as I feel her breasts and the rest of her body. Finally I come and then she nestles up against me, still caressing me. Sometimes I worry that others in the building have seen her come in and heard us; she promises not to tell anyone about our liaison.

From here my fantasy varies: Sometimes she stays the night and we fuck several times in the morning (something my wife doesn't like to do); other times we agree to keep meeting and she comes to my office regularly; sometimes I picture meeting her again a few years from now as a colleague, when she has her doctorate, perhaps at a meeting of some sort, and having a sexual reunion. Occasionally I imagine that after our first night she becomes pregnant, and as she walks about campus later on obviously showing and, later still, pushing our son in a stroller, only she and I are aware that I am the father. My wife of course remains ignorant of all of this as well.

This fantasy remains more of a daydream, although I sometimes call it to mind before retiring for the evening with my wife. She and I have discussed fantasies, but I have never told her this one, and in fact I am nervous writing it as she is in the next room at this moment. However, writing it out has been enjoyable.

P.S. I notice as I reread this that I am rather hazy on
the details of the actual sex. In fact, it *is* the situation and
the action *preceding* the sex that is most exciting to me!

If a woman asks a man to go down on her, is he passive
for following her orders? Or might it be said that he is the
one conducting the sexual proceedings, while she passively
accepts? A third point of view reverses definitions once
again: In sex performed this way, the woman will climax
while the man usually does not. Is she the more active sexual partner even though he is the one making it happen?

A more useful word might be to say that the man is not
so much passive as agreeable or *receptive* to the woman's
idea. Dayton (above) is invited into the bedroom, Rudy
(above) is literally kidnapped by a woman who leads him
into sex at eighty miles an hour. He says "She drives like a
man"—endowing the woman for once with the manly
qualities he is tired of carrying.

Lowry (above) sees himself in the position of the child.
The wished-for older woman does not tell him sex is a
naughty, but leads him into it instead, step by step—a fine
example of how fantasy uses the very stuff of everyday life
to work its magic, changing red lights to green, turning old
frustrations around so they become pleasures instead.

It is as if, entering the risky or forbidden area of sex,
these men want a masterful woman to show them the way.
Permission is often given in so many words, just at the
moment when the man is undecided about following
through on her seductive invitation. "It's all right," these
fantasy women say. "It's okay." From this realization of
men's need for permission, the next step becomes obvious:
Characteristic of fantasies like these is that the women are
often considerably older than the man, "old enough to be
his mother."

I do not wish to be understood as saying that the men in
this chapter are all looking for mother figures. What they
want is the kind of person mother once stood for—a powerful, grown-up woman. Someone they won't have to
worry about, who is capable of taking care of herself, and
even him, if need be.

These are very special leading ladies, prototypes not easily found in everyday life. Women have the milkman, the gas meter reader, the Fuller Brush salesman—men who carry the safety of the stranger we need never see again. Where is a man going to get the image of a woman who just walks up and rings his bell?

Enter the Avon lady, carrying a whole suitcase of tricks a guy doesn't even have to ask to see.

She is one of the great heroines of men's fantasies. Leaving out prostitutes—who come trailing an entirely different set of emotions—it is hard for a man even in our permissive times to get laid without strings. The girl he fucked the night before is already on the phone, saying she can't work today for thinking about him; but the Avon lady is too busy for all that. She has other houses to call on, other people to see, a living to earn. She comes and goes (all puns intended) just like a man

JASON

My fantasies take place on another planet. I board a submarine tied to a dock. It is usually night or dusk. I am Victor Laszlo without my wife, a lone fugitive—not from the law, but from life on shore.

The marvelous undersea cruiser has an all-woman crew, but I want nothing to do with them. I retire to my bunk and am asleep before we leave.

Sometime in the night the captain awakens me. I accompany her to the control room where she dims all instrument lights to a dull green and rolls back the protection from the windows. Suddenly we are in the middle of the alien sea. All around us a blue-purple glow spreads like static lightning across the water. Something in the ocean, some life form, glows from our contact and the energy waves spread out from us.

"Nice," she says, and hands me a lighted joint. We smoke and watch the sea burn its harmless flame around us. "The light show will last for hours," she says, and leads me to her cabin. The wide bed seems as big as the sea compared to my narrow bunk. A touched button opens a window that curves from the floor up over our heads. We seem to be hanging outside the ship, in the fire. We make love until the ocean turns out the lights.

ED

I am thirty-three and single. I'm five-eleven and weigh 160 pounds. I don't equate masculinity with sex whatsoever, and enjoy being aggressive as well as passive during sex. My fantasy is probably quite typical, as it involves a movie actress. The fantasy goes:

I'm a delivery man in Beverly Hills. I take some roses to an address in Bel-Air. When the door opens to my knock, Raquel Welch is standing there. I'm dumbstruck.

She invites me in and asks me to wait a minute as she disappears with the roses. She is wearing a tight pair of hip-huggers and a skimpy halter, and just the sight of her has given me a rock hard-on. After a short while she calls for me to "come in here."

I follow the sound of her voice and step into her bedroom; she is placing a vase upon a bed table. I stand there tongue tied. She looks at me and smiles, then starts walking toward me. She has noticed my awestruck attitude; she passes me and locks the bedroom door.

She walks over and sits on the edge of the bed, so I am standing just in front of her. She reaches back and unsnaps the halter, and I gasp as her lovely nipple-hardened tits are exposed to my sight. I fumble at my fly and take out my erect prick and start to masturbate. She motions for me to stop, then has me undress as she removes her pants.

She leaves for a minute. When she returns, she is carrying a small flight bag which she places on the bed. She motions me onto the bed and tells me to lay on my back, then she takes a pillow and slips it under my ass, raising me off the bed. She takes a jar of Vaseline and rubs my asshole with it, then takes a large dildo from the bag and straps it on. Then she bends down and takes my prick into her mouth. I come instantly.

She mounts me and eases the dildo into my ass; my

mouth seeks her gorgeous nipples, and devours them as she steadily eases the dildo deeper and deeper. I begin to moan and move my hips and she starts rapidly fucking me.

I have a large poster picture of Raquel in a bikini, and I often lie on the bed and fuck myself with a vibrator as a jackoff to her.

I know I can never act out this fantasy in reality. My picture, my vibrator and my imagination must suffice. Oh, well!

VERN

I'm a man in my late sixties—healthy, vigorous, and still very much interested in sex. My wife, age sixty-one, still enjoys sex to some extent—but too slight for my taste. My sex fantasies are myriad.

In one of my favorites, I'm a kid of about thirteen, and I've just found out what a thrill it is to jack off. My teacher is a doll by the name of Pennwell—we call her Penny. Every time she starts writing high on the blackboard her dress goes up, and every cock in the class rises in tribute. I've never seen a cunt but I daydream constantly of Penny's and every time I jack off I imagine I'm plunging into her.

One day I cut up in class—not unusual—and when the bell rings, Penny sternly tells me to stay. When everyone's gone, she tells me severely that she's got something very private to talk to me about, so we'll go into the anteroom, which is furnished like a sort of restroom with a couple of comfortable chairs and a daybed. Penny closes the door, sits in one of the chairs and makes me stand facing her about five feet away. She tells me she's heard something terrible about me—something I did with Buzz Jones in back of Dodge's barn yesterday afternoon.

"Now, Vern," she says, "I'm going to teach you a lesson you'll never forget. I want you to show me exactly what you did yesterday behind that barn."

I protest, but she threatens to tell the principal. It's too embarrassing, I plead. She answers that it will be harder for her than for me; I might find it embarrassing, but she'll find it utterly revolting. So, red as a beet, I reluctantly take out my prick. It's limp.

"That isn't all you did," Penny says. "Continue, please."

I drop my pants and shorts. "Go on," she says. "Do exactly what you did yesterday."

I implore, but she's adamant, so I start pulling my cock. Pretty soon I get real hot and I'm enjoying it—the more so now because Penny is watching. She stares at my rod. It's hard as iron. The veins are standing out. The head is purple and swollen so it looks like it's gonna burst.

"Imagine! Thirteen years old!" Penny murmurs.

I'm getting hotter by the minute. I can feel the flush in my face. I start to breathe hard. I can feel the pulsing and throbbing in my stiff cock and suddenly the thick white juice spurts out—shooting in an arc toward Penny. One gob lands right on her dainty shoe.

"Oh!" she cries, startled. "Very well, you may go now— dirty little masturbator!" Penny says sternly.

So I scram as fast as I can—but when I get a little way, I remember I left my cap and books. I hang around a while to give Penny time to leave, then I go back. She's not in the classroom, and the door of the anteroom is ajar, so I slip quietly in.

Penny's lying on the bed. Her eyes are closed. Her shoes are off. Her gorgeous satiny white legs are spread wide, wide apart and the knees are drawn up. For the first time in my life I see that most wonderful of sights—that feminine flower nestled in her crotch, the moist, soft, pink lips of it, framed in fragile curly hair, and the dark red of its depths. It's Penny's lovely cunt and she's masturbating it with her long, slender fingers for all she's worth. I watch fascinated. Suddenly she opens her eyes.

"Oh!" She's startled, but her fingers linger on her cunt. "Lock that door and come here," she says. I lock the door and approach her. "This is what you and all the boys want to see, isn't it?" she asks. I nod. "Then take a good look at it."

She spreads her legs more. I devour her cunt with famished eyes. I could look at it forever. It draws me as though it were the center of my being. She plays with it a little to show me the inner and the outer lips and the way they open up, and the clit and the little pee hole.

"It's just—beautiful, Miss Pennwell," I say. "I—I'd like to—can I kiss it?"

She whispers yes. I kneel on the bed and put my mouth right between her legs, right on that lovely pink twat that's the center of her femininity. It's soft, yielding, wet, and it has a musky odor. I press my mouth in gently. I hear something between a sigh and a moan. I take my mouth away.

"O, don't stop, don't stop!" she begs.

So I put my mouth back. Then she starts telling me how to eat her—how to flick my tongue gently around the lips and the clit, now slowly, now quickly; how to move it slowly from the bottom to the top. As I do it she makes sweet little excited sounds; she starts pumping up and down, fucking my mouth; my face is wet with her cunt juice.

"Can you fuck me? Can you get your prick up again?" she asks breathlessly. I tell her it's up already. "Wonderful thirteen! Perpetual hard-on!" she says. "Shove it in, then! Oh, God, fill me up with that male meat!" I slip off my pants and shorts.

She guides it in. I feel my rigid cock slide slowly right up to the hilt in the soft, warm, wet depths of her.

"Oh, jeez. It's heaven! It's paradise!" she whispers. "I can't wait—I'm coming—"

She's moving her hips in a circular motion, breathing hard. Her eyes get glassy. She shakes convulsively, uncontrollably, making little cries. I keep on pushing my prick in and out with long strokes and she keeps coming and coming. I speed up a little; I'm near the top. She's crying, tearing at me, digging her fingers into my back, biting me. She's shaking from head to foot. I feel the deep surge in my prick and with a long, pulsing discharge I flood the soft, wet, dripping honey mouth of my teacher's cunt.

That was a lesson I'll never forget.

BEN

I am at an elegant, formal dinner party in a large expensive home. It is outside the city and has gardens, a swimming pool in the back and a large curved drive leading up to the mansion. It is summer, and early evening as several guests begin to arrive in big cars. The men are all dressed in white dinner jackets with dark blue or black pants, and the women are wearing cocktail dresses. There are many beautiful young women there with low-cut, plunging necklines. There is all kinds of food and drinks and the people are just walking around in groups, sampling the food and talking to each other. I have found me a luscious companion and she is enjoying a drink and my conversation near the pool. She is wearing a high-necked dress, but the cloth is cut in front so that her bosom is almost totally exposed. The firm high mounds of her breasts are pushed up by her bra and I can almost see the beginnings of her pink nipples peeking out. She is close to me, talking low and stroking my chest and trying to press her body against mine. My heart is pounding, as she suddenly reaches down and finds the zipper on my pants and starts to unzip my fly. I have a partial erection, and I can feel it grow as her cool fingertips push aside my shorts and close on my swelling cock.

She smiles at me and licks her full red lips as she uses both hands to take out my stiff cock, squeezing the throbbing shaft and sliding her hand down under my balls. I just stand there, without a word as she rubs my "manhood." I have walked both of us into a poolside cabana, and I sit down in a canvas chair. The woman kneels between my legs and undoes my belt and opens my pants and begins to go to work on me. She starts by licking the head and then moves down the shaft; then she is kissing my erection and gently biting me all over, until her coral lips open and she slides down my hard cock, taking all of me into her mouth. I can feel the back of her throat as she plunges down on me, and as she pulls back, I feel the suction and the swirl of her hot tongue. My head is pounding as this beautiful woman skillfully brings me close to orgasm, but she slows her pace as I sense the sperm welling up inside me. My hands have found the zipper of her gown, as she "works" on me and I have drawn it down, folded back the cloth to expose her black lace bra. The back strap is unhooked and I soon have my hands cupping the firm, pink-nippled heavy breasts of this sexpot. She is moving me in and out faster now, and she is teasing my buttocks with her fingers and as she pushes her middle finger slowly up me—I explode in her mouth. Waves of pleasure throb in my loins as she drains me. I lay back dazed and exhausted—her face thrust between my legs. I open my eyes as I hear applause and talking and laughter. The whole side of the cabana is *open* and several people have been watching us in the dark as we "performed."

14

Sharing the Woman
with Another Man

Two sailors ashore decided to share a whore. They find
her, fuck her, and go back to the ship and forget her, their
friendship and feelings of masculinity somehow reinforced
at the woman's expense.

Drugstore psychiatrists wink at stories like these. What
these two men "really" wanted, they derisively explain, is
not so much contact with the woman, as feeling of greater
closeness between themselves: the prostitute was used
merely as a conduit to communicate emotions to one another that they'd become violent to hear named aloud.

That may be true, but it is only part of a large truth.
The two sailors may never have had an overtly homosexual
encounter in their lives, or a conscious homosexual desire.
Does that mean nothing? What is gained by hastily tagging
them "latent queers" or some other ugly and imprecise label that does nothing but express the anxious superiority of
the name caller?

Here begins one of the most highly charged (and misunderstood) themes in male sexuality: homoerotic emotions.
In the fantasies in this chapter and the four chapters that
follow, homosexual desires are sometimes openly acknowledged, sometimes not. I myself do not call any man gay
unless that is the name he gives himself.

What I feel is more important than mere pigeonholing is
the evidence, in my contributors' own words, of a new
awareness among men that traditional masculine attitudes
of isolation from the competition with all other men leads
to an impoverishment of the possibilities of life; the
strained, exaggerated effort to forestall even the merest
suspicion that one might harbor emotional interest in another man is an artificial stance too burdensome to maintain.

What I find really significant in these fantasies is not whether the men "really" want sex with one another, but how important—right in the heart of these homoerotic reveries—is the presence of a female figure. It is under her aegis that the male rapprochement takes place. Only in the avowedly homosexual fantasies does she not appear, though there are exceptions to this, too, even in the gayest of fantasies I've collected.

Coming out of a lifetime of predominantly heterosexual feelings and actions, many men are bewildered, puzzled and dismayed to find themselves heated by notions of including another male in their eroticism. To such a man, the inclusion of a woman in the scene is a sovereign anxiety alleviator. She allows him to feel things his conscious mind may ignore but his anxiety unerringly recognizes. Like a clever playwright who brings the star on stage in disguise, the fantasist may seem to indicate that the greatest intensity of emotion is being played out between the two men; the woman in these reveries may appear in the role of a second-class citizen. But she represents the wisdom of the unconscious.

In her omniscience and smiling compassion, she takes up arms on his side against his guilty conscience. She affirms life in all its bedeviling complexity. "Sure," she says, "I know you have these feelings about your best friend. I know you miss the easy horsing around you used to do with the other guys when you were a kid, and sex came without the strings that women attach to it. I know somewhere in you you're guilty about having done it then, and you're even trying to pretend now that it never happened. I know that while you are excited by having this other man in the scene, it doesn't necessarily mean you want to have sex with him. Maybe it does. Maybe it doesn't. In neither case does it mean you have to hate yourself. These emotions are playful, trying to see how this would feel, how that would feel. I understand these ideas, and there is nothing wrong with them. I'm here. I'm enjoying them as much as you. Everything is okay."

VANCE

My wife and I are both college graduates. We are in our
thirties and live in most ways in the mainstream of America. I commute to work on Wall Street, and she has always
been involved with teaching school on a full-time basis or
church work and community volunteer work on a part-
time basis. Our two children are in elementary school.

For thirteen years our marriage has been a rich, dynamic and joyful experience. Each of us has had rich fantasy lives, and we frequently discuss our mutual fantasies.
Once out in the open, we often examine them to try to
understand what meaning they might have. Sometimes one
of us has wanted to live out our fantasies; sometimes we
have wanted to keep them in the fantasy world.

This began when I once told my wife of a fantasy about
another couple our age. It led to a frank discussion of our
sexual attraction to others. In this way, I was able to lead
my wife into a more and more open marriage. My wife is
very attractive, vivacious and sensual.

Recently Jack came to visit us during a business trip. He
is an extremely successful businessman who lived near us
for a year. We had planned a big evening—cocktails, going
out to dinner, and good conversation. We started with the
cocktails and soon we were all getting relaxed and very
comfortable. We exchanged warm sentiments about our
mutual friendship toward each other and could have gone
on for hours, but we decided we'd better start thinking
about dinner. Since Jack had been traveling that day, we
offered to wait for him to shower before going out.

We have a large shower which we call our family
shower, and we both suggested he use that. Suddenly my
wife and I looked at each other with a knowing glance and
we realized we were both thinking of the possibility of joining Jack in the shower. Just high enough to make it seem
very feasible, I half suggested and half promised that we'd
join him. Jack is very uninhibited himself and it didn't surprise us when he laughed lustfully and said, "Great!" . . .
We did.

When my lovely wife walked into the shower, he immediately got an erection. Soon we were all laughing and sudsing each other. I began kissing my wife's neck and massaging her breasts, and soon her pussy. Gently but hungrily, Jack joined in. It was extremely erotic to see her pressed up against him. As she writhed under the growing excitement in our hands she reached for both our cocks simultaneously, masturbating us for a few crazy seconds.

As if she had gotten the last word, she coyly got out of the shower and started to dry off, leaving Jack and me standing with our hard-ons, partly to end the shower scene but partly also to suggest that if we wanted to get any "heavier" we should meet her on drier ground. We also got out then and started toweling her off, taking turns kissing her mouth and neck. I dropped to my knees, saying I would dry her legs, and started eating her. She went wild as Jack kissed her neck and I kissed her pussy. Then I said, "Jack, why don't you dry the other leg?" Instantly he was kneeling between her legs and eating her while I kissed her neck. Her hips were instinctively grinding in and out. Jack and I exchanged places one more time and soon, squirming and moaning, she exploded in a trembling climax.

That experience has been the basis of endless fantasies, when I'm out on the road, and on my commuter train. I fantasize that we will get together again and go further. She never gets enough fucking. So next time, Jack and I will begin by massaging her on a soft rug in front of the fireplace. Then we will undress her and take turns eating her. Finally we will take turns fucking her until she is totally satisfied—until she is begging for mercy.

Homosexuality is usually perceived as the greatest of all threats to the male psyche. In no other aspect of life are men so guarded. Everyone had parents of two sexes, everyone has introjected characteristics of both mother and father. Women will often say they are like their dad in this or that; the older I get, the more of my grandfather I see in myself. But it is the rare man who will say how many of his mother's qualities he has inherited. If lesbian contact comes up in feminine fantasies (as it often does), it is usually dealt with easily and in passing, with little or no disguises or excuses. But it is almost a joke how eagerly (anxiously) men pronounce themselves "201 percent macho he-male and a yard of barbed-wire wide."

The question naturally arises: Why, then, do so many men in this book introduce their fantasies by speaking about real boyhood encounters with other boys? I suspect that having read my other books on sexual fantasies, my contributors have decided I am nonjudgmental. If they can tell me everything about themselves, including homosexual ideas or history, the pressure to air these impulses will have been expressed; but their masculinity will have been reaffirmed. It is expected that, like the writer himself, I will take the confession as a matter of very little moment, kid stuff that happened a long time ago, boyish horsing around until the real thing (girls) came along.

Few boys get all the father-son closeness they would like. Dad works too hard at his job, is out of town on business, or just plain resigns the task to mother. The hunger for male companionship persists into adult life and is socially sanctioned in such forms as nights out with the boys or all-male hunting trips. But isn't this a charade of the passionate closeness boys once had together when their newfound camaraderie was life itself, and mutual loyalty forever was sworn with blood and campfire oaths—totems and emblems of entrance into the mysterious company of men and an identity greater than that of self alone?

I sense from my contributors that too much rivalry has entered into their relations with other men now that they have grown, too much competition, a loss of belief and distrust of emotion, especially between themselves. "Women feel, men *do*." Women may have access to intimacy with other women they may not have with a lover, but is women's cheek kissing and embracing anything like the innocent and heartfelt brotherhood young boys once shared? Even as a young girl I sensed boys had something together we girls did not, beginning with the simple fact that boys would tell lies to protect one another and we girls would have betrayed our best friend for the chance of a boy's heart. Having once had this closeness, can the grown man ever entirely forget it? By denying he has any feeling left for men, isn't he denying a part of himself?

It was for the love of women that men gave up their boyhood idylls. "Wedding Bells Are Breaking Up That Old Gang of Mine" goes the lament. How can men not be angry, at some level, that women have hoodwinked them into intimacy, offered them closeness without honesty, sex with guilt? Vance's fantasy (above) works toward putting that anger to sleep, reestablishing the good old days before friends became sexual rivals. He does not want to see the successful Jack as a competitor, but wants to feel as close to him as possible instead. With Mrs. Vance's agreement, the trio is fixed up in a moment. Jack and Mrs. Vance may be seen as Vance's two split selves. Sex—note that the woman agrees it is okay—makes him one.

TROY

I can hardly believe I've begun this, so the possibility remains it'll never be finished or mailed. Living in a small summer resort town whose businesses are open hardly at all during the winter, I'm incredibly horny. Nearly always. Some friends say it's because I'm a Scorpio with five planets also in Scorpio. It all means nothing to me, and I'm not sure the theory of astrology holds any water. I'm nearly twenty-nine, blond and bearded. Some women have said I'm very attractive, even handsome, yet being so damned introspective, it's honestly hard to believe. I wear a beard only to hide as much of my face as possible, which is only one facet of my hiding my true self.

As for sex, I love it. I've been with a woman now, off and on, for over four years. Very good at times, awful at others. She's run the gamut from the sweetest, most selfless person alive, to the most vindictive catty bitch ever. Sex with us, when we're okay, is fantastic. But in spite of her ability to make me feel incredibly good, I'm constantly fantasizing other scenes with and without her. I'll relate them in the sense of having happened already to make them less complicated to write.

Once while dressing for an afternoon out, she answered a knock at the door to find a black man in a utility uniform wanting to read the meter in the basement. When done, she offered him a cup of coffee, and while he was drinking it, she decided to seduce him. So sitting at the edge of the kitchen table, she opened her robe, smiling quietly, and leaned back, legs slightly spread, and began fingering her closely shaved, but not bare, cunt. Then she laid back completely, opened her lips and calmly said, "Please suck my cunt, just a little," which was an offer he couldn't refuse, and she held his head gently while he circled every inch of her pubic area and licked her inside and out with his tongue. She came in his mouth with a great sigh and more pearly white liquid than I'd ever seen before. Then she sat up and licked his mouth to taste herself, which she's always loved.

While he then sucked her nipples, she freed his great black cock, and gave a start for a second at the size of it. Then in a voice one ordinarily hears from the blonde on shaving cream ads, she asked him his name, which he said was Christopher. After barely touching his immense balls and tip of his cock with her nearly shaking tongue, she said, "Christopher, if I take your cock in my mouth and suck it very slowly and make it slide as far down my throat as I can, will you promise you'll come? Promise me you'll let yourself relax and let your cock squirt all of your come into my mouth? Please, Christopher. I love the taste of come, and your cock is so magnificent, I want you to fill my mouth with that hot creamy come." With his smile, she knew he was not saying no. So she began. Floating her tongue from his asshole slowly over his balls, up the underside of it, over the top and down again, over and over, rolling his balls in her mouth, and tickling his ass just enough to make him squirm a bit. She wouldn't allow him to hold her head, so he just sat back, lit a smoke, and enjoyed. Her skin appeared so white against his beautiful black skin, like lightning on a dark night. She'd by then forgotten I was even in the room.

Soon she began earnestly to take as much as she could in her throat, which was not more than half of that great, shining rod, and occasionally tickled her own clitoris with a free hand, as she raised to her knees and moved her ass in the air, almost magnetically drawing me nearer to fuck her from behind. Then, dammit, another knock at the door. I ran and answered it. Another utility man, black as well, wondering where the hell Christopher was. With a gesture of quiet and a knowing wink, I led him to the kitchen where Claire was alive with motion, and whimpers of pleasure I'd never heard before. Christopher had a glazed look on his face, but acknowledged the presence of his partner, who very calmly asked Claire if she would like to feel even better. Taking her flushed lips from Christopher's nearly bursting cock, she said, "Yes, please hurry. Fuck me anywhere," and with a wet groan slid back onto the shaft she hadn't let go of for a second. The newcomer removed his pants, knelt, and lightly tasted Claire's cunt, which was visibly moist and puffy, nearly speading itself in anticipation. His cock was nearly as big as Christopher's. He wet his index finger with her juices and slowly worked it into her ass, as his thumb enter her cunt. Her ass began to move much like a kite on a gusty day, as he seemed to be making up his mind as to which hole he preferred. Just as suddenly, he pulled his hand away, and without a pause at all, literally rammed his cock in her cunt so hard, it caused his balls to strike her tummy, and a low animal growl of pleasure emanated from her pelvis and erupted around the cock in her mouth.

Though I'd never seen her this way before, it appeared she knew exactly how to move her body to achieve full penetration of both cocks at exactly the same instant. I was beside them in an instant feeling every part of all of them, and stroking my own cock as near to Claire's face as I could. The floor actually trembled like a high speed train, as she brought everyone closer, closer, closer. Claire's eyes opened wide, wild with excitement, as she pumped that great black cock, her mouth stretched wide, but still smiling somehow. Her knees lifted off the floor with every powerful stroke of the man behind her creating slippery slaps, then finally, suddenly, loudly, incredibly, we all came at once. With the most unbelievable groan in her throat bubbling up through the come she'd wanted to swallow, her whole body off the floor, from the sudden implacement of the cock of the newcomer being violently, unexpectedly thrust in her ass just as he came, and Christo-

pher holding her shoulders, lifting her completely, her free
hand spread the come I'd squirted all over her face on her
swinging breats. Come drooled and dripped from everywhere, and everyone collapsed in a pile together with
sweet, insatiable Claire clinging to three cocks, with
mouth, asshole, and hand, soaked with come, whimpering,
drooling, giggling, spent. Four incredibly sexual people in
a pile, wet with sweat and come, panting, sighing, no
words being spoken, other than Claire asked how often the
meters were read.

VIRGIL

I have fantasized continuously since I was thirteen (I am
now eighteen, and I don't plan to quit. Most of my fantasy
life developed from books I read like *The Happy Hooker;*
ones with lots of sex in them. Here are a couple of my
favorite, overused fantasies:

Back in high school, there was a girl I knew who had a
beautiful mother with a fantastic body, and lots of guys
thought about her. The daughter was great too, but didn't
seem very nice. However, the mother liked people, and always wore very sexy clothes.

One day, my best friend and I ride somewhere on our
bikes, and we spot her with her husband and daughter,
also bike riding. We follow them and overhear that Mr. M.
and Laura have to go somewhere, but Mrs. M. is going
home. Dick and I follow her home, and we instinctively
know exactly what we are going to do.

After about ten minutes, we knock on the door; and
when she answers, we can't believe our eyes. She is wearing a stretch top with no bra underneath, hot pants, and
very high boots (maybe she knew we were coming).
Quickly jumping inside, Dick grabs her, while I shut the
door and close the curtains. She tries to run, but we catch
her and take her to the bedroom. While Dick holds her, I
remove all her clothes except the boots, and begin removing my own. Dick strips and moves beside her, while I am
on the other side, all of us lying on the bed. We both kiss
her face, neck and mouth while fondling her large tits; and

after a while, she stops struggling. When both of us suck on her nipples, she gets excited, groans, begs us to continue. I move to her cunt, licking her slit, finally sucking her clitoris. She locks her legs around my head, and Dick begins tonguing her ass, while she massages one cock in each hand. She starts begging to be fucked, so we switch, Dick fucking her, while she sucks my throbbing cock. She comes for the third time, which causes Dick and me to shoot our loads into her simultaneously. We quickly dress and leave the house, leaving her tired but contented.

Stories about two men and a woman often contain sadistic elements. The men do not like her. Sex is used to express contempt, and the woman is humiliated.

Such emotions are not what my contributors express.

I opened this book by saying it was about men who like women. In fantasies like Troy's (above), even though the woman is not experienced solely for herself, but also as the vehicle and permission giver for one man to enjoy otherwise taboo emotions about another man, it is important to the fantasist that he not lose his connection with her. She must like what is going on. Here is what Troy invents for his Claire to feel while she is sexually enmeshed with another man: "wild with excitement . . . smiling."

The only sadistic touch in this chapter comes from eighteen-year-old Virgil (above). At that age, a man is still so close to home—and the first great no sayer—that he is far from believing girls his own age will ever say yes. Force often seems the only way a man will ever get a woman to do anything sexual. Angry at women, angry at himself perhaps for still wanting some of the old homoerotic horsing around with the other guys—pleasures only recently given up—Virgil creates a fantasy in which he and his buddy force an older woman into sex. Do they hurt her? Does she react with pain and horror as most women would in reality? No. "She comes for the third time, which causes Dick and me to shoot our loads into her simultaneously." The woman ends up "tired but contented."

In these fantasies, the line between the woman's pain and pleasure, between the man's anger and desire, is deli-

cately, ambivalently balanced—but the creators of these
scenarios always make sure the final weight falls on the
side of the woman's ecstasy. In this way, she is perceived
as an all-wise mother who recognizes a small boy's in-
choate furies; one who returns them not with an aggression
of her own, but with love.

AUSTIN

My wife and I are college graduates, have teen-age children and are both employed. I am just past forty and my
wife is close to me in age. My parents were married quite
late in life and then were not able to have children until
several years after they were married. I come from a home
where sexual subjects were extremely repressed.

I had a strong sex curiosity as a child, in my erection,
the pleasure of stroking it and in girls and the clothes they
wore. I remember at age five finding a pile of my mother's
undergarments by her sewing basket and while fingering
them and putting on one of her long nylon stockings got
one of the hardest erections. With her occasional spankings
and enemas I also got the hardest erections.

It wasn't until I was eleven, and reading some of my
comic books with some erotic pictures and laying on some
inflated swimming inner tubes on the floor of the basement,
that I had my first climax. For this I could not have been
less prepared. I have fantasized what would have happened
if I had gone up and asked my mother about what had
happened to me. However, I overcame my fears and began a regular practice of masturbation. I would often think
of my mother, or look at the special comics and either rub
my penis against the sheet of the bed or use Vaseline and
my hand.

Something that my mother often enjoyed was to have
someone rub her feet while laying on the bed or on the
couch in the living room. This felt good after a long day.
She often liked it after a bath and before going to bed.

One day I actually did suggest giving my mother a foot
massage on the bed in her bedroom with the idea it would
be more comfortable. I suggested she leave her nylons on

and lay on her stomach. I see myself getting more onto the bed, and into the massage by extending more and more above the calf of the leg. I rubbed here for a while and was finally straddling one of her legs, on my hands and knees. As my arms reached forward I massaged higher and I was reaching the tops of her stockings where the garters were attached and where the white skin began. By now my penis is coming in hard contact with the calf of her leg and I started rubbing it back and forth. She didn't seem to notice and my hands were now high on each thigh until one hand was touching at the crotch of her panties. My feeling keeps getting better and I pressed on now. She can't help feeling what I am doing and without warning I have a pulsing and pleasing climax. She had stiffened her leg slightly but acted as if nothing had happened.

A shuffle is noticed behind me at the door and by a slight turn I notice my father is looking in the half-closed door and I think I am in for a scolding. He said nothing but came over to the bed. He looked at me as he moved to the place where I had been and he lowered mother's panties and parting his robe he took out his large penis and inserted it into mother from behind. I stepped back and realized the pleasure they were feeling. I grew more relaxed as I was not being noticed and began to take a greater interest in what they were doing. I became aroused at watching them move as dad would sometimes rise up and extend his penis out of mother so I could see it. I came closer to them and mother even took my hand as dad kept moving behind her and she smiled as he became still. He got up, exposing her, and I was urged to come closer and lay where father had been. The lump in my pants showed I had an erection again. Each encouraged me to take my pants down and although I was sticky from my first climax I was encouraged to lay against mother's exposed buttocks. As she was quite moist with a little squirming and the guidance of her hand she assisted me getting into her. My second climax came again very soon.

I often picture my wife being taken by another man in a swimming pool. An old boyfriend with whom she did heavy petting is the person. Later she calls me long distance and is fucked by him while we are talking.

In reality, her occasional dreams of sex turn me on. We repeat these stories during sex play, during mutual masturbation, and I tell and think about them to enhance our feeling. Here is one: She and I have come to visit her old boyfriend and we all slowly become naked. He fucks her first and she withdraws at his approaching climax as she does not want to become pregnant. I am excited and enter after he has climaxed on her stomach. She feels my climax coming and I know I can have it inside her. He has become excited watching this and is erected again with a large hard-on. She feels very sorry for him, knowing how he would have liked to have it in her. She remembers what good friends they were. I look at her, smile, and tell her it is all right. She doesn't encourage him to withdraw this time and he pumps his full climax into her.

SUSIE

I wanted to tell you about my ex-lover's fantasies, as he'd never write to tell you. The main one (and it excites me, too) was for him to invite his best friend over to the house on a hot afternoon; I'd be complaining of the heat, and my lover would suggest I take a cool bath. I went to "get ready," knowing that my lover would then offer me to his friend, who had been admiring my long legs and free breasts in my shorts and halter top. He (the friend) accepts, and I hear the bathroom door open, and see not my lover but his friend come in. He really wants to run his hands all over my soapy boobs and down in the water to my cunt. He gets so excited, he is panting and moaning, and we get together in just the right position to finally have a satisfying fuck in the bathtub, and we're sloshing water all over, and he drives deep and strong, til he comes. And here is my lover's part—I walk (stagger?) out of the bathroom, still full of the man's cum, and my lover picks me up and carries me to the bedroom and throws my legs over his shoulders and really deeply, and then teasingly, he fucks me after this man has fucked me. He really gets off on my having been fucked by another man, and then by him. I

come and come, and that is his favorite fantasy, but I like
it too!

I think we're all tired of the endless arguments about
whether men or women are more competitive. The issue is
not open to quantitative analysis. All that can be reasonably said is that competition is different for each sex.

For women, great fear attaches to the fact that the first
rival was mother—who, in life's earliest sexual battle, won
father hands down. How can a woman admit that the person she needs to maintain life is also her victorious foe?
What is even more difficult is that mother herself would
never name the tension. It was called "love" instead: Because she "loved" her daughter, she didn't want the girl to
wear attention-getting clothing, to childishly climb all over
daddy now that she was grown, and it was for the girl's
best interest that mother secretly read her diary.

The result is that women bury and deny competitive
emotions. When a man suggests that it would be fun to
make a sexual threesome, and asks his wife to invite her
best friend to join, she reexperiences all the old primitive
furies. She *especially* doesn't want to invite her best friend
because (like mother) this is the woman she loves more,
but also whose loss she fears most (like mother). Asking
the best friend to join a trio with the husband goes right to
the heart of feminine oedipal rivalries. How can you compete with someone and still keep her love?

On the other hand, men are encouraged to display their
willingness—their eagerness—to compete; but these feelings must not be given free rein. With their huge muscles
and identification of masculinity with force, uninhibited
competition between males can be dangerous. Boiling just
beneath the surface are angers that were never expressed
against father—that forbidding figure in the universal male
nightmare of oedipal competition. In its wisdom, society
has had to provide other outlets for forces that cannot be
dammed but would be destructive to loose. Games are invented.

Men feel unleashed on the football field, but they are

safe, too. There are rules, umpires and referees; protective padding and helmets are worn. And when the game is over, the code demands that all undissipated furies be turned off with a smile and a handshake. Every camp counselor knows that if two youngsters get into a feud, the safest thing to do is break out the boxing gloves. More often than not, they will leave the ring arm in arm. Murderous rivalry has been socialized through a special kind of aggressive male bonding.

In fantasies of sharing your woman with another man, sex, too, is turned into a game. The unknown rival, the man to whom your wife may be unfavorably comparing you, the man she secretly dreams of when she is in your arms, the superstud you fear can give her the orgasm you never did—is suddenly a competitor no more. The deadly oedipal triangle has been turned into a family circle.

The two men are no longer intent on beating each other out, but on joining together to service the woman. The fun of all three is a common goal. There is no showdown at the O.K. Corral, only mutual masculine identification.

Best of all, games don't count. They are not real life. When the game is over, the other man goes home. The woman stays with you. This release from competitive anxiety and fear frees an immense amount of emotion—which is expressed in heightened sexuality.

Hockey became a major spectator sport only when, in recent years, it slid over from being a contest of speed and graceful skating to become a brawl of armored bodies, sharp steel skates, and brandished clubs. "Kiss the bum!" men shout to their favorite player, who thus becomes a surrogate with special license to do to *his* rival on the ice what the spectator fears his rival in daily life wants to do to *him*.

When a woman is the prize, the competition is less symbolic. There can be no pretense that this is merely a game. Men may hate each other more when they are rivals in love than when they are competitors in sport; but they are far more inhibited, far more careful with each other. This is an index of how much they themselves fear the homicidal emotions just beneath the thin veneer. The fantasies in this chapter illustrate various strategies men use to hide their competitive fears and rages.

Austin (above) grew up in a house "where sexual subjects were extremely repressed." But then he describes a "real" situation: He is in bed with his mother when his father walks in. *His father doesn't scold him* or become angry, but instead gets into bed, too, fucks his wife with the little boy right there, and then both parents invite Austin to take his turn.

Can we take this indeed to be a real story—or, as is the case with many fantasists, are the events described so fervently wished for that the dreamer ends by deciding they really did take place? The borderline manner in which fantasy so often becomes indistinguishable from reality is fascinating; note how Austin mixes up his verb tenses—sliding from past to present.

In Freud's formulation of oedipal rivalry, not only does the son dream of killing and supplanting the father, but he also fears the father will reply by castrating and/or murdering him first. In Austin's fantasy, these fears are eased. Father and son do not see each other as rivals at all. Instead, they are aiding and abetting each other in their shared pleasures. *Male esprit de corps and camaraderie has replaced the expected deadly enmity.*

Men who go to stag films always want the hero to have a penis of gigantic dimensions. They don't feel jealous or inadequate while watching him—as they might in real life—because the film works like a fantasy. In their unconscious identification, they are the star of the movie. They are gigantic, too. It is my feeling that this is why sexual reveries of watching someone else go to bed with your mate are so much more prevalent among men than women. Men identify with each other more readily than women do.

A man may feel jealous when the other guy gets the promotion, but his next thought is not so much to kill the guy as to imitate and learn from him—"If he can do it, I can, too, even better!" Men feel envy of the guy who has a lot of women, but they don't exclude him from the group. They take his prowess as hope for themselves. On the other hand, a woman feels that when another woman wins—the job or the man—there is therefore less of the pie left for her.

In an S&M novel recently published, the heroine does

not object to her "master" chaining her up, or treating her like a slave. The one indignity she will not submit to, however, is allowing him to watch her masturbate. Chains were a demonstration of control; they were acceptable. Masturbating would present him with a picture of her out of control. That is unacceptable.

What the men in this chapter want to see is their women out of control. They yearn for terrific feminine sexual gusto, readiness to experiment, release from the tight confines of monogamous dependency. In real life they have chosen to marry the sexually timid woman. Given the opportunity they would probably marry her—or someone just like her—all over again. Only in fantasy can they enjoy what she cannot give them—and what they cannot allow themselves.

Grown men may smile when they tell about the time mom caught them masturbating. This does not mean they no longer feel the old inhibitions on a level too deep for words. The fantasy strategy for men like this very often is to invent women for whom one lover is not enough, who want two, three, or more at the same time. That's about as far from mother as you can get. The incest taboo is thus defended against, and only excitement is left.

THOMAS

My wife and I have been married for over twenty years, have three children, one still in high school, one not married, but on his own, and the oldest, a girl, has just recently married.

Our marriage has been a very rewarding situation for me from the very first, and my wife assures me constantly that it has been the same for her. My wife acquired her master's degree since we were married and has worked at her profession ever since. I have always worked at my job on the "swing shift" and taken care of a small business venture on the side.

Our working arrangements automatically put many limitations on our social life, and all through the week we aren't able to go to bed together at the same time or get up at the same time in the morning. Consequently, it is like having a "honeymoon" every weekend when I can be home with her and undress her at night and play with her.

She is a lot of fun. It is especially nice to take her to a dance. I can hold her close to me and feel all of her through her dress, and it is a real thrill to have her dance with other men, knowing they can feel all of her too. She invariably gives them a hard-on before they get through dancing together. She has a very prominent beautiful mound. I can actually see the impression of it through her dress and she has a way of pressing her partner with it at the most opportune moments.

Ever since I can remember, I have always considered the ultimate in a "Love Encounter" would be a handsome, loving, generously endowed black man on a beautiful, long-legged, loving blond woman!

This is my fantasy. Loving my wife like I do, and wanting her to have the best of everything, I want more than anything in this world to have an arrangement where "our friend"—this loving, handsome, well-endowed black man whom I will call Dick—can take her to bed with him every night until I come home. I think about being able to watch them through a one-way mirror, from the time he starts to undress her, through an almost endless lovemaking scene and be able to hear her moan when he lays her down on the bed and shoves it into her. I can't think of anything more exciting than to hear her say to him, "Oh, fuck me, fuck me," while she guides his big nine-inch black cock up between her long, lovely, well-spread legs.

I have a fantasy about coming home early from work one night, while she is at a PTA meeting. I lay down on the davenport to wait for her. Of course I dropped off to sleep. Directly across the living room from the davenport is a daybed sort of thing with a few nice cushions on it—ideal for fucking! I was awakened by someone talking just as they turned on the light in the hallway. It was Dick and her. They went into the bathroom and in a few minutes, they came out completely undressed. In the short distance from the bathroom to the daybed, they stopped three different times, to embrace, kiss and love each other. Knowing her, their kisses would have to be the deep, tongue-searching kind, that become more meaningful each time.

Dick had a terrific hard-on with a beautiful up angle to it—it had to be over eight inches long and perfectly proportioned. Each time they embraced, his cock would be squeezed between them with the head of his prick nestled in her belly button.

When they got to the bed, she lay down right away and scootched her ass over in the middle of the bed, and he was on top of her in one smooth move, resting his weight on his elbows and settling down on her while she guided his prick.

She had her long legs spread real wide and straight in the air while he literally screwed it into her. She pivoted her ass like only she can do. She is extremely tight so it always turns out to be a challenge to get into her. As soon as he made it all the way, she wrapped her legs around him and they lay there in an embrace for some time. I was almost afraid they had both come, but then I saw her start moving her ass and he started sucking on one of her tits and caressing her all over with his free hand, while he started fucking it into her with long, beautiful well-timed strokes.

(The light shined in through the hallway in such a way that I could see them very vividly, and still be in the dark so they weren't aware of me being there.) They both came together with a series of spasms that lasted for several minutes.

I have always shared my fantasies with my wife and have let her know how much time I spend thinking of all the details while I am at work and how excited it makes me to come home to her and hold her in my arms and love her. She has told me that she often thinks of Dick while she masturbates. The most fantastic orgasm I have ever experienced with her was the first time I asked her how she would like to have a real loving, handsome black man shove his big black prick into her.

MAC

I'm twenty-eight years old, married and have three children. We live in a large midwestern town. I work in a beef packing plant. I work the night shift, three thirty to midnight, so our sex life kind of varies.

In the ten years we've been married, I have had a lot of sexual fantasies. It seems like half of them I would really like to do, but the other half I don't think so. If for some reason making love to my wife is not working out the way I like it, I just turn on one of my fantasies and everything is great. When I masturbate, my fantasies are the key to my climax (yes, married men masturbate). The fantasies then would be me coming home from work and finding no one home, but hearing a sound from the bedroom. I go to look. Very quietly I turn on the light to the bedroom, and there in the bed is a man fucking my wife. It ends there. It's one that I never want to happen, but yet it turns me on, and isn't that what a fantasy is for?

JEFFREY

Let me begin by saying that our love life is no less than fantastic.

My wife was married for a considerable time to a man who was more concerned with his own needs than a mutual enjoyment in their sex life. In our seven years of marriage, we have progressed from shyness to open experimentation. We now enjoy oral sex, extended foreplay, mutual masturbation and occasionally, anal sex. June is thirty-seven, but has a body which is envied by women in their mid-twenties. It is hard to believe that she has a teen-age daughter. Just to see her walk across the room nude gives me an erection.

During the first three years of our marriage, I was away from home for extended periods and the total shut-off of our active sex was very frustrating to her. Because of her background, I had to convince June that masturbation would relieve her tension and, after a year of urging with many detailed letters, she had her first self-induced climax by clenching a pillow between her legs. Now when I leave, she uses water trickling on her clitoris or a vibrator for her relief quite frequently.

Our favorite position is with June on top and my dick deep inside her. I will caress her bottom and transfer her sweet juice from her pussy to her rear before I slide my finger in and out. She comes immediately and intensely when I do this and admits to fantasizing that she has her bottom full when she climaxes.

I love June and have had no other women since our marriage, as she gives me total fulfillment. She has been with only her first husband and me, so most of my fantasies involve things which I think would really turn her on. When I am on the road sometimes I will masturbate, and my favorite fantasy involves her accommodating two dicks. I imagine that she has told me she wants to feel a cock in her pussy and rear at the same time. I am behind the shutters in our bedroom, when she leads him into the room. As he pulls her to him on our king-size bed, he kisses her and his hands begin to softly caress her breasts and buttocks. She pushed him back and nibbles across his stomach to the base of his throbbing cock, licks it all over and lets at least half of it slide into her mouth. Her hands rub his balls as she straddles his face to allow his tongue to lick the wet folds of her pussy and her rigid clitoris. After a few minutes, she straddles his thighs, lowering her hips, and I see the cock disappear into her wet pink folds, inch by inch. Then she falls forward across his chest and starts that fantastic movement of hers.

I am sure that most men would like their wives to experience intercourse with two men at once. The sight of that wet white shaft thrusting into her tight pussy drives me wild. I am hot and hard as I move onto the bed and begin to kiss her twin globes and tongue her puckered rear. Then I transfer the juices at the union of her pussy and his cock to her behind, and to my eight-inch dick. I move between their legs, and begin to slowly ease into her. He moves all of his cock out of her, leaving only the head inside until I am fully into her rear and have given her a few gentle thrusts. Now we both ease up into her and they raise up a little so he can suck and kiss her breasts. Next we rock her back and forth so one cock is always penetrating while the other cock is withdrawing. Then she says, "Let's come!" and we both push in deep and spurt the wet sticky come deep into her, and she can feel each warm surge in her full bottom. I can feel the other cock throbbing and her bottom clenching as they come and it causes me to have a tremendous orgasm. Then we collapse for a few minutes and the other man gets up and leaves.

REYNOLDS

Most of my fantasies are about my wife Sophie. Although I have many without her, I like the ones in which she stars because she is the most important person in my life. I'll start with the first and most important fantasy:

I'm hiding in a closet when my wife brings a lover into the bedroom. They begin to kiss and fondle and take each other's clothes off until they are naked. He sucks on her tits and she just sighs and spreads her legs wider (they are standing on a rug in front of the bed) so he can get his hand into her cunt. Then she grips his dick which is thick and long and pulls him down on top of the bed. She starts to run her tongue around the head, then it slips into her mouth. I usually come by this time, but I can make it last longer by inventing more details.

Besides my wife and you, Nancy, only one other person knows about my fantasies. He is a close friend who married my sister. I told him everything, including the idea that I would love to see him fucking Sophie. This got him very excited, and he blurted out that he'd always had fantasies that my sister was not a virgin when she married him, and that I was the one who had taken her maidenhead. To tell the truth, exchanging these ideas got us both so excited, that we were rubbing each other through our pants before we finished, and have met a few more times since then to do a few more experiments in which we combine stories about swapping wives and jerking each other off. I guess maybe I'm bisexual.

When I have trouble getting it up, my wife will often tell me one of her fantasies about fucking some guy, and it jumps right up. There's one guy in particular who gets me all hot and bothered when she talks about him. He works with her and really turns her on, but she's afraid to pursue it much. She was a virgin when we married, and I'm the only guy who's screwed her. I wish she would fuck another man or woman and like it. That way I could act out my favorite fantasy and get her to make it with my brother-in-law. A trio would be heaven.

RODDY

Here's my fantasy:

Maisie and I have finally met a man who desires to fuck with us. I have had a curiosity about sucking a cock (in adult life, I have never had any contact with a male). He assures us that he is as horny, uninhibited and understanding as we are that sex for thrills is a perfectly good interest. We feel the taboo inhibitions waning as we all get into the shower, and I find that I am half throbbing from the thought of how much Maisie will love it, and half from the anticipation that I will now get my chance to suck a cock.

We couple in every way imaginable—Maisie sucks me while he fucks her, he sucks Maisie while I rub my cock over her eyes and nose, Maisie sucks both of us. I then realize that his cock is free while he's doing something to her and she is yelling loudly, "Fuck me! Fuck me! My God, harder, more!" And I suddenly think that I probably won't like the feeling of him coming in my mouth. But curiosity gets the best of me; and I take his big, beautiful cock into my mouth. At this moment I think of all the times I tried as a young man to get my own cock into my mouth, and was never able to reach it. Oh, how I wanted to suck myself off. But the best I could do was to turn backward into a half-circle, and masturbate until my semen dripped into my mouth and onto my face; and at those times, since I had already come and the lusty feeling began to wane, I did not like the taste. But now, I have his cock in my mouth, and I have not yet come, so I give him a blow job in the manner I imagine *I* would like, and he comes in my mouth. I don't like it really, but I don't dislike it either, but I am very pleased that I did it. I am so close to coming from this feeling of his cock in my mouth that I quickly move to where either he or Maisie suck me the rest of the way.

When I see Maisie's face reddened and perspiring from

all the sex she's had, I feel so good and so complete that
we look at each other and break out laughing in that manner that has always meant, "I love you, my darling; and I
will always be grateful that you have been so loving as to
allow me the sheer joy of sex with you, and with others, for
what makes you happy, makes me happy."

What the other man is doing at this point is of little
consequence.

CLAYTON

It's just growing dark as Vi and I return from a pleasant
dinner. We decide to sit on the steps outside my apartment
building for a few minutes. We look at the people walking
by, commenting on the ones we feel are attractive. We had
earlier agreed to try doing a threesome and tonight seems
like a perfect time. When I see an attractive man I'm familiar with, I wave him over and invite him to come upstairs
with us for a drink.

Upstairs, we sit and talk for a while, and listen to a record. I can see that Vi is nervous, but she has a couple
drinks in a row, and she calms down somewhat. I am
pretty sure that she will go along, so I tell the guy what we
have in mind. He looks at Vi and she looks at him, and
then he agrees to do it. We go into the bedroom and I
leave the door open so that the soft light from the living
room shows through the bedroom. First Vi gets undressed,
and we both sit and watch her. She sits naked upon the
bed and we all finish our drinks. Then it is his turn. Vi and
I both watch as he takes his clothes off. He is dark-skinned
and well-built, and I wonder if Vi is getting excited. He
lays on the bed beside her and runs his hands lightly
around her.

He is not hard, although I am by now. "I guess you'll
have to suck it," he says. She seems reluctant and she looks
at me and at him. I know that she won't go this far and
back out though. Then she bends over and takes his cock
into her mouth. Her eyes are closed and she slowly nibbles
around the head of it. He begins to get hard pretty soon,
and Vi puts more into it. I run my hand between her legs

and she is wet and slimy. She opens herself and I play with her clit while she plays with his dick.

After a while, she lies down on the bed and spreads her legs in welcome. It is a compelling sight to see her thus, and both he and I get hard as iron. He mounts her and she throws back her leg so that I can see him enter. He puts just the head to her cunt and it looks too big to fit in, but quickly it slips in by itself. I can see her pussy open itself up to take him in as he slowly slides the entire length down into her. I think that by the time he reaches the bottom, they have both forgotten about me watching. She sighs and clasps him firmly with her thighs as he begins to pump slowly and deeply in and out.

I become aware of her eyes on me, watching me watch them. I take her hand in mine, and it is as if the circuit is closed. Her eyes grow dreamy and her body begins to tremble. She is coming. He responds with more powerful and faster thrusts and her trembling comes all the way down her arm to the hand that I still hold, and then it is over.

He kisses her mouth for the first time as he pulls out of her cunt for the last time. His dick is withered and small and he takes his drink and goes into the other room to refill. I put my hand between Vi's legs and find her pussy so hot that she almost burns me. She is wet all over and it runs down onto the sheet. By this time my dick has been so hard for so long that it is beginning to ache. She is so wet and so open now that I slip into her cunt almost without any effort at all. As I touch her bottom, she locks her legs around my waist. She has not opened her eyes.

"Loving my wife like I do, and wanting her to have the best of everything," Thomas says (above), he wants to furnish her with a handsome lover—but he wants to be included, too. Mac (above) makes an important distinction between fantasy and reality: The idea of his wife and two men excites his imagination, though in actuality he would "never want it to happen." Jeffrey (above) says he is sure "most men would like their wives to experience intercourse with two men at once." Only when we get to Reynolds (above) do implications that have been resisted throughout get overt statement. He calls himself bisexual.

If a man wants to define himself as homosexual, bisexual, straight—that is his business. I accept his name for himself. What is of greater interest to me in these fantasies is how the presence of the woman enables the man to express his homoerotic needs while being able to avoid facing them at the same time. The greatest number of fantasies I received were from men like Clayton (above) who are genuinely fond of women, who love their wives—but nevertheless still want some male linkage, too. "I take her hand in mine," Clayton says, "and it is as if the circuit is closed." The circuit between him, the girl, and the other man.

To the men who invented these fantasies, the first likely association to the word *sex* would be *women*. This is not to say, however, that sex with women encompasses the fullest erotic experience they can imagine. Their scenarios tell us they yearn for something more; they feel something missing—some solidarity, even physical identification, with people of their own sex.

After all, a woman cannot give a man his sense of maleness. He can desire her, but not identify with her. At best, she can give him a negative identification: *I am the opposite of her*. This can be very thrilling, but still leaves him deprived of an object of positive identification. In the fantasies in this chapter, other men are brought in to fill the void. They provide contact with an element the inventor, consciously or not, knows he needs to assert himself as fully male.

On some dim livel, women—the people for whom he gave up his boyhood closeness with other men—are still taken to be strange, unfamiliar, unpredictable, censorious; heterosexuality, for all its satisfactions, carries a note of anxiety, danger, fatigue, and risk. Like a boy who hesitates to explore a haunted house alone, these men feel more excited, sexually more courageous—*more like men*—if when they are having sex with a woman, another man is there, too.

By joining in their sexual games, the woman grants absolution and permission. It isn't so much that these men use women to get to other men as that they need the woman to help break through the guilt barrier that blocks them from their *feelings* about other men. The woman's act in making it a trio provides a connection; a double charge of sexuality flies through. The men can face what is going on between them or not—as they need. For this freedom, this release from anxiety, of course they love her all the more.

15

Groups

How many make a group? If three is a trio, is four a group, or does it take ten to make an orgy? Whether you want to call the fantasies in this chapter group sex orgies, swinging, or swapping, it is significant that of the three thousand from which this book was distilled, I collected only one or two describing scenes of more than four people. Judging from my research, it is the rare man who dreams of mass bacchanals. What seems to be wanted in these group sessions is both variety and order. Wild, wonderful wicked, wet sex, yes—but also *control*.

Clubs like Plato's Retreat, which have begun to appear in cities across America, are subtly structured. They may be playgrounds for swingers, for orgies, swaps and group scenes among consenting adults who met only four seconds earlier; but there is a firm rule at the door (other than having to pay a handsome entry fee): Women can come in any number, but every man must be accompanied by a woman.

At first glance, this may seem unexceptionable. Unless you want to run a gay establishment, how can you have an orgy without women? But why does no one worry that there might be a preponderance of women over men? Why, in fact, is it felt *desirable* to try to make this happen?

It is my belief that—consciously or not—entrepreneurs of these places realize that women have psychological benefits to confer to the proceedings, benefits at least as important as their anatomical presence. Commercially speaking, if you are going to have swaps, daisy chains, or other varieties of group sex, male patrons must be offered the greatest possible latitude of choice. A less obvious reason is that since women are experienced by men as the censors of sex, women alone can legitimize it. Even men who love orgies don't want to feel they are a gang of dirty fellows imposing their awful desires on one or two stray, freaky women. The more women present, the more women who joyfully enter into these scenes, the greater the implied permission for the men. Hell, women aren't the prissy, jealous prudes men have always expected them to be; look, they're joining in themselves—and by the dozen!

We tend to measure the sexual revolution by changes in women's behavior. If the rate of male change is not yet equally rapid, it is perhaps because they don't trust that the new attitudes women boast of have become integrated on the deepest level. A woman may signal "I am sexually liberated" and still reserve to herself the right to retreat back into old-fashioned strategies of shock, tears, reproaches, and/or flight, leaving the man "out there," naked, exposed . . . perhaps with his arms around another man.

The delicate issue here is that if a man is turned on by a woman so sexually avid she will take him on in an orgy, he must accept the possibility—not as fearsome but as fun—that he will soon be sharing her with another man, or even rubbing up against the other man himself in the heat of the moment. Only when women are present (and the more the better), is the homosexual onus taken off such an event. If two men "accidentally" find themselves touching one another while both are having intercourse with the same woman, how can they be called "queer"? Only someone of an older, hung-up generation would use that label.

This may explain why I received so few group/orgy fantasies: The subterranean psychology of these events may still be too threatening for men to put into words. Even those who did contribute to this chapter are careful to have as little male-to-male contact as possible in their scenarios. They are a transitional generation, contemporary in their ideas, but still their mothers' and fathers' sons underneath. Most of them discuss how inhibited their early training was. Several were virgins when they married. Can you really expect that attitudes as deeply implanted as those we feel about our bodies, which were imbued in us by the most important people in our lives, are going to change in ten or fifteen years of liberal thinking? Out of this grows a conflict: freedom in the mind versus guilt in the gut. The fantasies in this chapter deal with the overt and covert satisfactions men find in sharing their women sexually, and the various strategies invented to do so without anxiety.

JUSTIN

Since it will not cost me anything to experience the "high" I get from recounting my fantasies, may I submit the following:

I am a Ph.D. and at forty years of age, I live a very happy and fulfilled life with my wife of eighteen years, Bess, and our four children. Bess and I were raised very much in an inhibited style, and although I had a small and lousy attempt at fucking at the age of twenty-one, we were both essentially virgins when we married. Bess was already a teacher and I was almost finished with my doctoral studies. Although her experience with masturbation, childhood look-and-touch games was very limted, *I* was a very inquisitive and horny cock-in-hand young boy who masturbated almost every day between the ages of ten and twenty-three.

As boys between nine and fourteen, we had reciprocal suck-off sessions at rare intervals, and though I enjoyed doing it, we never "came," so the interest kind of waned. At fourteen, the homosexual taboo ended this, and I passed the next twelve years with no interest in males at all. My desire for females with whom I might have a sexual experience was always very high, but my inhibited background prevented me from admitting it. From marriage until the present, I grew rapidly more confident, more sophisticated, and I quickly nurtured and encouraged the sleeping cunt I was married to, and she turned out to be a "diamond in disguise." She has eagerly accompanied me into every kind of contact imaginable: mate swapping, ménage à trois, etc. She has been friendly and understanding to many women whom I have fucked and sucked, but this was only after I was able to assure her that sex is sex, and I would never leave her for any thousand women in the world. I have had about twenty-four women, but I always insist upon a clear understanding of the limitations of a sexual relationship, and they all seem quite willing to accept that.

Here is my fantasy: Bess and I decide to return to mate

swapping (we did for two years, and kind of "retired" four years ago), but this time no separate bedrooms. We meet a group of decent, clean swingers and agree to have a full orgy in which everyone fucks and sucks everyone else at one time or another, all naked and sprawled out in our basement on the carpeting. I am fucking one blonde, sucking a negress, and as I peer out over her mons, I see my wife vibrating with joy as she sucks off two men alternately while a third is fucking her "doggy" style. Then we all switch and it becomes a kaleidoscope of cunts, cocks, tits, hairy chests, smooth faces, and on and on and on.

LARS

It is with my wife's encouragement that I am writing this letter to you. I am a thirty-two-year-old police officer, happily married for ten years to a wonderful woman who has given us four beautiful children. Our sex life is great. Neither of us has had affairs since our marriage, although the subject of swapping and affairs comes up regularly. I guess it's just the intrigue of wondering if someone different and strange would be exciting for a change of pace, but I doubt that any permanence would ever become attached to such an arrangement. That is why I would never worry or feel insecure if she were to go to bed with another man. After the initial excitement subsided, I am totally confident that she would return to me for the really good and thorough fucking which we have learned to give each other.

I guess what I am about to tell you will blow the image that some people have of the superstraight and conservative cop. I think it's about time that people learned that policemen are just as horny and down-to-earth as any other people. Living in constant fear of being shot tends to make some of us hard shelled and unsympathetic, but that's only superficial. I think the average cop is one hell of a lot more sensuous and sexually oriented than most people would imagine. How many times have we looked down into the car as we issued the citation to the speeder and seen her miniskirt hiked up to her crotch and her low-cut blouse or halter falling away from her beautiful boobs and wished and prayed that she would reach out and fondle our genitals and we could forget this bullshit and rush to the bushes for an all-out earth-shaking fuck? How many hundreds of opportunities have been wasted when I am out alone on the highway at night talking to a beautiful woman and saying, "Ma'am, I'll need your license and registration card please," when what I really want to say is "Baby, I want to suck those beautiful tits and roll your soft little clit between my teeth." But she's put off by the badge and uniform and I'm locked into my role as enforcer of the public law and safety.

My parents were very religious people who were good to my sister and me. I never had a sex education directly from my parents, but they had an old sexual encyclopedia printed back in the 1930s which I would read whenever I had the opportunity. The very first experience I can remember was when I was about five years old and I discovered that the rotating shaft of an old electric mixer without the beaters caused a pleasant sensation when I placed it against my penis through my clothing. I sat on the floor and experimented with it for almost a year before my mother threw it away.

I began masturbating when I was twelve years old. It took me about six months before I learned that if I moved the loose skin on my circumsized penis up and down with my hand the sensations were much more pleasant than when I rubbed the palm of my hand around on the head. I remember one summer night lying awake in my bed pumping up and down on my prick with my hand when I suddenly felt a strange and wonderful sensation. A wet substance came out of my penis onto my hand. I thought at first I had urinated, but it just didn't feel the same as urine and the sensation had not been the same as when I peed. I crept into the bathroom and turned on the light and much to my surprise and amazement, I found that I had had my first ejaculation. The ejaculate was clear and sticky, not white like my friends said it would be, but nonetheless I knew that I had finally "come." I very excitedly told my buddies about it the next day, and I felt much more mature to be in the select group of "comers." After masturbating to ejaculation several times over the next few nights, my ejaculate became a creamy white color, and I was relieved to know that I was completely normal. I continued masturbating an average of at least five or six times a week through my teens and until my early twenties. I still masturbate whenever I get the urge, but it's usually only once or twice a month these days.

When I was a boy, I would fantasize during masturbation about the girls in my neighborhood. I didn't have a completely accurate idea of what intercourse was all about, but I knew that I wanted to put my "prick" in some girl's "pussy." The girl who I most wanted to fuck was Joyce. I frequently visualized walking with her into the woods at the end of the street where she would lie back on the soft pine needles and pull off her panties. I would lie down on top of her and put my prick between her legs. I didn't know whether you were supposed to move or not, but technicalities didn't bother my twelve-year-old mind.

Now let me tell you about my wife and another girl at the same time. I have always been strongly sexually attracted to her sister. I imagine the three of us are on our king-size bed and my cock is buried to the hilt in my sister-in-law's cunt while I am sucking my wife's clitoris. All of us come in a frenzied screaming orgasm.

Another favorite fantasy is that my wife and I are swapping partners with another couple. She and her lover are fucking on the thick shag rug with only the firelight from the fireplace for illumination. The flickering light gives me fleeting glimpses of my wife's face as she throws her head back with her mouth gasping and her lover buries his prick into her cunt. I see the lips of her cunt clinging to his cock as he slowly pulls his penis out only to shove it back into her again. As I watch my wife, I am fucking a blond-haired and blue-eyed vixen with rather smallish breasts and a long slender neck and long legs. Her cunt is tight and her vaginal muscles alternately squeeze and release my prick. She is sitting astride me and we slowly fuck and watch the other couple. I come again and again, but we never stop fucking. I wish that imaginary stamina were true in real life. Two or three ejaculations a night is the best I can achieve now, and usually it's only one.

HARVEY

My wife and I are both upper-middle-class, college educated, living in one of the "affluent" suburbs. I have a responsible job as an executive of a moderately large corporation. I'm in my upper fifties; she, in her lower fifties. Married close to thirty years and parents of two children.

We've tried swinging a number of times but have been grievously disappointed by the unfeeling people we've met. We longed for a truly understanding, affectionate, long-term relationship with another couple who could be friends as well as bed partners, people to whom we could truly relate and with whom we could relax and feel at ease in an uninhibited relationship.

I learned a long time ago, back in high school, that I just can't screw a woman until there is some small element of a friendly and affectionate relationship between us. I don't have to love her, but I do have to like her. The prospect of cold, calculated, unfeeling sex leaves me unable to get a hard-on.

My fantasy involves the couple we've never been fortunate enough to find, and it goes like this. . . .

Their ad in the swinger's publication had sounded fine: intelligent, restrained, and discreet. The first phone conversation had been encouraging. Dick had a full, firm voice that smacked of self-confidence and assurance without undue aggressiveness—just the kind of man to take Betty in hand and put her at ease. Diane's voice had an innocent sexiness and a low, throaty laugh that hit me right in the crotch.

I opened the front door and watched them get out of the car. There was a flash of creamy thigh as Diane swung her legs out and then stood up, smoothing down her skirt. Dick and I sized each other up quickly as we shook hands. Just about my age and build. Good smile. The handshake was firm but with no attempt to crush any bones. I could not helping thinking that Betty would enjoy the feel of those firm but gentle hands on her breasts.

The martinis just hit the spot, and I was aware that they were relaxing from a tension that hadn't been apparent at first sight. I liked that too. They weren't so blasé that we were just bodies instead of people to them. As we chatted about life in the suburbs, an eavesdropper would never dream that in a half-hour or so, we were going to be fucking like four rabbits.

And Diane was worth everything a man could give her. Damn, but that innocent, little-girl sexiness was making me as hot as a blowtorch.

Most women like a certain firm directness on a man's part. I pulled the laces and kicked off my shoes. The hi-fi was loaded with a tape of Glenn Miller, Artie Shaw, Benny Goodman, Tommy Dorsey, and Guy Lombardo. I snapped the switches and "Moonlight Serenade" flooded the room from four speakers. Diane looked a bit puzzled as I knelt at her feet and slipped off her shoes. But she smiled gaily as I took her hands, pulled her to her feet, and into my arms.

"What are you thinking about?" she invited.

"That we were both naked as we dance so I could feel those full, lush titties rubbing against my chest and your warm, wet pussy moving against my cock.

"And when the music stopped," I went on, "I'd lay you down, slip in between those magnificent thighs, bury my cock right up to the balls in your luscious pussy, and fuck you until I pumped such a load of cream into your soft white belly that it would run out your ears."

I couldn't be mistaken. Her breathing *had* quickened! We danced a while longer. Sound crazy? She was such a good dancer, I didn't want to rush this. I liked this girl and would have enjoyed her company even if I knew I couldn't lay her. I glanced at the couch and laughed softly. I hadn't seen Betty move over to join Dick. Her blouse was open to the waist and Dick was sucking her lovely tits like a starving man going after twin sirloin steaks.

With my hands on Diane's luscious ass, we stopped dancing. I reached behind me and snapped off the hi-fi. Glenn Miller had done his job. The rest was up to me.

"I love to watch Betty getting fucked," I told her. "I'm never as proud of my wife as when I see how much pleasure she can give a man when she takes his cock in her warm, wet pussy and makes him spill his load in her soft, white belly."

Small, convulsive contractions were running through

those gorgeous buttocks that filled my hands as Diane began to gently hump her pelvis against me. "That's when I enjoy fucking her the most," I went on. "When I can slip my cock into her and feel how slick and slippery she is from the cream another man's prick just poured into her."

Diane slipped her hand down between us, got a good grip on Peter, and squeezed.

"When the evening is over," I said, "and I take Betty to bed, I hope I'm going to feel a good load of Dick's cream in her cunt. And when Dick gets you home and gives you the last fuck of the night, I hope he's going to feel a good load of my cream in your cunt. Every time your husband sucks your tits for the next mouth, he's going to taste my cream oozing out of your nipples."

She pulled down my zipper and Peter came out at her like a steel spring. She grabbed him and I could feel that the palm of her hand was wet.

I let go of her magnificent ass and pushed the blouse off her shoulders. I found the top button at her waist, then the zipper, and her skirt slid to her feet. Except for a black garter belt and stockings, she stood gloriously naked before me. I slid backward into the chair, holding her around the waist and pulling her into my lap.

I gently squeezed those fantastic tits and pinched the stiff, crimson buds. She was panting like a steam engine gone berserk. Her lush, ripe thighs fell apart. I touched her trigger lightly and she almost went off. Her pussy was as wet and slick as though she'd just been oiled.

I looked over at the couch. Betty was naked. Dick had pushed her back into one corner of the couch, her legs were draped over his shoulders, and he was slurping in her pussy like a drunk at the spigot of a whiskey barrel.

Groaning with the pain in my aching balls, I pushed Diane off my lap. I half led and half pushed her across the room to the other end of the couch. She took hold of the collar of my shirt and yanked. Buttons flew like hailstones and she ripped the shirt off. She dropped to her knees before me, pulled at my belt, and let the pants fall. Peter came up at her so fast and hard that if her face had been a few inches closer, she'd have gotten a broken jaw. Before she could grab the object of her affections, I put my hands under armpits and drew her down to the floor. I dropped to my knees, and her lush thighs came down over my shoulders. Grabbing one tit in each hand for balance, I dove tongue first into her dripping snatch.

My lips traveled over the velvety softness of her thighs, through the deep crease that framed her mound, across her lower belly, and down through the other crease to the other thigh. I took her succulent, plump pussy lips into my mouth, each in its turn, and sucked them gently. My tongue stabbed at the bottom of her love slit and traced its way up the dripping furrow to the little red trigger at the top. I licked it delicately and felt her jump. Her thighs were quivering uncontrollably.

I felt Dick's bare buttock against my own ass. Kneeling beside me on the floor, he tongued-lashed Betty's cunt. Her legs were splayed open, pulling her pussy lips apart. Her head was thrown back, she was panting, and I could see the telltale quivering of her thighs.

"Time!" I called. "It's our turn," I announced firmly. "You chicks work on us for a change."

"I was almost there," Diane complained reproachfully. "Another few seconds and I'd have had it."

"Just think of how good it's going to feel when you do finally get it," I told her cheerfully. "The longer you wait, the better it is. Now suck."

There's nothing subtle about my girl when she's trying to get herself fucked. She gobbled Dick's cock like a hungry trout going after a big, fat fly. Diane's experienced tongue traveled over Peter like a little red paintbrush. I felt the spasmodic clamping at the base of my spine. Her tongue was a small darting flame, scorching everything it touched. Her soft lips parted and encased the head. Her head went down slow . . . down and down and down until Peter bumped his head on the back of her throat. I groaned—a sound of pure anguish that started in my balls and crawled upward through my quivering body.

"Time!" I called again. I arranged them the way I liked best; lying side by side, pointing in opposite directions, each girl's head by the other girl's hip. I knelt before Diane as Dick knelt before Betty.

I leaned over and kissed Betty. "I love you," I told her. "It's so nice to have my cock in another girl's pussy while I watch you getting fucked. It makes me proud to see how much pleasure Dick is having with his prick in your luscious cunt.

"Dick, let's see if we can come together," I suggested. "I want to cream off in your wife's pussy while your prick is squirting in my wife's cunt."

The view was perfect in either direction, but what was I to watch? Dick's cock making those long, slow, deep strokes in my wife's cunt or my cock churning in circles in his wife's cunt?

I paced myself with Dick in perfect cadence. As he came up, I went down. I watched his stiff, throbbing cock come almost out of Betty, glistening with her juice, as my cock sank home into the sweet wetness of his wife. Then he watched my cock come out of Diane, wet and shining, as he sank his prick into the wet warmth of my wife's love nest.

I'd thought the bastard was going to beat me, but I outlasted him by a matter of seconds. He came up high, like a tarpon breaking water in its death leap, then stiffened and plunged, shaking spasmodically.

"There he goes," I gritted through my teeth to Diane. "Your husband's prick is squirting in my wife's cunt. He's pumping her belly full of thick, rich cream. Now I'm going to empty my balls in your belly."

She set her nails in my back and tore. Her body arched like a bow, her eyes bulged, and she screamed—a long, shivering scream that started in her cunt and ripped through her guts like a barbed spear.

My balls exploded and a geyser of sperm erupted from my cock, gushing into her spasming cunt like a tidal wave, and pouring through her belly in a hot, foaming flood.

Betty was laying on her back as limp as a rag doll. Her legs were still sprawled open as though she hadn't the strength to close them. Mingled sperm and pussy juice was trickling out of her cunt and down the crack of her ass. Dick lay limply beside her, his cock a withered and shriveled noodle, lifeless in the wake of total defeat. Diane groaned and dragged herself up on one elbow. Her luscious tits dangled and swung enticingly before me. I reached out and captured one, reveling in the feel of the soft, sweet flesh. "You are a glorious piece of ass, baby," I told her appreciatively.

The evening was over. Our new good friends said good night. We would meet again.

By the time I'd finished my shower and come out of the bathroom, Betty was already in bed.

I lit a cigarette and stretched out beside her. It had been a bitch of a weekend. We'd given the lawn its final mowing, taken the screens out of the storm windows, and replaced them with the glass panels. And she'd been with me every step of the way. Damned few wives work with their husbands the way she does with me.

I patted her lovingly on the behind. She sighed, curled up into a tighter ball, pulled the covers a little higher, and was asleep again. I didn't have the heart to wake her. My signal had gone unanswered, but I couldn't blame her.

I was probably too tired myself to be able to fuck, even if she'd wanted to. But Peter wasn't at all tired, and now he was standing up stiff and demanding.

There was only one way to be sure of a sound night's sleep. I took him in my hand and began to stroke him gently as my mind slid effortlessly into my favorite fantasy. . . .

ALLEN

I am fifty-five years old, a radical therapist, married seven years in my second marriage (twenty-three in the first), with four children and four stepchildren; my wife is also a radical therapist, and some of our work is collaborative. My wife and I have an open sexual relationship, and I really enjoy having a sexual experience with more than one person simultaneously.

My fantasies are always explicit, in that they always involve people I know and care for, rather than faceless strangers; in fact, the familiarity of the faces, and the changes in the faces as the people undergo increasing levels of sexual excitement, seems to be an important dimension of the fantasy. These are such important fantasies to me that I have even asked some of the people involved if they would be willing to act out my fantasy with me—

unfortunately, this has never happened. In any case, my fantasy:

Diane and I are with Mark and Jean—we have just played tennis together, then gone skinny-dipping, and all crowded into the Bensons' big bathtub. Now we are lying on their huge bed, all of us mellow and quiet. The peacefulness of the scene, the joyful experiences we have shared, and the beauty and vulnerability of the naked bodies of my friends around me arouse me. I start to make love to Diane—gently, slowly, I caress her feet, her ankles, and then move my hands up her calves, to her knees. I kiss her toes, very lightly at first, then with more hunger, more passion. All the while my hands, my fingertips, are tracing lightly over her feet and calves. She sighs lightly, and shifts her weight, opening her knees slightly under my caresses—it is all the encouragement I need! My mouth, my hands, my fingertips, my tongue, shower her toes, her feet, her legs and knees with little kisses, caresses, nips, and little licks as well. Her knees open wider to this loving assault, and I kiss her thighs, savoring, with my fingertips and tongue and lips, their smoothness and softness. Delicately, I kiss her all around her vagina, and then up the twin valleys between her belly and thighs; lightly, I bite through the pussy hair to the sweet mound it shapes.

Finally, after she has been urging me to for some time, by the silent and urgent language of her hands, and her undulating, twisting body, and her less-than-silent moans, and quickened breathing, I very delicately kiss the still-closed lips of her vagina; very slowly, very lightly, I touch her lips with just the tip of my tongue. Moving her body and her two hands, pulling me toward her, she tries to pull my searching tongue into her cunt. Finally, I can no longer stand to see her in the sweet agony I have created, so I plunge my tongue into her cunt. I search out every fold of those sweet lips, exploring with my tongue, planting deep, sucking kisses on the lips of her pussy, plunging my tongue deep into her vagina one minute, probing all the little precious corners another, sweeping from asshole to clitoris the next, until she is in a frenzy of passion.

By this time, her face and breasts are flushed with sexual excitement, her nipples hard and erect, and tiny beads of sweat have formed on her upper lip; and her noises! A more exotic song of lust and sexual hunger you cannot imagine! Moved by this emotion, Jean comes close to her, and cradles Diane's head against her breast, stroking her face and arms gently and lovingly. Diane reaches out her hands, and pulls Jean's mouth down to hers—at first, Jean is surprised by the passion of Diane's kisses, but soon she is returning them with equal hunger. Her hands are now strongly massaging Diane's upper arms; with my tongue still deep in Diane's cunt, I reach up and gently move Jean's hands from Diane's arms to her breasts—later we learned that never before had she touched another woman's breasts. I was struck at the time by the tenderness and hunger with which she explored the sweet mounds of Diane's titties.

Curious, and emboldened by the encouragement she was receiving from Diane's hand and body language, Jean began exploring Diane's belly, moving from titties to navel, and then down to that furry pussy hair I had not too long ago been playfully tormenting. For a moment, I left my sweet chore at Diane's cunt, and moved to kiss Jean full on the lips. Our eyes locked, and we both felt a closeness, a tenderness we had never experienced before. Eagerly she licked the pussy juice off of my lips, and sucked it from my beard; inspired, I dove down to Diane's cunt, and sucked up a mouthful of those sweet juices, to trickle it into Jean's mouth like a mother bird feeding her young.

Meanwhile, Mark has not been idle; he has watched all of the play and passion with a great deal of interest, but he can no longer remain a spectator. Taking his by now huge, red, and very hard cock in his hand, he drives it into Jean's wet and ready cunt. As she moved down Diane's belly with her trail of kisses, her sweet exposed bottom was too delightful for Mark to ignore, so the thrusts of his demanding cock, pushing deep into the wet hotness of her pussy, was driving her closer to Diane's cunt in total harmony with the pull of her own hunger and curiosity. As Jean was exploring Diane's body with her mouth and tongue, Diane's own mouth had not been idle; indeed, she had been savoring Jean's sweet flesh with as much hunger and delight as Jean expended on hers. Artfully she placed her mouth close to Jean's pussy, and without words, indicated to Mark that she wanted to take his cock into her mouth on

alternate strokes; he was quick to comply with her hunger
and pleasure. First he drove his cock, and a big cock it
was, deep into Jean's ready cunt. Then, equally slowly, he
withdrew it, and drove it just as deep into Diane's ready
and identically hungry mouth, side by side with Jean's
pussy. Slowly she sucked the Jean-juice off of Mark's prick,
to his great pleasure, and then sent him willingly back for
that sweet savory Diane found so delightful.

Jean, her body driven by Mark's thrusting until her
mouth was close to Diane's cunt, soon saw the waste of
using my mouth as the middleman, so to speak, so she
pushed me aside, seeing no need to wait for the slow transfer to those cunt juices via my mouth.

Diane, sensing the change, responded quickly with a similar idea for herself; pushing Mark's cock out of the way,
she pushed her face, her nose, her tongue, even her teeth
into Jean's cunt, licking, kissing, poking, biting with a
great deal of curious energy. She rubbed her eyebrows, all
parts of her face, into Jean's wet cunt, so hungry was her
curiosity, so passionate was her release. After a few moments of this kind of passion, both women, with an almost
painful slow tenderness, as if they had never experienced
such exquisite agony, licked and probed and nibbled, while
Mark and I, with some reverence, and a great deal of excitement, masturbated madly, until all four of us, with
screams and groans, exploded in a paroxysm of four, soar-
ing orgasms.

It is a cliché that a woman cannot have sex with a man
without falling in love. Very broadly put, women want a
continuing involvement with the men they go to bed with;
men rarely see sex as a basis for marriage. I find it interesting how men like Justin and Lars (both above), who have
fantasies about group sex, insist repeatedly how much they
love their wives. To the feminine mind, this seems contradictory. If his wife is so great and he feels so strongly about
her, why go looking for someone new?

Men are not raised on safety first. They are praised for
being adventurous, experimental, for wanting ever to climb
the next mountain. "If this woman of mine is so great," a

man might think, "wouldn't it be even better if I had two like her, if I could see her even more excited in the arms of another woman, or even another man?"

Marital fidelity is a positive, but so is sexual variety. It is a difficult equation, which everyone must balance for himself/herself: The more you have of one, the less of the other. In some future, more egalitarian time, wives may feel as free as men to suggest swinging their marriages. That time is not yet.

Many a woman has read a book or a magazine article and decided she is thus liberated. She wakes up in bed with one (or two) strangers the next morning and realizes that her earliest training in guilt and fear of uncontrolled sex is not shed so easily. Most women instinctively know this; it is usually the husband's adventurousness that brings the couple into experimental sex. The old solution was the double standard; the restless husband would have an affair on the side and tell his wife that he had to go out of town on business.

Current values say that honesty is all, even more important than fidelity. "Our love for each other will grow stronger because we haven't kept each other in prison. In our honesty is union and strength. We'll always come back to each other." Justin assures his wife that sex is merely sex; and that even if he could have a thousand other women, he would never leave her. It is an argument that women increasingly find impossible to resist—especially since a bit of unspoken blackmail hangs in the air: If I can't have an extramarital affair with your love and permission, I'll have it anyway, but secretly, and maybe leave you after all.

Men who believe in the double standard compartmentalize their lives. What has that little run-in with the summer stock actress in Canada got to do with his wife? Lars is a different kind of man. He speaks of his great love for his wife, and of their mutual happiness. His wife even encourages him to send in his fantasies. Is it a surprise that she is in both of them?

Lars reminds us that while men are raised less symbiotically than women, this is only a comparative statement. The little boy wants to feel free to roam the world, but also wants the feeling that mother is at home, waiting for him when he comes back. The most notorious philanderers are shocked and hurt when they come home one morning and find their wives have left. What men like Lars desire is to add sexual spice and variety to their lives, *but to maintain the love bond with the wife at the same time*. They are often so symbiotically meshed that even if an episode of infidelity is never confessed, it nags at the back of their minds. His wife has come to live in his conscience. She is so much a part of him, he feels she must somehow know what he is thinking, what he has experienced. The result is gnawing fear that somehow the wife will "know" there was a little episode with the secretary last Thursday night, and will leave.

If sex with someone else thus threatens the love tie, why not turn it around and make infidelity not a force of disruption but a shared, even more binding experience? Consciously or not, this is usually the reasoning behind swapping. Lars wants sex with a stranger, yes, but if his wife is having sex with a stranger, too, how can she get mad at him? What a relief to find that temporarily separating yourself from your wife—long enough to have sex with someone else, at any rate—does not bring retribution, loss, and hate! While swinging very often ends by causing trouble between partners, in all fairness it must be said that it need not. It can bring people psychic satisfaction—a sense of increased space in which to live (although I've heard from few such people).

When Harvey's wife joins in his fantasy infidelity, his relief at not being punished takes the form of gratitude and excitement. "I'm never as proud of my wife as when I see how much pleasure she can give a man when she takes his cock in her warm, wet pussy." Whenever he himself is with another woman, says Harvey, "I love to watch Betty getting fucked" at the same time. Even in fantasy, they fuck other people together, in the same room. By thus giving the man permission for his own sexual experiments, the woman becomes more united to him than ever. Symbiosis once again.

Harvey's highly dramatized fantasy reads like a *True Confessions* romance, complete with Hollywood effects and music sound track. But am I alone in feeling that behind all that liberated sucking and fucking, a lot of old-

fashioned moralizing is going on? Everything is so stren-
uously beautiful and lofty that only a prig would feel it has
anything to do with "dirty" sex.

In fact, isn't Harvey's flowery language being used to
cover up attitudes he might not like if they were to become
conscious? The description of his new friend at the end of
the evening sounds more like that of a defeated opponent
than that of a partner in pleasure. Dick's cock is a "withered and shriveled noodle, lifeless in the wake of total defeat," but Harvey himself is left "reveling" in feelings of
enhanced sexual desire, ready to have still one more go with
his wife. All throughout the evening, no matter how heated
he was by Diane, his eye rarely seems to have strayed from
Dick. "That's when I enjoy fucking her [his own wife] the
most," he tells us. "When I can slip my cock into her and
feel how slick and slippery she is from the cream another
man's prick just poured into her."

Harvey paces himself against the other man: "As he
came up, I went down." The contest is to see who can last
the longer—with the other's wife. Hasn't this fantasy begun
to sound not so much a playful game between boys and
girls but a match between two rivals to see who is the most
masculine of all?

In fact, Harvey's absolute control over the whole proceedings—interrupting other people's orgasms by calling
time, arranging bodies on the floor "the way I like best"—
reminds me of one of those whistle-blowing cruise directors
who infuriate everyone on board ship. This control allows
him to get as close to the other guy as he can tolerate—but
no closer. When Harvey mentions he can feel Dick's bare
buttocks against his own ass, it is very much *en passant*.
Otherwise, the men in this chapter do not touch at all.

The scene being created is a veritable *Saturday Evening
Post* cover for swingers: nice married couples getting together with other nice married couples. The closest the
men get to sexual contact is entering the woman while the
other's semen in her is still fresh.

In Allen's fantasy, the rules are even more rigid: The
main action is between the women; the men are largely
restrained to masturbating on the sidelines. The unspoken
emotion here is that while the other man is a partner, he is
also a possible competitor—and if he got too close, he

might even become a lover. The rules make sure that what the two men share are the pleasures of the imagination and the eye, not of touch. Close, but not too close.

These fantasies attempt to solve the problem of sexual variety and fidelity at the same time. In real life, my contributors tell me, it is rarely so easy. The Harveys, for instance, find that sex without emotion is a turnoff; but they never found a swinging couple with whom they could have a deep and lasting friendship as well.

Mr. and Mrs. Harvey may feel hemmed in by orthodox marital fidelity, but their solution is not to try for individual space for each within the marriage. This would threaten the symbiotic bond. What they want to do instead is extend the symbiosis outward, to include four people rather than just two. Since most people go into swinging scenes precisely to break what they experience as the suffocations of too close relationships, the Harveys never found what they wanted. Symbiosis between two people is difficult enough; trying to do it *à quatre* is almost impossible.

16

Straight Men, Gay Fantasies

Parents worry about masturbation, but anxiety about homosexuality is so great that it isn't even mentioned, lest the injunction itself "give the boy ideas." Kids who learn to masturbate on their own are thrilled and relieved to find the whole baseball team has been engaged in circle jerks for months. Goosing each other in the shower, mutual masturbation in the movies, reading dirty books and magazines together when there are no adults around—it's all just horsing around, breaking the rules—that's how boys are. Contrary to popular superstition, such early homoerotic play can strongly confirm gender identity. *"All the guys do it."*

Note the number of fantasies that begin with memories of real sex play with other little boys. The statements come in the context of early erotic gusto, kid stuff given as proof of virility today. They couldn't wait to get into sex and took whatever outlet was available.

This is not to say that these men feel no guilt or anxiety today about their homosexual memories or fantasies; after all, they're now grown-up, and know what society thinks of such ideas. But in their heart of hearts, they call themselves—and think of themselves—as heterosexuals. Even Wade (below), who feels it might have been nice if he had been born a girl, has a strong sexual preference: If he had been born female, he could have been a lesbian and had sex with women. But isn't that what he does in real life today?

Some men spend their lives "forgetting" early physical contact with their own sex. (Some men, of course, never had it.) The men in this chapter not only remember, but like to play around with fantasies that release those boyhood energies again.

Another researcher might have put them into the next chapter on bisexuals, or combined both sets with a third group who name themselves homosexual. This school of psychology is almost theological in conviction of sin: Thinking it is equivalent to doing it. If these men call themselves heterosexual, who am I to say I know them better than they do themselves? They have the courage to face the dark mysteries and alternatives Eros offers us all. Why should our response be a kind of flight from freedom, an automatic labeling that slams the door on further thought?

JOCK

I am a boy of thirteen and have enjoyed sex with myself from about the age of nine or ten. I remember back to when my sister and my friend used to play doctor and explore each other's bodies in the privacy of the bathroom. My sister and I used to take showers together, and I (at the time I didn't know what it was) got a sexual pleasure out of sticking my finger in her bare pussy when I got the chance.

My first sexual experience was at the age of nine when I was in the bathroom fantasizing about a girl I had a crush on in school. I placed a stuffed dog between my legs and was humping it—not knowing what I was doing—acting on impulse. Suddenly, to my amazement, I felt a strange, wonderful sensation pass through my body, and my penis began to quiver. Since then I was on my way to more wonderful years of playing with myself, which I do until this day—at least twice a day. I know that sounds like a lot, but I really dig it.

Since my first pubic hair sprouted, I was fascinated with pubic hair. I remember seeing a boy one summer with no hair under his arms, and the next year with an armpit full. I watched impatiently as the hair slowly started to sprout from under my arm. Every chance I get, I look under people's arms—especially boys and girls of my age. I just get some sexual pleasure at seeing their hair.

One of my fantasies takes place when I insert tampons in my anus, while I masturbate. I imagine one of my friends really giving it to me good up the ass. I'm not a homosexual, but I would love to really make it in every way possible with a couple of my friends.

In fact, a friend slept over one night, and asked me if I still jerked off (we jerked off together on another occasion), and I told him yes. We agreed we'd do it at his house that night. Well, I was all hot the whole day and in the back of my mind, I had the fantasy of us jerking each other off, then leading into blowing each other. When the time came, he was reluctant to jerk off (I was using suntan oil—the best). Well, let me tell you, that night my dick must have been a foot long, and I said to hell with him, I'm jerking off! Well, he watched as I slowly hand fucked myself and shot my come at least five feet in the air. Then he started to masturbate. His dick was so tiny—about 3 inches—he could handle it with one hand—even two fingers—when I had my hands full! He marveled at my whopper and asked what I did to get it so big. "Just practice," I told him. I really got hot watching him jerking off that little practically hairless three-inch jobber, and finally he came. He was inexperienced and asked if that was it. I told him I'd show him how to jerk off professionally in the morning, but we never got around to it. Next time we meet up, I'll be more daring and offer to masturbate him.

I always have dreamed of my girl friend and girls I know fucking, sucking, blowing and kissing me. Sex is on my mind constantly, but I'm still a virgin—not for long I hope.

CONNARD

I don't know if I had any sexual fantasies when I was younger—I'm twenty-two now. My dad left us when I was a kid and for most of my life, it's been my mother and me and a younger sister. We were raised kinda strictly in church with the hell-fire and damnation stuff, and it might have inhibited my sexual thoughts. I do remember an experience, though, that really happened to me when I was about seven years old. One day my mom took my sister to get some shoes in town, so she had the next-door neighbor baby-sit for me. I guess she was about thirteen or fourteen.

She and a girl friend played some games with me, and then she asked if I wanted to play a very special game. She and her friend took me out to their garage and took off my pants and tied me to the floor. They both played with my penis, and tickled the daylights out of me, and I got a little seven-year-old erection. I guess it wasn't good for much of anything at that age, but she took off her underpants and sat down on it for a little while. I guess it gave her some funny sensations (the same it gave me?), but she didn't say much; she just had a smile on her face the whole time she was touching me and playing with my penis. She kept me tied up for an hour or so; and when she let me go, she told me never to tell my mother or anybody what had happened. She told me it was wicked, a sin; and that if anybody knew I had done it, I would be damned in hell forever. Being a churchgoer, that scared me, so I kept my mouth shut and never told my mother. The girl never did anything to me again, and neither did anybody else that I remember, but it must have made me feel a little uncomfortable or I probably wouldn't have remembered it.

I don't think I was too much a sex fiend in my high school years. At least my friends tell me I was retarded in that area. I dated some but never pressured a girl too much, and it was an older woman who taught me the early pleasures of sex and balling.

I'm a singer, trying to make it from little clubs to the big time. If I had a fantasy now, I guess it would be to be Elvis Presley. Ever since I can remember, I wanted to sing like him and have people love me the way they loved him. I watched his TV special in 1968 and I wanted girls to scream for me like that and go crazy when I performed. I wear jumpsuits in my shows and since I already have long black hair and blue eyes like him, sometimes I do have people tell me I look like him. A couple times when I've walked from the stage to my dressing room, girls have reached out to touch me and some of them don't touch your hand or face, they reach for the crotch. I don't know if they get a thrill from it; but I must admit that sometimes when I get back to the dressing room, they have given me a nice erection!

I saw Elvis in Las Vegas a couple times, and I also saw him once at his Hollywood house. My girl friend and I

drove up there one day and he did come out, and he did
stop and talk for a minute. I feel funny admitting it, but I
half wanted to make love to him, even though we were
both guys. On the way home, my girl friend said she'd like
to ball him; and before I could stop, I blurted out that I'd
like to ball him, too. I have never had a homosexual experience before, but he was such a good-looking man, really
almost beautiful, yet masculine, too, that I just wondered
what it would be like to go down on him or feel his body
pressed up against mine.

When I'm with a girl, I don't really fantasize, but sometimes when I'm alone I do daydream about fucking Elvis
and how it would feel. And I daydream about being him,
and having millions of girls in love with me and wanting to
ball me all the time.

WADE

I am twenty-five, married two years. Both my wife and I
have college educations and enjoy a good open marriage.

My first awareness of sexual impulses came when I was
about nine. I would get a sexual feeling of excitement
whenever I changed into my bathing suit at the beach
change-houses. The feeling of the sand on my feet made
me feel hot and I would also fantasize about urinating with
my swimsuit on and feeling the hot, yellow liquid run
down my legs. I also thought about this while on a teeter-
totter in the summer. Usually it was with this one boy in
the neighborhood on whom I developed a crush. We would
be wearing our swimming trunks and I could feel the hot,
wooden board of the teeter-totter under me, and I would
wish he would let go and pee when he was in the high
position. I weighed more than him, and so I could hold
him up there and the warm stream would then run down,
and over my extended legs. This same boy was also the
subject of some unconscious sexual feelings which were altogether too vague and wonderful.

A couple of years later, I developed a tremendous crush
on a girl at school, for the simple reason that she wore
nylons in class, and I could see her legs. I guess I have
always been a leg man. I would stare at her legs all day. At

this time I began to masturbate regularly and fantasized from a list of about ten girls in my class. I would imagine a different girl every time. Then I would write their first names on the palms of my hands in ink, five on each palm, sometimes one to a finger tip, and masturbate about the one I could most easily recall at that particular time. Also, the cigarette played an important role in these fantasies. I would always look at the back of *Time* magazine to see the pretty girl smoking her cigarette. This aroused me. Although I did not know what girls' cunts looked like then, I would imagine my fantasy partner wearing a bikini, and wanting to hide her cigarettes from passersby, she would put them up her cunt. I would imagine myself walking along the river bank and finding her alone, I would proceed to feel her up and then I would discover two cigarettes in her cunt. The two of us would then enjoy a smoke with the permeating aroma of her love juices among the tobaccos.

Nothing much happened during high school, except that I continued to dream about this particular girl who wore the shortest skirts in the entire school. The next significant development was at university. A group of us guys decided to go to a movie. It just happened that there was a lesbian scene in the movie. This aroused me tremendously and even to this day, I fantasize continuously about lesbians. Before this movie, I had never even thought about homosexuality. Its existence had never even entered my mind. I began to read up on the subject, and I learned a great deal. It was only a short step before I began to imagine myself involved in male-to-male love relationships. This continued throughout my first year at university, continually alternating between lesbian and homosexual sex. Normal sex didn't seem to excite me at all. Although I would always get an erection when I thought about fooling around with another guy, and I often masturbated to this fantasy, as soon as I came, I would consider sex with a guy as being disgusting and wonder how anyone could ever have a male homosexual relationship. However, lesbian relationships continued to impress me. At times, I would think of sex with two girls. I would make it with both of them, and lie back and watch them go at each other.

Thereafter, I met my wife and thus never did get into a

homosexual affair. I know if the time had been right, if I had a private place and the right guy had come along, I would have been willing to give it a try. My wife knows of my lesbian fantasies, and I have let it be known to her that I would like to see another girl making it with her. Although she does not seem interested, I have some magazines and printed material on the subject of lesbianism, which she has looked at. At present, I still have some homosexual thoughts, and often put her panty hose on when she is not around, and I am feeling particularly horny. At times I have thought it would have been nice if I had been a girl, for then I could have been a lesbian.

SAM

I am twenty-five years old, heterosexual and single, although my girl friend stays with me and we will probably get married soon. We have both had many lovers, I myself starting at age eleven, when I was literally raped by a girl three years my senior. I am also a musician with a degree in electronics.

Usually my fantasy will begin as I am driving home in my car. I see two girls about my age hitchhiking. Both are very attractive. One has a large chest and the other is rather flat. (Don't get the wrong idea about my use of the word flat. Large nipples can be the most stimulating of all.) I start to rap with them after I pick them up, and we go up to my apartment to have a drink or smoke a joint. Eventually, the conversation turns to sex and since we are all sitting together on the couch, one or both of the girls start to rub my thigh. Naturally, I return the gesture, and we get into some heavy three-way petting and kissing. We retire to the bedroom, where I help undress the girl with big tits, while the other girl undresses me. The busty girl goes down on me and I remove the other's blouse and kiss and suck her nipples. I start to remove her pants, but before I can she too goes down to lick my cock and balls. I enjoy very much being sucked and licked, as I also enjoy making love to two women at once.

Both girls suddenly stop and the smaller one expresses a

great desire for me to eat her. I am extremely excited, and
eating cunt is one of my favorite pastimes, so I remove her
pants quickly. Imagine my surprise when I see a well-
formed cock where I expected to find a juicy cunt! Since I
have had a desire (and most men do) to suck a cock, I go
down on him hungrily. Soon I'm rewarded with a mouthful
of delicious come. The three of us fuck and suck each
other to many orgasms and get together quite often after
this first encounter.

I would like to point out that if homosexuality was not
looked down upon by society, everyone would be bisexual
to a great extent. My only encounter with a man occurred
when I was somewhat drunk. I sucked and licked his dick
a little, but he did not come in my mouth, although he did
suck me off to an orgasm. Usually my girl will save a little
come in her mouth when she sucks me off, so I have tasted
it and I do find it a pleasing experience. I have also eaten
her cunt after intercourse. The combination of tastes is fantastic.

DAVID

I am twenty-one years old. Like most young boys, I had
various homosexual encounters when growing up. Occasionally, I think about them. I fantasize sucking this guy's
penis, a guy I grew up with. His name was Mike. As kids
we would have sex together and this was my most recent
homosexual affair (maybe ten years ago). It is my only
fantasy concerning homosexuality and I don't use it too
often, probably due to a guilt of some sort.

Mike and I were neighbors. He was slightly younger
than I (I was around twelve). I recall going over to his
house frequently when we could be alone there. First we'd
strip naked and masturbate together. We'd suck each other
off or play with each other and I'd usually mount his ass
(but not penetrate it). We would rub genitals and this
would get me very hot. We'd think about fucking some girl
in the neighborhood and soon I'd be shooting sperm all
over him (he couldn't ejaculate yet). I'm sure he climaxed anyway because this is something boys do from a
very young age, or at least I did (six years old?).

I imagine sucking him off, but I don't know where he is now. I wonder sometimes if his penis continued developing in size beyond my own proportions and if he still makes it with other guys. I don't know, but it would be nice to re-live some of the good old times with him again. He's probably married with a couple kids . . . as I am.

By age thirteen, Jock (above) has learned that sex is dirty. But society has not yet taught him that masculine gender identity is fragile; he still dreams of boys and girls in the same fleeting moment. At his age, all things are possible. How many years does he have before, like the older men in this chapter, he will feel compelled to define and rede-fine his maleness every time he feels a tug of interest in another man?

Even the men in these pages who did not feel threatened by their homosexual fantasies nevertheless could not rest until they had assured me that their true preference was woman. Where do these anxieties come from? For once, women cannot be blamed. It is men who are hardest on themselves and each other in this competition to be the most he-male on the block. Oddly enough, fear and *avoid-ance* of competition are the very strands that often become woven into homosexual fantasies—the boy's fear he will never be the man his father was.

The unconscious statement being made to the other man is "Don't smash me because you think I'm your rival for the woman. I don't love her at all. I love you." If you can't beat him, join him.

Connard (above) is a fascinating example of this mecha-nism at work. Like his idol Elvis Presley, Connard is a guitar player and singer. He dresses and wears his hair like the late entertainer, and is proud when people say he looks like Elvis. Connard knows he has little chance of scaling the heights Elvis did. Does this mean he must admit de-feat? No. In making love to Elvis, Connard incorporates his hero, an idealized version of himself. Narcissism here has taken homosexual expression. Elvis is no longer an un-beatable rival. Elvis is Connard, Connard is Elvis.

Having given Freud his due, I still do not feel the issue

is resolved. Is unconscious fear of the father of twenty or thirty years ago enough to explain why men's anxieties over homosexuality never seem able to be put to rest today? Can it be that there is some ongoing process that continues all through life, keeping this fear ever fresh?

Once there was a time when boys were boys, and the other boys gave him everything he needed: camaraderie, physical closeness, reinforcement against women's petty nagging, the comfort and excitement of esprit de corps. To keep these feelings alive, grown men form groups that exclude women. The appeal to men of the 100 percent male society is so powerful that even in these egalitarian times, it took the power of the U.S. Constitution for women to have a martini in the Biltmore Men's Bar. Men feel they automatically belong, from birth, to some great, unspoken, and universal club the law can't touch: Drawing themselves up into ranks of solidarity whenever a woman approaches, they lie for each other to their wives without a second thought. *It is this undying call back to boyhood that is threatening,* the yearning to go back to a time when women did not exist, that keeps each man ever on guard against himself ("Oh, my God, I must be queer!") and against all other men, too ("That dirty little faggot, I'll beat his ass!")

Sometimes homosexual fantasies appeal to Wade (above), at other times they "disgust" him. What is unfailingly satisfying are scenarios about lesbians. There is a kind of role transference here: Watching two women make love, the fantasist can identify with one or the other as the recipient of all the sexual attention. But no anxiety attaches; it is not a man doing it to her/him. It is another woman. Sam (above) puts a similar mechanism to work in his scenario. The fact that one of the girls turns out to be a man allows him to have his homosexual fantasy without guilt. Nevertheless, the thrill is heightened by the fact that everything is taking place in the forbidden, homosexual context.

It is generally thought that women get the best of both worlds when it comes to closeness and affection. In addition to what they can coax out of men, women also have each other. With society's full approval, women kiss on greeting, walk arm in arm, wash each other's hair, hold each other while waiting for the jury to say guilty or not, rub suntan oil on each other's backs. Indeed, one of the revelations to me in researching *My Secret Garden* was the almost universal lack of anxiety with which grown women play with fantasies of sex with other women.

But women record their real sexual lives in terms of men. Whatever went on in those adolescent sleep-overs wasn't sex. In fact, my research tells me that young women have relatively little lesbian play with each other; it is mostly hugging and kissing—maternal stuff—that they exchange. As such, it carries both the good and bad emotions connected with mother: warmth, but intimacy always undercut by the threat of loss.

One of the great attractions of erotic horseplay between boys is its independence. Intimacy without strings or threat of loss. How could you not "love" such a person? Now wonder men's recounting of this early fooling around is so often lengthy and without regret. David (above) has always remembered sex with another boy. "It would be nice to relive some of the good old times with him again," David says, and adds, "He's probably married with a couple kids . . . as I am."

In the seven years since I published *My Secret Garden*, no one has criticized me by saying I had suggested that women were latent lesbians. Will I get off as easily if I suggest that men have at least the memory of having once had something fundamentally closer, more comforting, more exciting and intimate than women ever had?

EVERETT

I work at a little hotel as night security. I'm also a policeman in the daytime. When the hotel is closed, the restaurant has one young Mexican boy, eighteen years old, who looks like John Travolta and is built like a medium Mr. America. He does the porter work in the restaurant, cleaning the kitchen and store, and doesn't speak much English. So me and the night clerk take time and teach him. Naturally, we tell him who comes in to fuck, and about the hookers. He gets a kick out of all this.

Now I'm forty-five, three kids, and have always thought I was straight. One night this kid comes in and has to clean the stove hoods while standing on the stove. It was summer, he had his shirt off and white see-through slacks, and *The Most Perfect Small Round Firm Ass I Ever Saw.* I was standing behind him and I was as hard as a rock. He turns around and says, "Hi, Amigo," I said hi, but couldn't get my eyes off that ass. Then he said, "Hey, what is the matter, you no talk tonight, no feel good?" I threw him off and said yes. He kept talking while working, and I just agree with what he says, not really interested, but I still had my eye on his ass. Then he picks up, he catches me looking at his ass and he smiles. I get nervous and say I got to go check the lobby. I was so horny I wanted to jerk off right away, but the waitress was still in the restaurant. When she left, the young Mexican called me over to the stove to ask me something. Somehow his pants were down where I could see the crack of his ass. And he was really moving his ass, in a really sexy movement. I went to the coffee counter side (where the waitress calls in orders). I could see and talk to him but he could only see my head. I just had the feeling he was seducing me. I was hotter than hell and as I watched his movements I pulled out my dick and came off.

I must have sighed a little when I came because he stopped moving and smiled and I said, "I gotta go, I'll see you," and he said, "Anytime."

I'm a married man with several kids. It's very upsetting to me to find that when I masturbate now I think of this guy. Does it mean I'm homosexual? I hope not. I wouldn't know how to think of myself.

TEX

I'm twenty-three, male, and I work a blue-collar job and I'm also a full-time student. I started college in 1971 and dropped out in 1973 due to my then heroin addiction. I stayed strung out extensively for two more years, until I entered a closed therapeutic community *voluntarily* for a period of one year. I've been out of the program for six months. The program is centered on getting the individual in touch with his feelings and emotions, how they are acted out in both fantasy and reality, and how to alter these actions into something productive. Well, my particular case, my "reasons." for my drug addiction were twofold—(1) sexual inadequacy and (2) intellectual incompetency in college, as I was trying to become a doctor. Anyway, my sexual inadequacy was explored and here is where my trip of fantasies begins.

I did not experience orgasm until August 1971, when I "happened" to masturbate one night out of the blue. I did not have sex until April 1972, with a woman—the only reason then was she walked up to me at school and said quite bluntly, "I want to fuck you!" As I stood there shocked, looking at this beautiful woman, I could hardly refuse. So my sex life began. It was skimpy until the last six months since I've been out of the program. These are some of the fantasies which have held me together:

1. I'm not a homosexual, have never had a homosexual experience, but I do have a lot of homosexual tendencies and feelings, and I put them into fantasy, which for me is the most productive thing to do.

As I masturbate, I will close my eyes and think of fucking another man—a faceless, anonymous man—so as to be rid of any shame and/or guilt on my part—I think how beautiful it would be to just suck a big, beautiful cock till it comes and comes and comes. The reality of a homosexual experience is repulsive to me as I've had many chances, but I'd never give up my fantasies.

2. This fantasy is a real old one, but it's still around. not too often, though. I fantasize I'm a prisoner in a war camp run by women only—I'm like a "trustee"—I'm a servant, sexual servant that is. My job is to fuck and suck the women from the time I wake up till the time I go to sleep. After a while this fantasy altered occasionally with me being punished by being tied hands and feet to an upright pole—in the nude. And then the women would gather around to watch as one of them would go down on me and suck me till I came. As I would scream and groan in ecstasy, at that exact instant, the headmaster would take her knife out and cut off my dick and stick it in my mouth. I feel no pain in the fantasy and this is where it has stopped.

After eleven years of drug use, I'm now drug free and for the first time am experiencing what sex really feels like. I love it—sex, fantasy, any shape, form or fashion of the two together. Fantasy allows me an outlet for all my feelings and emotions that I am too fearful to release in reality. I've clearly determined my own personal cutoff point between fantasy and reality. I am a very open, intellectual sort of person, very passionate, very understanding (only bad thing is I'm ugly), and I also share my fantasies with my women and find it tremendously fulfilling.

JONATHAN

I am male, forty, and serving eight years for hash smuggling.

I have just finished your *My Secret Garden*. It filled me with excitement and admiration for the wildness and imagination of women's minds. Through the plethora of recent writing by women, I have learned more about them in the past three years inside than I did in my various thirty years outside. I have some findings of my own that I thought might be of interest to you.

In the first three to five years of incarceration, men's masturbation fantasies seem to be similar to those outside, i.e., the majority are almost unresolved situations of women they have never had any relations with.

After three to five years, however, the fantasies turn more to the remembrance of things past. Whether this is an attempt to recapture and confirm the existence of the outside world or whether it is because the old fantasies are so worn out from reuse, I don't know.

I have only met one other man besides myself who admits to having sex role reversal or homosexual fantasies. But I have not asked too many as I value the wholeness of my skin too much. I had a girl friend who was in a women's penitentiary for eighteen months. The ease and naturalness with which they are able to handle their homosexual relationships with one another could not be more opposite than the violent neurotic anxiety that pervaded men's institutions. It's the superbutch, black and white,

cowboys and Indians, all-American male attitude personi-
fied.

CHANDLER

I am a college teacher of philosophy, thirty-six, with a religious background. While I am creative, I am also a con-
formist in most areas as is my wife. Here are my fantasies:

1. This one I act out. I tie and gag myself in front of a
mirror. I lie on the floor in the sun which shines all over
my naked hairy body. I struggle and undulate against imaginary men and women, who want to use my semen
against my will to impregnate some women, so my sexy
body can be reproduced. Also, these people massage me
for pleasure.

2. Four friends wish to have group sex. One male is in a
female missionary position. The other male places his erect
penis between our kissing lips. The other woman starts
sucking the second male's cock on the head, while the man
and woman making love try to kiss each other around
the shaft of the intervening penis. All fondle the body of
the kneeling male gently. I would like to do both male
positions in this fantasy. I have told this one to a friend
who thinks it's original.

3. Sucking cock used to repel me. But having seen many
porno movies, I think I have acquired a desire to do this.
This is probably due to the sensual treatment of cocksucking and cock worship throughout porno movies. I wonder
if the recent fashion of bisexuality is connected to this phe-
nomena in porno movies? Speaking for myself, I would like
to love a friend sexually. But not if there is no mutual sharing of giving of pleasure. I have been exclusively heterosexual for thirty-six years.

The only image of male tenderness I know allowed by society is one of death: a soldier cradling a mortally
wounded comrade in his arms on the battlefield.

My contention is not that society would be better or

worse if it were more bisexual. Readers who fear I may be encouraging homosexuality would seem to have had too little personal experience with the erotic power of the male-female combination: Millions of years of human evolution guarantee that heterosexuals will never be an endangered species.

If we are not allowed—or do not allow ourselves—to face troubling feelings, they do not simply disappear. They surface later in distorted form. An example is the unreasonable hatred a man will evidence at hearing about a homosexual incident a hundred miles away. What he fears is that the homosexuality is a lot closer. Women may not like homosexuals for threatening their symbiotic needs for men's exclusive attention—but only another man brings a kind of uncontrollable rage to the subject.

I'd like to forward a hunch of my own here: It is exactly those men who hate homosexuals most who are also angriest at women. The man who believes lynching is too good for a faggot will also denigrate a woman as "just a piece of ass." A common resentment seems to be burning here: both gays and women can openly lust for men; the tough guy can't. Erotic feelings for other men would not be so threatening if he had not once felt them so strongly himself. If this is so, how can he not be angry at women—the people for whom he gave up the ease and kicks he once had with the other guys? Haven't women always met him less than halfway in all things sexual?

Beginning with adolescence, when the boy extends his hand to the girl in sexual friendship, he is met with fear and the anxiety of rejection. "Men are animals." And so, at times, he may act like one. But he never stops lusting after women, too: One half the man's feelings are expressed in heterosexual love. His anger goes underground to boil up again—very often, in another form of heterosexual love: sadomasochism.

17

Bisexuals

The fantasies that follow represent changing ideas of gender identity: the way we experience ourselves, at our core, as men and women. Though the contributors in the previous chapter had homosexual fantasies—even youthful homosexual experiences—it was extremely important to them to be called, and for me to know that they now felt themselves to be, *heterosexual*. It is not so vital to the men in this chapter.

To most people born before World War II, a bisexual was "really" a homosexual trying to disguise his aberrant tastes—which meant, to them, he was not fully a man. It is only in very recent years that official psychiatric thinking stopped labeling any man-to-man sexual contact as symptomatic of pathology.

This leaves a "middle-aged businessman" like Farrell (below) trying to straddle both worlds. He is like the men in the previous chapter in that, despite his twice-repeated insistence that he is heterosexual, he nevertheless has gay fantasies. Unlike them, he continues to have sex with other men to the present day: "I believe we all have a touch of the bisexual or homosexual in us." A "touch"—nothing more.

Farrell of course has a right to call himself whatever name he needs to keep himself in focus. I might even have put his fantasies in the previous chapter—these are always decisions about shades of gray—except that I wanted to contrast his point of view with fourteen-year-old Clark's (below). People of Clark's generation can more easily say they are bisexual without feeling they are thus diminished as men.

Clark's experiences to date have been only with boys,

but he feels that is because so far the girls he knows prefer "Jocks" and "superjocks." This much has changed: Bisexuality is beginning to receive social acceptance; a new kind of identity is being carved out of the space between straight and gay.

But the young men in this chapter still show some of the old insecurities. "I am primarily a bisexual," says Clark, "leaning to the heterosexual side." I think if he could find the right ruler, he would measure the degree of this "lean" just as he has put a tape to his penis. In his constant concern as to whether he "measures up as a man," Clark is not so different from previous generations.

The men in this chapter are still their fathers' sons. Behind their brave talk, I feel they are as tentative as any liberated woman trying to feel 100 percent confident in her new sexual equality. Things don't change that fast.

I don't care if Clark is 40 percent homosexual and 60 percent hetero, or the other way around. Numbers like these don't mean much. This transitional generation had fathers who taught them that homosexuals were mincing, effeminate fellows. Clark is trying to define himself as not one of these.

The fact is that a homosexual may look like the most virile fellow in the room. Many homosexuals take pride in their tough-as-nails demeanor. They dress as cowboys or leather-and-steel motorcycle riders not as a disguise, but as an outer, reinforcing expression of their inner feelings of maleness. The number of homosexuals who go in for drag is limited, and many men who do like to wear garter belts and satin gowns may never have had sex with another man. *Homosexual* and *transvestite* are very far from interchangeable terms.

On the other hand, the notion of closet queen rests firmly on the fact that many homosexuals are so indistinguishable from straight men that they can go through their entire lives with their secret unsuspected.

Ironically, among those with the most unshakable conviction of gender identity are transsexuals. Despite the supposedly incontrovertible evidence of anatomy, they remain convinced that they *are* the opposite sex, born into the wrong body. Nothing will deter them; they will undergo the most profound surgery to undo what they believe was nature's mistake.

Perhaps it is easier for women to feel conviction of gender identity. because you don't have to do' anything to prove you are a woman, just *be*. It is the rare man who, feeling an urge to put his arm around a friend, or give him a hug, can act spontaneously; the other guy might misunderstand. If a woman does it to another woman, she is just being affectionate—"that's how women are." Also, in a society in which being female is still close to second-class citizenship, threat of loss of the female label is not seen as expulsion from the ruling caste. It might even be said that to many people, for a woman to have homosexual feelings is regrettable but "natural"; the recent gay rights legislative battles show that most Americans think of homosexuality as a moral issue, a sign of weakness. Women are supposed to be weak.

But men must be strong. Manliness is held out as an achievement, a goal to be fought for—not given from birth. "Be a man," little boys are exhorted if they cry; they are being told that for the moment, at least, they are not being male at all. "We Make Men," the Marine Corps boasts. Masculinity seems to be something that you have to earn. It is fleeting, an uncertain thing that may be taken away next time you fail to charge that machine-gun nest, can't produce an erection on demand, or merely feel nervous about asking the boss for a raise. Have you ever heard a woman call herself "200 percent all she-female?"

Economic pressures—far more than the idealism of the sexual revolution—are forcing us to question rigid definitions of masculine and feminine. As both sexes take on work that used to be distributed along gender lines, there is a need to rethink how we feel about being men and women. A man who must share in the raising of his children is exposed to feelings he could have spent a lifetime avoiding. That does not mean he will become bisexual, or that if he does, he will be any less a "real man." It simply means he has choices his father did not have. ·

Peer pressure, too, is working to change ideas of sexual identity, denigrating masculine role playing, positing sexual experiment and rebellion as a way of life. As absolutes fade, anything goes. The men in this chapter refuse to ac-

cept those harsh definitions of masculine gender identity
that dominated (and shortened) their fathers' lives. It is of
the first importance for the reader to note that, aside from
Farrell, all the men in this chapter are young. This is not
due to my selection, but theirs: Fantasies on this subject
came only from younger men.

They leave me feeling optimistic. As a heterosexual
woman I do not feel threatened by the growing social acceptance of bisexuality. The harsh rules of adolescence
once strait-jacketed us by demands we be Boy Boys or Girl
Girls. How anxiously we tried to measure up, judging our
failures by the supposed success of others. Why continue
all that into adult life? I'm not the first person to note that
the more secure someone is in his/her gender identity, the
easier he or she is about ambiguities in someone else's.

Most of the grown men in this book turned from youthful homosexual play to heterosexuality. So may Clark. Or
he may not. Meanwhile he seems to feel that until girls
become available to him, he will pursue his alternative:
homosexuality. Whether he transfers his affections to
women later on is less important to my mind than that he
feels his sexual options represent a form of freedom, not a
reason for guilt.

FARRELL

I would prefer to ask one of my two secretaries to type
this, but they are both middle-aged married women, who
would be shocked at their boss's thoughts. I am a heterosexual, quite successful, middle-aged business man. It is a
second marriage for me; and my range of sexual experience has been fairly extensive. My sexual life with my present wife, Ellie, is essentially quite satisfactory, although
she is not as sexy as my first wife. That shows that sex
alone is not enough to maintain a marriage.

Even though I am heterosexual, I believe that we all
have a touch of the bisexual in us. I fantasize about one of
my sex experiences in this realm. A homosexual friend,
Gary, had an understanding that I could accept him fully
as a friend without any homosexual interaction. One night

away from home on a business trip, it was necessary for us to share a room and big double bed. I went right to sleep, but my body apparently became too much for him by morning, and he began to suck me while I was still asleep. He performed so gently that I did not awaken immediately. By the time I became fully aware of what he was doing, he had me so worked up and it felt so damned good, I didn't care what he did. For high quality, pure sensation, he was better at it than most women. He brought me to a convulsive orgasm with his mouth while he masturbated himself.

I let him have sex with me on two other occasions when he cleverly used women to stimulate me without my full knowledge. He got Jan, another friend, to begin the sex act with me; but then she conveniently arranged to leave and he came in and took over. It went like this: Shortly after she began, she suddenly remembered that she had to go pick up a prescription for her mother at a certain drugstore before it closed. He appeared on the scene then, and we discussed what a good piece she was because she had fucked him too. He said that many homosexuals fuck girls, particularly in between liaisons with other men.

Jan had told me Gary intrigued her too. Gary continued to talk about how he had fucked her. He got so hot in the process that he asked me to jack him off. Initially I declined, so he removed his clothes and began to masturbate while talking about Jan. Since he was naked beside me, I could see his nuts tighten within his scrotum as he proceeded. I knew what he was feeling because my own nuts do the same thing when I masturbate. He talked about how Jan's tits always drew up very taut and erect and stuck out at an angle when she got hot. He spoke of how she gyrated her pelvis and humped her ass. I could visualize her thrusting, cleanly shaven pussy and big clit sliding back and forth over Gary's prick. I felt his penis was mine and I wanted Jan to fuck me so much I couldn't stand it. At that point, Gary and I reached for each other's pricks. We fondled each other's genitals and our own alternately during the act. He shot off first, but I had to continue. As I neared my climax, I told Gary he could take me; and he did. I imagined my penis in Jan's pussy as he took me with his mouth.

CLARK

I am a fourteen-year-old boy, about five-eight, and I never seem to run out of fantasies, or a strong urge to have sex with somebody.

I am primarily a bisexual, leaning on the heterosexual side. Unfortunately, my resources in the area of heterosex are limited, because I am one of a group of "intellectuals" in my school. As almost everyone knows, you have to be a "Superjock" or a "freak" to get any free sex at my age. Meaning: The girls who are close to me in emotional thinking are not very permissive. And only a small percentage of those even look at me! So, my first sexual experience was with a boy somewhat younger than I. We had been actively discussing sex, since I started helping him on his paper route. Between us, our comments were usually heterosexual. Seeing as neither I nor he had any female outlets, we began to "play" in a shed in the back of our house. We had several mattresses, under which one of us would get, and the other would jump from a low shelf and pretend to hump him. Finally, he asked if I wanted to really fuck him, and without waiting for an answer, took his pants down. I was pretty large for him, he wasn't even into puberty, and was quite short. I was exhausted when we finished. Enough biography, I guess.

As to fantasies, I have one about an Arab boy who recently moved to this country and my school. He wants me badly, but I am afraid of going up to him and seeing what his real desire is. In other words, I really can't be sure of what he will do. He thinks I am strange, and spreads the word around the school that I am a homosexual. Anyhow, my fantasy is this: I am brave enough to ask him to come to my home for a sleep-over on a Friday night. I find his intentions are good. When I say "yes," he gets in the bed with me. A few minutes of his rubbing my genitals, and he rolls me onto my stomach. I have not seen his penis yet, but when he thrusts it between my thighs as beginning stimulation, I reach around and feel his penis. It is about 8 inches long and pretty wide. After I felt it, I turned around to look, and verified my measurements visually. I have about the same size penis, larger, but I let him do the honors. After a few minutes of thigh stimulation, he vigorously enters me. Through the night I discover his erection just doesn't go down, while in the process of sex. He fucked me throughout the night, over and over, endlessly.

We began to go on bike-backpack trips, to which he brought some friends—two of them. At night, a couple of miles from civilization, they all mount me in turn. Sometimes they have contests to see who of them can enter me in a specified amount of time. Occasionally one of them will switch places with me, and when I am doing the entering, I almost always win.

Oh, I neglected to say earlier, that one of the two "newcomers" is a powerfully built thirty-year-old man, the other is a seventeen-year-old boy. My original partner is fourteen, as I am. The seventeen-year-old has a penis which is in between the sizes of my own and my partner's, and the thirty-year-old man has the largest of all. As my fantasy skips months, I see that we are all building ourselves up through exercise of weights, jogging, sports, etc., making myself and my original partner the envy of our school, and considered highly desirable, bull-strength intellectuals by the school girls. Of course, I can't resist having sex with the most beautiful of the girls, who allows me to go far just to be able to truthfully claim that I considered that particular girl desirable. Eventually, I lose interest in homosexual activity, but I don't cut it out completely.

Other than these two homosexual fantasies, I have established dozens of heterosexual fantasies. My favorite follows:

It is an earth type planet two hundred thousand light-years outside the earth's galaxy. No animal or insect life exists that is potentially highly dangerous either to other animals or vegetation. I have found a way to freeze my aging process, and have frozen the aging of my five or sex intellectual best friends, and that of my cousin, Adrian, and some local female friends, I guess two or three. (I discovered my planet by a special gadget I invented a year ago on earth, and made a superfast transporter capable of sending me and my friends to and from earth in a manner of seconds.) I have built a super mansion (filled with electronic stuff in half of it, for living in the other half) of my own architectural design. I allow my friends to bring their own best friends, male and female, but past that, I allow no more. I am always with my female friends, my friends are with their own. Sex is gentle, free, and meaningful between myself and my girls. It is paradise, no other word for it.

In his desire to differentiate himself from homosexuals, Farrell (above) brings special definitons of participation into play. An enduring idea among male prostitutes is that if they remain passive during the act, their heterosexual status is not threatened. "I'm only in it for the money." To remain completely detached, with never an answering caress, while the customer goes down on you, maintains machismo.

Farrell, too, makes little mention of reciprocation when he has sex with a man. At an exuberant moment, he may fondle the other's genitals, but at the climax, Farrell is once again in command, *even though in the passive role*. He gives his homosexual friend permission to "take me." He allows it to happen, but the tone is as if it were merely a favor he is allowing a needy friend.

If Farrell is more open to these sexual experiments than most men his age, his actions still run along lines dictated by his generation's notions of gender identity. The younger men in this chapter may also be a bit reluctant to initiate the action—fear of rejection is always with us. But their hesitation is not meant to show they don't care if the sex takes place or not. They want it. Once things are under way, notions of activity versus passivity, and whose idea was it in the first place, are soon forgotten. Andre is twenty-four, Jones's college days are not far in the past (both below). For them, sex—with either sex—is just "all very healthy and fun." Everyone does, and is done to. Turn and turn about.

JONES

My wife and I are both twenty-seven. She claims that she has no fantasies (sexual, that is) but occasionally has romantic ones with no sexual overtones. Oh, well . . .

I fantasize sexually a lot. I'm turned on by porno and reading about others' sexual fantasies and experiences. Lesbian pictures and scenes especially turn me on. From what I've read, most men are supposed to be turned on by the sight or thought of two women making love. I wonder how many women are turned on by the thoughts or scenes of men making it?

With that unanswered question, let me tell you about one of my homosexual fantasies. I guess I'm somewhat bisexual as I get turned on looking at pictures of guys with hard cocks and I have had two occasions where I sucked guys off.

My fantasy is rooted on a roommate I had for one semester in college. We were both addicted to pornographic stories and he enjoyed reading and jacking off to them as much as I did. One night I retired early but Ken proceeded to dig around the room looking for my supply of dirty books. He found them, sat in the easy chair dressed only in his shorts and proceeded to read and rub his dick through his shorts. All the while I kept tossing and turning. The light on in the room coupled with Ken's getting turned on, gave me no desire for sleep. But it did give me a big hard-on. Ken said he wasn't embarrassed, so I got out of bed, nervously picked out a book, watched Ken's reaction to my cock, then got back in bed to beat off under the covers while reading. Damned Kenny pretty much ignored me until I came and reached for a Kleenex near my bed to wipe myself off. Then he just sort of giggled. He then went to bed but disappointed me further by not beating off. I really wanted to get up, go to his bed and engage in mutual masturbation or to blow him. But it never happened. After graduation we never heard from each other.

My fantasy takes place in the present. I'm in an adult bookshop looking over the selection of gay magazines when who should also be there but Kenny. We strike up a conversation, quickly going over the years since college.

Ken tells me that he never married and had a nice place nearby and that he also has a good selection of porno. I ask to see it and we go to his place.

Once there we have a drink and begin telling about our sex lives. I ask where he keeps his supply of porno and he leads me to his bedroom dresser and opens a drawer which is half full of gay magazines and also has women's underwear. I pick up a black slip and hold it to myself and ask Kenny if he'd like to get dressed up. He's not too enthused but finally agrees. "for kicks." I go to the other side of the bed and strip, pulling up dark nylon stockings, black nylon panties, and turn to face him as I'm pulling a full black slip over my head. Kenny has put on nylons with garters and is pulling up his panties. His cock is half hard and mine is pulsing like it is now as I write this. As he gets his slip on I walk over and caress his sides and ass, pausing to rub his cock through the silky nylon. We put our arms around each other and engage in a long soft French kiss, rubbing our cocks against each other and the super feel of the nylon underthings we're wearing.

We fall on the bed rubbing against each other and making out. I slide down the bed, push up his slip and lower his panties. There after all these years is his beautiful hard cock. I suck and lick every inch of it. Finally, he comes in my mouth and I drink every drop. I lie back and light a cigarette. No one has said a word. He slips down the bed and proceeds to blow me just like I blew him. It's great. He asks me to stay the night (the first time anyone has spoken), and I gladly agree. We remove everything but our slips, then lie with his back to me, my hard cock against his ass and my hand curled around his dick. He asks me what I want to eat for breakfast. I reply, "Your cock."

In the morning, we wake about the same time and reach for each other's cocks. We walk to the bathroom that way and hold the other's dicks as we piss into the toilet. While drinking coffee on the couch, we continue to fondle each other; and I tell Ken how I'd like to be fucked up the ass. I get down on my knees in front of him and suck his cock till it's good and hard. Then I lie on the rug, place a pillow under my rear; and he kneels between my legs, slipping his cock in ever so slowly. When he's all the way in he begins

slow in-and-out movements while I reach for my own cock
and masturbate to the same rhythm. As I feel his cock
stiffen in my ass, I speed up my hand on my cock so that
we come together, Kenny in my ass, I all over my chest. I
reach down with my fingers and dip them in my white
come, hold them to Kenny's lips, and he licks my fingers
clean then leans down and we French kiss, passing my
come back and forth in our mouths.

You have no idea how much I'd like this to come true!
If not with Kenny, then with some guy in his late teens or
twenties. It would be great to spend the day blowing each
other, dressing up, making out, and having a great time
with no guilt, no fear of getting caught. I'd also like to
make it with a bi guy and two bi gals in the same room
with everyone switching off.

ANDRE

I'm twenty-four years old and was raised in a conservative,
middle-class family in small towns in Iowa. I am presently
managing an apartment complex in a metropolitan area,
but also have a degree to teach school.

At age fifteen, I started dating girls and had a steady for
four years. I did some outside dating but stayed pretty
loyal to my girl friend. At the end of four years, my girl
friend called it off; and I started running a lot. I enjoyed
picking up a girl in a class at college, in a store, or in a bar
and seeing how far I could get with her. I usually did
pretty well, but also had my share of disappointments.

A common fantasy for me was to be out somewhere and
be approached by a very attractive woman. I liked women
who were aggressive enough to let a man know that they
enjoyed sex, too. It was a kind of a treat to have a woman
look at you in the same manner that you looked them
over. In my fantasy, I would usually be in a bar or a store
and have a woman start talking to me. They were usually
single and interested in me stopping by their place so we
could get to know each other. Once in a while, it would be
a married woman who would want to get together after
explaining that she usually didn't do this type of thing with

anyone but her husband. A couple of times I was actually approached by women who wanted to get to know me because they said I had beautiful eyes and a nice smile. One of these women was a stripper from Chicago. That was quite a dream come true.

During my senior year of college, after my twenty-first birthday, I had my first sexual experience with a man. A woman I was seeing at the time introduced him to me, knowing that he would make advances. She was bisexual, and we had talked about it some, so I was curious. I enjoyed the experience but didn't have another one for three or four months. Then, another four months after my second experience, I decided that bisexuality might be the answer to the boredom that I was encountering in heterosexual experiences. My sex life and fantasy life have both been expanded to include men now, and I'm very happy that they have.

I enjoy a masculine, aggressive man when looking for a gay encounter. I have a recurring fantasy which usually involves a heterosexual male friend. In it, my friend and I are often roommates. After an evening out on a double date where we were both unable to get a bed partner for the night, we return to our apartment. He goes to the bathroom while I fix myself a drink and turn on the stereo. When he comes out, he asks me to fix him one too, and he goes into the bedroom. He calls out that it is probably best that neither of us had scored that night because there is something he wants to talk to me about. I tell him his drink is ready on the bar, and I take my turn in the bathroom. He is standing by the bathroom door waiting for me when I step out. He then leans over and gives me a quick kiss and tells me that he has wanted to try that for a long time. I nervously (but excitedly) move into the living room to sit down. He then tells me that a few days earlier a friend of mine had told him that I was bisexual. That got him thinking that we should be more than just roommates. We then spend the night making love like we had never done with any woman.

With bisexuality I don't have to limit my sex to the opposite sex. Sexual liberation has been something that I have preached and lived for three years now.

Andre (above) states an argument with which many bisexuals would agree. Despite an active heterosexual life, he found staying with one sex "boring." He is "very happy" that he opened up his appetite to include both men and women.

Andre is not married, nor does he speak of love—both of which may be preferred by some people to games of change-your-partner. But if it is a varied erotic life you desire, and if, like Andre, you can move in and out of homosexuality without anxiety—bisexuality is one very good answer. In our society, men are more quickly susceptible to a casual invitation than women and attach fewer strings to it. The bisexual who seeks a change from the emotional complexities that most women bring to the bedroom finds it in gay episodes. He can have it both ways: emotional satisfaction with women, uncomplicated sex with men.

Homosexuals may or may not have as hard a time in maintaining relationships as popular wisdom says—but what if there is a time in someone's life when emotional ties are not what he wants? In Turkish baths frequented by gays, for instance, it is not unknown for a man to take a room overnight and have ten different men enter before morning and do ten different sexual things with them, no questions asked—perhaps not even a name exchanged. A heterosexual's chances for that ever happening with ten different women is zero.

This is not to say if you were brought up by parents who had watertight definitions of masculinity and femininity, you would find it easy to change your mind now and enter into carefree homosexual acts. Gay people like to say that any straight can be seduced under the right circumstances, but watch out for the anger with which he will get out of bed the next morning. The basic building blocks of character are not always mere prejudices.

Conditioning is not changed by fashion; but if fashion continues long enough, it becomes custom, and then hardens into what people take as commonsense reality. "That's how people are." The tough who brags that he is all man, and who likes to go around beating up gays, would perhaps be gay himself if he'd been brought up by sexually amorphous parents. His genes would be the same; his sexual tastes would be different.

BLAKE

Sometimes when I masturbate, I get confused as to who (what) is masturbating what (whom). I love the firm fleshy tower that juts off my body at its crazy harmless angles. With both hands I caress my balls, cock, nipples, thighs, asshole. I visualize my hands running over my body. As I get myself more and more excited, my mental picture of my cock gets larger and larger. It is so big I am hugging it, and soon I'm dwarfed by it. My penis, I want you to know, is a very friendly and talented organ. As it gets incredibly large, it flies and takes me on rides. I haven't been able to see any far-off places yet, but that's okay. I love the feeling of being surrounded and protected and loved by my cock. (The feeling is most reciprocated.)

I'm twenty-one, have had lots of quickie affairs and several longer ones. Most have been with women, but several have been with men. I don't consider myself "experienced" because women's cunts are always a mystery to me. No matter how much I peek and poke and suck and play, I simply feel insecure as to my ability to handle a cunt well. More than anything (at least recently), I've enjoyed eating women out.

One of my childhood fantasies is as follows: My sister and all the neighborhood girls have flies in their pubic hair. They tell me and I, as a seven-year-old doctor, prescribe the following for one week: They must parade around my office with only strings tied around their chests, going over their nipples. At the end of a week, I inspect them again, and on it goes. Sometimes, I shave their underarms and pubic hair. It's all very medicinal; especially the parading. I remember how I used to linger over the long examination periods, changing from one patient whom I fancied to the next. Just a curious, horny, seven-year-old junior gynecologist.

One thing I want a lot of right now, is for a beautiful man, muscular and dark (as I am) to walk into my house, stand me against a wall, and slowly, forcefully, almost brutally, fuck me while telling me how much he loves me.

JEFF

I've been involved with the men's consciousness-raising movement for over three years, and I feel a book on men's sexual fantasies should be edited by a man. However, as I know of no man who's compiling such a book, and as I feel it's equally important for men's fantasies to come out of the closet as it was for women's, I've decided that I want to contribute.

I'm twenty-three, have a master's and additional graduate study in education and law. Most of my sexual experiences have been with myself or with women, although I've had a number of sexual encounters with men.

Most of my fantasies are about women, although, as has happened during other periods of my life, sexual fantasies with me and another man are becoming more frequent. I hope to explore this area of my sexuality more in the future, and that it will one day be an integral part of both my fantasy and actual world.

Most of my fantasies with women involve women I know, as friends, people I work or go to school with, and women I've seen who turn me on. I frequently have a variation of this fantasy:

The woman and I have had a fantastic conversation. Though we've had different experiences, we view the world very similarly and the effortless joy of deep communication fills me with the exuberant liberation I feel when I bare and share myself openly with a person whom I trust. I am literally shaking with emotion. I ask the woman if she'd like to make love, and she's turned on too. I gently take off her clothing, and then slowly remove mine, all the while we smile deeply and playfully, look into each other's eyes. Without speaking, I ask her to trust me, and she nonverbally says she does.

We embrace and hug and kiss deeply, tongues exploring

mouths, faces, necks. I begin kissing lower, gently touching her all over her body, gradually learning the places and kinds of touching she likes best. Then I am down between her legs, and I gently and playfully lick the insides of her thighs, sometimes brushing against her vulva with my tongue or lips. After a while she starts twitching and moaning, trying to kiss my mouth with her cunt. Suddenly I press my mouth against her clitoris and cunt, as my tongue shoots up her vagina, and wiggles around. She is really going wild as she opens to me, and I continue caressing her, switching to my hand around her clitoris as I come up to her face, kissing her gently. I ask her if she'd really like to let go. Oh, yes! Quickly, before she fully realizes what is happening, I have staked her out—tied down to the corners of the bed. She is shocked and at first scared, but as I gently caress her all over, she begins to relax and let go again. I teasingly explore her body slowly, just with my tongue and mouth, and then go down on her vigorously, lightly, touching her all over with my hands. She comes several times, then I play with her clitoris with my cock, which is lubricated with her juices and my saliva. She begs me to put it in, and I manually play with her clitoris with one hand, and with the other, slowly guide my cock into her. After slowly fucking for a while, I know that she and I are ready and we vigorously fuck till we both come, crying out together. She, like I, is dripping with sweat, and I quickly untie her and then, exhausted, fall back on the bed. We hold each other and hug.

One fantasy I've been having a lot recently involves me anally fucking my lover as a handsome man with a long (but fortunately not too thick!) cock fucks me up the ass. While masturbating to this one, I often stick my finger up my ass and simulate being fucked.

I enjoy dancing with women and men, and I fantasize that I'm stoned or a little drunk at a dance, and I really get it on dancing with a slender, but strong, man. We do some fast dances, and then we leave and go to his place, where we smoke some dope, and lie in bed nude, gently kissing and feeling each other's bodies, learning the similarities and differences. I go down on him (I've always gagged when I've tried in the past), and am able to take it all. Then, after I've sucked him off for a while, he turns me over and spreads my legs, parting my ass cheeks and licking and kissing my asshole. Although I am afraid because his cock seems large, I begin to loosen up and open to him. He tongue fucks me and then slowly gently pushes his hot throbbing cock in. It's easier than I thought to take him in, and we gently, then violently, fuck while I jerk off, and we finally come together, me using my ass muscles to milk him dry.

I hope that one will become real soon!

Youth cuts both ways; so does the sexual revolution. Previous generations may have been straitjacketed by sexual stereotypes, but when they lived within these narrow definitions, they were reinforced by them, too. If you lived by the rules, they worked for you.

An experienced older man might relish a sexually aggressive young woman; he'd know exactly what he wanted from her. But twenty-one-year-old Blake (above) finds such a woman makes him insecure. He retreats into the narcissistic self, finding safety in a fantasy of being "surrounded and protected and loved by my cock."

Uncertain of what "being a man" calls for, anxious that he will not measure up to this mysterious standard, Blake goes on to another narcissistic fantasy, one in which he is raped by a brutal figure, as "muscular and dark (as I am)." The underlying desire here is relief from anxiety about what it is to be a man. This powerful other person knows what the masculine rules are, he measures up to them, and he is going to force them onto Blake. Psychoanalysts call this "anal incorporation of the masculine role model." A pretty exact description of Blake's fantasy.

Can it be an accident that the new statistics on rising impotence among young men have started to come in at the same time as the rise in women's sexual assertion? I don't think so. It is impossible to go from patriarchal attitudes to sexual equality without casualties along the road. But nothing is without price. What must be asked is, Was the patriarchal society itself so free of costs to both men and women?

To blame women for the rise in masculine impotence is

to miss the point. It is to ask women to go back to the time when one of the principal definitions of womanliness was to act in such a submissive manner that men achieved an artificial, unrealistic, and grandiose picture of their erotic powers. The cost to women was apparent, but little attention has been paid to the price of this status to men. *If women lived up to their side of the bargain, men had to live up to theirs*: to produce instant, never-fail erections whenever in bed with a woman. Noblesse oblige. I hope we are moving into a time when if a man does not become erect, it will not be seen as a failure, merely as a sign that he is not in the mood at the moment.

Perhaps the difficult period of transition we are going through is easier for women, since they are the activists, intent on throwing off notions of inferiority. What the new equality asks of men is more difficult: to give up exactly that position of inflated superiority on which their sexual self-assurance was based. Unfortunately, I am not aware that history has ever recorded the voluntary resignation of any ruling class.

I always enjoy reading and rereading the fantasies in this chapter; on the whole they are more fun than almost any other category I have collected. It is not surprising that such a high proportion of their inventors would like to live them out. The average reader may not wish to go where these men are—into bisexuality—but we must all envy them their freedom from guilt, the great enemy of sexual pleasure.

WILL

I am now twenty-seven, white, a sort of former "hippie," very much interested in the back-to-the-land movement. I can just remember finding out about sex, when I was about eight or nine years old, which is when I began to masturbate. It was also at this time that I was "discovered" by my father. Although neither of us said anything about it, I instinctively felt that it was wrong. Not that it stopped me, but I felt guilty about it. I have a sister who is one year younger than I, and I used to lie awake nights when she had friends stay over, and imagine doing things with them, as I listened to them in the other room, while I jacked off. I never really had a clear idea of what I meant to do, only that it involved their falling in love with me. Probably because I felt myself to be ugly, and was not "in" socially.

At about twelve or so, I had a few episodes of mutual masturbation with a friend of mine, and had a brief affair with a boy when we were both about nineteen.

I finally lost my virginity when I was twenty-one, on a night when we were tripping. Luckily, she knew what she was doing, because I sure didn't. I didn't even come from fucking her, because I didn't know I was supposed to, but she didn't mind, because my cock stayed hard for six hours!

After that, I lived off and on with three other women, and was enjoying myself. Then, while on a visit to some friends, I met a woman, went to bed with her that night, moved in with her the next week, and we got married three months later. I was lucky, and after three years, we are still both amazed at our luck, and our love for each other. However, after about two years, we both felt that something was missing. We wanted to avoid getting trapped in traditional man/wife roles, but were both afraid of "losing a good thing."

However, about my fantasies. Here is one I use while masturbating:

We are at a party at our house, with lace curtains, oriental rugs, plants everywhere, candles and kerosene lamps, just three of us, my wife, myself and a male friend. I play my guitar, songs of love, songs with and without words, where the whole atmosphere is overwhelming love. I sit on a chair, while he and my wife cuddle on the couch. Then I put down my guitar, and we go into the bedroom, and spend what seems like hours kissing, touching, caressing. At first each of us is concentrating on my wife, then slowly I start touching him more openly. I lie on the bed, with my legs on the floor while she sucks my cock, and touches my balls and ass, and he is behind her, slipping his cock inside her, and his cock is huge. Then he starts to suck my cock, and I move around until his cock is in my face, and it's

nine inches long, and wet from my wife, and for the first
time, I start to suck a man's cock, not a boy's, and I love it
and won't stop. And then I start to fuck my wife, while she
sucks his cock, and I watch him getting ready to come, and
he uses his hand to help her because she can't get all of his
cock in her mouth, and I keep fucking her pussy. I feel her
starting to come, and I see him come, with his cum shooting onto her face, and she's desperately trying, then suc-
ceeding, to get it into her mouth, swallowing it, sucking
him dry, and she's coming, and I come and fill up her
sweet pussy with cum.

JIMMY

I am a thirty-year-old man living in Carmel, California. I
studied to be a lawyer, practiced for a year, and dropped
out to crew a yacht to Hawaii. Since then, I've been something of an adventurer, getting involved in mountaineering,
and traveling extensively. I'm also a french translator, spe-
cializing in books about the sea.

Sex has always been a happy, satisfying part of my life. I
lost my virginity at fourteen.

I'm going to talk about a rich, recent fantasy about making love to a man; but first, I want to deliver myself of a
paean to women. They are wonderful! In all shapes and
sizes, in ways that never fail to move me. A partner's orgasm can be so beautiful that it often seems more important than my own.

My current lover is one of the most erotic women I've
ever known. She has "the divine gift of lechery," and our
sex together is fantastic. She comes explosively, and I feel
like Superman. We've expanded our own considerable field
of experience with anal sex (a bit tight for her), a brief
entanglement with mutual bondage (very exciting), and
have recently started looking at our friends as sweet victims of joint seduction. We also share a sexy interest in our
own sex, and will probably act out our fantasies before too
long.

In this department, I have a better chance than she, as I recently became friends with a man whom I like tremendously, and who also turns me on. After weeks of my suspecting, he recently revealed that he was gay. I'll call him Chris.

Well, what's keeping you back, you might ask. Shyness is part of it. I had a number of sexual experiences with men when I was in my teens and enjoyed them. But I was always the passive partner, letting some other man suck my prick. To suddenly become the seducer, to imagine taking hold of a man's prick, putting it in my mouth, or even (ouch!) my ass, well . . . that's a bit of a leap to take.

Recently I was driving into San Francisco to spend a couple of hours with Chris; and as I bumped along in my VW bus, I got more and more excited. I could visualize walking into his apartment, confidently reaching for his crotch, and letting it all happen. In my mind's eye, I could even see his penis, which I'd decided was probably circumcised (a pity; I know more about cunts than the average woman, but next to nothing about pricks). I decided that I could manage to take it into my mouth, and could probably even let him come in my mouth, though I've never been very turned on by the taste of my own sperm. Would he let me fuck him? I wondered. Chris is so un-gay in his behavior that I had no idea whether he preferred the "male" or the "female" role in gay lovemaking. What if he wanted to fuck me? That made me a little nervous. I like my lover to put her finger in my ass while we're fucking, but I know from experience that assholes are tight little things; I've caused pain to the two or three women I've fucked anally, though they've generally enjoyed the result. All these thoughts rolled around in my head as I got closer to his part of town. By the time I reached his apartment, I was as hot as any sixteen-year-old *demi-viérge* who'd decided that this is the day to go all the way. I was ripe

So what happened? Exactly nothing. Chris was his usual quiet, charming self; and as time passed, I felt the opportunity drift away from me. The more I delayed making an overt move, the harder it got. Finally, Chris announced he had to go to an appointment, and left me to masturbate by myself. He may never know that I came twice in an hour, on his own bed, thinking about him. I still masturbate to the fantasy of what might have been and have come to believe that given the chance again, I will not let it pass. Bisexuality is not so much threatening to me as novel; after all, I love my own body, why shouldn't another man love it too . . . and me his?

18

Homosexuals

NICK AUGUST

My father, well, I can't even remember him much. After twenty-five years of practicing homosexuality, I have come to see it for what it is. Homosexuals are men who are so terrified of their sexual feelings for their mothers that they have spent their whole lives proving they don't have any feelings at all for women. The whole idea of homosexuality is just to deny an erotic lust, a feeling for women, namely one's mother.

Other fears are involved too, like the fear that your penis is too small to satisfy this huge woman in your life, and the fear that your father will kill you. I have never met a homosexual who is willing to discuss these ideas with me. I think it's very dangerous for a homosexual to discuss his sexual fantasies because he has to get to women eventually. I will tell you about all the levels of my male fantasies, but what they come down to is women. We have an elaborate network for not letting us get in touch with our feelings about women. I think that it why you have had such a hard time getting fantasies from homosexuals.

Look at all the homosexuals who take out beautiful women. As they drop the woman off, they go and have sex with a man. Meanwhile, they have just spent four or five hours experiencing sexual feeling for this woman; they are not aware of this. They would deny they had these feelings. I ask homosexual friends how they feel about women; and they go, "Yuk! I wouldn't touch her!" There are a lot of homosexuals who won't even be in the same room with a woman. There is a tremendous undergound of homosexuals in this country who don't even deal with women. It's a whole world where women do not exist.

I think most men are angry at women. Mothers give so much to their little boys, and then there is this cutoff at night, when she goes with father. Anger.

I think that all homosexual fantasies have to do with the cock. The cock worship in homosexuality is unreal. It's obsessive. I always say to myself, "I could sleep with any woman in the world, so long as she has a cock." In homosexuality, the cock is like an altar. Asses are terrific too. Jock straps for instance, the way the straps cut and the ass comes out, it's like the ass is being served up for you.

I've been to bed with lots of married men who are really like nymphomaniacs. They are cock crazy. They seem desperate for it, perhaps because they get less chance than homosexuals to fulfill their fantasies. When you meet a married man who is traveling, who wants to be pissed on or fucked, it's usually someone with three children, who is a pillar of the community.

I don't think any man really ever forgets the pleasure he once enjoyed with boys when he was very young. They just get to a point where they know they aren't supposed to do it, but they don't forget it.

I think most men—under the right conditions, and if they trust the other man—can be seduced. I went through a period in my own homosexuality of being very turned on with getting someone to have sex who didn't want to—someone "straight." It's very easy to do. There are a lot of men who will go with you for money—like cab drivers. You say, "You want to make an extra twenty dollars?" But I don't think that is why they are doing it. Taking the money means they aren't gay, they aren't a faggot. I think that is why so many homosexuals get murdered. These people get very very angry at you afterwards.

No woman has ever told me the size of a man's penis. But that is all men talk about. They remember every other guy they ever knew or saw who had a cock bigger than theirs.

In *Saturday Night Fever*, John Travolta says to the girl, "You gotta decide now in your life, Annette. Are you going to put out? You're either gonna be a nice girl or a cunt." Women are stuck with this idea. But I think men

are even more stuck than women. Being a man is a difficult thing. You are this little boy, you've got this little
cock, you wet the bed, there is this big woman who is taking care of you, and there is this big man who appears in
the evening and takes your mother away from you. You are
scared of everything. Then suddenly, you are thirteen.
You're never supposed to be weak or frightened. You're
supposed to be the warrior, the breadwinner. I think homosexuality is a harbor, a safety, for all these frightened
boys. Homosexuality keeps you a boy forever.

If you're a homosexual, there is no responsibility, no
children; you never have to be the daddy. It's safe. This is
what you get for being a homosexual: You get to keep
your cock, no one's going to take it away from you, you
stay a little boy forever, which is keeping your mommy
with you forever. You always have the fantasy that you are
momma's little boy. All homosexuals are trying to prove
they are not by sleeping with men all the time. The whole
elaborate homosexual network is built on this one thing
. . . being afraid of having sexual feelings for mommy.

As difficult as it is to get heterosexuals to discuss their
homosexual feelings, it is just as difficult to get homosexuals to discuss their true feelings for women. They refuse.

I came from a very poor straight-laced neighborhood,
basically Roman Catholic. There was this beautiful woman
there who had left her husband, a saxophone player, for a
drunk. It was very scandalous. I was about four. My
mother went out to play bingo with this hot redheaded
woman; and her new boyfriend, the drunk, baby-sat for
me. I can remember having very strong sexual feelings for
him. I didn't know it then; but I was in a very aroused
state about him, my first sexual feelings I can remember. I
got undressed for bed and he was watching. I don't think
he was interested at all—but I was aroused.

When I was twelve, one day I was playing in the park
and a man came up and told me he was a photographer
and was doing a special issue on boys. He wanted to take
some photos of me peeing, he said. He wanted me to take
my clothes off, and I got very frightened and ran away . . .
even though I was very titillated by it.

A couple of years later, I was playing around with
everyone in the neighborhood—we were all jerking off to-

gether. But these boys didn't appeal to me. I had movie fantasies—Marlon Brando and James Dean. I came from a rough neighborhood, but there was even a rougher part— guys who wore leather jackets and rode motorcycles and were older—I had fantasies about them. I used to masturbate thinking about them.

My breakthrough came when I was about thirteen or fourteen. There was this older boy in my neighborhood. I'd had this adolescent, homosexual adoration of him. He was tall and athletic, blond, and his family had a little money. I think there is this period of time when all boys worship other males, athletes, Greek gods. Remember the move *If,* when the young boy watches the older boy gymnast and worships him? I think all boys go through that; and it is why even grown, straight men still love to watch male athletes.

So one night this older boy was walking me home from baseball; and I'll never forget, he asked me if I'd ever ejaculated. I didn't know what the word meant. He explained what it meant; and the next night, we jerked off together; and we kept that up for two years. We touched each other. We got dependent on the relationship. There was love and sex mixed together; it was my first real homosexual relationship. When I look back on it, it is all covered with a lot of fantasies. I still have a lot of fantasies about him. He had a huge penis—although today I might not think so. But in my fantasies he does.

I fucked a lot of girls when I was a teenager. Then I started to get more interested in the men I was friendly with. We'd take two girls to the drive-in, and I'd fuck a girl in the backseat, and he'd fuck a girl in the front seat. But I was always more interested in what he was doing and catching glimpses of that. It was almost as if I was having him through that experience.

I like it when men resist. I like it when I have to turn the man on. I feel very powerful that way. In my fantasies the men are always very gentlemanly and proper looking on the outside—but very hot inside. I like it when they do it on my terms.

I fantasize about men I have had, am going to have, or have just had . . . how we met, the undressing of them, what happened. I sometimes keep the person's underwear that I've been with; and the next morning when I wake up, I like to masturbate and smell the sexual aroma, remembering what actually happened.

Sometimes I fantasize things that never happened, being with certain athletes I've seen in gyms or on TV. Or being in a construction workers' hut with all those sweaty bodies. I once read a poem about some guy who dreamed of being a nurse who was in a hot steamy sewer in the summer with ten magnificently built construction guys who had stripped to the waist, showing their naked, hairy chests beneath their hard hat helmets. . . .

The trouble with a lot of homosexual pornography is that there are homosexuals doing it. When I see a gay porn movie, I'm very conscious of the fact they are two gay men. I find heterosexual pornography more erotic. Seeing straight men doing things together is more exciting to me.

I have a lot of fantasies just walking around on the street. A gorgeous cop with a helmet and goggles. He would have no personality. He would be sitting on his horse and I would be sitting in front of him, facing him. It would be very important that he have all his clothes on. His cock would be out, and I would suck him off on the horse. Or I would like to be behind him, sucking his ass. But in my fantasies, he practically has nothing to do with it, he is just there for my purposes. I have a lot of fantasies about chauffeurs. I've acted a lot of these out. Uniforms turn me on, all the paraphernalia—West Point cadets, sailors.

When I'm walking down the street, I look into parked cars and always hope I'll see a guy with his cock out. Many men do that, they drive around, jerking off as they look at women in cars. So I have this expectation of seeing one.

I have this black tie fantasy. In it, I am in black tie. I'm a little stoned. I might have gone to a big dinner party, and I would be looking like a prince. I will be perfumed and maybe I've had a joint and have enough drink in me that there are all these levels going on. There is this chauffeur driving me. My fantasy, which I've acted out many times, is then to seduce the chauffeur. I don't want the chauffeur to get out of the car, to come upstairs. My fantasy is to go down on him in the front seat, in his uniform.

When I masturbate, I have a succession of movies going on in my head. It's hard to maintain just one. I use a lot of things. I will fantasize about a young guy I once saw masturbating while he watched a beautiful girl at a filling station. I was masturbating watching him, and I'll remember that. But I won't sustain it, other images will enter. Like maybe I've just been walking down the street that day and seen someone walking toward me whom I want. My fantasy is that I'll lie right down on the street and he would lie right down on top of me. I have that fantasy a million times a day walking down the street. I just see people, and I want them. I'll be going down an aisle in a restaurant and a waitress will be bending over and I'll just want to stick it in her. I have an instant gratification problem. I want it that second.

I never have S&M fantasies. I don't like pain. I don't even like it when somebody squeezes my nipples. That's very big now. But once I feel pain, I am turned off. There's too much degradation, say, in pissing on people. I'm too much of a romantic. I like the masterful feeling of fucking, of shoving it in; but other than that, I don't like inflicting pain.

I'm beginning to fantasize that maybe there is this gorgeous man who has had this operation to become a woman, but has still retained his penis. A number of my homosexual friends have recently married women. These are men who were much "gayer" than I. They seem to have wonderful lives; and I say, I want that to be me. I have these fantasies now where I want children, and I want to be a man and not be a little boy anymore. A lot of this new thinking is due to my analysis. My analyst has told me to try self-hypnosis. We all think we are a product of our past, conditioned like Pavlov's dog. Well, you can be reconditioned too.

One last favorite fantasy of mine is an imaginary name I have long hoped could have been mine. I'd like it if you would call me Nick August.

The majority of men in this book had read one or the other of my previous works on women's fantasies and responded to my request for contributions. The problem then became an embarrassment of riches: to select, from the thousands of fantasies that came in, those that best represented the themes that had begun to make themselves evident.

But I heard from so few homosexuals that I cannot presume to say this chapter is representative of the gay population as a whole. Why would homosexual men want to read a book about female fantasies? And if they did, I suppose they would be reluctant to reply because they were not sure of my sympathies as a woman. I sought the help of various sex therapists and psychiatrists who do homosexual counseling. They put my request to their patients, particularly those living with another man. "Why ask *me* to contribute on that subject?" was a typical, indignant response. The inference was that their sexual preference at the moment did not yet definitely name them, in their own minds at least, as homosexual. I also advertised in widely read homosexual periodicals and had requests posted on gay discussion group bulletin boards.

I received not one reply from any of these sources.

If I had persisted, had searched harder, I am sure I would eventually have collected more material for this chapter. If in the end I decided not to, it was because I feared all this effort would distort the tone of this work. The men in all the other chapters had essentially come looking for me.

Many men will march in a Gay Pride parade because of the inherent group reinforcement. To sit down all by yourself and write candidly to someone who is, by definition, an outsider is perhaps too much to ask. "There is a tremendous underground of homosexuals," Nick August (above) writes, "a world where women do not exist." Perhaps in the future, someone will give the subject of gay men's fantasies lengthier treatment than I have been able to, but which it deserves.

In all the other chapters in this book, I usually had dozens and dozens of fantasies to select from, and the only problem was deciding which were the most representative. The theme of homosexuality presented me with no such choice. The fantasies in this chapter are the total number I recieved on this subject. If I have gone ahead anyway, it is because I felt it would be better to proceed even on an admittedly narrow basis than to ignore an important section of the male population just at a time when they are trying for increased public acceptance.

Nick, whose interview is taped, volunteered to come speak to me. While he did it mostly for personal expression, he also did not want homosexuals to be so comparatively few in my book.

And yet the fact that he *would* speak to me, that he is in analysis and so perhaps more self-aware than most people, puts him in a special category. If I have printed what he has to say at length, it is not because he speaks for all gay men but because what he has to say is so fascinating.

I have called this a book about men who love women. Nick tells us that many gays despise women. He does not. In the end, perhaps this chapter's brevity, in a book by a woman, makes its own point.

JONAS

I'm a homosexual male, sixteen years old.

My fantasy:

This young male asks me to come to a party at his house, so I go, and he and I are the only ones who are gay. The rest of them are regular. Well, about when the party is over, we're going into the bedroom. We undress each other. Then he goes down on me and I go down on him. I would like this to happen, but not now.

TOMMY

I am only sixteen and very horny. I really couldn't care less who I got it on with. But I prefer well-hung men. I have had sex with both sexes. I have this hang-up about being raped by a good-looking guy, black/white, so long as he's good looking and male.

My fantasy starts when I am walking home from baby-sitting. I have some guy come along and grab me, take me to his place. Then he strips me and kisses me all over my body, while he does it. He then lays me down on his bed and sucks my cock, till it gets real hard. Then he gets some friends (three) and they tie me down and take turns with my body. One would blow me to make sure I stay hard, then leave, then another would feel me up and kiss me French style, while I go into fits of ecstasy. Then he would go after the first guy and the other two would kneel over me. One with my head between his legs, so I could suck him off, and the other would shove my hard cock up his ass and go up and down. They would kiss each other until the guy I was sucking was ready to come. The guy sitting on my cock would take it out of my mouth and start sucking it and spitting it out all over me.

I hope you will publish or print this, so people will know sixteen-year-olds also have secret gardens and forbidden flowers.

PHILIP

I am seventeen years of age, an Hispanophile and an Anglophile. In my fantasy, I am transformed into a handsome young man with a moustache and a flowing beard. I am, in the beginning, at a party in London. There I meet a beautiful young woman. I find out that she is a peeress in her own right, and in addition to having money and property of her own, is administering the estate of her stepbrother, aged fifteen. She invites me to a house party at her country estate. I accept. When I arrive I am assigned a strikingly handsome Argentinian as my "man." The house party lasts several weeks, with people coming and going. (Including the hostess, who goes to London Mondays, Tuesdays, and Fridays to attend the House of Lords.)

One day I come up to my rooms (a parlor, a dressing room, a bedchamber and a bathroom, also a priest's hole and an entrance to a secret passage) after having a swim. I find my "man" there.

"Manuel," I say in Spanish, "come here."

"Yes, sir?"

"Manuel, you are a very handsome man."

"Really, sir?"

I reach out, grab him, pull him to me, and kiss him on the mouth. There is a struggle, but when I get him out of his livery, and myself out of my trunks, he becomes agreeable, although he still is resistant. I shove him onto the bed and shove my penis in his mouth. He sucks me, kneading my buttocks, thrusting a finger in my anus. At this point, Her Ladyship bursts in from the secret passage, naked, and throws herself on me, while I'm still "riding" Manuel. He ejaculates, and so do I. I release myself from his mouth and plunge into Her Ladyship, while she blows him. Then Her Ladyship and I do sixty-nine, while Manuel copulates anally with first Her Ladyship, and then me. Manuel and I then exchange places, then we "go doubles" with her—first with me in front and Manuel behind, then the other way around. We then form a "daisy chain" in various ways.

This scene is repeated with variations. Sometimes Manuel is replaced by the stepbrother, or a guest. Sometimes Her Ladyship is replaced by a maid, or a guest. Sometimes it's me and the stepbrother, with Manuel watching from a "squint" in the priest's hole, or with me in the secret room and Manuel with the boy. Sometimes both Manuel and I seduce the boy. Sometimes Manuel and the stepsister, sometimes . . . etc.

Another one that I have is that I am with a friend of mine in the woods camping. We are swimming and bathing in an old swamp. As I come out (he is already), I slip. He catches me and lifts me. The contact of our naked bodies does something. First we simply hold each other, kissing. Then he gets a jar of Vaseline from the first-aid kit, and stroking my chest and kissing my neck, plunges his penis into me. His hands leave my chest and he jerks me off while I put my finger up him. We both come, and, after laying in each other's arms for a while, we repeat it, exchanging places. We then go back in and blow and jerk off each other underwater.

RED

I'm twenty and a junior in college. I'm of average height, weight and intelligence. I consider myself homely (most persons won't disagree). I have a little penis under six inches, but lovers have said it seemed larger.

For the last year, I've been exclusively gay. I would be less gay if I weren't afraid of women. Men are easy to cruise because it has no emotion to it, and usually consists of a quick suck and fuck. Women are more emotional and deeper in feelings, possibly causing a long-term affair and not a quicky.

When I cruise men I do it only for sex; with women I usually get to know them and then feel guilty about wanting to ball them. If I don't know her, I think she's a whore (that is if we ball), and I despise whores.

Last night while thinking of new fantasies to beat off to, I thought about my sex life to date, and the many fantasies I've had and the events that caused them. The first fantasy I remember is a variation of an experience that happened when I was twelve.

I was at a basketball court near the woods, playing by myself, when older guys (high school seniors) took the ball and ran in the woods. I chased them and they cornered me. They said if I didn't lick their dicks they'd deflate the ball. I was afraid to have the ball deflated and got on my knees and licked their dicks. They left after that, and quit picking on me. I fantasize about that a lot.

Years later, a classmate and I would masturbate each other. I felt guilty about this and told him to forget the sordid affair and never saw him again. But I think about him when I masturbate.

Not long after that time, I began heavy necking with a girl in my class. I did feel her tits, but that's as far as I ever got. I give this information to help you possibly understand why I have the fantasies I do.

Back to last night. Out of this contemplation, I received two fantasies—one old, one new.

The old one: I'm in a busy building and see people (male and female) I want to feel up. To fulfill my desire, I wave my ass twice in a circle, and point my cock at the building. This puts everyone inside in a state of suspended animation. Then I feel up some people, others I strip, some I even pose in sexual positions with others. This is where the fantasy ends. I had this around fifteen or sixteen years old.

The new one (it's an update of the affair with the girl I mentioned above): She comes to my room in college (she does live on the same campus), and we talk about old days. She mentions she remembers my lying on top of her and feeling her boobs. She particularly remembers I had a hard-on and says she's fantasized of it for years. Then she reaches between my legs and feels my cock. It becomes instantly hard. She then rips off my pants and sucks me off, then rapes me.

ARTHUR

I'm fifteen and gay. I've never admitted this to anyone before, but after all—ANONYMITY GUARANTEED—what's to lose? Actually I don't give a damn if anyone thinks I'm queer or not . . . I sure as hell am not gonna fake like I get a hard-on every time I see a bra strap!! I'm no hypocrite! Guys just turn me on—sexually at least. It's funny, but I don't think I could actually feel *love* toward another male like I have toward certain girls. You know— a warm wholesome emotion. And yet, girls don't excite me when it comes to sex. Look, don't bother with a psychoanalysis of my situation—at least, hear one of my sexual fantasies first.

I am most highly attracted by cool-looking guys about my age, you know, teenagers. Lots of times when I masturbate, I imagine that I am in a high school locker room with all these guys around me. At first they're all jeering and poking at me—"the fat kid." Then they start to pull my pants off. To make it look good, I thrash around and swear a lot, but in the end, I just lie back and let them strip me. Naturally I have a huge erection and for a second, the gang is stunned. They just stand there in silence, and gape at my groin. Some of the guys are breathing hard and move closer. I push my dick toward the cutest one, and rub it slowly. He looks around at the others, and they just shrug their shoulders. Slowly he takes my penis in hand, and starts jerking me off. I close my eyes and thrust upward to meet him. Then I pull him nearer and prop my legs on his shoulders. Now he's staring down at my balls and asshole. Suddenly, he goes wild and buries his head between my legs. Now he's sucking and rubbing and pulling and grunting. Then he starts ripping off his own clothes, and I see he has a flaming hard-on. I get down on my knees and under his crotch. He brutally pushes his prick into my mouth and holds my head there. I start sucking on it like a milking machine and stick a finger up his hairy ass. He shudders and I feel his hot sperm shoot into my throat. Finally his dick goes limp and he sighs contentedly.

I get up and see that the others are all naked and balling each other. I go over and get my dick up one guy's asshole, and start pumping. He's bouncing around in joy and playing with my balls. I feel it coming, so I freeze until it passes. Then I lay my playmate down on a bench and rub my hand all over his thighs. He spreads his legs to me and I press our balls together. Then we jerk each other off. Just before I shoot, he catches my dick in his mouth and my jism squirts like a geyser.

My fantasy hasn't come true *yet*—but who knows!!?

Every psychiatrist has had the new patient who announces in a panic that he is homosexual because he just had a fantasy about sex with another man. What is ignored by the patient is his own panic. If the idea were really attractive to him, why would he come rushing to the doctor's office to be "cured?"

I don't think it an accident that most of the men who labeled themselves as belonging in this chapter are so young. In our teens and early twenties, we've had so little real experience, have such tremendous needs to measure up, that we are quick to name ourselves, even if it is with a name we fear. Anything seems better than the anxiety of not knowing who you are. A label gives you something to hang on to, a sense of direction and maturity. "That's who I am, and that's where I'm going." My own feeling is that in another five or ten years, several of the men in this chapter may well have changed their minds.

During his mid- to late teens, a boy's sexual powers are at peak, almost awesome in their drive for expression. The

timing could not be worse: The girls he grew up with have
suddenly matured at a rate faster than his, and are looking
for "older" men. Younger girls are scary, too. A seventeen-
year-old can barely handle his own anxieties about sex.
How can he take care of a fifteen-year-old who is more
frightened than he and so looks to him for absolute guidance, sophistication, and responsibility?

Obviously, most seventeen-year-olds do find partners,
but what happens? The girl has had little experience with
anyone (herself included) touching her. When he puts his
hand between her legs, she is shocked and cries out that he
is gross. She feels less loved now that he has "spoiled" everything by doing this awful thing. Either she wants to be
taken home immediately, or demands that he atone for his
terrible behavior by being sweeter to her, more romantic,
more huggy, more kissy . . . less sexual.

Angry at being made to feel guilty, humiliated in his
own mind by comparing himself to his supposedly more
successful friends, and—perhaps most important—still
frustrated sexually, the boy in his rage can easily turn away
from troublesome women, back to that earlier, free-and-
easy kind of sex he had with the other guys. "I don't think
any man really ever forgets the pleasure he once enjoyed
with boys when he was very young," said Nick August at
the beginning of this chapter.

The male split between "good and "bad" girls never
seems so irreconcilable as it does at this time of life. Red
(above) explains his homosexual choice this way: "With
women I usually get to know them and then feel guilty
about wanting to ball them. If I don't know her, I think
she's a whore (that is, if we ball), and I despise whores."

My usual practice is to accept whatever definition people
give themselves, but in most of the fantasies above, I am
not so sure. Sixteen-year-old Jonas and Tommy and
seventeen-year-old Philip (all above) could each indeed
become confirmed homosexuals, especially if a strong male
love interest should enter their lives at this time. But it is
equally possible that this love may arrive in feminine form,
swinging them the other way . . . or both. There may be
a prejudice of my own at work here. I am only too aware
of the coercive power of words in print. If I agreed with
these young men that they were homosexual, they might

take it as confirmation of an identity they may later wish
to change.

Arthur (above) seems to present a less ambivalent problem. He wants to put it all up front. He's not going to
pretend that women excite him at all; and indeed, in my
reading, he seems more defined in his sexual preferences
than some men in this chapter who are older than he. "I'm
no hypocrite!" he sternly tells us. I don't think he is. But
he is also fifteen. His tone of voice carries conviction; but
at his age, perhaps he himself is still too young to know
what he is going to grow up to be.

FRITZ

I'm a bachelor and I'm also a homosexual. I've been gay
since I was a young boy. I still remember my first homosexual experience, when I was twelve years old, and sucked
the cock of my boyfriend, who was the same age. I love to
suck cocks and taste and swallow the come juice out of
them. While I prefer to give a cock a blow job, I like to
take it up my asshole, too. The muscle in my ass is
stretched and I could easily take up to twelve inches.

I jack off quite a lot and when I shoot, I eat my own
come. A day doesn't go by that I don't have sperm to
drink. I love to eat semen.

When I was in service, I was stationed in Germany.
There was a men's room in a PX that was plenty wild.
There was a suck hole with some great action. The guys
would line up to get sucked. One was a sergeant who came
about four times a week to dump his load of come. His
wife and three kids lived with him. I sucked him off many
times through the hole, and would see him about the base.
He never knew I was the one. It was an assembly line basis.
The most cocks I ever sucked in one sitting was about
twenty-five. I'm counting only the ones I got loads from.
Now and then a guy would put his dick through and pull
out before he shot his wad. I used to like to see the variety
of shapes and sizes, cut and uncut, and the differences in
the volume of their loads.

I really dig married trade. Not far from where I live

there's a chain of discount stores. On Saturday afternoons, I go from one to the other and man the suck holes. Lots of married men come there shopping with their families, and while the wife and kids are out in the store, they come in and stick their dicks through the hole and dump a load in my mouth. Many times the pickings are poor, but there are days when it's a bonanza. I've gotten ten loads like that in one Saturday afternoon. I also get a kick out of sucking a guy and later seeing him in the parking lot with his family, getting into the car.

Because of the fact that I'm a cocksucker, I have one fantasy that I wish would come true. I equate come juice from cocks with mother's milk from the female breasts. I think of how beautiful it would be if there were one hundred naked boys between the ages of thirteen and fifteen standing in line with big wonderful hard-ons. I would be on my knees on a soft cushioned conveyor belt, stopping before each lovely hard-on and then proceed to suck the heavenly come out of each cock. I would even suck and swallow the remaining drops of come juice that were still in the shaft of each cock after it had shot its wad. I would also want one hundred boys behind me, fucking me in the ass, while my mouth was getting fucked.

JETHRO

I am a homosexual boy, seventeen years old, and am presently a senior at a rural high school. I've been gay for as long as I have been aware of sexuality and have no desire to change. My parents acknowledge homosexuality, but refuse to accept it as something good. They know of my homosexuality.

Now my fantasies. I guess you could say that I am a sadist. My fantasies all deal with some form of domination; either by me or by someone else. All my fantasies deal with someone being raped by me or someone else. The victim is always someone younger and weaker than me. Sometimes even a cripple, or a person with some kind of handicap. And the victim is always a boy.

In my favorite fantasy the boy is either tied spread-eagled on my bed or else I am straddling him and pinning him down. My victim's clothes are off and so are mine. I walk teasingly around the bed listening to him plead with me to let him up. When I am good and ready I jump on the bed and if he is tied down I kneel beside him and look him over while playing with my steadily growing penis. If he is not tied down I jump right up on his chest and begin. I immediately start torturing him: spitting in his face, pulling his hair. and sitting on his head. After I've done these things I usually have a tremendous hard-on. (When fully erect, my penis measures about seven inches. Though not as large as some I've heard about, it serves its purpose very well.) The boy struggling beneath me makes it even harder.

I force his mouth open and shove my prick in as far as it will go, pressing his face into my crotch with my hands behind his head. I can see and hear him choking and gagging and this and his efforts to get up are just about making me go crazy, but I don't let up until I've shot my whole load down his throat and made him swallow every drop. I then sit back and look at his face dripping with my come and relax a minute. Then I move up and sit square on his face, place my anus over his mouth, making him smell and tongue me. I then pull back and let my balls fall all over his face, jamming my prick into his nose and eyes, making him beg me to stop. If I have to piss, I either go all over his face or else I force his mouth open again. stuff my prick in and piss down his throat, making him swallow all of it. If I really feel nasty I will take a shit on his face and either smear it over his face or make him eat it.

Sometimes I pretend that the boy is my lover and lick all over his body, fondling his penis, kissing his mouth and sometimes just lying on him and holding him tight in my arms, feeling his nervous warmth.

I often fantasize about watching a group of two or three boys raping a young boy. The boys are seventeen eighteen, nineteen, or twenty and have beautiful lean and muscular bodies and thick long hard pricks. They fuck, shit on, piss on, force to suck and degrade the boy, all to my arousal.

Sometimes I fantasize about being raped the way I rape the boy. I think about an older teenager straddling me and forcing me to suck him. Even though I know it hurts, I become very aroused knowing some beautiful male is coming or pissing in my mouth. I lie there watching his body convulse and pump his climax as he forces his prick down me and comes. I try to imagine what he is thinking and how he feels as he pisses on me. I feel a kind of joy knowing that through me he is being sexually satisfied.

In all my fantasies someone is straddling someone else. Ever since I can remember I have always become sexually aroused watching older boys wrestle and sit on each other, especially if the guy on top has his crotch up close to the face of the guy on the ground. I guess that is the feeling of domination that I get from this position.

In all my fantasies it seems as though I am brutally hurting the boy, yet in real life I would never think of beating anybody or causing any kind of physical harm.

In real life I am in love with another boy at my high school. I would do anything for him. It seems strange but I would never dream of doing the things I do in my fantasies with him. He is the most beautiful person in the world and I feel toward him like no other person. My parents know how I feel but I can't tell *him* how I feel. He is presently going with a girl; and though I am upset, I am also glad that he is happy. I will probably never be able to tell him how I feel and will always be only a buddy. Some day I will find someone I can love freely and honestly, but until that day I will have to keep quiet about my preferences and not broadcast them around school, especially the one I attend.

JOE

I'm fifteen, in the middle of my adolescence, and gay. I've kept it to myself except for one other guy who's bi. I haven't let it out for fear of ridicule. I masturbate once, twice, or sometimes three or four times a day, and love it. I don't fantasize too often when I'm beating off, but sure do during the day, at school, home, wherever I am and happen to see one hell of a good-looking hunk. I always come when I jerk off, no matter how long it takes.

My fantasy is about a guy I've never met, but just put together in my mind. It starts out with me going to some club (I don't belong to one) where there's a bunch of athletic shit going on and I'm going to go for a swim. I go to the locker room and just one guy is there. He's around thirty. He's a hunk, he has a beautiful build, he's got a great tan, and we both begin to take our clothes off. I soon find out his tan is everywhere, which begins to drive me wild. His chest has just enough hair on it, not too much, not too little. He takes his shoes and socks off. Then he goes for his pants. He takes his time. I go wild although I try not to show it. He slides them down slowly, beautiful legs, not to mention what's hiding under the underpants. He's wearing tight white low-rise briefs, God how he fills them! He begins to notice me, especially because my underpants are sticking out. He gives me a little smile, but not enough to go for. I see his briefs getting a little larger than before. Suddenly he turns around, just before he takes the last stitch off, as if to tease me. The moment I've been waiting for is stopped short! But to make up for some of that he starts to take his underpants off with his nice round ass toward me. Slowly he takes it off, God what a nice ass! It's so perfect and smooth. His ass is just as tan as the rest of him, it's enormous! My dick is as stiff and large as it can get.

He goes to the showers, I follow. His cock slowly gets harder and bigger, I can't stand it! He starts to wash himself (I'd gladly help him if he'd just ask) with a bar of soap. He starts out with his hairy chest, then he moves down toward his crotch. As he washes his cock it gets even bigger and harder! Until it's as big and hard as it'll ever get. I follow him out to the pool. We're both nude. He dives gracefully into the pool. Nobody else is in sight. We start swimming around, he makes long graceful strokes. He begins to follow me. I "casually" slow down until he is finally swimming along beside me. I can see his gorgeous cock is still erect. We start swimming toward the shallow end until we're in about five feet of water. We both stop swimming and stand up. He moves toward me, grabs, and embraces me! We start necking. I pretend to fight it a little and then surrender. I can feel his huge warm prick against mine. We move toward the edge of the pool, still embracing, and get out. We rinse off a little in the showers, then go toward the locker. I start to fondle his cock, teasing it, rubbing it, licking and sucking it. He loves it. Then he fondles me for a long time. He drives me wild, licking it all over. Then he starts to suck it. He goes up and down on me, flicking his tongue around the tip of my prick. Then I let go and come more than I ever have before.

I just lie there for a few minutes, then I see he's horny as all hell, too. Then he takes me back to the shower and soaps down me and himself, fondling my cock again. Then he shoves his cock up my ass and goes in and out a bit. It feels great. Then he pulls it out and lets me do the same to him. I love it! I pull out and start to suck him off until he comes and comes and comes in my mouth. He puts some more soap on his prick and then walks out of the shower. He lies on his towel face down. I butt-fuck him until I come, wow! Then he lays me face up and gets on top of me, puts his enormous soapy cock just below my balls in between my legs and tells me to squeeze my legs together. We start necking. He begins to move his hips up and down, rubbing my balls as he does this, then he starts pressing harder and going faster, driving me wild. I can't hold on, I say I'm going to let go, he goes faster and harder! Then together we have one hell of an orgasm! We just lie there, frenching for a few minutes, then stand up and start to dress. He gives me his address, says I was great, and leaves.

If I could ever meet a man like him, anywhere, I'd love to fulfill that fantasy. I'm sure there's a lot of people like me who would love to read this, if I could only meet them.

While most psychiatrists no longer label homosexuality as pathologic, they nevertheless usually say it is psychologically determined by fixation at an early level of development. Put another way: The fact that someone has oral or anal problems does not mean he will be gay, but the reverse is usually true—if someone *is* gay, oral or anal ideas will hold a strong glamour for him. The fact that S&M plays so large a role in the gay life is usually given as additional evidence that homosexuality has its root in the pre-genital stage of life dominated by spanking, discipline, punishment, and details of excretion.

Homosexuals themselves, on the other hand, put the emphasis on sexual preference and possibility. Their focus is on the mouth and anus, yes—but that is merely due to the fact that "you have to use your imagination on what you've got," as one homosexual explained to me. "One opening in the body is as 'natural' and erotic as any other. If this weren't so, you wouldn't experience going down on a guy, or taking it up the ass, as a sexual kick. Hell, even women feel that way."

Life is all about choices.

19

Transvestites

The moment a baby is born, pink or blue ribbons are displayed. In identifying a stranger, the unknown's gender is perhaps the first piece of information given. There is a primitive need in all of us to assign everyone his or her correct slot. The sexual confusion of long hair—"making boys look like girls"—caused more turmoil in more families than almost any other manifestation of the sixties.

Cultural notions of masculine vs. feminine signals may change—among the English Cavaliers, for instance, long hair was the very mark of a man—but there is a strong biological reason for anxieties about one's basic sexual identity. In the animal kingdom, males and females are as vividly differentiated as manes, stripes, plumage, antlers, color, and odor will allow. The preservation of the species depends on sexual signals being unmistakably clear. Of all creatures on earth, only human beings deliberately blur gender distinctions. Sometimes it is done in the service of fashion, fun, or excitement. At other times it can arouse horror, confusion, anger, and embarrassment.

It all depends on context. For instance, what are we to make of these people:

—the Yale halfback dressed in sassy skirts and net stockings, high kicking in the chorus line of his college musical.
—the beautiful boy wearing full makeup and a sequined Jean Harlow satin gown at Mardi Gras, New Orleans.
—the feminine figure pouring tea in her angora sweater, skirt, and pearls, who used to be a man before undergoing surgical transformation.
—the father of three children, prancing in his wife's underclothing before the mirror, his penis engorged with

blood and excitement, but his heart in his mouth lest someone come home early and catch him.

Are these people gay or straight? Are they transvestites, transsexuals, or just fooling around? The only thing we know about them right now is that for reasons of their own, they are wearing women's clothes.

The football player is doing it for a laugh. The idea that anyone might think a supermacho stud like him "queer" is the joke.

The young boy in New Orleans may well be gay, but his joke is that he's not hiding it. Flaunting it, making oneself into a caricature of both women *and* homosexuals, is one of the definitions of camping. He is not a true transvestite because it is not wearing women's clothes per se that sexually excites him; the attention it gets him, outraging the solid citizens while his cohorts cheer—*that* is the charge. Public knowledge (or suspicion) that there is a penis under all that exaggerated female finery is the essence of drag, and the drag queen *does not want to be a woman*. None of this should be taken to mean that all homosexuals have a secret yen to be drag queens, but merely lack the nerve. The average homosexual would rather be hit by a truck.

To the transsexual pouring tea, her feminine clothing is the outward guise of what she inwardly feels herself to be heart and soul: a woman. She has often told friends that if not for the operation, she'd have committed suicide. She is proud of the vagina that surgery gave her.

To the man wearing his wife's clothing, the idea of such castration is horrifying. Medically speaking, he is the only true transvestite in the group above. Seeing himself in the mirror in panties and bra gives him an erection he is proud of.

Some transvestites are gay, some are not. The fact that a man gets a kick out of wearing feminine attire in itself is no proof either way. Joey's fantasy (below) combines elements of cross-dressing with a homosexual experience, but many transvestites are husbands and fathers who never had a homosexual encounter in their lives. George (below) was able to give his wife such ardent proof of his heterosexuality that she was happy to join in his games by giving him a pair of her red lace panties to wear.

While the drag homosexual feels there is no point in dressing like a woman unless he can go out and show it off in public, it is enough for the true transvestite merely to see himself in women's clothes; even if he is all alone in his bedroom, he feels unparalleled excitement. The drag queen has fantasies of the applause his act will bring. Some men are terrified that anyone—even a trusted, beloved wife— might find out. Nevertheless, cross-dressing holds such infinite allure that I have never heard of a transvestite who has not acted out his fantasies to some degree. It is ironic that of the four categories named above, only one is suffused with guilt about wearing feminine apparel. Trembling and eager to play with fire and yet afraid of being burned—this combination of excitement and guilt is the mark of the true transvestite.

JOEY

I enjoy getting dressed up as a girl. First I smoke a little pot to help get rid of inhibitions, then I put on a pair of stockings, garter belt (black with red bows), bra with socks stuffed in to give fullness, white lace panties, a half-slip and a pretty black dress. My hair is long and I put a little nail polish on my fingernails and toenails. My frame is slight and my ass and legs look feminine. A little makeup and I can pass as a girl. I look in the mirror and usually have a hard-on from the soft panties and the novelty of looking so cute. I take a pillow and put it down in my panties between my cock and my belly so my penis will rub against the nylon. I lie down on the bed and start fucking the pillow and dream something like this:

I am sitting in a wide chair that is suspended over a naked man who is lying on a cushion on the floor. The chair has a canvas bottom with the center cut out. I am tied to the chair with my dress pulled up, sitting cross-legged and my pantied ass bulging through the chair pointing down at an eight-inch black boner. The chair can be worked by manipulating the rope which goes through pulleys in the ceiling and this is shown me. They are playing a game with me and every time I give an incorrect answer, I will descend one inch toward the awaiting penis with the game starting at ten inches above his cock.

As can be expected, the questions are loaded and the rope and pulleys creak as my butt nears humiliation. They tease me and a seesawing motion jiggles my anus over the tip of the cock as I get one question right followed by a wrong one. Black hands from below wiggle my lace panties up so my bottom is fully exposed. I can't believe it, as I descend the next inch and the Vaseline-covered cock makes contact with my asshole. The questions are all tough now and he palms my cheeks as his cock goes in. It feels like a thousand pricking needles as the head stretches the walls of my anus. To add to the excitement, one guy holds a mirror and I watch as the prick goes in, inch by inch. Finally his balls come into contact with my hole and he is moaning. He is all the way in.

I feel strange feelings. Pain and pleasure overwhelm me. I am naughty for allowing myself to get into this position and they laugh in derision as I am raised and lowered. I watch in the mirror as the cock goes in and out. The black guys keep calling me a punk, sissy and fag. The one fucking me calls me a bitch and I feel his bird start shooting thick cream into my rectum. In the reflection I can see him fucking me and the white stuff is starting to dribble out of my ass down his cock to his pubic hair. There is a slushy, sound as he wriggles against me. In a few minutes they raise the chair and the limp penis slides out of me.

During this fantasy I screw my pillow and when I feel ready to come I put Vaseline or spittle on my penis with a Baggie over it and pump back and forth until orgasm. It's a nice randy diversion when you are afraid or unable to find the real thing.

GEORGE

When I was about ten years old, during the war, when things were scarce, I only had a couple of pair of undershorts to wear. One time after my bath, I discovered they were all soiled. As the family was to go out for the evening, my mother told me to wear a pair of my sister's panties, until she could wash the laundry the following day. As I recall, those pink panties really felt good and I enjoyed wearing them, although I didn't admit it at the time to anyone but myself. That experience was then forgotten for a number of years.

When my wife was in the hospital for a month, I was alone in our apartment. My wife had asked me to bring her some clean clothes to the hospital and do laundry for her. In handling her panties and other underthings and being alone, I remembered wearing my sister's panties, so I just slipped on a pair of my wife's panties after undressing completely. I finished doing the wash wearing only my wife's panties and having them on gave me an erection. So I masturbated in them.

From then on, whenever I was sure I could be alone at home, I would put on a pair of my wife's nylon panties and masturbate. I looked forward to the day when I could discuss this with my wife and longed for her to be able to share in my panties thing. My dream has come true.

A couple of years ago, I started to put a little extra weight around my stomach area, and when I would wear certain sweaters, this would show. On several occasions, my wife would jokingly say she was going to make me wear a panty girdle, if I didn't hold my stomach in. One day when we had been standing all day, I had an ache in my back. My wife rubbed my back and said her back wasn't too bad from the standing; the reason, she said, is because she wore a panty girdle, and it helped support her back. I asked her if she would mind or think me funny, if I were to wear one of her panty girdles to help my back. She said no, and immediately gave me one of her panty girdles to wear the following day. It really helped my back and made me feel good. I also like the idea of my wife wearing an identical panty girdle at the same time.

One day we were out shopping and while walking through the lingerie department, she suggested we purchase a panty girdle for me. If hers had helped my back, she said I should wear one more often. About this same time, the unisex underpants came on the market and I pur-

chased a couple of pair. They were more trim and comfortable when wearing the panty girdles. My wife objected to
them, saying they looked too much like panties because
they didn't have a fly. I told her they didn't and proceeded
to slip into a pair of her panties in front of her to prove my
point. She objected again and made me take her panties off
immediately. We then lay in bed and discussed men wearing women's clothes and women wearing men's clothes.
She thought all men wearing women's clothes were homosexual. I reassured her this was the farthest thing from my
mind and would never think of being homosexual. This put
her mind at ease and the subject was dropped.

A couples of months later, after an hour or two of sex
play and intercourse, we went into the bathroom and when
she and I finished giving her a douche, I said I had forgot
my underpants. Would she go to the bedroom and get them
for me? To my delighted surprise, she brought back her red
lace nylon panties she had taken off earlier in the evening,
and handed them to me to put on. What a thrill after all
the years of masturbating in her panties without her knowledge! Here I was, both of us masturbating me in a pair of
panties.

Then one day I complained my legs were tired. We
talked about support hose for tired legs, and I purchased a
pair of men's knee-length support hose. But they didn't
seem to help my legs above my knees. My wife suggested I
try ladies' support panty hose. We purchased a pair of the
massage-type support panty hose. My wife showed me how
to put them on. But my nylon Jockey shorts bunched up
under the panty hose, and were uncomfortable. The panty
hose really helped my legs, so next day, I tried a pair of
panties under the panty hose, and have worn them this
way ever since.

My wife and I love each other very much, our sex life is
varied. We like oral sex, masturabation, regular intercourse,
and a lot of foreplay. We take baths and showers together
and have since we were first married. We have been married twenty years, have three children and are both forty-
two years old. Two children are in high school and one in
elementary school. We are happy, and the kids know I
wear panty hose for my tired legs. My parents know I wear

panty hose, and so do several other people. I don't know where my transvestism will lead, but I would like someday for my wife to dress me in a bra, slip, panties, panty hose, body suit, blouse, skirt, wig, lipstick, eye shadow, and the works.

———————————————

Research shows at least two different ways to understand the psychic pleasures of transvestism. Let's start with the Freudian: The first time a little boy sees his sister naked, he feels a shock. There are people who have lost their penis! Did father do it to her? If the older man got angry at his son, would he do it to the boy, too? In fact, isn't father somehow already angry because of what the boy feels about mother?

The transvestite does not necessarily want to be a girl. What he does want is a specific defense against castration anxiety. The notion of dressing in women's clothing presents itself as a solution. In essence, the unconscious message is "Don't worry, nobody really loses his penis. Even girls have one beneath their dress. Look, I'm wearing a skirt, and I still have mine . . . so there's no danger I will lose it."

The transvestite often reinforces this defense by inventing fantasies in which he is not father's competitor, but the darling of his eye; dressing in a satin gown abets the scheme. However, the desire to avoid masculine competition by becoming the male's love object is not true only of transvestites. It is a dynamic that often applies to homosexuals, either with or without cross-dressing; heterosexual men, too, may play with these ideas in their fantasies. In fact, fear of the oedipal father is taken as a universal by the Freudians; it is only the individual expression this anxiety takes that differs from man to man.

As I've said, the above is a fairly orthodox analysis of transvestite fantasies. You may prefer the ideas of psychotherapist Dr. Leah Schaefer, who has had extensive clinical experience with transvestites. Dr. Schaefer's ideas do not so much contradict the Freudian reading as supplement them in a more everyday, commonsense context.

"When I meet a transvestite," says Dr. Schaefer, "the first thing I ask about is the relationship to the father. Most often they turn out to have had violent, demanding, temperamental fathers. In time, these sons may also grow into hard-driving, hard-working, successful men. But there is a kind of plaintive note running through their lives: 'Why does masculinity have to be so hard? Being a woman is so much easier.' "

Society agrees. Women and children get off sinking ships first. If danger or difficulty arises, "Be a man," we say. "Swim through the ice and polar bears to get help." Dr. Schaefer reports that "transvestites seem to end up being worn out by this notion that masculine life is an unending endurance contest. Wearing women's clothes is not so much expressive of a homosexual yen as of wanting a respite, a vacation from the tough, combative need to prove you are a man. I don't think it is a coincidence that the desire to cross-dress usually hits most irresistibly when these men are overworked, under intense pressure to perform well in some testing area of life."

Under stress, the alcoholic reaches for a drink. The transvestite puts on women's clothes.

DAYLE

I have just finished powdering my nose and touching up my eye makeup. Along with adjusting my Hanes panty hose and my noncling slip, I am ready to chat.

I have just returned from Aurora Mall, where I bought some Elizabeth Arden nail polish and matching lipstick from the cosmetic center. The girl who waited on me also had gorgeous long, mesmerizing nails. We chatted about various nail polishes and agreed that Elizabeth Arden was by far the best. We compared nail lengths and shapes, and agreed that the artificial nails in the new nail salons are very beautiful and cannot be belittled by any means.

My first stop this morning was the nail salon where a gorgeously dressed lady did my nails. They are beautiful, particularly now as I write. My next stop was Baker's where I bought a beautiful pair of wood-heeled pumps.

The shoes feel as if I were in another world, as I walked down the mall at 11:00 A.M. With my skirt whispering against my freshly shaven legs, with my long black wig trailing, my scintillating walk is indeed an experience to behold. What a joy it is. I'm fooling the world.

Yes, I am a transvestite. I enjoy nothing more than dressing to the hilt. My wife is now making me a new skirt and blouse. The material is fantastic.

When I am not in women's clothes, I have fantasies of being in them. You could say that I live my fantasies.

HOWARD

All my life I've wondered how someone acquires a particular set of fantasies, especially ones as peculiar as mine. As far back as I can remember (possibly as early as age three) I remember having to sleep with my older sister. She must have wanted a sister very badly because I invariably awoke in the morning with an article of her clothing on, usually rayon panties or a slip (I couldn't have thought of that myself, could I?). When her girl friends visited, they helped her put me in girls' attire and took me strolling with them.

As a consequence, I suppose, I've always looked forward to any opportunity to wear women's clothing. When I started dating, I always searched a girl friend's bathroom for her stray lingerie when given the opportunity. With a pair of soiled panties over my head, I could come off into the toilet in ten or fifteen seconds. Fresh lingerie was for trying on *carefully*, so as not to leave evidence.

When I was twenty-one I started masturbating. We were living on a farm. Often I used to let a calf suck me off and when none were around, interrupted my chores as often as six to eight times a day to jack off into the hay. We had mares but I never quite figured out how to mount one safely. Thus my first piece turned out to be a milk cow that I had managed to corner.

Before my wife and I were married, I attempted to give her some hints as to my tastes, especially my affinity for everything lovely that covers a woman's body. We were sexually active for about a year before the wedding and I would invariably put on an article of her underwear before or after intercourse. Without fail she would awaken to find me clothed in her nightgown and panties. She seemed surprised at first but also tolerant.

The longer we stayed married, the less understanding she became but that wasn't her fault. I had graduated now and never passed up an excuse to don her stockings and garter belts as well as corsets, panties, bras, slips, nightgowns. My most blinding orgasms came about when we both had on stockings, garter belts and nightgowns.

With time my taste became more discriminating. Her clothes never really fit me all that well and her rather plain tastes didn't coincide with my affinity for sexy, very frilly, prissy-looking items. At any rate it wasn't long before I began assembling my own special wardrobe. I still buy a few things by mail order but rarely pass up a chance to buy in person, usually on the flimsy pretext that it's a gift. An overpowering thrill seizes me when I can discuss the acquisition of a new garment with a pretty salesgirl. Then I can hardly wait to get home and see how I look in it and feel it on my skin. There have been times when I couldn't restrain myself and put on an item under my street clothes (when I could find the privacy) when I had to remain at work too long.

Before we were divorced, my wife became enraged and horrified on the several occasions I really "made myself up." When I was sure that she was asleep and wouldn't interrupt me, I would shave my face closely after bleaching the beard and carefully depilate my chest, arms and legs. After I had removed all of the rough skin, I applied full makeup, eyelashes, wig and painted my toe- and fingernails.

The following day I could look forward to parading around the house all day, changing at leisure into each one of my outfits before I was finished. By this time I had acquired skirts, dresses, shoes, accessories and even mastectomy breast forms to fill my brassieres. When I look in the mirror, I scarcely recognize the "other person" I have become. At other times, it becomes an effort to avoid collapsing or fainting with ecstasy because by now I am quaking and trembling all over.

I desperately want to make love (maybe it should be "be made love to" since I adore being seduced by women) while in this state. The woman who loves me would have to regard all this in an admiring, sympathetic way or else with mock severity. By the way, my wife never laughed at me when I was "made up." I'm rather attractive as a "girl" so maybe she viewed me as a threat to femininity or hetero-sexuality (hers).

Yes, I've tried men (how else can you really be sure you're not gay!) but am not interested. Nothing compares to an attractive woman.

Getting back to my "hobby" though, whenever I have a "fashion show" (only before the mirror now) it takes several hours to change into all of my outfits and I proceed leisurely from daytime things to evening wear and finally my great fascination—sleepwear. The end of the charade finds me wearing three pairs of stockings supported by two garter belts and a long-leg panty corselette, the top of which is filled out by my breast forms. Under that I have on three pairs of nylon-satin briefs, the first and second pair worn with the crotches alternating on either side of my prick and balls, the third pair covering it all. My five-inch-heel maribou-trimmed mules, costume jewelry and long, luxurious nylon chiffon peignoir set complete this stunning ensemble in which I practice posing and walking in front of the mirror. Finally, I no longer postpone the inevitable climax. Lifting the gown, I draw my stiff and straining cock through the corselette's split crotch, letting the outer panty cover my balls. Carefully tucking a few inches of the gown's underskirt into the edge of the corse-lette over my cock, I allow the rest of the peignoir and gown to fall around my well-stockinged legs in soft caress-ing, clinging folds. The movement of my prone body (by now practically transfigured) up and down the sheets and across and into these soft and yielding garments is next to effortless. When I've fairly fainted with pleasure, the shat-tering crash takes place, leaving my adorable outfit soaked in sweat and semen, my makeup running and the pillow covered with lipstick.

Is this too heavy for *any* woman? I desperately hope not.

CRANE

I am forty years old, born and raised in a rural area, with a conservative political religious background. I am married, have two children. I am a clergyman with a major pluralistic denomination of the reformed tradition. And I have a great investment in and love for the work of the church. I have a string of degrees in business administration, theology and pastoral counseling and enjoy education.

Much of my early life is still a fog. I think that I developed fantasies very early in life, and used them as hanging hooks to suspend the conflicts that arose concerning my psychosexual development. It was my fantasies that gave me pleasure for years. It also was my fantasies that were sources of conflict and alienation because I would not share them with anyone.

Stage One (7–10 years of age): My parents were divorced and my mother, two sisters and I moved to the maternal homestead in a very rural location. My nuclear family lived in the great parlor, with rugs hanging from ropes suspended from the walls to make for privacy. I developed a fantasy about being Wonder Woman with her magic truth rope, getting tied up, under beds, in corners and so forth, and then escaping from the Nazis. I had a cover story about Roy Rogers in case I was caught, but cannot ever remember having to use it. I found relationships with teachers easy to develop—all I had to do was be smart. It always had been tough to relate to peers, however.

Stage Two (10–17 years of age): My father and paternal grandfather died within days of each other soon after this move, and when my body began to work through puberty, the fantasies erupted again. The power of Wonder Woman was gone, and I was angry toward my sisters. Somewhere around age twelve, I began to dress in my sisters' jeans and other clothes and have fantasies that I was tying them up and punishing them. Then one day, the delicious thing happened—I came! I was scared at first over the mess. But I loved the feeling. I quickly developed a surreptitious system in order to have more experiences like that. I practiced different kinds of variations four or five days a week, fantasizing first one sister, then the other, or perhaps one of the girls I liked to look at at school. Since my buddies began dating, and I was too shy to ask, I began to think that maybe I wasn't likable—or that I was bad. I come from a very quiet family, except when we are fighting, so had no permission to ask about my feelings.

Stage Three (19–34 years of age): Upon graduation from high school, I fled into the world—to freedom from the confines of rural life, and to privacy, I hoped. This was the stage where I spent time in college, in the armed forces and employed in the secular world. It meant money, and though it took a lot of effort I was able to go into public stores and by concocting embarrassing stories, I was able to purchase the things I always had wanted to wear but couldn't. It pretty much was confined to sports clothing— women's jodhpurs, halters, ski outfits, jeans. Only a couple of times did I wear anything in public under my regular clothing. It created a lot of anxiety on my part and I can remember just barely making it to some private spot where I vomited. I fantasized myself as a woman, sometimes as a man who had been changed into a woman, or as a man who was wearing special skin that hid my penis until the right time when I would turn the tables. Most of the pleasure came in the preparation, planning and executing the plan that led to the ejaculation. It was downhill and damned depressing from that point onwards. After marriage it became less frequent, and I began to develop the anxiety that led me to therapy and a different way of handling my fantasy life. I disliked myself, I was becoming self-destructive. Even my relationships with the women in my life could not seem to extinguish this passion I had for masturbation and transvestism. I had a number of minor auto accidents, and suffered from a variety of viral illnesses. I was scheduling myself to die before the age my father had reached.

Stage Four (1972–present; 35–40 years of age): This is my therapeutic age. I defused my fantasies and convulsions. I wanted to be castrated. I had been preoccupied with crotch watching and feeling guilty about it. After some intensive therapeutic experiences I got rid of the guilt that went with the fantasies.

What was emerging was a new way to use my creative

imagination. My fantasies are still with me. I use them to
grow, and to get the old pleasure if I want it. Recently, I
gave the "woman" in me a name. And I made friends with
her—in a therapeutic setting of course. Now she helps me
in my fantasies. We take turns being dominant or coopera-
tive in my fantasies. And she wears a dress! That alone, for
me, is significant in the way I feel about myself. I don't
have to disguise my creativity to myself. I can take advantage of it. The future is open for me. I can look forward to
a better understanding of my masculine and feminine
parts—which really are just me. And I can praise any
Christian God for the total image which I think I now have
of him—a great gentle, strong force that led us all to seek
him out in our own private experiences.

LLOYD

I should like to relate a fantasy I have had re: cross-
dressing as a woman. It excites me, and I usually masturbate while having it:

I am twelve years old, and going to a small, private,
nonsexist school. The headmistress of the school is fat,
jolly—a grandmotherly woman. One day while we are in
class and discussing sexual stereotypes, such as girls' games
and boys' games, one of the boys blurts out that he would
like to learn how to sew. I sympathize with this wish, and
would like to sew even girls' clothes; but the other boys
immediately tease and ridicule the boy, much to the dis-
tress of the headmistress, who wants us to give up stereo-
typed roles. I join in the teasing out of fear.

So the next day, she announces that the boys will be
required to attend the girls' home economics and sewing
classes; and more, each boy will have to produce as a project a skirt, circular and full; and the girls will grade them
upon craftsmanship, at a final session at which the boys
will *model* them. The boys, needless to say, protest; but she
gradually overcomes their objections, saying things like
"I'll bet lots of you have wanted to try on a skirt, to see
how it feels, and won't admit it." She asks for a show of
hands on this question, and eventually most of the boys

reluctantly admit to wanting to try on a skirt at one time or another.

So, soon the class is in full swing; and as the boys enter into the spirit of the thing, they find that they like sewing and want to outdo the girls at it. I like to imagine them working on their skirts, comparing them with each other, and lastly, trying them on in front of a mirror to adjust the length of the hems, blushing and giggling as the girls would.

Finally comes the big day: the modeling of the clothes made in the boys' and girls' home economics classes. As a special surprise, the headmistress has provided frilly half-slips to wear under the skirts; and some of the boys elect to wear them. At first the boys feel very self-conscious, appearing in public in their skirts, but soon become very used to it, and behave naturally. Several of the skirts are praised by the girls and get high marks, and then there is a party with lemonade and cakes, and a good time is had by all—especially me: I even dare to appear wearing a stand-out petticoat lent me by a girl, and a pair of high heels, and no one puts me down for it.

I'm sure if my parents knew that I wanted to wear skirts and petticoats, they'd be sure that I was becoming gay—which I sensed even when small. I used to sneak up to the attic and try on my mom's old skirts and dresses.

I don't see why people can't just wear what makes them happy, without labeling them as "homosexual" or whatever. Whatever bisexuality I may have only seems to be accentuated by the societal pressure that identifies cross-dressers as "queer." If my desires as to dress had simply been accepted, and something I could do without fear or ridicule or arrest, I think I'd be much more "normal" sexually, although that may seem a nutty statement.

If gays can have rights, then I think cross-dressing males, whether they want to be gay or straight in their life-styles, should have that right too.

The drag queen or female impersonator wants to show off what he is doing, but to the average transvestite, the thought that he might be discovered is unbearable. Dayle's

joy (above) at fooling the world with his womanly disguise
is in proportion to how sure he feels he will get away with
it. Cross-dressers often argue that their desires are harmless. This is not quite true. Their pleasures are often bought
at the price of living with fearsome guilt and shame. Crane
(above) allows himself only the most masculine of wom-
en's sports clothes, but his anxiety is so great that on at least
one occasion he vomited.

Such a burden can be too great to carry alone. If only
someone else knew, someone who didn't mind, didn't call
the man names—even joined in the fun—the relief would
be marvelous. Whom can he trust if not his wife? Mrs.
Dayle is so far from condemning her husband that she
even sews for him. In this, she takes on the role of one of
the enduring heroines of fantasy: the permission-giving
woman.

If a man can limit his transvestite desires to the privacy
of his own home, he can go for years (even his entire life)
without being found out. The fact is that this kind of man
is often a hard-working, model husband. Living up to the
high performance standards that he sets himself as *the*
mark of a man makes him a good provider for his family;
it also wears him out to the point where, as Dr. Schaefer
says, he feels he has earned the few hours vacation he gets
from the masculine rat race by putting on women's clothes.

The wife's position can become very anxious and complicated. As if to emphasize how difficult it was to be a
man, Howard (above) seems to have entered into competition with his wife about how easy it is to be woman, wanting to prove he could be more feminine than Mrs. Howard,
more beautiful and glamorous. In Lloyd's fantasy (above)
the boys "find they like sewing, and want to outdo the girls
at it." Not only must the woman endure the violence done
to her own ideas of gender identity in finding herself married to someone who wears lipstick and panty hose, but she
must accept his competitive putdowns of her femininity,
too. Howard's wife became enraged and left him.

"In my personal counseling," says Dr. Schaefer, "what I
try to do is help the man rid himself of his guilt. As he gets
easier about cross-dressing and stops thinking his wife is
judging him harshly, he in turn usually stops putting her
down. The therapeutic idea is to make cross-dressing not a

guilty secret, but a part of life. Do it as much as possible. But I always remind him that while it may be a big thrill to go out in public dressed lke a woman, it is also a big thrill to drive a hundred miles an hour. Both are dangerous. If he confines his cross-dressing to the home, he will be safe. Once it becomes a part of their life together, the wife may become less anxious about it; and he can stop resentfully telling her he would make a better woman than she. What they end up with is a special sort of spice that is part of their own private lovemaking, and nobody else's business."

I have always admired Dr. Schaefer's generosity of spirit in all things sexual. Her advice is sound, but I know in my heart how difficult it would be for me if my husband loved to cross-dress. Heeding Dr. Schaefer's admonitions may help you to keep a marriage you want. But if you cannot, it does not mean you are a failure as a woman . . . or a man.

20

Breast and
Vagina Envy

The debate over the significance of penis envy—a notion
born early in psychoanalytic history—still goes on. Orthodox Freudians believe women unconsciously fear that they
have been deprived: They long to get back the penis they
feel was taken away in some mysterious past. Various traits
are usually cited in evidence: women's belittling of their
own sex, competition with men, negative self-image, resentment of the feminine role leading to frigidity.

More recently, the idea has come to be taken less literally: the male organ is seen as a symbol of the power and
control men are given by our society. Women do not resent having a vagina; they resent having it posited as a sign
of their inferiority.

Little credence is usually given the parallel phenomenon
in men of breast and/or vagina envy. To say that in our
male-dominated culture a man might covet a part of the
female anatomy is thought ludicrous. Psychoanalysts report
that while women often fantasize about having a penis, it is
the rare man who mentions any desire to have breasts or a
vagina. For a woman to dream she has a penis is to dream
of strength. For a man to dream he has a vagina is to lose
his.

These prime female attributes were not always seen as
diminishments. Psychoanalysts often take extreme male
chauvinism—with consequent denigration of women—to
be evidence of, and defense against, fear of women. Wasn't
there a time in every man's life when woman—mother—
was the most powerful person on earth?

Early on, children of both sexes develop awe of the
breast at a level too deep for words. Mother's milk eases
hunger, pain, fear. If it is withheld, suffering, even death
can follow. My own guess is that women covet a large

bosom not only to attract men, but also because the breast is the most salient symbol of female power. In this, are they so different from the men in this book who measure their penis presumably to satisfy women, but also in fear that they might be deficient in size compared to the gigantic father-penis of childhood?

Breasts are beautiful. They have mystery and power, too. And while little children may not know exactly how babies are born, they soon sense it has something to do with that secret place between a woman's legs. Next time you see a child staring at a pregnant woman, take a look at his face. There is power in that idea too.

ALEX

I'm writing this for both my wife and I. My wife is twenty and I'm twenty-one. We've been married two years and one fantasy we have a lot is the exchanging of sexual organs. She loves to fantasize that she has a long, thick cock and is filling the depths of my cunt, and giving me the pleasure I give her. Meanwhile, I'm imagining I've got a hot, wet pussy, just waiting to receive her cock. We both get a thrill out of this. Often she will call me a cocksucking cunt, while I'm telling her what a throbbing dick she has, and then we'll have one hell of a come together.

BREWSTER

Some of my fantasies involve me as a female. I think this is one of the neat things about fantasy, the fact that one can interchange the male-female role. I suffer from "pussy envy" anyhow, I think the female anatomy is so great. I also admire the multiple orgasms a lot of females enjoy.

I once had a short affair with a woman who enjoyed sex more, and more often, than any one man could possibly keep up with. After four or five hours of being eaten, fucked, and masturbated, until I was so worn out I simply couldn't make it anymore, she would still lie there and masturbate and keep on coming over and over. The first time I saw her do this was one of the most exciting experiences of my life. Although I had already come five or six times, and was so weak I could hardly walk, watching her gave me another hard-on and I masturbated and climaxed again. She would lie there oblivious to any external distraction, her eyes closed, completely engrossed in herself, one hand busily engaged with the middle finger going in and out of her hole as the flat of her palm rubbed her clitoris, and the fingers of her other hand fondling her nipples. She would softly moan, "Oh, no—oh, no," over and over as her climax approached, then this would turn into a sort of guttural grunting as her legs stretched out and she tensed up through a climax. Then the whole bit would start all over again as she relaxed and her legs separated. I don't know how long it was possible for her to keep this up, but I do know that as I quietly dressed and let myself out the door, she would still be going and apparently not even aware that I was leaving. One of my great fantasies is for me to be her.

Of course I can't come over and over as she did, but I have developed the ability to bring myself right to the verge of coming, let it squeeze just once, then let it subside a little, then bring it back to that point again and again. I can keep it right there for some time, just letting it come a drop or two over and over until I just can't stand it any longer, and I have a really mind-blowing climax. Then it is wonderful to lie there in a sort of weightless afterglow and without moving a muscle just drift off to sleep in whatever fantasy happens to take over. I can really get into this fantasy, to the point where my nipples are sexually sensitive, and the sound of my own voice moaning "Oh, no" really turns me on. Once I have brought my cock to this condition, it takes only the lightest, slowest rubbing on the head to keep it there, so it is easy to imagine I am rubbing my clitoris. None of the cock-in-fist masturbating in this fantasy, I'm just lying there rubbing my clitoris.

Also in this area of role reversal, my wife does a thing that is great for both of us. When we are fucking with her on top, she will sometimes assume the male role, putting her legs together inside of mine and fucking me. Although we have never talked about it (it isn't necessary and I don't want to take a chance on losing the magic of it for either of us), I'm sure that I am, in her mind, a female. Whether she is a male, or just being herself making it with another female, I don't know. I don't really care either, as I can have her be either one in my mind as the mood strikes me. All I know is she becomes the dominant one, kissing me with her tongue going in my mouth and not letting me do any tongue penetrating, sucking my nipples, and wanting me to lie still and let her do the fucking. I sometimes wrap my legs around her and can imagine that I actually feel her fucking up inside me. The only drawback is that it is so exciting for both of us that it doesn't last long. She won't quit fucking me when I tell her I'm getting close, in fact, fucks me harder. I like to think that she is fantasizing that she has her cock up in my pussy and is excited by the idea that her fucking is making me hot enough to come with her as she squirts her come up inside me.

She may have had a whole bunch of goodies going for her in her fantasy during this bit. I'll never know. Asking her about it would probably take the spontaneity from it, and this is what makes it great. Along these lines, I think this is an important part of why people fantasize. In fantasy, the egotistical "I" or "ME" is the center of attraction. We all have the need to be wanted and desired just for ourselves, just as we are. Consequently, in our fantasies, we are automatically desired by whomever we wish, and they always just spontaneously do to us, for us, whatever we want them to do.

HORATIO

I am a Caucasian male in my forties, college educated, and happily married for seventeen years. I have masturbated since puberty and still do so, mostly when I travel. The sight of large-breasted girls really turns me on and I know that many women get turned on by the sight of an oversized penis. This then is the basic theme which runs through all my fantasies, the most elaborate of which I enjoy while masturbating.

Since adolescence I've always imagined myself developing huge, gorgeous female breasts, but otherwise keeping my normal male figure, except for a more enormous cock. I like to enhance this fantasy by stuffing my shirt in front of a mirror. After climaxing, I feel quite disgusted, but I still come back again and again to the same fantasy. Sometimes, I have this fantasy when my wife performs fellatio on me. While she is sucking my huge cock, my fantasy becomes so intense that I can actually feel my large breasts resting on my chest, and partly hanging down to the sides, while my hard oversized nipples are pointing straight up. I am trembling for my wife to reach up, touch and massage my gorgeous tits and then move up and suck them, until she draws milk. At this moment, I usually come.

The following fantasy is much more elaborate. To be honest, the weirdness of this fantasy bothers me:

My wife has somehow obtained two bottles of a miracle drug that is used to enlarge human sex organs. One is used for women to enlarge the size of their breasts, while the other is used to increase the size of a man's penis. We decide to have some fun and try it right away. We both empty half of our bottles with the expected spectacular results.

However, my favorite variation of this fantasy is as follows: We have just emptied half of our bottles, when I go to the bathroom. I really was expecting my penis to grow, but nothing is happening. I am very disappointed and walk to the mirror. I am stunned when I examine myself. I notice a definite growth of my nipples which are poking from below against my undershirt. Also, the surrounding areas seem to swell. I am fascinated and keep watching. Soon, two firm breasts have developed with hard nipples, almost poking through the material. They still grow, and I feel my shirt getting awfully tight. By now, my shirt has been stretched to the point of bursting open. I walk back to the bedroom, when my shirt tears open, and reveals two enormous gorgeous tits, firm and proudly protruding forward. My wife has been sitting in her gown reading, and looks up when she hears my shirt tearing open. She screams out with surprise, "By George, what happened to you?!" She is not really expecting an answer, because we both realize that we must have got the bottles mixed up.

The drug had such a tremendous effect on me, what happened to her? She must have read my mind and lifts up her gown to look. As I had expected, she has grown a penis. I am shocked by the enormous size of her cock hanging down limp at her knees, while resting on a pair of oversized balls. She moves her hips and her cock swings like a pendulum. I have come closer and she slowly pushes my head down to her knees. I have never seen such a huge penis and begin to move the foreskin back and forth. It starts to swell and I take as much of it in my mouth as I can, and start sucking. She moans with lust, removes the remainder of my torn shirt. Then she lifts up both of my huge breasts, puts them together in a way that the two nipples are close to each other, and starts sucking both at the same time. She gets very excited. Her cock is too big now for my mouth, and I have to let it go. She stands up immediately, still holding on to one of my breasts. It hurts, but I do not mind. She is still wearing her gown, but the penis sticks out for almost three feet, keeping her gown lifted up. She walks over to our large mirror, parading her cock, which whips slowly up and down. I have dropped my under pants, and look at my fully erected penis, which looks like a dwarf compared to hers. She notices it now too, and starts making fun of it. I cannot take this, and reach for her bottle, emptying it in one gulp. I feel the warmth getting into my penis. It is a wonderful feeling. It keeps swelling and stretching like an erection that is not going to stop. It keeps growing until it has surpassed my wife's cock's size. I move it up between my breasts. There it is kept in place, but it sticks out almost to the tip of my nose. I can lick the giant head with my tongue, but cannot get it into my mouth. I remember the other bottle and pass it to my wife. She does not want it, and says that she is satisfied with the size of her breasts, but wants to save the drug for our friends.

She walks to the phone, her cock still sticking out like a pole, and calls up two of her lady friends. She asks them to come over to witness a miracle. Then she goes to the living room, prepares two drinks in which she puts the remaining fluid of the bottle. She finally manages to hide her cock under her gown (it must have become a little limp) I hide in the bedroom, but can watch through a gap what is going on. The bell rings and Ruth and Norma, her best friends, enter the living room. Norma wears a skirt and a pink blouse, which really does not have to hide much, since she is quite flat chested. That is one of her hang-ups, because I know she envies my wife. Ruth is flat-chested too, but she tried to make as much of it as possible, and wears very tight sweaters and pants. They sip their drinks. Ruth notices it first, and puts her hands on her breasts, feeling them swell. Her tiny tits have grown to a handsome size, pushing her sweater forward, and are still growing. As she removes her hands, one can see the elastic material of the sweater stretch to its limits. Her nipples have become hard and large, one almost poking through. Norma must have felt something too. She has unbuttoned the top of her blouse, and looks in disbelief. Her breasts have become huge and are filling her blouse fully. The blouse is stretching to its limits and has slipped out of her skirt. The restraining materials on both girls' cannot hold any longer, and burst open. Two pairs of tremendous tits pop out. Both seem to enjoy the new features of their bodies. My wife's gown is bulging, her huge erection is returning lifting up her gown. The girls are stunned. That's when I enter the room.

I am naked and make a few quick steps. My huge breasts bounce while I hold my penis up with both hands. My wife's friends are fascinated and get aroused. They quickly undress. Norma comes over to me while Ruth joins my wife. They try to put the penis into their vaginas, but realize that this is not possible. Norma gets the idea first, and mounts my penis, leaning with her back against my enormous tits. Ruth mounts my wife the same way. They have to use both their hands to span the circumference of each of our cocks. But they hold on and we are galloping through the room. They rub their vaginas back and forth, moving the foreskin of each penis in the same rhythm. My wife and I have reached for our friends' huge tits and massage them. It is heaven. We all come simultaneously.

"I suffer from 'pussy envy,'" says Brewster (above). "I think the female anatomy is so great."

Little girls in the midst of their toilet training traumas

envy their little brothers' "handle." Imagine having something like a faucet; how easy it must be for boys to turn it on or off and so never ever again risk mother's censure, loss of love, or public humiliation.

Boys and girls grow up and go to bed together. How can women who enjoy sex not continue to marvel at the continually unfolding mysteries of the workings of the penis? I love it that my vagina and breasts give my husband so much pleasure; how can I not help wondering at times what it must be like to be him? But most of us cling so desperately to our gender indentities we cannot allow ourselves to play with these questions.

We have all met men who send out Johnny-One-Note signals: "I am never jealous" or "Nobody can hurt my feelings." Not much insight is necessary to sense that an opposite fear is being defended against. Flexible personalities like those of the men in this chapter can take troubling aspects of life and find satisfaction by reversing them in fantasy. Men who must ever boast "I am the biggest, 200 percent male macho stud you'll ever meet" get no rest. All they can do when their anxiety button is pushed is repeat their stereotype, only louder.

In a restaurant, if someone else's order looks better than our own, don't we often ask for a taste to appease our envy and curiosity? If a man likes women, and enjoys their breasts and vaginas, isn't it logical that he might occasionally fantasize about what it might "taste" like to have female organs for himself for once?

Fantasy has the power to take us back to that magic time of childhood when it seemed possible to have a penis, *and* a vagina, *and* to be a blue pony, too, all at the same time. Alex's fantasy (above) fits right into this mood; what a romp to have both a cock and a cunt. Brewster covets the multiple orgasms "a lot of females enjoy." Neither of these men gives me the feeling he would like to be a woman; on the contrary, they seem so strongly centered in their masculinity that they can toy with an idea that would give most men the shudders: swapping genders. Whatever anxiety is present in these fantasies has been turned around, expressed, and made into an Alice-in-Wonderland trip.

If Alex and Brewster make games of their fantasies, Horatio (above) approaches his like a roller coaster . . . first there is fear at the bottom of the stomach, then the dare is taken, the ticket bought, followed by a ride of ever-increasing excitement. Having a fantasy in which he himself had enormous breasts was anxious-making at first for Horatio; the thought "disgusted" him. But he finds the idea thrilling, too, and is determined to pursue his wild ride of the imagination to the end. In a fantasy foursome, he grows enormous breasts, his wife has a giant cock, and all the rest, he says, is "heaven"—one of the most unusual and imaginative fantasies I've ever heard.

"JOAN"

I am a male but have always wanted to be a girl. Not that I would go for men, though I do hear how wonderful it is and wonder what it would be like. Nevertheless, I still ardently prefer women.

I think I was about eight when I first discovered girls wore garments described as "bloomers," not the gym knickers type, but pink silk ones. These and long stockings I would have given my eye teeth to wear. If I were single and young, I should have a sex change operation. What about a six-foot female with measurements of 44-38, and a face like a horse?

I have come a long way since those early days, and climb into female gear whenever the chance presents itself. I love the marvelous tight feeling of a long-line bra and panty girdle, and/or corsets. The strange feeling of a tight stocking top around the thigh and the brush of one silken clad leg against the other really sends me. I have walked over the hills on a moonlit summer night in girl's clothes, including high heels and full makeup.

This is my favorite fantasy: I have been invited to this gathering of girls (anonymously) and go out of curiosity. It is a beautiful house in about ten acres of grounds at the cliff edge.

There are eight girls when I enter. Two are sitting naked

by the fire rubbing each other with oil. The organizer, Helga, says, "You must meet Connie. This is her house. She only joined last month and doesn't know anyone yet. So I have asked her to look after you today."

Connie is slightly on the small side, just my height, her hair a mass of tight black curls, contrasting with my crimson mane, and what a figure, it must be 37-22-36.

"Right," says Helga to me, "you can take your clothes off, after all, we are all girls together."

I am a bit mystified.

"Come along to my bedroom," says Connie, "you must hang up that long dress and also check your makeup. There won't be another chance." I go along. She is wearing such pretty blue frilly underwear, I feel a sudden urge to throw my arms around her and hug her. What a pair of tits she has. They are beautifully sloped, hard and firm, and the nipples are standing right out. Actually our figures are exactly the same and neither of us has a hair on our bodies. With a bag over our heads, you couldn't tell us apart. Although I haven't looked, I can tell my nipples are as hard as Connie's.

She comes over and plants a soft kiss on my lips. This time I yield to the temptation. I fling my arms around her and hug her close. "Oh, Connie," I say, "what is going to happen?"

She just leans against me, soft and warm. "Don't worry," she says, "you are going to enjoy yourself." She catches my hand and we return to the main room.

I am sitting in the center of the settee, Connie on my lap. She puts her arm around me. "It's all right," she says, "I had to go through it last month, but it's really quite nice."

I don't know what it is, but don't worry.

She pulls gently as I close my eyes, and I lie back against her. I can feel her hot breasts against my back. Her other arm is round me now feeling the other tit. "I think," she says, "that from your reaction, you are going to enjoy your initiation more than all the rest of us put together. I was a virgin," says Connie, "as I think you are, and the gag was quite necessary. I should have screamed the place down. They left me with the vibrators going for half an

hour. Then they let the men in. After they had tossed me
up and down in a blanket for fifteen minutes—"

"Men!" I scream and struggle.

"Yes," she says, "that's why we have to gag you. Anyway," she whispers in my ear, "I have organized it so that
you can't be screwed by the men either. The others don't
know about this yet!" I can feel my nipples standing
straight as she presses against my tits.

Next the girls drag me forward. My body is suspended
from the rafter and I am hanging by the wrists. Now it is
about to happen. Another pull and I am swinging like a
pendulum, twisting and turning. At last, they lower me till
my feet are on the floor, my hands still high above my
head. It doesn't hurt my wrists, as the straps are so well
padded. The girls rub cream all over my body. They are
quite expert, the sensations are fantastic. Between them,
they keep me just below coming for an hour. I am mad
with desire.

Someone is running a finger up and down the nylon covering my sex. I scream and struggle, but am firmly held.
Connie redoubles her efforts with her mouth. The shooting
stars all seem to go off at once. It takes a tremendous time,
my mind is blowing for ages, but suddenly I come.

They take off the gag and one girl gives me a stiff drink.
I am so dizzy, the whole room seems to be sliding sideways. They release my wrists and ankles and carry me
over to a cushion-strewn table and chain me out in an X to
the extremities. I am too dizzy to resist.

I can see Connie has an enormous artificial penis sticking out in front of her. You couldn't get one of those into a
girl, I think. With a shock I realize it's for me.

Now she is lying on top of me squirming. She darts her
little tongue into my mouth. I wish it would go right down
my throat.

"I love you, Connie. I love you!" I murmur.

"I love you too," she whispers. She lines up the device.
Four girls get behind her while another checks the line-up
and applies some more grease. Then the girls chant, "Ten
. . . nine . . . eight . . ." I shall know exactly when it is
going to happen, what will it be like? Then I think: Something I can never get back will be gone in a few seconds. It

seems an age between each count. "Two . . . one," and the four girls all rush together. My single shriek is cut to a gurgle at this most exquisite moment. I feel I have been transfixed by an artillery shell, which turns into a tree trunk as it slams home.

I must have come. I scream once more and realize Connie is on top of me still going. Her eyes are glazed and mouth open. Her tongue goes right down my throat. What a sensation! I kiss Connie, her hands are on my tits, pushing them backwards and forwards across hers. The rest of the girls watch fascinated.

"Stop it, you two," says Helga, "the men are coming in now." As the men enter, Connie and I are stood up, still chained to one another. The other girls pair off with the men. Rough hands reach for me and Connie and we hug one another, pressing our tits together, our tongues intertwined. The men enter us in the only available place. It hurts, but the two of us cling together. Eventually the men leave. "I've never seen anything like the two of you lovebirds," says Helga. "I think you were made for each other. You will never be subjected to men again."

Helga and the others leave. Connie and I decide to spend the rest of our lives together.

As you can see, I am an out-and-out lesbian.

DEAN

I am a forty-year-old male.

My sexual fantasy is to have my hand inside my panties, with my palm on my mound of love and middle finger between the lips of my pussy touching my clitoris.

I believe I am transsexual. Ever since reading about Christine Jorgensen, twenty-five years ago, I have wanted to be rid of my dick and balls and that muscle root where a pussy should be.

I want to lie on my belly in bed and rub my mound of love against the mattress. I want to walk briskly and have a feeling of freedom and nothingness between my legs. I want to cross my legs tightly and squeeze an empty crotch.

I want to run nude and swim nude, free of confining

clothes and free of the dick and balls I have hated so much
for so long. I want a mound of love I can shave . . . and
oil . . . and powder . . . and love.

"Joan" (above) has always "wanted to be a girl," and even
chooses a woman's name for signature. But the fantasy itself is about sex with a woman. "As you see," says Joan, "I
am a lesbian." The usual name for someone who has a
penis and desires sex with women is *man*. Joan may have
strong transvestite desires, but nowhere in "her" long fantasy is there a word about the over-riding passion of the
true transsexual: hatred and loathing for one's own penis.

In 1952, moved exactly by this fierce dislike of the male
organ, the woman we know today as Christine Jorgensen
went through the first highly publicized sex-change operation. In a recent newspaper interview, Christine was asked,
now that she has lived so long as a woman, would she
undergo the operation if she had to do it all over again?
The answer was an unhesitating yes. This is gender identity
of a very high order—psychological belief so strong it absolutely denies anatomical evidence.

The only man in this chapter who does voice hatred for
his penis is Dean (above). He won't touch it, even when
he masturbates. Says psychotherapist Dr. Schaefer, "Rubbing up against the sheets in bed is a common form of
masturbation among transsexual men. They don't want to
see their penis, they don't want to acknowledge it the way
you would if it were handled."

Another trait Dean has in common with most transsexuals, Dr. Schaefer continues, is that his fantasy is not so
much about *sex* as a woman as *life* as a woman. "Transsexuals are gender oriented," Dr. Schaefer says, "much more
than sex oriented. Their fantasies may more often be about
darning a man's socks, or cooking for him, than focused on
going to bed with him." Dean's imagination is gripped not
so much by ideas of sex as by the pleasures of feeling oneself female.

Dr. Schaefer continues: "People who are searching for
identities are quick to grab any label, even an unflattering
one, to tell themselves who they are. I can understand that

they want to end their frustrations, their gnawing feelings of bewilderment; but it is a very dangerous game. All the men in this chapter play with the idea of being women in one way or another; but in my professional opinion, Dean's fantasy is the only one that might signal a therapist that here is a transsexual."

21

Sadomasochism:
The Chains of Love

Enslaved in Egypt, the Jews cried out, asking why God was so cruel. The prophets replied that the punishment must be accepted; because He loved them so, God was disciplining His chosen people for their own good.

Faced with the problem of what gift could be made as proof of devotion to an omnipotent Being, the Christian saints offered up their voluntary suffering.

The idea that love and pain are inextricably mixed is enshrined in the Bible itself.

I have always hated the cliché that women are the masochistic sex. I am not excited by movie violence, and the emotions of shame and humiliation trouble me more than any other. Again and again as I went over the material for this chapter, I almost gave up the effort to understand the devil's rage of S&M fantasies.

And yet, if we could come to see how pleasure can be born of pain, if we could make contact in ourselves with that left-handed love that makes a man dream of degrading the woman he desires most, couldn't we understand almost anything else in human sexuality?

To begin, I had to move from the point of view of the shocked judgmental observer; get rid of the relentlessly egocentric picture of myself as possible victim. I was to enter a make-believe world of mirrors, contradictions, and opposites, of children's nightmares played out with the physical strength and passion of grown men.

It is humiliating to be told our adult anxieties are rooted in childhood. Is it possible we are still repeating scenes first played at two, four, or eight years of age, only this time the role of mommy is being acted by a lover, wife, or husband?

Perhaps the idea most difficult to understand is that sexuality can be tangled up with nursery emotions. Dear God, if we aren't separated from childhood when in bed with our lovers, when does adult life begin?

I personally have resisted this inference all my life, and assume most readers have, too—especially men, who are supposed to have cut the cord to home and mother so much earlier than women. But no understanding of these fantasies of torture masters, groveling slaves, and pain can be reached without accepting that they are both infantile and grandiose at the same time.

Beneath their wildly differing and exotic details, the common denominator is fury at the loss of authority and control to women. In our society, father usually abdicates the raising and discipline of small children to mother. You may remember father as harsh or kind, but all of us tend to forget how relatively late he enters our emotional lives. He is not usually the one who feeds and nurtures the baby, covers him when he is cold, picks him up when frightened—or punishes him into acceptance of civilization's first rules.

"Don't do this," mother says to her little boy. "You must do that." Sit, stand, eat, sleep—the commands batter his self-esteem all day long. Eventually, the child digs in his heels and says NO. "Do you want to go to the park?" "No." "Do you want to stay home?" "No." It is the child's effort to recapture infantile omnipotence, to assert his independence in the face of life's overwhelming pressure to conform. The boy's rage against mother's rules is evidence of his struggle to preserve an emerging sense of himself as his own man.

Tired of the battle, he removes himself from mom's control by spending more time out of the house, in the anarchic freedom of boys his own age. Dad and society encourage him to be a man, to be adventurous and assert himself—to be as unlike mother as possible. The young man's sport of "mooning"—dropping one's trousers to flash a naked rear end in the face of an astonished public—is a playfully defiant gesture; it asserts the mooner's right to masculine behavior "no matter what anyone thinks."

Can anyone imagine a girl mooning? When women are involved in the young man's assertion of sexuality and daring, the matter becomes less playful. "You filthy, terrible person!" the girl cries when he gathers up nerve to put his hand between her legs. "I never want to see you again!" He feels the beast for having tried to be a man.

In our society, saying no to sex is usually the feminine role. The girl's outrage at the boy's sexual advances comes from trying to be as much like her mother as possible; those are her rules for gender identity. "If anything bad happens," mothers warn their daughters, "I don't care why or how, it is the girl's fault." Controlling men, denying men, offering sex only with strings attached, confusing it with love, romance and marriage—that becomes second nature, the very mark of a lady.

The damage done to the feminine psyche is considerable, but not the subject of this book. The result to men is that while biology drives them to seek sexual satisfaction, they feel they must "attack" women to get it. Fortunately for the survival of the human race, the sexual imperative will not be denied. The girl who at fifteen made him feel like a beast capitulates when she is twenty. But there is a price. "No," she says, "only if you love (and/or marry) me." "No," she says as a wife, "I don't feel like it tonight because you were mean to me yesterday." "No," she says, "I will never try that because it is disgusting."

The husband feels a familiar loss of power, a frustration of desire, a damming up of his most central self. He is regressed back to those angers first felt when he was so little he had to do as women ordered. Some men may put the resulting frustration and rage into their work or into extramarital affairs. Others may run away or just have a philosophical drink with the boys and forget it.

Some men cannot. Their angers are too heated to be forgotten or released through ordinary channels. S&M fantasies provide a safe outlet, reversing old positions of dominance. "They assert your right to be yourself no matter what others say." (Eliot, below.)

The man is taking revenge for hurts he has felt ever since he was a boy.

ELIOT

I act out my fantasies with submissive females. They're still fantasies nonetheless; but, for example, this actually happened:

A matron of fifty-five or so answered an ad I had placed in a swinger's newspaper. All her life, she had had fantasies of masochistic submission but had never dared act them out. She is married with two children. Finally, she got up the courage and made an appointment. She came to my studio in town, and soon I had her on her knees, her hands tied behind her, naked but for a garter belt and stockings I made her wear (to make her feel more self-conscious, more naked than naked), and a dog collar and leash around the neck. I sat on the bed as she knelt before me, the other end of the leash in one hand, a cat-o'-nine-tails in the other, and told her what I was going to do with her. At first, of course, she was terrified, not only with fear of pain but with a sort of residual common sense, and more: the fear of the unthinkable. But as I tell my girls, it is because you don't dare do it that you must do it. This is the ultimate fascination.

Well, I calmed her fears so that she could enjoy herself, tied her down spread-eagle on the bed and whipped her, insinuating the rhythm of the whip gently into her body rhythms and building from there. As soon as she realized it wasn't really going to hurt, and that nothing terrible was going to happen to her, she became more sexually excited; and the experience blew her mind.

Now, this was a fairly typical S&M experience. They are not all that numerous, I admit; not nearly as numerous as those of dominant women, though it occurs to me that a great many men who go to "dominant damsels" may not really be all that masochistic; if they could easily find submissive females they would do so. It isn't easy; but I am patient and persistent, and now have several female slaves. Those who talk women's lib, crying "male chauvinist pig," often make the best slaves.

But you asked for a fantasy; well, I often fantasize punishing Barbara Walters, Luciana Avedon (of the Camay commercials), Anne Francis, Elizabeth Montgomery,

Bernadette Peters—and Nancy Friday. . . . Though I
must admit Baba Wawa is my favorite, let me state the
complete fantasy in this way: Nancy Friday reads this letter and feels a pang of impulse she never felt before; it
becomes an obsession; her husband can't satisfy it; he's just
the old husby, not the Demon Lover. (Most of my women
are married, and not unhappily.) The impulse haunts her.
At last she writes and makes an appointment.

At my studio, she is sent into the bathroom to change;
then she walks into the studio wearing only a garter belt,
stockings, and shoes, tingling all over with self-
consciousness; she is required to parade up and down before a fully clothed man this way. Now totally aroused, she
is tied over a bar; her stomach rests on the bar, her wrists
and ankles are tied together; she is in a calisthenic exercise
position of one bending over and touching her toes without
bending her knees; and she cannot move. I then attach a
pair of moderate-strength nipple clamps to her nipples;
they hurt just enough to give pleasure.

Going around to the other side, I anoint her vulva, from
anus to clitoris, with "orgy butter" (no kidding, there is
such stuff in the sex boutiques). This is very soothing, and
our Nancy is now aflame with desire, all caution and inhibition gone, she is now totally spontaneous; which of
course is the whole idea, not only of my exercise, but of
lust, even of sex itself. . . . While she watches, I take a
cat out of the drawer; now the big moment is coming! She
attains a new level of apprehension. She is required to say,
"I've been a bad girl, so please whip me." I caress her back
with the whip; it is an indescribably sensuous sensation.
Then, as described above, I whip poor Nancy mercilessly
(well, not really), and soon she begins to cry out—not
with pain but a series of soul-wracking orgasms . . . After
this, she must kiss the hand that whipped her and say
"Thank you for punishing me," and she promises to forward to me all letters from masochistic females; she makes
an appointment to return next week. . . .

All I will add about myself is that I was happily—and
normally—married for some years; my wife died of cancer.
After several depressing years on the "singles scene," I find
this both more fulfilling and more rewarding than trying to
marry again in a fragmented world; these experiences

really are liberating and cathartic, they assert your right to be yourself no matter what others say; it is the most intense experience a human being can have—which is no doubt why many shy from it. And it expiates guilt. I do not proselytize; I do not justify. I only say this is the way it is, and it is a good way. And that is why my several ladies, in search of a supreme catharsis, find it when they visit

> The Master Rod
> (AKA Eliot).

Fantasies like Eliot's (above) illustrate men's ultimate love/ rage polarization. The inner logic has been pushed so far, become so exaggerated, that it has entered the absurd. While S&M may be the most terrifying aspect of the erotic imagination, it allows us to examine the masculine conflict on the largest possible scale.

Here men are, pursuing both ends of their ambivalence at the same time: lusting after women, but also angry at them. Wanting their love, but wanting to hurt and humiliate, too. Men trained by our culture to think of women as pure, asexual creatures, but dreaming of turning them into sexual animals as "dirty" as themselves. Men *forcing* women to love them, whipping them into sexual happiness. Heart on the sleeve, the torturer's mask on the face.

A cartoon-simple notion of the sadist would start with the idea that he has no concern for how his victims feels. In fact, wouldn't the ultimate refinement be, not that the victim grows to love her pain and finds orgastic relief in it, but that she hates it so much it finally breaks her? After reading a few of these fantasies, however, a surprising picture begins to come through. Again and again, we find that underneath the sadistic facade the fantasy has a contradictory story to tell: The man seems to be saying that he inflicts his will on the victim not to be cruel, but to force the inhibited woman into pleasure she could not accept in any other way. Eliot hurts his sexual partner "just enough to give pleasure. . . . Soon she begins to cry out—not with pain but a series of soul-wracking orgasms." He selflessly mentions no orgasm of his own, only the satisfaction of helping the woman "expiate [her] guilt." Eliot signs

himself with an aggressively masculine *nom de guerre*, but
doesn't the picture he gives us have elements of a mother
giving a child a dose of bitter medicine "for her own
good"? Is it possible that one element of the sadistic character is based on identification with a female model—
mother herself, the Ogress of the Nursery?

Eliot gives us another insight into the inversions of
power so characteristic of S&M. We need not expect fantasies to follow the unities of Greek drama, but out of what
motivation does the woman in his story suddenly say, "I
am a bad girl"? There has been no preparation, she has
done nothing wrong. Then we realize these four words are
a stage direction from her to him. *She is telling him she
needs to be punished.* He has her *permission* to proceed. If
Eliot is the actor, she is the playwright.

Instead of Eliot feeling he is a bad boy because he wants
to express anger and get sex, the woman takes all the
blame and initiative. Women have always denied him sex;
this woman now begs for it. Eliot whips women in revenge
for the suffering they have caused him, but his cruelty
arouses no fear of retaliatory anger. He has constructed his
fantasy to emphasize that the woman is a volunteer. He is
not forcing her to do anything; he is merely carrying out
her orders.

This is very curious. Since fantasies from men like Eliot
take as given that men are imperious, powerful, and superior to women, why do notions of guilt, of needing to appease the victim with pleasure—even a suspicion of fear of
the woman—so inexorably enter? Why do these fantasies
tell us again and again that only superficially is the man
the "master," that underneath he is the woman's servant?
Is it his will he is serving here—or hers?

TOD

I'm a very very happily married male, aged thirty-three,
educated, in business for myself, and I never let a fantasy
pass me by. I share it with my wife. We hold nothing back
from one another.

I was a battered child and a fantasy was a normal thing.

It was a necessity. But out of this constant came the realization that my mind was totally capable of producing any ideal I wished. With this realization came yet another, the detail. Given quiet time I realized that I could build any amount of detail into any fantasy. Instead of spending five minutes inside my mind I could spend ten times the time and really make the fantasy come alive. Out of this thought came an obsession with detail.

An example: She pulled her panties down. Not enough, leaves too much to chance. What color are the panties? How did it sound? What room was she in? Exactly how did she pull them down, fingers, thumbs, one hand, two hands, were there lights on, what did her face look like, how did her hair hang, did she have other clothing on?

The point of all of my fantasies is to make the woman feel touched by a gentleness and sensitivity not always associated with the male animal. I have a need to please the woman but I need to be pleased too. For myself I need to know the intimate secrets this marvelous creature, woman, keeps for herself. The following fantasy is a favorite:

There is a room somewhere where there can be total privacy. It is white with a padded table that can be moved and adjusted into numerous positions. On the table is a woman about forty-two who owns a local bookstore. Her hands and feet are tied with soft padded straps, her eyes are blindfolded and a soft white cloth covers her mouth. She is awakening from the influence of a mild drug . . . apparently induced to get her to this place. She suddenly begins to struggle as she becomes aware of being tied down. I speak to her slowly and softly, telling her she will not be harmed and will be set free some hours later. I tell her she is beautiful and I want to know her but that she would never let a relationship develop normally. I tell her to calm down and relax. I tell her over and over again she will not be harmed. She finally realizes it is useless to struggle. I tell her I will remove the covering over her mouth if she'll not scream. She shakes her head and I remove it. She's nervous, crying, fearful. She asks many questions and begs me to let her go. I tell her I am going to love her and that I want her to be calm and relaxed and to just let it happen. She calls me a perverted rapist. I tell her I am nothing of the kind. That such a person would do his thing only for himself and not consider her. She acts like someone being violated and it hurts me not being able to convince her otherwise. She will not calm down and so I cover her mouth again. She is dressed in a white blouse and tan vest buttoned over her small breasts. She has a full medium-length dark brown skirt with brown high boots and black stockings. Her hair is long and dark brown with a touch of gray. Her frame is small but not stubby looking. I move to her side and touch her breasts softly telling her how beautiful they are. I unbutton her vest and blouse, pull them both apart and kiss her chest and neck. I tell her she shouldn't wear a bra, that she really doesn't need one, that her tits are small enough to support themselves. I put my hands under her, slowly, and somehow unfasten her bra. She fights me as much as she can. I am gentle and slow-moving and I talk to her, telling her she will not be harmed in any way. I lift her bra up and reveal her little tits. Her nipples are quite large for the size of her tits and are brown. I kiss each gently and play with the nipples with my tongue. I tell her I've wondered what her tits looked like and who has felt them before me and who has sucked on them for her pleasure. I ask her if her husband likes them. She is still, so as not to give me any reply.

I tell her that no matter what, I won't harm her, but that before she leaves me she must tell me about her masturbation . . . how often, what positions, what she wears, where she does it. I become very detailed in what I want to know and I tell her over and over that she must tell me before I'll release her. I continue to lick her and tease her, occasionally playing with her nipples which now grow hard with my touch. I slowly work my fingers in and out of her cunt and ask her to tell me what I want to know about her masturbation. At this point in the fantasy she changes completely into total cooperation and tells me in vivid detail about her masturbation. She doesn't stop struggling against the bonds or give into me but she does soften and tell me what I want to know.

As she finishes I am licking her cunt furiously, lapping her juice and she is shuddering and responding to my tongue. Suddenly her hips raise and she comes. But she tries to hide it a little and with a shaky voice tells me to please stop and let her go. She promises not to mention it to a soul. But I tell her I am not finished and that I must have my cock inside her as I will never again have such a superb opportunity. I undress and release my swollen cock. I move to her and touch the tip on her cunt hair. She tells me to stop.

I continue to play with her tits and I raise the front end of the table so she is sitting up. In this position, I slowly untie one arm and slip her vest, blouse, and bra off, redoing her arm afterwards and then doing the same to the other. She is nude from the waist up. I return the table to the reclining position. She tries to talk me out of what I am doing but I tell her she can't. I put my hand on her crotch over her skirt. She tenses. I can feel her mound even through the skirt. I tell her that I like very very hairy cunts and I like them dripping wet. She begs me to stop. I ask her if she has a hairy cunt. She is silent and still. I lift her skirt onto her stomach. She is wearing panty hose over a very normal pair of white panties. She has a very tight body and her mound is quite prominent as is a delicious space between her legs. I touch her cunt, cupping it. She attempts to squirm away. She tells me to stop. I tell her that of all the men she has ever known that I have an appreciation of loving and of woman that no other can ever comprehend. I pull her panty hose down to mid-thigh and nuzzle my face into her cunt. I breathe her body deeply. I kiss her cunt through her panties. She keeps telling me to stop but she is careful not to raise her voice. I tell her her cunt smells delicious. I grasp the sides of her panties and slowly edge them down, then the first cunt hairs appear. I gasp and tell her how beautiful it is. Her cunt is, indeed, quite hairy and I quickly but gently pull the panties down and off. And there it is, hairy, thick, long, and very black . . . her cunt, her physical secret! I tell her how beautiful and soft and lovely she is. I tell her I want to make her feel good and that I wouldn't dream of harming her.

I drop the leaf on the table and raise it so her cunt is at the right height and her legs are hanging down. I spread her apart and examine each fold, I kiss it, lick it, bury my tongue in her vagina. It is just barely damp and very tight. I marvel over the amount of hair that hides her secret entrances, I am mad with desire but in control of myself for her. I am slow and easy and soft. I lick her clit and tell her how exciting it all is for me. I ask her if anyone has licked her cunt like me. She is purposely silent. Her juices begin to flow and I feel her responding to my tongue and fingers. While I am licking and sucking her I ask her things . . . how many cocks she has had, how she likes to be sucked and fucked, how often she plays with herself. (This is a fantasy all to itself . . . a woman loving herself in her own privacy.) I spread her wide apart and slowly push my cock into her warm secret place. She is still and silent. I feel as though I can't hold it so I pull out and lay my cock on her mound. Her cunt hair is so exciting and it feels so erotic on my cock, and my balls are dangling on her cunt lips which almost makes me shoot off right there. I move to her side and then climb onto the table so my cock and balls are softly brushing her tits. I press it down onto her chest and ask her if she's ever known a cock that hard. I move up and drop my cock and balls onto her face and neck. I want her to suck me but I know it wouldn't last but a moment. I ask her if I should come inside her cunt. I ask her if it's okay. She is silent. I get off and go back to her hairy cunt. I look at it, spread it apart and I can't resist sucking it again. I clamp my mouth over it and she breathes heavily saying that she's too spent to have me down on her again. I continue, lost completely in the slippery, hairy cunt. She is moaning and crying and heaving her body away and then hard into my face. I feel her beginning to come again. I stop and quickly inserted my cock to the hilt. I begin to fuck her harder and harder and she moves with me instead of against me. In seconds we are both lost in a fantastic orgasm. I feel like my cock will never stop pumping come and I pull out and spurt the last of it onto her cunt hair.

Time passes while we regain ourselves. I bring a bowl of warm water and wipe her cunt slowly, kissing it occasionally. She is silent, not moving or saying a thing. I carefully untie her arms, lean her forward and retie them behind her back. I then untie her legs and have her stand. I pull her panties on, her panty hose and her skirt. I finish dressing her, taking special care to lay her tits softly and gently into her bra. Suddenly she says she has to pee, that if she doesn't she'll burst. I led her into a white bathroom with her arms tied behind her. I stand her in front of the toilet, reach under her dress, pull her panty hose and panties down and sit her down. I hold her legs apart and her dress up so I can watch the stream of yellow pee come out of her. I am hard again. I tell her that I want her to suck me and that after she's finished I'll let her go. She says nothing. I wipe her cunt and as I stand I gently pull her head toward my cock. The tip touches her lips, I moan and she opens and takes me in. I move back and forth slowly and her mouth moves with me, not against me. I feel myself coming, I tell her I am. She tightens her grip and surrounds my cock with her tongue. A final deep thrust and I empty my cock in her mouth. She sucks and sucks, a drip of come slithers out of the corner of her mouth and down her chin.

I tell her what a lovely sensuous woman she is. I withdraw my cock, she stands, and I pull her panties up, letting my fingers feel for the last time. I finish dressing her. And the fantasy ends. The come spurts from my cock with such extreme pleasure I think the fantasy has actually happened. The conclusion is a deep and wonderful, restful sleep.

LARRY

My wife and I share a good sex life and frequently spice things up with variations and new ideas. Liberation will take time and patience. Women, however, will lead the way. What many good, not very chauvinistic, and loving men need is PERMISSION. Both men and women have been victimized by previous generations. We treat women we love with too much care of their lady-like sensibilities (due to our *mothers,* not our fathers). Most men are more aware of what they *can't* do than what they can do. Strangely, there are many men in my age group (I'm twenty-six, postgrad) who are afraid to ask their wives for a blow job!

It's been said, "99 percent of a hundred men masturbate, the other one is a liar." And during masturbation, if not during actual fucking, men do fantasize.

Now for my fantasies:

I am called by a friend and hear that Harry's wife has been bad and needs discipline, so come over. We (three or four) sit in the living room, and Harry comes in and explains some trivial offense. She comes in and pleads guilty. We are stuck by her sincerity and get up to leave, saying she's been sufficiently embarrassed. Harry agrees; but his wife shouts "WAIT!" She loves Harry, feels guilty, and needs discipline. We're confused, and she says the obvious punishment is to be our sexual slave for the afternoon. We're hopeful, but reluctant. Harry says that is great. She walks up to each of us and leans close, giving a pleading look, and fondles our balls or places a hand on her breast or cunt.

We retire to the bedroom, where Harry commands her to strip, slowly, with us echoing the order. She blushes when one man demands that she kneel at his feet and suck his sock. She really gets into it, but he pulls his cock out and spurts all over her face and breasts. Another man tells her to rub the cream into her face and breasts, and moan. I tell her to get on the bed, on all fours. We all examine her and comment. We probe her and slap her behind a little, and ask her if a good gang bang will serve her guilt. She says yes, breathlessly. Each man fucks her in turn. Finally, I approach and spread her cheeks, eat out her ass. I then plow her cunt till she comes with a shudder. I pull out and slowly ease my cock into her ass. She becomes amazed at the easy penetration. I finger her clit, she comes as I push all the way in. She screams for more and to make it harder. We repeat the whole process with her on the bed, her head on the pillows, with her hands tied behind her back, and on her knees. She finally thanks us, asks Harry's forgiveness. They embrace and never quarrel again.

There is an interesting parallel between women's rape fantasies and male S&M scenarios. Not one woman I have ever met actually wanted to be raped in reality; what she wanted from a fantasy of being forced was release from responsibility. "I'm a good girl, but he made me do it. It's not my fault." The men who invent these fantasies don't want to be blamed either. It is the woman's stubbornness that is forcing them to take drastic measures; even then, they declare, the whip is used lovingly, lightly. In Tod's fantasy (above) the woman's flesh is so beloved that he uses padded handcuffs so as not to bruise her. He is merely being cruel to be kind; doesn't "really" want to inflict pain, but to force the woman to relax, lose control, experience passion, lust, filth, perversity, depravity—all the orgasmic emotions that have been rolling around in the man's unconscious in one big undifferentiated stew labeled *bad*. Even in chains, the woman is placed in a judgmental role. If he can force her to join him in these forbidden pleasures, his anxiety will be appeased: Women like sex, too.

It is not his fault if she will not easily admit that she is aroused and he must go to extremes to break her inhibiting chains. *She is making him do it!* If she were free and non-judgmental, spontaneously erotic and all-giving, he would not have to use force to get her to admit she secretly loves the orgastic pleasures she pretends to hate. What he wants is not the "ouch!" of pain, but the shuddering "OOOOHHhhh!" of lust. This tells the man that control of the sexual situation has passed from the woman to him. The little boy has grown up.

Larry's fantasy (above) of the woman as "sexual slave" goes further in expressing the contradictory notion of forcing your victim not to hate you, but to love you. What men need, he writes in capital letters, is "PERMISSION" from the slave.

But why? How could a slave hurt him? Why does he need her "PERMISSION"?

These questions cannot be answered on the level of every day logic. Only when we remember that the woman in the fantasy has symbolic meaning can we begin to fathom her retaliatory powers.

During the first months of life, mother bends every effort to see that the baby experiences no fear at all. If he is wet, hungry, cold, or lonely, all he has to do is signal his discomfort. Immediately, the malaise is fixed. One cry from him and he is fed. Magic! At this stage, he is so symbiotic with mother, he feels they are one; her powers are his.

As time passes, the infant's growing ability to perceive more of reality and how it works ironically brings him realization of his helplessness. He is not mother; mother is not him. She has power, but is separate from him. The world is not waiting to fix itself just because he cries.

Mother has a will of her own.

The object of the baby's love has thus also become the focus of his fear. Maternal care and solicitude may put this fear to sleep for a while; and in the happiness conferred, a basic balance is struck. Contrary to popular superstition, mother doesn't have to be perfect. If she is what psychiatrists call "a good enough mother," the child will come to see life as something more to be trusted than not. Fearful things may happen, but mother can soothe them away. Thus encouraged, the child moves outward, into life. He has learned that if he is obedient, doesn't lose his temper, and does everything mother wants, he will be rewarded by her love. If he is bad, gets angry, or throws things to express frustration, he will be met by another mother, the one who frowns. This is the origin of the conflict: the good mother and the bad one.

In the second year, a traumatic war breaks out. Psychiatrists call this phase of life "the Terrible Twos," when the child finds his will pitted against his mother's in the battle over toilet training—one of the universal traumas of life everyone "forgets."

Like S&M fantasies themselves, it is a conflict that mixes love and fear, rewards and punishment, anger and affection, discipline and freedom. Not every atom of our being is beloved by mother! In fact, there is this other, furious side of her that does not like us, that disciplines and controls us because she thinks we are shitty. How dare she! we feel, but are too scared to say.

Sphincter control is difficult. How many of her frowns and punishments must we endure before we learn self-discipline so iron-clad it never relaxes even in sleep? We hate this bad side of mother but must obey her. What if she got angry and withdrew her love? We are diminished. One day, we will get our revenge. . . . Is it surprising that so many S&M fantasies dwell on details of excretion?

The battle of the chamber pot is not the only defeat we suffer as children, but it can be taken as symbolic of the many other conflicts we must lose in the (alas, generally thankless) parental struggle for the child's socialization.

When I first read male fantasies that confused love and sex with shit and piss, I wanted to cut this chapter down to a bare minimum. "Who wants to read about something like that?" I had to get past my own prejudices—stemming from my own training as a little girl—before I could come to see that S&M fantasies express an aspect of male experience that women do not go through.

When young girls cross over to the love of men (father), they get a kind of fresh start. But men remain in love with women all their lives; leftover angers against mother get transferred onto the no-saying girls of adolescence and then onto the women of their mature years.

Girls are taught that surrendering their autonomy wins them something more valuable: They will be called "womanly" and attract someone to love and take care of them. The little boy is taught that love, while important, is not so sexually defining as independence. That is his gender identity.

He may have made some concessions to women, but he wants them to know it was against his will. "If you really love me, you wouldn't demand that I be clean." He never fully accepted feminine rules. Alone together, men reinforce in each other the desire to show the war still goes on. They piss in the sink at the hunting lodge, don't shave, drink from beer cans, and eat off dirty plates. If a woman visitor registers shock, the men smile. From these emotions arise S&M fantasies in which women are not allowed to object to men's obsessive use of details of excretion, but are forced to love them instead.

To the psychoanalyst, the compulsion to bring scatology into sexual matters is evidence that S&M fantasies are the work of a two-year-old mind surviving in a grown-up man. The preoccupation itself is a method of giving in to mother's demands, but expressing forbidden anarchic anal impulses anyway. Instead of the imagination being left wild and free, the mind is controlled by an obsession with detail. Some sphincter of the imagination is at work. It keeps the focus of the fantasy narrow and limited, but nevertheless preoccupied with the forbidden. If urine and feces were what the early struggle for autonomy was all about, they continue to be its weapons today. Since these emissions from the body become eroticized by S&M logic, is it surprising that semen often becomes a "dirty" weapon in the fight, too? Once, long ago, a woman would not allow him to discharge these emissions from his body as he willed. Young girls found his semen distasteful and ugly. Now the feminine sex will have to take these awful manifestations of his body into their own.

All children suffer injuries to the will. Therefore, why aren't we all turned on by S&M? Because many parents—most, I believe—temper the inevitable disciplines and frustrations of growing up with love and tenderness. On the other hand, if humiliation, beatings, or other punishments were the principal tools by which a child was taught, he is a likely candidate to become an S&M dreamer—his parents' offspring in this as in everything else. It is no accident that Tod (above) tells us he was a battered child. It is a truism among social workers that most parents who batter their children were themselves beaten up by their parents when they were little. Violence and its fantasies are passed on from one generation to the next.

MATTHEW

Whenever I have unchanneled nervous energy. I always turn to masturbation. My fantasies center around domination and rape. My wife, Kathy, likes to be submissive.

When I fantasize, I start out thinking about Kathy, but it quickly turns to her being some bitch that I hate in real life because if things get rough in the fantasy, it would be a real turnoff to see Kathy getting hurt.

I start off by imagining my friends and I are in a theater. We spot a girl sitting by herself watching the movie. She doesn't mean to, but she looks a little bit trampy because she is wearing a skirt that rides up her thigh when she sits down and a sweater with a low neckline. From where we are sitting, a couple of rows behind her, she shows a lot of cleavage. We separate and walk down the aisle toward her. Each of us coming down from a different direction, we surround her. There's one of us on each side of her and a couple of guys behind and in front. The theater is not too full.

I put my arm around her and she starts to protest, but Jerry, the guy on the other side of her, pulls out a gun that I didn't know he had and tells her just to sit there and enjoy herself. She is scared and just sits there while I continue on and say pretty incriminating things like "You fucking hole! When we get down with you, we're going to pass you around the theater and charge for it! Maybe a quarter!" And Jerry is pulling the neckline of her sweater down so that it exposes her tits and holds them up proudly (she is wearing no bra). Jerry holds her face with his hands and squeezes it roughly, so he hurts her, and says to her, "If you're a woman, you should show your tits so no one has any doubts." By this time, I imagine it to be some bitch who is flat—because I want her to be the opposite of Kathy, who is a 36C. Anyway, Glen, the guy in front of us, has taken her legs and put them up on the back of the seats in front of us where he is sitting and spreads them wide. I am kissing her roughly and shoving my tongue back to her tonsils and running my hand up her right leg and Jerry is sucking her nipples and running his hand up her left leg and we discover that she is wearing garters and nylons instead of panty hose. This is too good, a dream come true! We are really exciting her by stimulating the inside of her thighs, because by the time we get to her pussy, it is warm and juicy. Glen reaches back and pulls her panties off and starts jacking off in them. (He has that fetish.) Jerry sticks two fingers in her butthole and uses his thumb to stroke her perineum. I shove four fingers in her cunt and use my thumb to get her clit. She comes two or three times in a row. By now my cock is killing me, so I undo my fly and push her head down in my lap. She sucks me off while the other guys turn to each other for relief as my fantasy fades.

HANK

My sexual fantasy is about me and my wife. We are having a real large party and we have invited some couples, including this Negro man. Me and my wife are sitting in the bedroom talking, and I excuse myself. She stays in the bedroom. The black man is taking a shower, and he comes into the bedroom to dry off. He sees my wife and she gets up and runs to the door, but he gets in front of it. He yanks her dress off and lifts her up and carries her to the bed. She is fighting him, so he gets some rope and ties her hands to the bedposts, and ties her legs in a spread-eagle fashion. And then he gets on the bed and puts his cock on her panties, right on her cunt. The panties are the only thing separating them. He is teasing her, and she is crying for help, so I go back in there to see what is going on. When I walk in, he is taking off her bra. She sees me and says, "Knock him off me," but I just watch. He then grabs her panties and jerks them off, and she is fully exposed. Her cunt is jiggling, which makes him hard. She is squirming and jumping like hell, and he then slaps her cunt and says, "Be still, white whore" and then he spreads her cunt lips, and she screams "Help!" and I say "Give it to her," and he crams his cock in her cunt, and fucks her, and she keeps calling my name to help her, but I just keeping saying, "Give it to her. Give it to her." And eventually he fucks her till he is tired. And that is my fantasy.

ROCK

I am white, twenty-two years old, a mass communications student here in Toledo, an athlete (on the rowing team at school for five years). I have danced classical ballet for two years. I play guitar, like to read.

I was fat and sexually repressed when I was in high school. When I was in the tenth grade, I had a girl friend. We would manually stimulate each other a couple of times a day, when we could be alone. Then one night she and I and another couple were at my house alone. I suggested that we change partners. She hit the ceiling. She yelled "I hate you," and that scene closed me into a shell for many years.

Many girls came and went through my college years. This seems to conflict with my earlier "I was sexually repressed." Allow me to change that to "emotionally repressed." I had a thing that I could never tell a girl "I love you." If I did, I was afraid that she would get as close as the one girl did and "hate me," when I wanted my freedom.

This all sounds like I should be telling it to a shrink. But it is the background that contrasts with how I feel about myself today.

My fantasy is about a rapist. A guy waits till he sees a girl's light go out in her bedroom. He sneaks inside and through the house. I build the suspense on this one like I would if I were shooting an Alfred Hitchcock movie. The event is second to the buildup. The slow creeping into the back of the house, then stealthily opening the door. The agonizing pain of wondering if she has heard you. Creep. Creep. Stealth. Stealth. Silent footsteps moving along walls, testing the floor for squeaks. This suspense gets me excited. If I don't come yet, I continue. He gets to the door of her room. Silently, slowly tests it. It's open. He moves slowly to her bedside. Puts his hand over her mouth so she doesn't scream, and wakes her. He sticks a knife in her face and tells her to do what he says. To save details, she gets tied down. She blows him. He fucks her.

"No, you are not in control," the sadistic fantasy declares to the woman. "I am. You do not hate sex. I will force you to show how much you love it. The whole female race has been saying no to whatever I wanted. Now, I will discipline and control you. And you will not hate me for it, or call me bad. You will beg me to do whatever I want; and when I do, you will not be angry, but get excited with pleasure instead. You will love me for it because I'm going to force you to have the dirty orgasm you used to pretend to know nothing about!"

When these emotions are decked out in the dread rapist's flesh of fantasy by men like Matthew, Hank, and Rock (above) my reaction is anger and fear so instinctive and immediate that I do not want to publish them. I must remind myself of my own basic perception: Fantasies are not necessarily suppressed wishes. These men are not describing real acts of rape. Doesn't Matthew say he loves his wife so much that he can't bear to hurt her even in fantasy? It is some anonymous "bitch" he conjures up to humiliate in his mind. These three men are the only ones among the thousands I've heard from whose fantasies run to rape; but even in their fury, they show strong elements of inhibition: Every single one of them brings in a surrogate to do the dirty work!

And yet, and yet . . . I remain deeply disturbed by what they say. I can hear accusations that these ideas may be taken by other men as encouragement for real rape. My ambivalence led me to seek advice from several psychoanalysts whose professional judgment I've come to respect.

They told me what my intellect already knew: It is not surprising that these stories aroused childish terrors in me. It is not the mature mind that is being addressed here. In these fantasies, it is the infantile male ego speaking, still burning over defeats suffered at the hands of a woman long ago. Defeats of a specific kind: Matthew, Hank, and Rock do not want to tear the woman limb from limb, but to force her to say yes, to make her give them her orgasm, as if it were the very crown of manhood which she has been spitefully withholding. These are fantasies, images not so much of sexual desire as sexual revenge.

In the end, this is either a book about men's sexual fantasies, or a book about the way I'd like them to be. Some men have these emotions, whether I print them or not. Why some men put them into action—the mind of the rapist—is a subject for someone else. To omit fantasies merely because they frighten me would be to play the ostrich, to pretend that if we ignore facts, they will go away.

VINCE

I'm twenty-two years old and have recently started my own industry. Marriage is still far off. As for my sex life, it's okay, I guess. Usually all my sex, foreplay and afterwards, is what you could call straightlaced (imagine no oral sex at all!). Mostly my fantasies are either masochistic or sadistic, and my fetish (fascination of the female's naked foot) is always included. I am an avid bondage enthusiast.

Now let me tell you something about my fetish. It really

turns me on to lick the soles of a female's feet, to kiss
them, love them, and do almost everything with them. I
like soft white slim, rounded, dainty feet, which look small
and delicious with neat slim ankles. If I see a girl with nice
feet and particularly the arched instep and the feet sort of
restrained in their footwear—oh, boy! it's something out of
this world for me. I'd then like to hold the feet next to my
face and lick them, suck on the toes and sometimes, I like
to paint them with jam or jelly, and lick them clean of
each and every drop. Boy! if I could only treat a lady to
my licking session! Most of my fantasies consist of this fetish, in which I am generally restrained and made to kiss
or lick female feet. In the sadistic version, I have a beautiful girl all tied up and I can do whatever I want with her
feet and her also. So all my fantasies are a mixture of bondage, masochism, and slight sadism.

Fantasy Number One: I am driving on a lonely road,
when I am kidnapped at gunpoint by four masked men.
They take me to a van where the leader asks me to strip. I
want to refuse, but the gun makes me strip, and I'm left
stark naked. One of the guys puts a steel dog collar around
my neck, and then snaps it shut and gives the key to the
leader. The leader then explains that the ring can be exploded by means of an electronic control, and he shows me
the control. He tells me that I have to act a slave for seven
ladies for as long as they want to keep me. I am stunned,
but can't say anything. The van stops and I am asked to
step out. It is an unknown countryside with an isolated
home. There are seven ladies waiting (all have beautiful
feet). All are very lovely and look rich and youngish. They
all have the electronic control. They look me up and down
critically, and I'm left with them, entirely naked. feeling
odd. One of the ladies puts a leash on the collar and leads
me into the home, where she tells me I'll be a dog for them
and please them any way they want. I am not to speak
unless asked, otherwise I must nod. She tells me I shall be
punished for any wrongs I do, and I shall always show my
affection and respect by licking, kissing, loving their feet.
Then I'm fitted into my dog's costume, after they have
shaved me entirely, leaving only the head and my eyebrows. My knees and ankles and also my hands are
chained around my waist and neck in such a way that I

can only trot around like a dog. Then they all sit in the drawing room, and I start licking their feet one by one. I kiss them, lick the soles, and then suck the toes and caress them, and love them. Anytime I touch them with my teeth, I'm whipped on my back and ass. They are all in seminude dress, and are generally wearing the sadomasochism dress, and my organ is erect and stiff. They just kick me around exactly like a dog.

Next, one of the ladies says that she did not like my kissing, so I shall be punished. I'm lead to an inverted U-rod, over which I'm pushed, so that my face is facing the ground and the erect U-rod is under or around my cock, and my ass is protruding up. My feet are tied to the ends of the rod, and my face is pushed toward a small velvet-cushioned stool, and my hands are tied around it, and handcuffed, and now the lady who wants to punish me sits on a chair in front of me and places her feet on the cushioned stool. Then one of the ladies gets a cane and the other a whip, while another brings two foot screws and puts both my feet in foot screws. Then they start on me. I start kissing and licking the feet of the offended lady. They ask me to beg her pardon, so I start by saying, "Please madam, have mercy on your slave, forgive him." All the time, I'm being whipped, caned on the buttocks, and foot screws are tightened. I am aching all over, and it's an hour before they let me walk around, but again as a dog, and with a leash. I have already jerked off twice. During lunch they make polite conversation with each other, and I trot around licking their feet, and eating the crumbs they throw for me. Next, after they have finished, they think of my lunch. They proceed to bring a bowl which is filled with sweetened milk, which is placed in front of me. Then one of the ladies places both her feet in the bowl, so that they are partially immersed. They then tell me to lap it up. I start, and keep licking the lady's feet and with it I keep drinking the milk, till I lick dry.

In the evening they tie me up to a cross, and make love to me, i.e., they satisfy themselves with my cock. After this, they go for a walk and again when they come back, they say they have dirtied their feet, so I'll have to give their feet a wash. So they lead me on a leash to the bathroom, where they sit on a comfy chair, and I am again thoroughly restrained, so that my hands can move about, and my mouth. So I start with soaping their feet and caressing them, and lovingly cleansing them, and all the time, I keep kissing and licking them, and I especially caress their soles with my face. After cleansing, I wipe them lovingly with a towel and then give them a massage, and sprinkle powder.

Another thing they all love to do is to tie me up in a kneeling position, my hands behind my back, with thumb screws and foot screws, and they sit on a chair in front and make me go down on them, and they keep increasing the torture till they get an orgasm. Many times one of them keeps sucking me off. This is how it continues for a week or two, and after that, when I am thoroughly used to being a dog, and their slave, I'm suddenly picked up by the same person and dropped off at my house, all dressed up as I was. On reaching home, I find a package which I open and find consists of movie reels. I put them in the projector, and find that all my enslavement has been captured in them. Next day I get a letter telling me to keep quiet or—. And so the affair continues.

Fantasy Number Two: I am a Roman lord and have my own soldiers and palace. Everyday I get a new slave girl for my entertainment. This girl is a wild sort of a thing, and very arrogant. My soldiers drag her by chains and bring her to me. I order them to take her to my chambers. She is now tied to the wall with chains, her hands raised above her head, so that only her toes graze the floor. Now she looks scared. I then slowly start undressing her. First I remove her garments, then her underclothes. She gasps and goes red in the face. Then I move on to her shoes. I remove one shoe and then gently caress her foot. It is beautiful, with a soft pink sole, and small dainty toes. I start kissing and licking it and she just moans. I do the same with her other foot. Now she is standing stark naked with her whole weight resting on her toes. I look at her pussy. It is beautiful, with soft curly hair, but I don't like the hair, so I start shaving it. She starts crying and begs me to let her go, but I don't listen to her. I then expose her cunt to its full glory. It's pink and pulsating very excitingly. I then go down to her and lick and kiss it, and probe it deep with my tongue. She starts squirming and tries very hard not to show her own excitement, but then loses all control and has a wild orgasm.

Next, I have her spread-eagled on a table, similar to an operating table. All the time, the girl keeps begging me to let her go, but I don't listen to her. After I have licked her hands and ankles, I start licking and kissing her feet. Then shackles make them look all the more small and lovely. After I am satisfied with the kissing, I slowly mount her. Now she is really scared, and starts screaming, but I don't stop, and my manhood is erect and throbbing. I slowly enter her and she screams again. Then I start working over her and she starts enjoying it too, and wants to join in by pulling at the chains, but there is no release for her. After that, we turn her around and she is made to mount me, and at the same time, one of my men takes her in the asshole and another asks her to suck. We all jerk off on her and then leave her tied in chains. At night I give her her freedom, but first I give her a beautiful bath—soap her clean and kiss and lick her feet in the bath till they are pink and tingling. Then I take her to bed and caress her feet and make love to her and give her all the pleasure I can. Then she is set free and sent back to her slave den. The next day starts similar to the preceding one. I take a new girl.

ROD

I am white, twenty-eight, and live largely for my work. This is due in part to the fact that I am very shy, and therefore rather solitary in relation to other people, especially women. I feel sadness knowing how unlikely it is that I will ever find emotional and sexual fulfillment. It is so "chancy" a thing to find someone with whom you are genuinely and wholly compatible. We just dare not go around baring our innermost secrets to strangers. Even with acquaintances, it is terribly risky to disclose oneself. Here are some of my fantasies.

The woman or women—one at a time, usually—in my "dreams" are actual people I've known, at least on sight, sometimes quite well. There is usually a very clear division between who is dominant and who is submissive. When I am dominant, the woman does what I tell her, although she is very willing to submit. She is naked, except that she is wearing one of those black bands that women sometimes do, around her neck, and nylons, but no garters. Her sex is always smooth shaven, as this is something I love in women. She lays down on a platform or bed with posts, and I tie her so that her arms are outstretched above her, and her legs are drawn up against her body, slightly outspread, tied so that her legs cannot move. I then say to her—and this is important in setting the tone for this fantasy—that she is most completely feminine now, her beautiful, naked sex totally open and available, her voluntary submission to whatever I might desire, the most arousing of all things she could do. I then tell her that I am going to whip her on the mound of her sex, with a very light whip, that will not mark or injure her in any way. (The thought of mutilation or injury disgusts me.) In this, too, I tell her, she is most essentially feminine, her moans and cries, like the moans and cries of passion, serving both as a token of her submission to me, and as a mode of arousal for my passion. Then I whip her, slowly and rather ceremoniously, gazing alternately from her sex where the whip rises and falls, to her beautiful face, eyes closed, head moving slowly from left to right, and back again, her mouth emitting soft groans that occasionally suggest a greater intensity. Usually, if I just follow through with this part of the fantasy, dwelling on it, I will come. Sometimes it goes further with my fucking and sucking her. The curious thing in all this, I suppose, is that I am always very tender, telling her how much she arouses me, and never injuring or bruising her beautiful flesh.

In fantasies where the woman is dominant, she is above me, moving her smooth sex over my mouth, rhythmically, back and forth, dwelling in pleasure, giving me her taste and scent. (This is a position in which I would dearly love to lick a women.) Sometimes she fucks me—anyway, I do whatever she likes. That is the important thing. The turn-on for me is her unhesitating, straightforward expression of her desires, and her enjoyment of her pleasure.

GERARD

I am a thirty-year-old white, divorced male and a psychotherapist.

My turn-on is spanking. Mostly to be spanked but occasionally to be the spanker. The fantasy has a thousand variations but the common theme is that I am bending over someone or something with my ass bare and my feet off the ground. I am helpless and vulnerable. The fantasy is always with a woman. She is not brutal or angry although she may tease me. I've been naughty and getting what I deserve. I always agree with the punishment. The ritual (in whatever form it takes) is very important, the bending over, or tying me up, especially. All *that* is really loving and caring. In fact that is the whole theme. When she begins, with a switch of her hand, she starts gently and slowly. It makes me want more. Eventually she builds up and it hurts. It's like a climax. The physical contact is an act of love. It reflects (literally) the caring and affection.

These fantasies are masturbatory. I have them also when I am making love and really want to act them out. Occasionally I have with different lovers and some of these experiences have been exciting. I am very risky. I know that some woman have their own fantasies that are similar to mine. That is when my needs are met in the best way.

Despite my relative ease in writing this and the fact that when I have been in therapy I have shared these fantasies with groups and even acted them out, I cannot get over feeling deeply ashamed about my fantasy.

Our society says that it's not okay for a man to be submissive and helpless. We're supposed to be tough and domineering. I can do that; it would be easy to project that image in the community where I live and work. But I don't want to. The men who are my friends are struggling with new definitions and roles for ourselves. We want to be soft, gentle, and tender, caring, authentic and whole. I certainly do. Perhaps one day it will be more acceptable to feel that my fantasies as a man are okay and that coming across as a wrestler in bed is not what men and women want or need all the time. Getting there (feeling that it's okay) is my personal work to do.

NIGEL

My fantasies revolve around being sexually dominated by women or groups of women. My fantasies rarely include actual violence and pain—whenever they do I usually substitute another man into the fantasies—but rather emphasize humiliation, obedience, and dedication in providing women with sexual satisfaction. Here are two of my favorite fantasies:

1. I am the sexual "slave" of a well-built, and good-looking, but tough young girl (say about twenty-six or twenty-seven) who is a secretary or a nurse. We have known each other for several years, and although our relationship began more normally, it has evolved to where she controls all our sexual activity. I come to her apartment and live there with her for extended periods whenever she wishes. Our sexual activity boils down to my satisfying her through cunnilingus and analingus, primarily. Initially she would masturbate me, but then she trained me to perform autofellatio by lying on my back and jackknifing my legs over my head. She also mastered the technique of fingering my ass and making me come by massaging my prostrate glands. In fact, the rules are that when I perform autofellatio I'm not allowed to come until she initiates it via my prostate. Since I obey all her commands, I do not hesitate one day when she decides to demonstrate our unique sexual practices to her girl friend. This girl enjoys this performance so much, and becomes so stimulated that I am required to satisfy her orally and she convinces my girl to put on regular shows for groups of women. One thing leads to another and before long I'm putting on weekly, and then even more frequent shows in my girl's apartment, for groups of four to five women (some of whom are single "career" women, college students, or horny married women's libbers). The demand is so great (all by word of mouth) that my girl is soon earning lots of money by charging admission at twenty dollars a head. The show consists of four acts: (1) After all the audience has arrived and has become acquainted, I must strip down nude, masturbate to an erection, and let each person inspect me any way she wants. (2) I perform autofellatio on the floor,

with my girl finally letting me come by massaging my prostate, and then I must let the semen dribble out the sides of my mouth. (3) I perform cunnilingus and analingus on all the girls present—but this is done in a special way: Each girl was previously told to come to the "party" wearing a long full skirt, with nothing underneath. This way I can satisfy them with my head buried underneath their skirts, while everyone remains in the room, watching and talking while I satisfy each girl in turn. (4) In the final act, each spectator gets to choose an unusual act for me to perform, such as screwing me anally with a vibrator or dildo, my pissing in a bottle, or urinating on myself in the bathroom, my receiving an enema, etc. A favorite request in this portion of the show is for a repeat of analingus as many of the girls have not experienced this before, and find the act very stimulating. There are many demands for me to be "rented out" but my girl has not *yet* agreed to this (it's not up to me); although this is "hanging over my head" and some of the things the women want me to do are extremely humiliating (but yet exciting to me).

2. I fantasize that I am the sexual slave of another woman (this one is usually a little older than the one in fantasy number one). I am usually married to this woman, am the wage earner, but perform all household chores as well. At home I am always kept in the nude or dressed in some humiliating costume with my genitals showing. I am required to parade around this way even when she has guests over, even when I am serving a dinner party to mixed company. When I come home from work on certain days, she has her bridge club at the house, and as soon as I walk in I'm ordered to strip down, crawl on all fours over to my wife, and kiss her feet and ass. She then removes the metal "thimble" she has fastened to my penis which I am required to wear at all times when she's not with me. This device is attached to my penis by a wire which goes through two holes she had pierced into my foreskin. The "thimble" has a small hole so I can urinate with it on, but can do nothing else while it's on. The other girls are always fascinated by this device and the way it permits my wife to maintain full control over me even while we're apart. (I cannot remove it myself, since it must be done with a small key that only she has.) Once the thimble is off, I am told

to masturbate myself and ejaculate into a plate with every-one watching. Then I must lick up the semen from the plate until it is dry. Then I must perform cunnilingus and analingus on all the women present beginning with my wife. They either sit on my face or kneel with their asses up in the air for this purpose. After that's all done, she has me lie down on the floor on my back (on her expensive Persian rug), squats over me and pees in my mouth. She really prides herself how she has trained me never to miss a drop, and she calls me her "walking toilet." She then invites the other women to use the "facilities" which some then proceed to do, in the same fashion as my wife has just done.

Although my fantasies probably seem very far-out, I want to let you know that, except for my sexual fantasies I'm a very normal person. I am thirty-three years old, have had fantasies such as these for about four of five years. I'm married, with two kids; college grad with a good profes-sional job. Although I haven't ever shared any of these fan-tasies with my wife, neither have I ever lived out any of these fantasies, or had sexual relations with anyone in what would be considered an abnormal or unusual way.

DOUGLAS

I am forty-two years old and married to a twenty-five-year-old woman. It is my second marriage and hers also. I was married to my first wife for eighteen years, and we learned a lot together. We shared our fantasies and even tried a lot of them out. Her main complaint was that after she told me about her fantasy, it would no longer work for her. So I'm sure she never told me all of them. (Not that it mat-ters.) A lot of times I could guess what some of her fanta-sies were.

My fantasizing started before I knew what sex was all about or what masturbation was. I can remember being excited from seeing drawings in history books depicting cruel acts. For instance, Indians scalping someone, an old-time sailor being keelhauled, Christians being nailed to a cross. At the time, I didn't know why they excited me or what to do about it; but I would fantasize myself in the picture. Sometimes as the victim, sometimes as the perpetrator. Later I would use similar fantasies to masturbate, but usually my thoughts were of making it with a girl or woman I knew.

I devised ways to act out some of my sadistic fantasies, using myself as the victim. Occasionally I could be alone in my grandfather's garage. I would strip naked and run a rope over a rafter and fasten it around my cock and balls. Then I would wrap a rope or belt around my wrists and pretend they were tied. Then I would pretend I was being tortured and beaten, causing me to pull against the rope around my cock and balls. Sometimes going so far as to fall down so my hips were held off the floor by my cock and balls. These would end by me masturbating to climax with the rope still tied in place.

I remember a couple of times enticing a fellow playmate to play my games with me. There was an old unused barn on our property. I devised a pirate game that we played. My friend was the pirate and I was a captive he was making walk the plank. Naturally I had to be naked to walk the plank. I would tie a rope around my cock and balls and then he would tie my hands behind me with the same rope. He would push and prod me out onto a plank we had set up and then with a play sword, keep stabbing me until I walked off the plank, falling into a pile of straw. The pull of the rope and the sticking of the straw would really get me excited. I don't remember ever masturbating in front of my friend or with him, but I received sexual pleasure from playing the game.

My teen years were spent in trying to fuck a girl and having fantasies about it. Only occasionally would old torture fantasies pop up. When they did, they were still similar to my earlier ones except usually my torturer was female now. I don't remember having any fantasy where I was torturing a woman. I was always the victim.

Then about a year or so after my first wife and I were married, I got to thinking about tying her up. I don't remember any particular fantasy about it, I just wanted to put her in bondage (of course, I did not know it was called that, then). We talked about it, and she agreed. We tried it, liked it, and were into a whole new thing that lasted the remainder of our marriage.

From then on, my fantasies were of me having a slave girl to torture and fuck, or a victim of some kind, always female, to misuse and have sex with. I drew pictures, wrote stories, and finally began taking Polaroid pictures with my wife in bondage. These all helped my fantasies which took place while I was working, driving, or just goofing off.

The fantasies I have these days are more like daydreams and are always about my wife. She is my slave and is sucking me, or I am whipping and fucking her in front of someone. Most of the time, I do not masturbate with my fantasy but use it to add to my sexual excitement before starting anything with my wife. I don't use them because of a lack of sexual satisfaction but to enhance our sexual encounter. Nor do I need them to get excited. All my wife has to do is cuddle up to me, and I have an erection. She can get me hard by just looking at me in her own sexy way or by pursing her lips like she was sucking my cock.

PETER

A couple of times I made up fantasies for my wife as we made love; it seemed to work pretty good. I know that when she performs fellatio she likes me to put my fingers in her rectum and vagina and she becomes very excited. I suspect she is fantasizing about being loved by three men at once.

I and two close friends talk a lot about having a big love-in with our wives. But when we approached the girls on the subject we were met with very cold interest.

I am white, thirty-one, blond hair, blue eyes, five-nine, one hundred forty-five pounds, not ugly. I'm a Leo by sign, but not a dominant male, at least not in reality. I love sports but I'm not usually a winner. I'm a loner and am fairly timid around women. I once called myself a professional soldier, but I sickened of what I saw and did in Vietnam, so I left active duty and entered the reserves. I'm now a federal police officer and go to college part time.

I started masturbating at about fourteen and didn't have

my first real fuck till I was eighteen. I went straight into the army from high school. From the army I went into marriage (girl next door). We now have two children, good sexual relations and I'm dissatisfied with my life. Is this all there is?

I was never a bachelor in the true sense. Never got the chance to chase around and have lots of lovers. I think I got married too soon. Of course my loss is self-imposed, we live in a liberated society, but my wife doesn't accept it. I really wish I could openly seek sexual relationships with other women, but my wife would never consent. I keep hoping that she will open up and take a lover. As far as I know I'm the only man she has ever fucked. I think that's a sad way to go through life. It would add lots to her life, our marriage and her womanhood if she did take a lover once in a while. I'm not afraid of losing her. I've had four lovers since our marriage and I haven't left her, so I project that she is also capable of multiple sexual relations.

My sexual fantasies started in preadolescence. Primarily: I am kidnapped by an older woman who steals my clothes, keeps me tied up and plays nasty games with me. Later I expanded the theme to being paired with a beautiful young girl, tied together and forced to do lots of neat acts. From the beginning of my puberty period till marriage at twenty-two, my fantasies were never very developed. Usually they were simple lovemaking scenes with the girl I was dating.

We got married in 1967 and it took quite a while for us to get used to each other. Neither of us was very experienced with sex. After two years of marriage I had slowly introduced my wife to fellatio, cunnilingus, fucking during her period, and I'm still working on anal sex and groupies. She is more timid than I am and I have to be the leader in all things we do. It's a disappointment to me. I think I could really dig being dominated once in a while, or at least told what she wants and when she wants it. Our lovemaking is very silent and almost never discussed.

After two years of marriage I began to masturbate again, usually when I'm away from home. With the return to masturbation also came the need to develop fantasies.

My job requires me to be away from home periodically, anything from a couple of days to a couple of months. I really develop a sex urge when I'm gone from home, it's always great to get home to mama. At army summer camp for two weeks I go out of my mind. I guess it's being totally cut off from women and living in a barracks full of men. I find that when I'm a long way from home, with a very stiff cock, my fantasies are very vivid, strong and extremely stimulating. My fantasies almost always deal with kidnapping, bondage, domination, and forced love, but never pain. My fantasies are generally very elaborate and detailed in how the victim is obtained and controlled.

As soon as I get home, or have an orgasm, I lose all interest in them, in fact they even repulse me. The female public is safe from me and my fantasies. I use them as a tool, and while they are very vivid and strong at the time, as soon as I reach my orgasm they are instantly gone. I try to avoid fantasizing while actually making love. Fantasizing usually causes me to orgasm way too soon. I may use a fantasy to get myself interested, but I immediately try to get rid of it so as to prolong my fucking endurance.

In brief outline here are some of my favorites.

1. I stop to pick up a beautiful young girl hitchhiking by herself late at night. I'm in uniform and I step from my car, telling her that for my safety I have to search her for weapons. I make her spread-eagle outside the car and then I search her thoroughly, even under her clothes. I then handcuff her. As soon as I have her in the car I blindfold and gag her. I then take my beautiful and helpless victim to my secluded home where I imprison her in my dungeon basement. From here on it's routine bondage and forced sexual acts, which she always ends up enjoying. After a period of days I always turn my victims loose. Sometimes I elaborate the scene to the captive being fat and ugly. After her capture I force her to diet and exercise. When I release her she is beautiful and sexy.

The next one I have given consideration to acting out with my wife. Sometimes I get the impression she might be receptive to a little domination. So far all I have tried is some mild tying up—it wasn't much of a turn-on for me but my wife seemed to enjoy it. I think I could really enjoy it if there was more realism involved. But my fear is that it would be much too much for her. That would be leaving the world of fantasy and I don't think I can allow that to happen.

2. I capture my wife any number of different ways. Primarily, I come home late at night, sneak into the bedroom and subdue her before she knows what's happened. Blindfolded and gagged she would be at my mercy. I would then carry her to the basement and leave her tied to the rafters. Then I take the kids to their cousins for a few days and have the house to myself. The script from here on would be very much like *The Story of O* except that the punishments would be in much milder form. One variation is to strip her and put her in a poncholike cloak she has, tie her underneath and take her to a motel for some forms of bondage and public exposure.

I derive pleasure from giving my partner pleasure. It's really wild to manipulate a woman after she gets really turned on. I dislike fakers though. Actually I wouldn't mind being the victim myself. At least it would be nice to be tied to a bed and sucked to orgasm.

Thank you for the chance to write in: It feels neat and a little sinful.

Dictator psychology is not hard to understand. The aggressive drive to establish authority over another person through sadistic acts is cruel but recognizable. But why would anybody want to be a slave? *Why did I in fact receive far more fantasies from men that express masochistic desires than the other way around?* The ratio was four to one, totally at variance with our cultural edict that men must be tough and independent. One of the people I heard from in preparing this book was a call girl. She described a dozen S&M scenes in which men paid her to sexually abuse and mistreat them. "More men like being dominated," she said, "than the average woman would believe."

Men like Vince (above) say they get as much pleasure in submission as in domination. Even Rod (above), who begins with fantasies in which he is the aggressor, ends with an admission that he wouldn't mind being the victim. Rod does not give us details about his masochistic dreams; perhaps, like the enlightened Gerard (above), he is too ashamed of desiring submission to spell it out. But he twice mentions that he has such fantasies.

Fear and guilt about going too far; anxiety that what he wants of women is dirty and evil; fatigue with the responsibility of initiating sex—all these seem to go into the construction of Gerald's fantasy. "Our society says that it's not okay for a man to be submissive and helpless. We're supposed to be tough and domineering. . . . But I don't want to and I won't." In his fantasy, he no longer has to struggle against his conscience, which tells him it is bad to want sex; he no longer has to risk rejection by being the one who initiates it. He accepts judgment. He is naughty and must submit to the woman's discipline. But when she spanks him, "the physical contact is an act of love." He has pleaded guilty, accepted punishment, paid for his pleasure in advance. Now he can demand his orgasm with a clear conscience.

That masochism offers subtle rewards begins to be evident; but still—why is it *preferred* by the majority of sado-masochistic men? Sadism is best understood as a rage for revenge, the man's passionate wish to assert the ego and will that were curbed in him as a boy. Are we to understand that the majority of the male race, like the majority of my contributors in this chapter, do not wish for autonomy after all?

In my understanding, the answer is no. The masochist's fantasy illustrates an inversion of anger, but is born of the same rage against the parent as the sadist's. The sadistic personality is bolder; but as earlier fantasies have shown, even he suffers an underlying fear of the power latent in his victim. The masochist is even more inhibited by dread of the symbolic figure.

What chain could hold back someone as omnipotent as the mother who lives on in the infantile part of his unconscious? What rope or gun could force her to love him if she grew angry? To complete the picture, I think we must also take into account the masochist's fear of his own rage. It is so volcanic by now—after all these years of repression—that it could lead to murder. He shuns the confrontation that would allow the destroying demon out of the bottle.

"Have a nice day," people ritually say to each other after the most appalling business meetings. The furious guy who cuts into your lane has a bumper sticker asking you to

"Be Nice." Ours is an angry society that wears a smiling mask.

Some people turn their aggression back on themselves; stomach ulcers, migraine, and other stress-related symptoms are the evidence. The masochist does the same, using other people to satisfy his need for pain. If he asks someone to play the sadist, if he pays a call girl to abuse or humiliate him—isn't she doing what he wants? Behind the façade, he is running the show. Like the sadist's, the masochist's dream is to express his rage, but in the way he chooses. He has found it safest to do it against himself.

Only on the surface does the idea sound bizarre. It is actually rooted in a special reading of a lesson all children are taught. If you return mother's anger with defiance of your own, that only makes matters worse. But if you accept her punishment, it will be followed by love. "This hurts me more than it does you," she'd say; and if our cries were in part for our own pain, they were also an effort to arouse that forgiving love of hers that could only stand so much: We knew her breaking point.

More often, she would leave the punishment to dad. "Wait till your father comes home," she'd say. As the hours passed till the dreaded six o'clock, we could sense her anger was already turning into fear he would hurt us too much. "You've been punished enough," she'd say, looking at our long face, and not tell him. If she did tell him, she'd intercede for us in almost the same breath. How many fathers have been put in the thankless role of disciplinarian, only to stand bewildered as the mother kisses away the tears of the child *she* set up for punishment?

By the time he is ready for girls, a young man has learned that women like you to show repentance. Let the girl see how miserable you are, that you hurt her feelings, went too far last Saturday night. Women love to forgive, love to say "there, there"—once they've seen enough unhappiness. At the bottom of the masochist's soul is a smirk: *knowledge that his suffering manipulates the aggressor's anger into love.*

By the time he is married, the man knows better than to try to argue with his wife when she declares he has hurt her feelings, said this wounding thing, forgotten that important anniversary. He also knows what his punishment will be—no sex—and that it will go on and on, no matter what anger or logic he brings to his side of the argument. "I'm sorry," he says, "I'll never do it again." The balance has righted itself in his wife's mind; the situation has been restored to her control. She takes him to bed for the best sex they've had in weeks.

The old lesson is being retaught: If he is careful, if he listens to the woman's rules, suppresses his anger, and accepts her discipline, he will be rewarded with sex and love. *It is the formula for masochism.*

Nigel (above) is not the only man who told me his masochistic fantasies began after he married. The husband's rage at being controlled needs a target. To vent it on his wife is only to start up the entire cycle again. It is safer to make himself the victim. Douglas (above) is a bit braver than Nigel. When he was little and dependent on women, he played the masochist. It was only after marriage, when familiarity with the female sex bred—if not contempt, at least an abatement of fear—that he "got to thinking about tying *her* up." Isn't that what he really wanted to do all along?

Peter's early fantasies (above) were about being kidnapped by older women so powerful they could force him into nasty games. His sadistic fantasies turn it around so that he forces women to play *his* fantasy games. In the end, though, he adds a plaintive note: He wouldn't mind being the victim himself. Women gave the boy the feeling that when he became sexual, he became isolated from them because they were pure, he was not. If only he could meet women who *were* nasty about sex, they would be like him, he would be like them. His lonely feeling that sexuality separates him from women would be healed.

This desire to be tightly meshed with a woman haunts Peter even when adultery is on his mind. If only he could have other women, with no threat that it would cause his wife to leave him, then it would be "great to get home to mama." He wants what he wants—but he needs his wife's permission to want it. If only she would commit adultery, too, she would be revealed to be just like him. They would be united even in their dirty desires.

Men like Peter illustrate a common facet of the masculine conflict. They long for the swinging life, but want to hold on to "mama," too. Their solution is often to go in for orgiastic scenes, having talked their wives into going along with them.

DR. LEWIS BROWN

For me masochism is a real turn-on, especially humiliation—*as long as it stays a fantasy.* I have had a "dominant massage" and found it to be only painful. The only turn-on was in my fantasies about it. I have never had any homosexual experiences.

This fantasy really gets me on, either for masturbation, or, even more, when my wife and I playact it out.

Fact: My wife has a friend named Frank, whom I have never met, but who is totally in love with her. He would probably do anything to get rid of me because he thinks my existence is the reason Sharon won't go to bed with him (that's probably true).

Fantasy: Sharon and Frank become lovers, but after a while he becomes very angry at having to meet surreptitiously. At each of their very frequent meetings, he gets progressively more angry at me for making it difficult for him to have her as much as he wants. Finally he says to her that he has made up his mind to murder me. Sharon is upset—although she prefers him sexually, she still likes me; so she tells him no, that she has a better idea—and whispers it to him. He smiles, is delighted and agrees.

Sometime later Sharon and I are at home quietly reading when the doorbell rings. I answer it and Frank is at the door. He is dark, stocky, has cruel eyes and is wearing an ironical grin. He says, "Hello, Lewis, I'm Frank." I am first surprised, then rather amused. I confidently ask him to come in. As soon as he is in he says, "Sharon and I are lovers and we want you to clear out now!" I laugh and look at Sharon who is watching us both very closely—she has a shy smile. I say to him, "No way, buddy—now get out!" He says, "Fuck you!" and starts throwing punches. The ensuing fight is very vicious. Although I am quite a bit smaller than he, I am much more agile and am giving him quite a beating. Just as I am enjoying it the most, I make an error and he lands a solid blow that staggers me. Now he is on top and beats me unmercifully.

Sharon is watching and is totally fascinated by the raw animal sensuality of the beating. As he beats me he starts to undress me—tearing the clothes off me—this really turns Sharon on as she sees her lover first physically destroy, and then totally humiliate her man. Finally, when it is obvious that there is no more fight in me, the beating stops. Frank looks me up and down and sneeringly says to Sharon, "How could you have ever let that impotent asshole have you?" He picks me up like a dead chicken, drags me off to the bedroom and throws me on the bed. He and Sharon then undress and make love with tremendous passion right next to me. Their passion is heightened, knowing I am there watching and hearing them and totally powerless to do anything—although their lovemaking is choking me with rage and passion.

After fucking her multiple times, he seems even more sexually vigorous than before starting. His penis is immense. He notices that I am moving about a bit more, so he stops fucking her and he stands me up and punches me a few more times, until I go limp and helpless again. Then he turns me over, mounts me and fucks my asshole. Even though I'm thoroughly beaten, I still have to scream in agony—but both Frank and Sharon notice that while he is in me, I, in turn, develop my own huge erection.

When he's finished with me, he throws me off his cock and looks at me lying on the bed bleeding from my ass. He laughs roughly at my helplessness and says, "Don't get tired yet, Lewis, the fun is just beginning."

He then flips me over onto my back and he and Sharon begin to tie me up, such that they pass a rope behind each knee and pull my knees up over my head, knees apart, and tie the ropes down so that I am spread-eagled, but with my knees drawn up. My wrists are then tied down so my arms are spread straight out. Finally, a rope is passed across my waist, so I can't move or squirm.

Frank grins like a little boy and admits to me that he had wanted to kill me, but Sharon had a better idea. What they are going to do is castrate me and amputate my scrotum! He explains that due to the humiliation I would never report them, and being a eunuch, I couldn't compete for

Sharon's attention. As a final ironical blow, they would keep my scrotum and testicles in a bottle and blackmail me by threatening to disclose my condition—unless I paid them all of my income.

I start to swear—say they can't get away with it, but Frank only laughs. I look to Sharon but she just smiles and says: "Why don't you just be quiet, Lewis?"

Frank gets sterile towels and instruments (we are both physicians) and starts washing my scrotum and penis with alcohol. For some reason, my courage seems to have returned, and I tell him his plan is fantastic; that he'll never get away with it; that I shall report him and they'll toss him in prison.

Now he is silent as I continue to berate him . . . he just keeps washing and preparing me. He puts gloves on, but no mask. He then seats himself in front of my balls and instructs Sharon to hold my penis up so it won't get in his way.

For the first time the full impact of what is really about to happen comes crashing down on me—and I totally panic I plead; I cry; I scream; I threaten; I try to squirm and thrash, but am tied too securely.

Frank just smiles and, holding a scalpel and forceps, says: "I'm going to castrate you without any anesthesia, Lewis, because I want you to feel everything—especially that moment when you lose your last ball." Throughout the operation I continue to scream, cry and beg pitifully, but to no avail.

The surgery begins with Frank grasping the left side of the base of my scrotum with a toothed forceps—I feel white pain! He then slices in with his scalpel—I'm nauseated. He directs Sharon to hold my penis up just a bit more. She is watching the surgery with intent fascination. When the incision is large enough, he reaches in and pulls out my left testicle. He loops two sutures across its stalk and cuts between them, freeing the ball. He shows it to me—I babble incoherently. Sharon, however, notices that I am becoming erect. Frank drops my ball in a bottle of formaldehyde—with a loud plunk! Smiling, he next slices the front and continues around to the right side of the base of my scrotum, letting it fall back in front of my asshole. Working slowly, he throws two sutures over the stalk of

my right testicle. Then he holds it up and, placing the scalpel where I can see, he says, "Okay, Lewis, this is it!" and
with me watching he completes my emasculation. That ball
also gets dropped in a jar as well as the scrotum.

The moment of emasculation is very powerful and very
primitive. The inevitable and ultimate result of the struggle
of two savage males competing for one female. The finale
is total, as one savage completely defeats the other and
takes his strength—his maleness—the ultimate in domination—the ultimate in defeat and humiliation.

The entire operation is bloodless, but when he cuts me
loose, he has me hold a large pack over the scrotal area,
presumably to stop bleeding. With me so occupied with my
loss and postoperative care, he and Sharon proceed to fuck
next to me again, and both notice that their fucking gives
me a monstrously large erection.

As the fantasy closes, Frank is inside of Sharon and she
is amazed at the size of my erection. Frank, beaming with
self-satisfaction, says: "Yes, but it's his last!"

RONALD

My fantasy consists mainly of being completely dominated
by the opposite sex, to kneel before a lovely tall, long
blond-haired woman (about six-three, wearing a black bikini). She has stripped me completely nude, and tied my
hands behind my back, and with clippers and razor shaved
my head totally bald, and plucked my pubic hair with
tweezers, until I look like a newborn child. Then, she leads
me down the street on collar and leash (with my hands
still tied, of course), with the sidewalk lined with hundreds
of girls. The blonde is barefoot. Her feet are lovely and she
is walking on her toes. She leads me to a huge town
square, also crowded with thousands of women. She sits
above me in a large chair in the center of the square, and
forces me to kneel before it, making me keep my knees
open wide so all can see my swollen penis. She now points
her finger down at me and shouts a command heard all
over the square, to kiss and suck her bare feet, which I do
obediently, for eternity, while all the women look on and

laugh and cheer. I remain there on my knees kissing the
feet of my queen, bound, naked, and shorn for the rest of
my days.

When we are told a story about a witch changing a man
into a dog, we smile. It is merely a fable. A story about
how a man gets sexual pleasure by wearing a dog collar
and groveling at a woman's foot horrifies and fascinates,
repels and attracts; we want to hear more. The sexual desires of men like Dr. Lewis Brown and Ronald (both
above) may sound like the love life of Martians, but they
touch a chord in us all.

Humiliation is such a powerful emotion that it literally
makes some people want to die. "I wished the ground
would open up and swallow me." A boy who is shamed by
his parents or schoolmates, *but who is powerless to retal-
iate,* must develop subtle defenses: Fantasies of humiliation
begin when the child decides he cannot affect the intolera-
ble outer reality in which he lives. He changes his emotions
instead. While the sadist identifies with the aggressor, and
so comes to be one himself, the masochist learns to love
what he is expected to hate, thus consolidating his own
identity, even if it is as a victim.

It is a strange victory, an acceptance of death-in-life over
death itself. How this happens, how pain can be used to
lead to orgasm, remains a mystery.

Dr. Lewis Brown's fantasy tries to work out a way to
bear unbearable defeat. The woman is taken away from
him by a more powerful sexual rival—just the way dad
took mother away from her son every night. When Lewis
tries to fight back, he is beaten, humiliated, and finally castrated—the very fears Freud names as felt by the little boy
who is angry at his big, strong father. In the end, however,
fantasy works its magic, reversing the flow of power. Does
the sight of his tormentors happily fucking away deliver
the final crushing blow to the castrated Dr. Brown? No, it
gives him his penis back, with a "monstrous large erection"
at that!

Ronald's scenario suggests an even earlier time of life; it
is dominated by a female giantess, with no other men

around. She undresses him like a baby and even puts him back to the time when he had no pubic hair. In his fantasy, "I look like a newborn child."

What better revenge on all women in his life who made him feel ashamed of his naked sex than that the woman herself "force" Ronald to display his swollen penis to all the world? He has rebelliously turned women's authoritative *no* into an absurdist farce, where the more she insults him, the more she arouses him. "You can't hurt me," says the masochist's fantasy. "In fact, you may think you're punishing me; but instead, you've given me such pleasure I've just had an orgasm!"

It is a strangely triumphant world the masochist lives in. Despite all outward appearances, he is never defeated. He always has the last laugh, an orgasmic one.

CLIFFORD

Here are two of my fantasies. (They are only fantasies. I'm sure I could never fulfill them, even if I got the opportunity.)

I am a white male in my mid-twenties. I am a graduate student in geology. Though recently married, I could never tell my wife about these secret dreams. I don't think she is ready to share such thoughts. We have a great sex life, even if it is rather conventional.

Most of my fantasies center on female domination and mild forms of bondage. I am not masochistic; I don't relish pain, only the thought of being dominated by women. I don't consider myself a latent transvestite, although the thought of dressing in women's clothes excites me.

The type of woman that attracts me is either older or much younger than I am. In my fantasy, I meet a beautiful woman at a party. She takes me to an empty room where she hypnotizes me. While under hypnosis, I tell her all about my secret desires.

The next evening, I get a telephone call from the woman. She tells me that she is going to a costume party in a few days and wants me to go with her—dressed as a woman. She asks me if I have ever worn women's clothes before, and I tell her I haven't. Then she reads me a list of items to buy and to bring over to her place the next evening.

The following evening, I go to her place with the items. She tells me to undress, take a hot shower and shave twice. Then she comes into the bathroom and inspects my nude body. She comments about how small she thinks my cock is and says how it will be no problem to conceal.

She then has me put on the black lace bikini panties that I had purchased; she helps me put on makeup: eyeshadow, false eyelashes, mascara, and bright red lipstick.

Then she helps me put on my long blond wig, my black bra and falsies, my black mesh stockings, and black lace garter belt. And then I put on the white frilly blouse with long sleeves, a skirt, and high-heeled shoes. And to finish my costume, she has me put on bright red fingernail polish. After my nails are dry, she teaches me how to walk in the high heels; and I parade around the house for her.

Then she drives me home. On the way to my place, she jokes about what would happen if the car ran out of gas— that I would have to walk to a service station in my costume.

At my house, she comes in and tells me what other outfits she wants me to buy and then she takes all of my undershorts from my drawer and tells me that from then on I must always wear women's panties instead of shorts. And she tells me that as soon as I get home from work each day, I must change into women's clothes and wear them for at least an hour. She says that at night I must wear women's nighties, and she takes away all my pajamas to make sure.

After a week of following her instructions, she calls me and tells me to dress up and come over to her place in costume. When I get there, she tells me that she has been checking up on me and that I have been a very good "girl."

She then makes me take off my panties. Then she opens her purse and shows me a number of obturators. They are all made of white plastic and have varying lengths and diameters. But each one has a wide flat base and a slight knob at the tip. She says we had probably better start with the smallest, so she takes it from her purse, dips the tip in a jar of Vaseline. Then she has me bend over and she inserts the white shaft all the way into my asshole. She then has me put my tight bikini panties back on which keeps the obturator firmly in place.

She then takes me next door to meet her girl friend. The thrill of being shown off to a beautiful girl in my costume is greatly increased by the constant feeling of penetration—the penetration of the shaft up my ass.

In the following weeks, she keeps increasing the sizes of shafts and starts having me insert them myself. Finally, my asshole is stretched enough to accommodate the largest obturator she has. After wearing the largest shaft for several days, she calls to tell me to come over in costume that night for a special surprise. When I arrive, I find about a dozen other women there with her. After parading me around, she announces her reason for inviting them there—that I am going to put on a special demonstration for them.

With the women all sitting on chairs in a circle around me, she first makes me lick her pussy and every other pussy in the circle. Each woman makes sure that I give special attention to her clit; and when each woman is turned on by my cuntsucking, I crawl to the next pussy. After I complete the circle, she makes me remove my blouse, skirt, and panties. Then she takes something out of her purse. It is a large dildo, as large as my own erect cock. But the dildo is not just an imitation cock. It is as lifelike as can be. Flesh colored, with even the bulging veins of a throbbing real male organ. It even has a scrotum with balls.

After pointing out to the women how much better the dildo is than my limp prick, she makes me crawl over to her and kiss the dildo. Then I take my tongue and start to lick the large glans, the head of the huge cock. Slowly she starts sliding the cock in and out of my mouth. With the dildo slick with my own saliva, she has me insert it in my asshole. And while shouting encouragement (like "Fuck it!" and "Shove it up your ass!" and "Fuck, fuck, fuck!") I fuck myself and love every inch of it.

ROY

I am white, married, male, age twenty-five with two children. My wife is twenty-five also. I envision the following fantasy before sexual intercourse and sometimes during the day when my thoughts turn toward sex. I rarely fantasize during sex because I'm usually living the emotions and feelings of the moment. I have always entertained the idea of bondage and submission so in my fantasy my wife plays the role of "boss." I often imagine what the beautiful body of a young girl looks like as she walks down the street, but I like my wife in my fantasies, because it makes them seem more real to me.

I imagine that my wife (Jane) enters a room where I'm reading or eating and announces that there are things to do around the house that I've left undone. She explains how this type of behavior is a direct challenge to her authority, and that she sees no other choice than to punish me for the work I have left undone and also to demonstrate that she is in charge. I am startled and my face becomes flushed, for I had no idea that I had done wrong and am almost amused at this blatant display of power. Jane doesn't look amused, however, and orders me to remove all my clothes. I stand up and comply, thinking that I'll go along with this game just to see what happens. When I am naked, she quickly ties my hands behind my back. She then raises my joined arms over my head and ties my hands to a rope hanging from a nine-foot ceiling. At this point I am really hoping this *is* a game, for if it is not, I could be in a very dangerous position. My cock doesn't seem to care one way or the other because it grows until it is fully erect and throbbing. Jane, with a black leather riding crop in her hand, points to my erect cock and says, "I don't remember giving you permission to get hard, Roy! This is a punishment, not sexual intercourse!" She then whaps my cock on the end with her crop. It stings and I instinctively try to cover my genitals by raising my legs, but to no avail. Then she lectures me on the sound practice of completing all household chores before indulging in any other type of activity. While saying this she smacks my ass, thighs, nipples, stomach, legs, back, even slaps my balls once. She tells me that I will have to experience many things before I am purged of guilt. I also realize that this is *really* punishment and not a game at all (but I also love it).

Jane then takes a ten-inch candle and while she's greasing it in front of me she explains how I'm going to feel, what it's like to be fucked. She orders me to lean forward slightly, which the ropes allow me to do, she spreads the cheeks of my ass apart and slides the candle up my anus little by little. She asks me how it feels to be fucked and slaps my cock with her hand. I yell and she puts a piece of tape on my mouth, "to shut you up!" She then places two spring clothespins on my nipples. I squirm and squirm and my cock gets harder and harder. I just wish she would touch my cock, suck it, pull on it, anything so I can squirt and have relief. She senses my urgency and announces that she will not pull me off because it "makes such a mess." She then begins to take off her clothes, piece by piece, caressing herself, spreading the lips of her cunt apart, and using a large dildo on herself. Seeing this makes my cock jump up and down and makes me want to come all over her. She holds her wet fingers under my nose, exciting me all the more. She walks behind me and pushes the candle in my anus another inch, which makes my cock jump again. Clear, sticky fluid appears at the tip of my cock, dripping down to the floor. Jane sees this and tells me I've just earned further punishment and places a large rubber band tight around the base of my cock. Just to make sure that I don't make a mess, she places a smaller rubber band around the head of my cock and begins to pour oil all over my cock and balls. She massages my cock with both hands and pulls on my balls, watching my face contort with pleasure. In a few seconds, orgasmic spasms shake my cock, but no sperm squirts off. Jane laughs and says, "What's the matter? Don't you know how to come?" My body aches, especially my balls because my sperm was trapped inside of me. She eases the candle in a little further and readjusts the clothespins. She then cuts the rope that held my hands over my head and lets my arms fall behind me, hands still tied. She then secures a small nylon rope back behind my balls and over the base of my cock, grabbing all my genitals tightly. She has a lead rope to hold on to and gives the rope a couple of jerks, forcing me to do her bidding. She

rips the tape off my mouth and tells me to suck the dildo
she had in her cunt. I hungrily open my mouth and suck it
like it's candy. She pulls it out of my mouth and tells me to
suck her cunt. I get on my knees and suck and suck. Jane
comes on my face and makes me lick her very clean. She
turns around and bends over, saying that her asshole needs
cleaning also. I begin to lick her anus, discovering that it's
clean; she just wants to humiliate me though and makes
me lick it and stick my tongue inside.

My fantasy usually ends here because Jane makes me do
things like this for hours, never letting me come. I would
not like to manifest the fantasy physically, because I
wouldn't like some of the more severe pains; however, a
little pain would be fun, I think.

ZACK

In reality, I'm a very gentle person, with no desire to hurt
anyone (or have anyone hurt me). But in fantasy, the
opposite can be exciting. A lot of times when my wife
seems unreasonable and cranky, I have no desire to make
love to her. In fact, the natural inclination is to strike back,
which I simply don't do. Little does she realize how drasti-
cally she is punished when she is out of sorts (as we all get
at times). This happens to her when she isn't even here.

You see, I have this little soundproof room that contains
a hospital delivery table and a little hand-cranked electric
generator (the generator being of the type I've read about
some of our neighboring countries to the south using for
torture). I also have these neat little attachments for the
generator, custom made, naturally, for an exact fit in or on
any portion of her body. (I really don't know where this
room is in our house; but believe me, it's here.) Sometimes
when I take her in there, she doesn't know what is going to
happen and goes right along with the whole bit. Other
times, she has been there before, and I have to force her
into it. Either way, she is put onto the delivery table and
strapped down fore and aft so that she is spread out wide
and vulnerable. I have this little suction device that I put
on her clitoris, attached to one wire, and a large bulbous

dildo that completely fills her vaginal cavity attached to the other wire; and as I put the one on her clitoris and force the other up her cunt, she notices the wires and starts to get an inkling of what is coming. I, in my sadistic excitement, enjoy tremendously the sight of her naked body so helplessly spread out before me; and her pleading voice only adds to my pleasure. I watch her closely as I give the crank a few slow, experimental turns to judge how much pain or discomfort the electric shock will cause. She twitches and cries out in surprise; and as I slowly increase the speed of the generator, she strains against the straps; and her cries get louder, her whole body convulses and then relaxes as I slow down the crank, then convulses again as I speed it up. Her voice becomes a scream as I keep up the speed; her body is one big tight muscle; and as the electric current keeps flowing between her clitoris and the whole wall of her cunt, she screams, "Oh, my God, I'm coming, I'm coming!" I just keep cranking until her long sustained wail starts dying down. I stop the crank and watch her as she twitches involuntarily and slowly relaxes. Her relief is so great that she so completely relaxes that she no longer has any muscle control; and her anus opens up and voids, just as the piss quirts from her little peehole. Little does she realize, as I clean up the mess, that her ordeal is far from over. I unstrap arms and upper body, and tell her she must lick her holes clean. She refuses (of course she thinks she can't bend over this far, but this is my fantasy and she can do anything I want her to do) to so degrade herself, so I quickly put my little nipple suction cups on the wires and attach them to her nipples. Only a few cranks and she gladly bends down and licks her holes clean and ends up sucking her own clitoris, as the idea of what she is being made to do excites her. I now strap her back down to the table and remove the nipple attachments. Her fears start anew as I put on two different attachments, one a long, slim one that I slide into her peehole, and one a dildo that I push into her asshole. By now, whatever masochistic tendencies she has have been multiplied many times; and she starts to get excited by these actions. As I start turning the crank and the electricity flows through that part of her body, she once again starts convulsing over and over. I slowly turn the crank and watch her and listen to her moan as she comes again and again, almost continuously, until she is completely satiated and passes out. Conveniently for me, she always passes out at exactly the moment I need all my concentration for my own mind-blowing climax.

For me, it is a very useful type of fantasy. In addition to being a big sexual turn-on when I don't feel very loving toward females in general, it also has the very useful effect of ridding me of any feelings of hostility toward my wife. Really, it works wonders. She will never know how I can stay so calm and accepting of her bad moods. Little does she know how I've used her. Anger just doesn't last long at our house.

There is another side of the coin. Sometimes the fantasy goes just the other way, and I am the one strapped to the table. She has a ball with me, forcing me to drink my own come as she aims my cock so that it hits my mouth (huge, unreal squirts of come that almost choke me), then the same with my piss, all the while rubbing her clitoris and coming continously until she has to let go of the crank and grab a huge dildo and fuck herself as she keeps rubbing her clit through a big, final climax. Again she passes out completely following this, as always just at the very moment I no longer need her. Isn't she considerate? I also think it's cool that the one being tortured ends up getting excited and coming, and not really being hurt at all.

When I began this book, I was so naive and confused about S&M that I tried to break it down into neat, separate chapters. My contributors even gave me the titles, complete with capital letters: "I am into Bondage . . ." and so I would open a file marked Bondage. "What turns me on is Spanking . . ." and that's where he went. But then I would hear, "My scene is Flagellation with Transvestite overtones, and I also go in for Golden Showers and Enemas while wearing a policeman's uniform. Sometimes I do them . . . sometimes they are done to me." My contributors knew what I had to learn: These highly specialized notions easily change from one to the other because they have one central idea at heart—the delivery of all forms of sexualized pain, physical or not, in the service of expressing dominance or submission. If this chapter is longer than others, it is not only because I received more S&M fantasies; it is because the complexity and power of S&M would be lost in any effort to see any one aspect as unrelated to the rest.

Before I began this book, I thought sadomasochism was about whippings and red-hot irons; now I know that even in fantasies in which there is little or no physical violence, psychic humiliations are all any of us need know to understand hell. Clifford and Roy (above) have fantasies in which they are feminized. This does not mean that either of these men is necessarily homosexual. They mention being married; their sex scenes are mostly with women. Of course, gay men also marry sometimes, but my feeling is that if the men above could be easier about accepting the more "feminine" components in their characters, which society has denied them as "real" men, they would not choose loss of gender identity as the most shameful torture they could imagine.

It is also fascinating to see how subjectivity carries all before it, even in S&M. Heaven and hell are both in the mind. To a transvestite, Clifford's fantasy (above) might be a kick. Clifford is not a transvestite; for him, cross-dressing is the most abject humiliation.

The notion of bondage runs throughout this chapter. It, too, does not have absolute meaning; ropes, manacles, handcuffs, mean different things to different people. The whole fantasy can be about the pain of the ropes; sometimes being tied up can be mentioned while passing on to descriptions of an entire host of other things that are done. To one man, bondage expresses power—"You are my prisoner." To another, it says, "You are so precious to me, I cannot bear to let you go." To the masochist, chains can be a symbol that the jailer cares.

When we were little, we may have resented mother's rules; but unless she limited our freedom, we felt she didn't care if we lived or died. Who wants to be free to play in traffic? Rebellious and difficult as adolescents may seem, they also want parental boundaries—if only to cross them when they are ready. "Why not?" the seventeen-year-old boy asks the fifteen-year old girl. "My parents won't let me." To the grown-up ear, that sounds feeble. To children, it carries power.

I think that chains and ropes carry another significance in these fantasies, one difficult to explain because it operates on a level of body consciousness words can only approximate. How can anyone prepare a young boy or girl for the intense eruptions of emotional and sexual energies in adolescence? Something is going on in their bodies they don't understand. The overload of sensation in the nerve endings is frightening. Many young people report that their first orgasm made them think they were going to die.

The total loss of control that is the sexual high can also bring a fear of loss of personality, of going beyond familiar limits, exploding, being annihilated. Defenses are set up— not always the easiest to live with. Some people keep a tight grip on themselves because they feel no one else will. They cannot let go even for orgasm. For these people, outer symbols of containment are reassuring. Held tightly together by the ropes and safeguards provided by someone else, the fantasist isn't fearful he will lose his freedom. He has lost only his anxiety. He is safe to let go, to explode in sexual release. Ecstasy means the state of being outside the body. The chained dreamer need not fear he will go outside too far. He is held in by the chains of love.

Open any page in the Brothers Grimm and you will find blood, dungeons, ogres, evil witches. S&M fantasies begin in horror; but like the fairy tales beloved of children, they, too, journey to the desired goal: "Believe it or not," says Vincent (below) in discussing a fantasy in which he is slapped by his wife, "this is a tale of love." It is a commonplace that parents tell children their discipline shows how much they care. Sometimes it is. Sometimes it is an expression of the parent's anger. In the end, with the child's instinctive radar for what people important to him are feeling, he figures out the truth.

More often than not, parents wish their children well, but no child grows up without an occasional hurt during the necessary processes of socialization. In our culture, the job of inculcating those disciplines which will make the child acceptable to society is handed to mother. The child may think she is arbitrary and motivated by personal malice; the truth is, of course, that mother is merely passing on the rules by which she was taught herself. If her ideas of conduct are bewildering, they merely mirror conflicts of the society for whom she is acting as acculturizing agent.

If at times I have referred to mother as the Ogress of the Nursery, if—especially in this chapter—I have seemed always and inevitably to be blaming mother, it is because I am giving the child's point of view; I have tried to describe, analyze, and explain, not make judgments.

A more reasonable society would have reacted to the unenviable position mothers are put in, and found a way to have fathers share the burden, both of love and of anger. Ours has not. Nor has our culture resolved its double messages and conflicts about sex so that mother is not left in the ambiguous position of saying sex is lovely, but acting in such a manner that the child perceives she really feels it is dirty.

And so while mother may act with all the love in the world for her children, it's often a lonely, thankless task. She is not raising her children to live in some ideal freedom of the future, but to live in the world as she perceives it today. Her problem is how to civilize her son without crushing his spirit. In this dilemma she gets little help from our culture, which mostly offers only puritanical solutions toward coming to terms with our animal nature.

How can a child understand that it is not mother, all by herself, who has decided sex is dangerous, but that in this, as in so much else, she is reflecting what she perceives is reality? And if, after making sexual experiments, the child finds that mother first grows angry and punishes him, but then repents and shows him her love in atonement, how easy is the next step: A woman's punishment *is* a woman's love.

After such realization, how can rage at women not follow?

The happy ending in fairy tales is reassuring to children because it says that the dark forest will eventually end and they will all live happily ever after. The orgasmic end of S&M fantasies is no formal convention either; it reassures men that their pain will be rewarded. The convoluted train of dread events, the hidden contradictory emotions that seem to have been inverted in a nightmare mirror, have succeeded: The past has been avenged and made into pleasure.

VINCENT

The resumé of the writer:

A. From birth to date—solidly heterosexual; at once revolted by and compassionate toward any who are otherwise. I consider myself to be a highly moral individual who obeys the Golden Rule, the Scout Law, and my Conscience.

B. Between ages eight and thirty-five—troubled, tortured, and tormented by both guilt and fear due to masturbation and fantasizing. At eight, I had already developed two contradictory fantasies: One, which I have succeeded in actualizing, was to find the best woman in the world, court her, marry her forever, and raise a family. At the age of eight, this was no less a fantasy than the other, which remains pure fiction: to be attacked, overpowered, and disciplined by one or more beautiful women, always wearing long, black kid gloves. By about fifteen, I had, with the help of society and Mr. Webster's dictionary, classified myself as a sexual pervert—specifically, a masochist! with a fetish!! who masturbated!!!

This period of my life included two years in the navy during World War II (throughout which I feared a dishonorable discharge should I be discovered), a college degree, and my first ten years of wedded bliss.

C. Thirty-five to mid-forties—The discovery of pornography and the fact that there are others like me. I was able to reclassify myself as merely a deviate with submissive fantasies and a hang-up about kid gloves. The torment disappeared, but much of the guilt remained.

D. I am convinced that I am one of many, many normal males who is turned on by his fantasies, which, incidentally, include specific costuming. I am not truly a masochist, because I don't desire pain—only playful domination. I am not truly a fetishist, because I function quite normally without the presence or thought of the specific object. As a youth I prayed that my fantasies and desire to masturbate would disappear; now I pray that they do not.

E. My wife and I enjoy an extremely satisfactory missionary sexual relationship. Unfortunately, she does not fantasize, and cannot be comfortable humoring me with my fun and games. For this reason, I seldom star her in them. The enclosed fantasy is an exception, but is still indicative of the type of tale that turns me on.

What actually happened:

We were having almost two dozen people for Thanksgiving dinner at six PM. We had been preparing since Sunday, when I shopped for the nonperishables, and my wife (who worked full time) began baking. My son got me up at seven A.M. on Thursday to set the two tables, as a surprise to my lovely wife. He and I both helped her throughout the day. I grated two quarts of carrots, loaded and ran the dishwasher at least five times before and after dinner, and helped serve and clean up afterwards. I love my wife; I enjoy helping her whenever I can. Pleasing her makes me feel good. She loves me too. My favorite benediction to newlyweds is, "May your lives together be as beautiful as ours." Along about eleven P.M., however, with still a sixth load of dishes to be washed, my back began to ache so badly that I decided to go to bed. Just at that time, my wife suggested that she could help me move the tables back and fold them up, and put away the chairs. I really did not feel up to it and grumbled a bit, but we did it. My back was better in the morning; I got up before my wife and loaded the last batch of dishes into the dishwasher.

When I climbed into bed Thursday night, my wife said to me, "Thanks, honey, you were a terrific help today. Lie flat on your back like I do when mine aches, and I hope it will be all better in the morning." We hugged and kissed awhile, and went to sleep.

What I invented in my mind: She says, "You didn't finish the dishes yet, and you sure were grouchy about putting the tables back! And I'll bet that bit about your back was just a hoax! In fact, I'll know it was if it is better in the morning. I'm afraid I'll have to give you another lesson in discipline when I wake up. You haven't had one in quite some time, and you're beginning to slip!"

Returning to the bedroom after loading the dishwasher

in the morning, I find her smoothing on her long black kid gloves with a determined look on her face. She says, "I gather your back is okay now, so it really couldn't have been so bad last night! I'm sorry that I have to do this to you, but you know you have it coming. Now, are you going to walk over here and accept your punishment gracefully, or must I drag you over here?" I slowly approach her and allow her to position me on the bed face up so that she can straddle me. The sentence is sixty slaps, to be firmly delivered, yet with compassion, in the following manner: With my left cheek cradled in her warm right palm to prevent my head from rolling with the slaps, she slaps my right cheek thirty times and then reverses hands. After each solid, deliberate slap, her hand remains on my cheek for about ten seconds, as if to reabsorb some of the sting. At the conclusion of the lesson, she asks if I will now behave as I should. I agree. We embrace.

PLEASE NOTE: Believe it or not, this is a tale of LOVE. It is imperative my wife knows that I know that she is, in fact, more than pleased with my help for the day. I could not enjoy the beating if she were unhappy. I would have left her long ago if she were actually of this nature, and treated me as depicted above outside of love games.

BOYD

I'll tell you a little about myself and then tell you one of the fantasies I have when I'm bummed out by something.

I'm twenty-three, five-eleven, one hundred sixty-five pounds. I "lost it" at the age of sixteen. I now am forced to live at home because I was laid off about a year ago and no longer get unemployment payments. I like to read "men's magazines" but mostly for the stories; the girls in most of them look too unreal to turn me on. I like women with some kind of imperfections, especially young ones. My favorite music is David Bowie which might have something to do with my fantasy. I am completely heterosexual.

My fantasy starts with me standing underneath a streetlight on a dark corner. I am wearing makeup, white face powder, green eyeshadow, mascara, and red lipstick. My hair is cut in a rooster cut and is dyed blue. I am dressed in very tight black leathers and knee-high red boots.

A plump blond lady steps out of the shadows and walks up to me. She has a very worn looking face, and looks like life has kicked her around a lot. She silently looks me over and then takes twenty-five dollars out of a tattered purse and hands it to me. I take the money and follow her to her dumpy apartment.

The next part of my fantasy is always different, depending on my moods. Sometimes the lady wants me to whip her and piss on her. Other times she wants me to eat her. This fantasy always ends with me driving her up the wall with pleasure and then fucking her so hard and long that she screams for mercy. She then tells me how great I was and gives me another twenty-five dollars. I laugh at her and go out to find someone else.

I don't know why I always fantasize about being a male whore, but I know that if I ever had the chance I'd do it. I've always satisfied all my women, mostly because I take their feelings into account as well as mine. I think I'd make a good whore.

BENJAMIN

I am a thirty-three-year-old, white construction worker. I've never been married, though I've considered it. I have lived and worked in more than twenty states extending from New York to California.

I have about two years of college which I acquired mostly in night school. Though college has helped me earn higher wages, my work is still very physical. I'm also very athletic and still participate in contact sports such as football. I stand six foot two, and weigh over two hundred pounds. I'm elaborating on the physical thing because of my fantasies. I have a very wide assortment, but these are my favorites:

My first fantasy starts in an office building where I'm doing remodeling work. The office workers are having a party. One of the bosses invites me to join them and I accept. I meet a girl who tells me she doesn't know what she is going to do on the long weekend coming up. Since I don't have anything planned, I invite her to my place for drinks and dinner later. She accepts. When we arrive, I take her sweater, and put it on a chair. I then start taking all her clothes off. She is startled and I tell her she might as well be comfortable. When she is completely naked, I tell her to fix the drinks while I hang her clothes up. When I return, I put on some music and take her on my lap. I'm still fully clothed. We finish our drinks, and she dances on the coffee table. The music stops and I examine her body, feeling her all over. I pick her up fireman style and carry her to the bedroom. I tell her to kneel. She does. I tell her to take my penis out and put it in her mouth. I tell her then to undress me without losing my erection. If she loses it, she gets spanked. I then put her on the bed and make love to her.

This fantasy occurs sometimes when I am making love to a girl who is slow to climax, or needs excessive foreplay. It also occurs, of course, when I'm working near pretty office girls.

Fantasy number two starts at home. I am home with my lover. She is pissed off at me about something. I want to kiss and make up, but she calls me a bastard and slaps my face. I get mad. I grab her, strip her, and tie her to the bed. She is spread to the point of being uncomfortable, but not really hurting. I then tickle her with a feather. This makes her furious, which is what I want. I then masturbate her until she begs me to enter her. I tease for a while longer, and then take her rather roughly. She climaxes several times. When I have climaxed, I dress her, and take her on my lap. She is very quiet, but no longer angry.

This fantasy occurs when my lover is feisty or cocky. It occurs, too, when a girl such as a waitress or grocery clerk is unnecessarily sarcastic.

Fantasy number three: I am shopping in a slave market. The girls are naked and tied to posts, which form several rows. I have a reputation of being a kind master, so they all try to get me to buy them. I *do* buy five or six of them, and take them to my domain. They are bathed, fed, and given medical treatment. I select one to sleep with me for the night. The others are locked in comfortable rooms. I will use them later.

This fantasy occurs when a waitress, office girl, or any working girl is very pleasant and is trying hard to serve me, as efficiently as possible. It may be a hidden desire to take her away from all this.

This last fantasy usually occurs when I am alone and feeling lonely. (Men *do* get lonely sometimes.) It started when I was in the army on field exercises. There were many nights I had to sleep rolled up in a poncho, while it rained like hell.

The fantasy goes like this: I am walking through the woods on my way back to my weekend cabin. It's pouring rain even though the weather report didn't call for it. I come to a small clearing where I find a girl naked, gagged, and tied in a spread-eagled position. I untie her and carry her to my cabin. I have all the conveniences of home. I let her shower, while I get dry clothes for both of us. (I have no women's clothing, so she must wear mine.) When she finishes her shower, I fix her hot soup and coffee. When she eats, I give first aid to her. (She has insect bites and rope burns.) She tells me she doesn't know who did this to her, or why. I show her to her bed and tell her to call me if she needs anything. In about two hours, she calls. I go to her bedside. She pulls me into the bed. She tells me that I am extremely kind. We make love. It's raining harder than ever. Listening to it makes both of us appreciate the warm, dry bed and each other even more.

I wish you luck on this book. It may be more difficult since men are shyer about sex than women. In looking back over this letter, I find that I've used very little profanity. I assure you even though it may not sound like what you would expect from a construction man, it is quite authentic.

22

Virgins

VERNON

I'm a boy, fifteen years old, soon to be sixteen. I, unfortunately, am a virgin, though not by choice. I'm too shy to approach girls, but I am trying to overcome this.

I like *nice* girls, but I still want to get laid. I doubt that any of the better-class girls I know would make love to me, but I bought condoms just in case. I've read *Cosmo's Love Book* and *The Joy of Sex*, so I think I could satisfy most females.

Well, on to fantasies. I've been skinny-dipping a few times at a motel, and I really wish I could make love nude in a pool with a girl sometime. All my fantasies I would like to act out. Especially screwing in a pool or on a beach, and maybe in a forest or outdoors someplace in a wooded area. I prefer fair-skinned blondes, but right now I've got a crush on a brunette in my summer school class. (I didn't flunk, I'm picking up extra credits so I can graduate early.) The thing is, I don't *know* her, and I don't know how to introduce myself.

I often masturbate while thinking of certain girls I like, and dream of performing on them. I would also enjoy rear entry and breast sucking. I have a special passion for the female rear end, and I go wild watching them in bikinis at my apartment's pool. Big breasts don't impress me much. I like them, of course, but they don't really matter when I see a girl I like. Maybe you could drop me a note and advise me how to approach a girl I like. I know what to do in bed, but I don't know how to get there. Before I read *My*

Secret Garden, I didn't think nice girls (or women) ever thought about sex.

"People ask me if I can briefly define what Freud has done," psychoanalyst Dr. Helene Deutsch told an interviewer,* "and I say, 'Oh! only very little. He only found that children are not saints, and [discovered] the meaning of the unconscious.'" Just as children resist seeing their parents as sexual, so do parents refuse to accept that their darlings of five or fifteen touch themselves and dream of even more.

The young men in this chapter speak to me with enormous resonance. I groan, I sigh, I die a little over their laments. Women understand virginity. All that adolescent romance when everything seemed possible in the sweet confusion of love and sex. Deciding how far to let a man go, how far to go herself, weighing the pros and cons of every centimeter of maidenhood lost along the way.

All that power.

For how many women, I wonder, were the adolescent virgin years their best?

Sex is supposed to be power for men, but it is (ironically and logically) their very powerlessness at this time that stings teenagers to shame and fury. Studies at major universities are beginning to show how much has changed in our sexual values . . . and how much has not. In an era in which we think "Everything is different for young people now," it is essential to understand that there are at least three ways to measure change. A change in *attitude* can happen quickly—an influential book, a conversation with a powerful speaker. Our *behavior* changes more slowly. You may approve of the new freedom, but somehow are reluctant to put it into practice. Slowest of all to change are *notions of right and wrong,* which we get from our parents. You act on your new liberal attitudes, but deep inside you feel anxious, guilty. These feelings can take generations to change.

* "Helene Deutsch and the Legacy of Freud," by Suzanne Gordon, *The New York Times Magazine,* July 30, 1978.

For instance, young people today seem to be unanimous in their public professions of belief in a single standard for both men and women. This is an enormously important change in attitude. And if it were genuinely integrated, it would be a radical, evolutionary step toward sexual equality. But like people who tell sociologists that what they like best on television are the documentaries on noncommercial stations, but turn on *The Love Boat* when home alone, men like Vernon (above) are evidence, in my research at least, that in their secret hearts, men haven't changed all that much. Vernon tells us he wants a nice girl, but also—equal and opposite in his mind—he wants to get laid, too.

Vernon is so candid about the conflict that you don't know whether to hug him for being such a little boy or punch him in the nose for being such a jerk. It never occurs to him that the nice girl and the one who will have sex with him might come in the same package.

The young men in this chapter broadcast their tension, their agony and fury at being frozen by assumptions that they know "everything" while they still have no experience at all. Nor can many of them look to parents for a solid base line—even if only to push off against.

Ask someone if he has talked to his children about sex. "Oh, it's not necessary. They know more than we did at their age. They pick it up in the streets or the movies." And yet read the words of the young men in this chapter. Do they sound so cocksure and all-knowing? In fact, do they sound very different than you did as a teenager?

Somewhere between the sexual rules taught when they were young and the sexual revolution their children are living in, parents have lost authority. Some have surrendered, mouthing their children's inane slogans, imitating their styles and attitudes. Others just throw up their hands. Difficult as was the Victorian Silence, at least it had the virtue of consistency. The modern silence is correctly read by children to mean that parents today are so confused they say nothing for fear they will be laughed at as wrong, harmful, misguided, repressed, or square.

Some parents do try to pass on a more loving, guilt-free ethic to children about sex; but to the boy or girl listening to their supposedly liberated 1980s message, what most often comes through is confusion: The parents' words (atti-

tude) say one thing; the deeper music still carries under-
and overtones of unresolved anxieties mom and dad got
from their parents.

I hope this will not be read to mean I am against trying
to prepare children for their sexual lives. I believe in it
profoundly. The danger is that parents will tell children not
what they really feel but the brave new way they would
like to feel. Out of this gap, inauthenticity grows, paralyz-
ing the child, pushing him/her in two different directions
at the same time. The result is that young people are left
on their own to figure it all out, pooling their anxieties and
fears, their half-truths and rock lyric slogans under the pa-
thetically inadequate banner "all you need is love."

This makes our time particularly difficult for young
men. The same studies that reveal both sexes say they believe in one standard nevertheless often show that the boy
is still expected to take the sexual initiative. He is the great
sex expert.

Reading these pages, we come to understand the crushing weight this imposes on male virgins. They aren't even
into sex yet, but great things are expected of them. How do
you go from uninitiate to sophisticate with nothing in between? The boy who is still timid about asking a girl to go
to the movies is supposed to show no fear of rejection
about inviting her into the bedroom afterwards; once there,
he must display all the technique of a gynecologist.

Questions about the first step, worries about the First
Time, unresolved, unmediated emotions of love, lust and
anger come spewing out all at once. How cruelly these
young men describe girls who put out, even as they dream
of the nice girls who never will. They write down measurements of the penis they've never used. This is the age of the
pill, they've read all the books, they can spell cunnilingus,
they die for sex, all around them the whole world is Doing
It, but they call a girl who does "a pig." The boys/men in
this chapter are under such pressure that they have become
conscious of both halves of the male paradox: They love
women, they lust for women, they dream of going to bed
with women . . . but they also dread women, fear and are
in a rage at them for the frustrations and anxieties they
inspire.

In time, as sexual experience is gained, some of the heat

will go out of the conflict. If it were possible to interview these same men in a few years, they would probably look at their words in these pages and smile with disbelief. "Did I really say that?" Their everyday sexual experience will have become their reality in an unexamined way. Knowing how to do it—doing it regularly—how could they justify any leftover anger at women for frustrating them? They are now potent, powerful; proud of their sexuality. "Anger at women?" they'd complacently say. "Not me. I'm a lover, not a fighter."

But the fantasies in this book tell us something else: The rage is still there. *It has merely been repressed again now that the man has safely maneuvered his first sexual experiences.* Even a psychiatrist colleague of mine, a man usually sensitive to emotional issues, preferred not to think about the dilemma of the men in this chapter. "This stuff is boring," he said after reading these pages. "These men are all virgins. So what?"

EDDIE

I am a twenty-two-year-old white middle-class college-educated virgin. Male. *Virgin.* How that word fascinates me, with sick, gnawing despair, hysteria, amusement, awe. How often it seems Eternal, a Cosmic Condition, and this sex everybody is always babbling about is nothing more than fantasies. And yet, at other times, sex seems very real, and I feel that not only could I be a great lover, I *am*—I just, in my leisurely way, have not gotten around to sexual intercourse yet. Hopefully it won't last much longer. I am getting ready to finally cut the family ties and take off for the West Coast, where I feel that I can really begin to develop my life-style.

I have read [sic] a very introverted life intimately involved with books, science fiction and fantasy especially. Thus, fantasy is one of the most important aspects of my life, and always has been, on every level, and naturally sex hasn't been left out. Most of my "daydreaming" revolves around artistic triumph and cosmic adventure, and is at least as real to me as everyday life. Perhaps I'm insane:

people don't seem to think so but they can't see The Real Me (credit to Pete Townshend, one of my heroes).

Since I almost totally lack experience with women, my most common fantasy involves My First Fuck. A typical situation would be: I am out selling products door-to-door (that's how I worked my way through college), and come to a door which is opened by a young, attractive housewife, who smiles warmly and invites me in. She is still wearing her houserobe, or a bikini, or a short skirt and loose-fitting, open blouse. As she is pretending to look over the products, she takes every opportunity to bend over and give me a good look at her generous (but not sagging) bosom. She has no bra, so I can see her nipples—stiff, taut. If she's wearing a skirt or robe she moves her legs around carelessly, giving me many hot glances of her thighs and "mons veneris." If it's a bikini she behaves freely, aware that she's driving me wild and loving it. Soon she finds an excuse to sit next to me, pressing her hips against mine. Despite my virgin terror, I can no longer resist the temptation, because she has made it clear that she wants me. I brush the outside of her blouse, casually, she smiles knowingly, and my hands slip into her clothes to caress her firm, warm breasts. She sighs with pleasure, her mouth opens, and I kiss her passionately (how else?). My hand darts down to her groin, rubs it so that she begins to squirm; my fingers plunge into her hot, moist cleft and bring her to a rapid, violent orgasm. She is now completely out of control—she tears off my clothes, popping buttons, abrading my skin—but do I notice? All I'm aware of is her fiery, frantic mouth, her eager hand guiding my erection into her. We fuck vigorously, and I come soon but lose no stiffness, I just keep riding her, as she writhes and gasps with intense pleasure, panting, "OOH! Fuck me, fuck me! Harder, oh, harder, it's—so—GOOD!" We keep at it on and off for several hours, fucking and sucking and coming, until her husband is about to come home and she has to let me go—after we exchange telephone numbers.

Often I imagine that, while we are still in the midst of sexual abandon, the woman's surprisingly ripe and nubile daughter comes home early from school or work, discovers me, and thinks, "Far out! Here I've been feeling incredibly horny all day, and mom has a fine young stud all ready to shtup me!" Her mother defers to the daughter's acute need, and soon I am deliriously fucking an even hotter and wilder version of the mother! Our arousal is so intense that the women lose all inhibition and start making love to each other as well as me. The sight of the lovely mother and daughter kissing and fingering each other excites me unbearably, and I began fucking them even harder than before. Soon we are all exhausted and slick with the various juices of love, idly nibbling my cock, massaging a clit, sucking a teat, frenching, gliding over each other's tingling bodies. Afterwards the women talk about their luck at having such a fantastic lover just happen to ring their bell. I assure them that any man would be fantastic with such voluptuous women, and next thing you know we're at it again, and again, and . . .

I pride myself on being relatively nonsexist, since what turns me on is not women's bodies, but their reactions—how much *I* turn *them* on. I am a likable, reasonably attractive person; my lack of experience is entirely my own fault. These scenes could be memories if only I weren't so inhibited. My upbringing was not at all strict, but asexual—my parents were nervous and unsure about sex and never mentioned it. It's hard to explain, but everyone in our family seems very conventional, considering our intelligence and awareness; unwilling to push at the barriers of life to see what we can make happen. Sure, this is a very common failing—but the fact that most other people are worse off than I has always failed to make me feel better about my own feelings.

I guess all my First Fuck fantasies are generally the same—initiated by a sensitive, seductive woman, usually not a stunning beauty, because I find the perfectly beautiful, *Playboy*-type sex objects too unreal to interest me as much as the attractive women I see around me. Our sex is outrageously successful, and is usually joined by a second very horny woman after a while. Afraid I'm too selfish to imagine myself with a woman and another man, but then it is *my* fantasy. I am not sexually attracted to men, and rather hung up about that since I believe that ideally anyone should be ready to accept and give love to anyone. However, when I do have a homosexual fantasy occasionally (almost never about a man I know, just a general

Guy), I can get a hard-on, so I guess there's hope for me. I'll be ready for anything if I can just get some experience with women under my belt (heh-heh).

Although the Seductive Woman is my most common fantasy, I can also get very aroused by imagining myself as the aggressor, especially in a public place. I love to think about walking up to a nice bookwormess in a library and putting my hands up her skirt (or, more likely these days, down her pants). I would love to goose some of the women I meet going door-to-door, but I'm sure I never will, I'm such a chicken. I don't care so much anymore about getting into trouble, but am afraid that she will have a very uptight reaction and make me feel like a crude sick pervert and very impolite at that; or even worse that she will respond warmly and instead of being turned on I will be frightened by not knowing what to do, and thus find myself impotent. It is all too easy for me to imagine myself starting something that I can't finish.

Where are all these liberated women the media are always panting about? Even at school I found them frustratingly inert. There must be something about my attitude that scares them off; indeed it is hard, torturously hard, to show a woman you like her when you're terrified by the fact that you want sex so badly! It's the most vicious cycle imaginable, which I have been trapped in all my life.

I know that I could handle a relationship if I had one, but how the hell does a guy start in this lousy society? I have so many adolescent hang-ups to overcome, yet I am intellectually very mature, so I despair of ever being able to find a woman who can even begin to understand me. An agonizingly frustrating damnable situation that has me chronically depressed and near to tears right now.

But no! Men must keep a stiff upper lip to keep from rusting their typewriters.

OMAR

I'm white, Christian, Republican, fifteen years old, and a damned virgin. I will be sixteen in October. I have never even dated a girl because I am too shy to approach them. I know plenty about sex, and I wish I could put it into practice, but rejection kills me.

I wrote to a girl whom I'd heard liked me, but she wrote back saying she didn't. I love girls, and collect girlie magazines, but my lack of confidence keeps me from finding a girl friend. Also no girl has shown much interest in me since third grade. I'm near six feet tall, one hundred thirty-five pounds, blond with brown eyes, and reasonably attractive (maybe) except for a few fucking pimples. One girl pursued me through a female cousin, but she laid it out plainly that sex was not her bag. When I made a date to take her to the movies (twice), she said yes at first, but at the last minute came up with a really flimsy excuse. Even my mother told me I had been kissed off, though not in those exact words.

My mom's a real puritan where I'm concerned, but she's taught me about sex right and she likes men plenty well. My father died a long time ago. I believe in sex before marriage, though not adultery. My mother would be horrified to know I'm trying to get laid. She disposed of my magazines once, too. She only believes in marital sex. S&M and male fags disgust me, but lesbians do not. Pictures and the idea of two nude women (white) making it turn me on. Orientals also turn me on. Twins (both female), nude and screwing really drive me wild. I'd love to screw twins at the same time. Also sex on a beach or in a pool would excite me. Mostly I fantasize about doing it with a classmate or store clerk while masturbating. I never use my hand while masturbating, I stick my cock between two pillows.

If I could only meet girls and get to know them, I'm sure I could satisfy them sexually (or I'd sure as hell try!). I'd eat them or whatever they wanted indefinitely, if that's what it took to satisfy them. A friend of mine got laid last Saturday. He didn't enjoy it a whole lot, because (quote): "She's fat and even her tits are ugly. When I put it in she bled like the pig she is all over the floor."

BUDDY

I am just fifteen; however, my fantasies always make me feel like a twenty-year-old. I have always had fantasies, but I never told anybody of them. I come from a religious family and sex is a "no-no." I have an older sister who is twenty and still unmarried.

My first fantasy is about my thirteen-year-old cousin. We have always been very close and we used to play "house," where we would kiss and make believe we'd fuck. She's very pretty. We never did it! In my fantasy, she is sixteen and a virgin. She has large breasts and sexy legs. She wanted to remember old times and asked me to play "house." I agreed. When we kissed I pushed my tongue into her mouth. She got turned on. With my hands, I unbuttoned her blouse. She didn't stop me, and I undid her bra and fondled her large tits. Her nipples were erect. I kissed them. With her hands, she took out my erect dick and rubbed it. She urged me to go on: "Suck me . . . fuck me."

I put my hands under her skirt and I felt her wet panties. In my excitement I ripped the material with my fingers, and I fondled her clit. She unhooked her skirt and let it fall to the floor. Immediately, I pulled down her panties and buried my face in her pussy. She had a big bush of hair and it smelled good. I flicked my tongue in and out of her cunt until I heard her *ooohs* and *ahhs* and felt her come flood my face. When I mounted her she told me she wasn't on the pill or anything, so I shouldn't get her pregnant. I heard her but I came in her and she got mad. She got pregnant, and I thought it was all over, because she'd tell her parents, but she got an abortion.

My second fantasy is about my sister. She has large boobs and a round, plump ass. She's a virgin. I have seen her in her bra and panties, but she doesn't seem to want me. I saw her naked once, when I passed her room. She looked radiant. She covered up when she saw me.

In my fantasy, I am naked in my room reading a porno book, and she comes in wearing a sheer nightgown. Instantly I cover myself, but she sees my erect cock and she says, "What have we here?" She pulls my pants away and looks at my cock. "You like it?" I ask. To answer, she would close the door and pull down the straps of the gown, and let it fall to the floor. I leap up to her and pull her on the bed. I suck her tits and move down to her dark black pussy. I get between her legs and lick and suck her clit until she comes. I fuck her with my eight-inch prick and make her want more and more. From then we fuck regularly. She's great.

In my next fantasy, I have a harem of chicks. I like blacks the best. Their skin is so slick. I go into my apartment and fifty girls leap out from hiding. They rip my clothes off and make me fuck each of them. All those wet cunts. Tits flying all over. There are five girls on me at one time, while the rest finger-fuck themselves or fuck each other.

Another fantasy is me raping Raquel Welch. I would take her to a country house and gag her mouth. I would rip her dress apart. She wasn't wearing a bra and her tits sagged a little, her nipples were pink and already erect. I told her, "You bitch, you want it. Look at your nipples. I'll bet your cunt is dripping wet." Sure enough, it was. I sucked her muff until she urged for me to fuck her. I didn't. I played with her, getting her more and more excited. She had come twice. Then I put my cock in her moist cunt. I kept her there all week and she and I have a fucking great week in fantasy.

Every chick I pass on the street, I look up and down. I like big tits in a tight sweater. I wish I could go over to a blond chick on the street, and put my hand in her blouse and fondle her big boobs. Then while everyone watches, I strip her and myself and fuck her in the middle of Broadway.

SHERWIN

I am eighteen and a college sophomore, but I have only begun to relate to women sexually (dancing, a couple of dates), in the past year. As I was very introverted and ill

at ease with other kids until a few years ago—when I went
away to boarding school—this isn't surprising. You have to
crawl before you can walk. But because I reached puberty
early and always identified with older kids intellectually,
and because of current norms for teen-age sexuality, I have
hurt a lot inside.

I had romantic feelings about girls as far back as I remember, but my earliest specifically sexual fantasies came
when I reached puberty at eleven. Those fantasies were
still basically romantic and conventional images of lovemaking (gleaned mostly from books and magazines),
somewhat hazy, but sufficient for masturbation. They began to change when I turned fourteen, after a couple of
girls rebuffed my clumsy, albeit thoroughly romantic and
unphysical, approaches. My masturbation fantasies shifted
to less threatening material like incest, rape, pedophilia,
even incredibly gory sadistic fantasies. At least I didn't
want to actually realize these fantasies, whereas the old romantic conventional dreams of girls reminded me too
much of my real world failures. I feel guilty about some of
these new far-out fantasies, but at least I know now, after
reading your books, that I'm not the only one to have
them, that I'm not so weird after all.

While I'm a believer in sexual egalitarianism, and the
abolition of sex roles—I wish women *were* free to make
passes at men—there's another level where I blame women
for my frustration and would like to make women pay for
it. Hence my homosexual fantasies, fantasies about female
homosexuality and about women and animals (none about
men and animals—I think it's another antiwoman fantasy).
They've almost all been tried in both first and third person;
third person is especially good when something makes me
feel too guilty in first person.

Until last winter, I was confident that my homosexual
fantasies were as improbable as the others. Then I got
stoned with some kids (which I do very rarely—the kids I
usually hang out with don't smoke), and suddenly I had
the hots for this guy whom I'd been avoiding all semester,
because (I'd told myself—and it may've been true) I
thought he had designs on *me*. I was very upset for a
while, but finally I accepted, at least intellectually, that I
was probably potentially bisexual—at the same time as I

promised myself I wouldn't express it, if at all, until after I'd confirmed my "credentials" for heterosexuality. There are too many things I want to do that can't afford the label "queer."

One of my favorite "conventional" fantasies a few years ago was based on the movie *The Effect of Gamma Rays on Man-in-the-Moon Marigolds*. I imagined that I met a girl like Matilde, about twelve, very bright, neglected. We became friends and very slowly became closer and after a couple of years, we became lovers. Finally I turned eighteen and married her and took her away from her awful home. But the erotic part was just before that ("happily ever after" isn't sexy).

Last summer I lived under the same roof as my sister (age sixteen now) for the first time in several years. There were no other teen-aged females in my life at the time, and I became aware that she was very sexy and started to fantasize about her. I'd imagine that she would suggest that we get stoned together. We would, and then I would have sex and I would spend the night in her bed (this one still makes my pants rise). Naturally, I never told her any of this, though I'd lie there each night thinking about her on the other side of that wall. I'd be frightened that she would be upset with me if she ever found out how I felt, because I'd like to know her better as a person.

I will describe one fantasy I got into after I accepted my possible bisexuality. I would meet a guy in his twenties in a café. We would start rapping and he would invite me up to his place. Once there, we would have something to drink, and while we were talking he would unzip my fly and masturbate me. Then he would ask me if I wanted to stay the night, and I would say yes, and he would teach me all kinds of sex.

P.S. My parents broke up when I was seven, were formally divorced four years later. My father remarried, had two kids, is getting divorced again. Both of my parents have liberal values both sexually and politically, but my mother didn't feel comfortable discussing sex with me, and after the breakup, I had a poor relationship with my father—who is a very pushy person. My sister and I lived with our mother, spent many summer and other vacations with our father. Last summer my father told me I ought to go out and pick up a girl on the street.

"Virgin. How that word fascinates me, with sick, gnawing despair, hysteria, amusement, awe," says Eddie (above). "How often it seems Eternal. . . . It is hard, torturously hard, to show a woman you like her when you're terrified by the fact that you want sex so badly!"

For eight years I wrote about women's plight, women's enforced passivity, women's needs and fears, and the injustice of it all. It was only around the sixth or seventh year of research—two and a half books along the way—that I got this feeling of something left out, something missing, something I cared about a great deal: men.

As Rev. Jesse Jackson often preaches, you can blame somebody else for getting you down, but you can only blame yourself if you stay there. Blaming men and putting the boot in their face (for a change) will accomplish for women the last thing most of us want. I for one do not want to live separate from men, even if I live there in moral triumph.

Can anyone, male or female, read Eddie's words and not empathize? What saddens me is that Eddie is probably more open to his own real feelings and to women now—while still in his deplored virginal state—than he will be later. Why is it that sex so often distances us, leaving us less in love with the reality of ourselves and the other?

Buddy's spontaneous use of the word "radiant" (above) to describe his sister when he catches a glimpse of her naked is a lovely tribute from a fifteen-year-old, suggesting all the sweetness and surprise boys and girls can hold for each other.

He is furious when she covers up. The idyllic moment is lost. In retaliation, he constructs a fantasy in which she comes into his room and seduces him. Not only does the fantasy guarantee he will not be rejected again, but he has punished this chaste, superior creature by making her a bawd.

Buddy's next fantasy about his cousin takes anger a step further. When the girl asks him to stop because she fears pregnancy, it must be remembered that her fear is *his in-tention*. If she is frightened, it means he can be masterful, to the point of blandly going on with his fucking despite all her protests.

In Buddy's final fantasy about Raquel Welch, the con-flict of love versus rage intensifies: He wouldn't talk to his nice sister the way he does to this sex queen movie star. A girl is either a lady or a whore.

"Rejection kills me," says Omar (above) whose mother taught him that nice girls don't do it. She herself "likes men plenty well," but is "a real puritan where I'm con-cerned." When his mother found him reading girlie maga-zines, she threw them out. Mother taught Omar about sex; but her second, contradictory message was that it was not for him. One result is that Omar remains "a damned vir-gin." The undercurrent of revenge and hostility toward withholding females spills out in the story of his friend's sex with the ugly girl: "She bled like the pig she is."

Sherwin had always been a romantic, he tells us; but at fourteen, girls began to rebuff his "clumsy albeit thoroughly romantic and unphysical approaches." Another boy, an-other temperament, might have gotten over these turn-downs; Sherwin brings a deeply wounded history to his emerging adult sexuality. His fantasies have now turned to "less threatening material like incest, rape, pedophilia, even incredibly gory sadistic fantasies."

What are we to make of this startling statement? Is he joking when he calls such fantasies "less threatening"? Sherwin's own explanation is touching: This dungeonful of imaginary horrors is safe because he is not impelled to try to put them into action—as once he did his romantic fanta-sies. In his last paragraph he says, "last summer, my father told me I ought to go out and pick up a girl on the street."

What a job it is to be a man! He has to live up to his father's macho demands, while still carrying the anxieties about sex learned in the first years of life. Even if Sherwin summons up all his courage and tries to approach young women, what happens? They laugh, recoil in fear, reject him, call him filthy. A cry echoes throughout this chapter, as one young man after another protests always having to be the one to make the first move, always to be the one who risks rejection. "I wish women *were* free to make passes at

men," says Sherwin, "I blame women for my frustration
and would like to make women pay for it."

Can it be so surprising that often the solution is to angrily turn your back on women and all the conflicts they
pose, and make the easy slide into homosexuality as Sherwin describes in his last fantasy?

ANDREW

I am a boy fourteen years old and a virgin. I have a good
sex outlet because there is a pool at our house, and I have
holes to look into the dressing room which is next to my
bedroom. I get to see a lot of cunts and tits this way.

I have many fantasies of which I will tell you a few.

A lady I baby-sit for is a big fantasy. Usually after her
son falls asleep, I go into her bedroom, lay on her bed and
pull my pants down. Then from her dirty laundry basket, I
get out a pair of her worn bikini underpanties. I rub it
against my dick for a while, and then sniff it for a while,
then I stick the crotch area around my mouth and suck
and lick the partially dry vaginal juices into my mouth, as
though I were eating a cunt. I do this until I come.

By the way, the underpanties of a woman are the most
stimulating thing for me and I always try to see them
through girls' pants.

On with fantasies: It's a Friday night and I'm in a Volks-
wagen buggy with the lady whose underpanties I masturbate with. She's a close friend of my mom's and I have to
spend the weekend at her house, because my parents are
going away. This lady, whose name is Ann, has a husband,
but he's away on business. Anyway, in the car Ann says,
"Andrew, how would you like to spend the weekend making love?" I grab one of her tits, fondle it and say yes.

She parks and in her house, I start feeling her butt and
cunt. Once in her bedroom, she strips me and kisses my
seven-inch-long erection (we measured). Then I take off
her shirt and bra, and start sucking her tits. She has an
orgasm, and I can feel the dampness through her pants.
Then she pulls off her pants and I pull off my pants. As I
start to eat her out, she turns me around and starts sucking

my cock in the sixty-nine position. We go on and have a simultaneous orgasm. We spend the rest of the weekend fucking away.

Fantasy Two: A family friend of ours is alone at our house with me. She is lying in the sun reading *The Happy Hooker*. She is wearing a dress with no panties. I am reading near her. When I look at her, she is fingering her cunt. Then she sits up, looks at me, asks me if I "want a taste," and then spreads her legs. I go and eat out her super black-haired cunt. I flick her clitoris with my tongue, until she comes in about four minutes. Then we start walking to her bedroom, my finger banging her all the way. Once on her bed she takes off my bathing suit and gives me a fantastic blow job. After we rest a while we fuck in all sorts of positions. I even butt fuck her.

We get dressed because my mother is coming home.

Fantasy Three: There is a special whorehouse where the whores are cheerleaders at my school, and the madam is the girls' PE coach. My entire identity is changed. An hour with one of the girls costs only a quarter. The patron gets to strop and screw them. This proves very funny, because I know all the cheerleaders very well.

SHEP

I'm 16, son of an ex-minister. I mean "ex"—because he passed away a little while ago. I played baseball for a while, but we moved.

I've been wanting to express my fantasies to someone, but thought that if I did, I'd be called a queer or something.

I had one exciting thing happen to me that I still wonder about. I was in the seventh or eighth grade and I was walking down the hall. As I was nearing the girls' restroom, there were a lot of people in the doorway. Some girl I didn't even know called me over to ask me something. She was older and big. She grabbed me by the arm and pushed me into the girls' john, and the girls inside slammed the door, and tried to keep me from getting out! I musta been an idiot! But I finally got out and raved about what I saw (but I didn't see a thing). But I keep fantasizing about what could have happened if I had stayed. I'd let go of the door and start to walk around the restroom. Most of the girls start screaming, but the others tell them to shut up. One of the girls is one good piece. She tells me to come here, so I walk over and she and I start kissing. While we're kissing, I'm unbuttoning her blouse and she isn't wearing a bra and was she big! I turned her around so her back was to me and pulled her to me that way, so I could massage her breasts and kiss her on the neck. But then we get carried away, and she takes my arm and guides my hand down her pants. Wow! She was wetter than a whore and panting like a dog in the sun. Some other girl came over and started taking down my pants. And then another girl came over suddenly and yanks down the first girl's pants and starts giving her head, and she's moaning and groaning and I'm going out of my mind with horniness at this whole thing. So I just grab the nearest thing which happened to be a very pretty girl who was a cheerleader. She was excited by the whole thing she saw, because she was breathing heavy and besides, I could see her out of the corner of my eye when I was massaging the other girl's tits, and she was masturbating. So I just grabbed her and we were on the floor next thing I knew. I thrust it in and were we flying! Then we rolled over with her on top, which I enjoy (in the fantasy, because I've never fucked before, but look forward to it very much!). And I've heard if you work a finger up a girl's ass while you're fucking, she'll climb you all the way. But in fantasy, we both climax together and of course there's a commotion at the door, which scares me shitless, and I yank up my pants and go to the door, and pretend I've been trying to get out all along.

Most of my fantasies involve relatives (sisters, sisters-in-law and their sisters, etc.), and they about all go like this: We're all at a reunion and we're walking around and we go inside where it's cooler. (In this fantasy, Ive never been at this house before.) I catch sight of a *Penthouse* and leaf through it. For some reason a young niece wants to look too. So we're sitting pretty close and looking at nude women. I see this picture of a guy holding a woman upside down licking her cunt, while she sucks him. I show it to her to see how'd she react. "How about trying it?" I'm no fool to pass this up so I say yes, but I'm stuttering. But we gotta go where we're not seen. They got a big closet which has a chair in it to reach up on the shelves. So we go in there. We undress each other and I sit in the chair and pick her up by the waist and up she goes, putting her knees on the side of my head. I almost die of a coronary, because the door opens suddenly and it's my sister's girl friend. Why she came I'll never know. But she's one piece! She smiles and quietly comes in and closes the door, and undresses, and joins us. She's so beautiful, I just have to stop and work on her. I kiss and lick her nipples until they stand out like bullets. Then I kiss and lick down her front to her crotch. My first friend is masturbating, but comes over and grabs this girl's tits. After a few minutes, we're in a daisy chain, fucking, sucking and licking, till everybody is exhausted.

I've been writing this in front of my whole family while watching TV, but nobody knew what I'm writing.

MILT

It would please me immensely to know that I have shared my thoughts with other people and maybe even helped someone.

I was a bit hesitant at writing you because I am only fifteen. I have had "dirty thoughts" as long as I can remember. I explored sexually with some little girl friends of mine from the time I was four to nine. I kind of forgot about it until I discovered masturbation at eleven. I have a very powerful sex drive, but I am still a virgin. I have engaged in relations as far as one can go without actually having intercourse. After each of these sessions, I have to masturbate to relieve my pent-up desire.

I think there must be others like me, but I'm not always sure. I masturbate quite often, whenever and wherever the desire hits me. I masturbate more than anyone I know, a minimum of once a day, an average of twice to three times a day, and on some days, four or five times. Only two of my friends have ever told me they masturbate, but neither of them mentioned fantasizing, although I'm sure they do.

Neither of them masturbate nearly as much as I do and showed a little surprise when I told them of my activities.

My fantasies range far and wide, from animals to girls to other guys. Sometimes I know the people, sometimes I don't.

1. Our next-door neighbor, who I make much more desirable in my dream, is sunbathing in her backyard. I climb the fence and watch her for a while. Her family is conveniently away. She is on her stomach, but she rolls over on her back. I approach from the direction of the sun and kneel down and put my hand between her legs. She never looks over, but parts her legs wider. I caress her breasts and clitoris until she is quite lubricated, and then I perform cunnilingus to her and then fuck her. When I am done, I climb back over the fence, all the while she never looks to see who I was.

2. There are two girls on my swim team who are thirteen and just starting to mature. They are under my command, and I tell them to strip for me and the one who strips the best gets to be in charge of pleasing me. The first girl, Penelope, who is not quite as pretty, slowly strips down to her minute nylon panties which I have seen her in and displays her budding breasts. Kim is prettier and I have already decided she will win, even though Penelope is trying hard. Kim strips down to her small bikini briefs and displays her better figure and firmer breasts. Penelope then turns around and pulls down her small panties, revealing her tight little ass. She turns around, exposing her almost hairless cunt and sits down next to me and spreads her legs. Kim, not to be outdone, does the same, but her cunt is more hairy and to me more stimulating. If I have not come by now, they both sit down next to me and play with my cock and balls until I come.

I don't enjoy fantasizing about masochistic or sadistic actions, but I do occasionally think about other guys and the size of their cocks.

I know I would enjoy enacting all of my fantasies, except the homosexual fantasies.

CECIL

I am sixteen and still a virgin. My family is very religious and sex is a "no-no." To overcome my desire for sex, I fantasize. It is not the best replacement, but it will have to do. While I fantasize, I usually masturbate. I started masturbating at the age of twelve. From then I have had a wide selection of fantasies to choose from.

I live in an apartment house. The family on the floor above me are married for about five years. The man is an average-sized man. He is not sexy at all. His wife, however, has beautifully round, full tits. She is also packed with a great, sexy ass, and fully formed hips.

As I go to sleep at night, I see their bedroom light on. It remains on deep into the wee hours of the night. The curtain is partially open, but I cannot see anything from the lower floor. As I watch the light, I fantasize what the couple are doing. In my fantasy they are both naked, sprawling on the bed. He is between her legs, sucking her pussy. The more he sucks, the more she wants him to fuck her. He doesn't stop. He licks her clit while inserting a finger into her asshole. She comes after a few minutes, and he sucks her juice up.

As if they read each other's minds, they both got ready to fuck. He was on top of her, his prick erect—only five and a half inches, but it was very thick. He got right down to work. In ten minutes, they were finished fucking. They were both fulfilled.

I fantasize that I go on the roof to see what they are doing. I see the act. But when they finish, he goes to the john; and she goes to the window. She looks up to the roof and sees me. Our eyes meet, and we look at each other for a few seconds. Then she goes back in, closing the curtains.

The next morning, I go to their floor and wait till the husband leaves. After he is gone, I knock on the door. She opens the door and sees me there. I put my foot in the door before she could close it.

"You fucking bastard," she called me, "what the hell were you doing up there last night?" She assaulted me with a row of curses as I pushed my way into the room. She kept on cursing. When she finished, she was nervous and out of breath.

I put my arm around her waist. "How about a drink?"

She agreed, saying that she needed one. She went in the living room and told me to fix her the drink. I did, brought it to her, and sat down next to her. I put my arm around her and cupped my hand over her soft, pillowy boob. I told her that she was beautiful and that I loved her. She kissed me on the cheek, and I returned the kiss—on the lips. The kisses became frequent. I got a big hard-on. As I started to take her blouse off, she regained her senses. She told me to stop. Of course, I didn't stop. I pushed her on the couch and jumped on her. I removed her blouse and started taking her bra off. Again her personality changed, and she helped me get it off. I got up and we went into her bedroom. It was a spacious room with two double beds. She got on the first bed, half-naked, her tits blossomed with small, pointy, brown nipples. I put my head into the softness of her breasts, kissing each nipple. Her nipples were at least an inch long. I squeezed her tits together and licked the valley between them. She was feeling around, trying to get my cock out of my pants. She fidgeted around and worked my boner out. It was bigger than it is in normal life (six inches)—it was eight inches long. She rubbed it in her hands and felt my balls.

I got her pants down, and she removed her panties herself. She had a gorgeous cunt. She was very wet, and her dark pubic hair was soaked in her juices. I told her to wait a second as I stripped. I got between her thighs and I started fucking her. Up and down with my eight-incher, I fucked her for a half-hour straight. I made her come ten times before the half-hour was over.

I would come up every day after this and fuck her—a new method each time. I'd suck her, fuck her doggie style, let her fuck me, fuck her ass, and any way we knew how.

By this time I have masturbated all over the place.

I have other fantasies, but they are all quite similar. I never fantasize about homos though I like reading about lesbians.

DALE

In essence, I have one favorite fantasy. It is entirely fictional, as I have never been married:

I was living with a woman who I had never had sex with because neither of us had taken the initiative. I, for my part, was shy and reserved; she was afraid of becoming pregnant or losing her virginity or some such funny notion. A friend I talked to often was aware of my situation and thought it rather strange that for five years of marriage my wife and I had never copulated. So, without my knowledge, he arranged a meeting in this sex court, where sex problems are worked out. The day after he did this, he made a date for himself and his wife and me and my wife for dinner. When the day arrived, my wife and I went to the predetermined place. I parked the car and we went inside, expecting to see a restaurant as the sign outside implied. But to our amazement, we saw what resembled a small courtroom. Presiding over the judge's seat was an attractive woman of about thirty-two years. When we stepped in she said, "You must be Mr. and Mrs. Robins," to which I replied, "Yes, we are." She motioned us to be seated. Also in the courtroom was an old girl friend of mine who had left me due to my failure to establish a sexual relationship. She had developed, since our last meeting, into a strikingly sexy lady. The woman who was acting as judge then began the proceedings.

"I am Rose Chancy," she said, "and your case has been brought before me by a friend of yours."

Upon hearing this statement, I remembered my date with my friend and then realized that this was his doing.

"It has been brought to my attention," she continued, "that your marriage lacks a very essential element: sex. This hearing is to hear the facts and remedy the situation."

At this, I glanced over at Sarah, my ex-girl friend, and I received a wink.

"What do you have to say for yourself?" Rose inquired.

"Nothing, Your Honor, I mean Miss Chancy," I replied.

"From here on you will address me as Rose. Is that understood?" she asked.

"Yes, Miss Cha—I mean Rose," I stammered.

"Okay. Now, Mrs. Robins, what do you say for yourself?" asked Rose.

"Only that I love Dale but do not desire sex with him," she answered.

"Well! How can you love a man and refuse him sex?" demanded Rose. "I am afraid, Mrs. Robins, that you do not deserve to be married. Therefore, I now annul your marriage. Will you please rise, Sarah?"

Sarah rose and awaited Rose's verdict.

"Sarah," said Rose, "will you please state your relationship with Dale?"

"I was once his girl friend," stated Sarah.

"And your reason for leaving him?" inquired Rose.

"Rose," replied Sarah, "the reason I left was because my sexual appetite was not being cared for."

"Dale," said Rose, "will you please stand next to Sarah."

I did as she asked and wondered at the events taking place.

"Now," said Rose, "what do you feel for Dale now, Sarah?"

At this Sarah reached down, unzipped my fly, and withdrew my dick for all to see. It immediately achieved a hard-on as she held it in her hand.

"Okay, Dale," purred Rose, "what would you like her to do?"

I whispered to myself that I must be dreaming; nothing like this could be happening to me.

Sarah heard me, and she merely said, "If you wish to think this a dream, feel free. But let's be sure it's a pleasant one." At this she knelt on the carpet and started sucking my cock. Rose looked on happily and my wife, Jenny, stared in amazement. As Sarah was working me up for a climax, Rose stepped down from the judge's seat, came over to me with her dress lifted exposing her delicious cunt, and got on her knees over my face. At this, I stuck out my tongue and started lashing at her pussy. She moaned in ecstasy as her love juices started pouring. At this time, my dick exploded in Sarah's mouth and she gulped down the hot cum eagerly.

Jenny, meanwhile, seeing what was taking place, got up and stormed out of the room and my life. Rose, when she saw this, said cheerfully. "Good riddance. I believe we have remedied the situation." We all chuckled at this.

We continued our ménage à trois for approximately two more hours, at which time Rose announced, "Dale and Sarah, by the enjoyment we have received, I now pronounce you husband and wife and may the bond of love which unites you never be broken. I shall, when time warrants, drop by for more mutual enjoyment."

At this I replied, "Thank you, Rose, for all you've done. You've really helped me more than I imagined possible."

"Oh, it was nothing," smiled Rose.

With that, Sarah and I departed for home and were happy ever after.

And so there you have it. An inner look into the way my brain works. To date I am still a virgin, awaiting anxiously the day when I taste my first pussy. As my dreams tend to indicate, however, it will have to be the female who initates the act of love as a result of my passiveness. I'm twenty-two years young and live alone.

FOSTER

I only recently read your books on women's fantasies. It was quite a shock to realize that *I* fantasize! I'd simply never thought of it before. I've discovered that just about every encounter I have with a female becomes a sexual experience . . . in my mind.

Before I go on, you should know a little about me. I'm a slightly overweight but very athletic white male. I have earned a B.S. degree in Education, have a very poor self-image, am thirty-three years old and a VIRGIN. Nobody suspects in the least. Even if they did they wouldn't believe it. I'm hoping to find "Miss Right," but the hope fades every day.

My fantasies are two basic types. For some reason I'm erotically attracted to young girls. Invariably they are pubescent, innocent virgins. Ten to fourteen is probably the age group. I constantly undress them, and if I'm attracted, want them to be totally one within me. It's as if I want to absorb their beauty and innocence through every pore. I

even find myself hoping that they feel the same toward me.
I want to be their whore, totally desirable, and they are
mine if just in fantasy. Secretly they crave my permission
to approach. They want to consume me sexually, but as I,
they cannot show it when we are together or just passing.
I find myself very aroused but very fearful of *discovery*.
I know if I let it show I would turn them off. Any time I
make a favorable appraisal, there is an immediate desire to
know them as a person, to know their minds as well as
their bodies. There is *never* any physical contact.

Until two years ago my fantasies always failed to include
definite female genitals. An encounter with an X-rated film
enabled me now to imagine a cunt and what you really can
do with it. It has to be the most beautiful pleasure center a
man or woman could wish for. When I was five or six, I
heard about "fucking," and wondered about it a lot, but
my fantasies were always incomplete. Just when I'd get to
the "good part," I'd come back to reality ALWAYS. Since
seeing the film, I want to go down on women very very
much; intercourse plays a minor role now. Regardless, my
fantasy ends just before any intimate physical contact can
occur. I think this happens because I have no real experience, no real sensory information as to how it will be. It
must be so fantastic though. Fear plays an important part
also. I am terrified that any offense to their minds or harm
to their bodies might occur. On my part, I could not be
more considerate of their well-being. Their excitement,
their pleasures are paramount always.

My second type of fantasy has me always as a boy. I
have reached puberty, and an older woman, a "Mrs. Rob-
inson," is turned on by my innocence. She is gentle, persuasive and very horny. She wants to seduce me, she wants
my virginity. She has done this before to others, she
knows how many times and with whom, she never forgets,
she is an EXPERT. I am both fearful of the unknown
(what will she do?) and terribly excited. She teasingly
masturbates me by hand, time and time again bringing me
just to the edge of coming, but not quite there. I want to
explode and try to come, but she senses exactly when to
slow down. She seems to want to suck my cock but never
does. My never having seen such activity probably causes

this. I have no real information to act on. I masturbate to this fantasy to a beautiful climax.

It just occurred to me that the second fantasy has me completely reversed in roles. In the first I am a leader, in the second I am led. In real life I am a loner with careful selected friends, yet inside I am turned on to everything and everybody. However, any sexual feelings I have are about girls. Just the thought of "Gay" men makes me feel like throwing up. Oddly enough, lesbianism doesn't seem repulsive at all. I think I could learn from them. Who really knows better how a woman feels than another woman?

Could my fantasies ever become reality? I doubt it very much. Absolutely, the other person would have to come on to me; I've been rejected, it seems, my entire life. The thought of someone I worship rejecting me would cause such heartache and dejection, I would not want to live any longer. Nobody has ever been interested in me, I'm sure, and never will be. There is nothing worse than loneliness. Just writing this has my insides knotted up and tears in my eyes. To know me you would never suspect my unhappiness, for my whole approach to the real world is but a fantasy, and I've practiced it to PERFECTION. If only someone would really care. I would do anything to be loved and able to return it a thousandfold. *I* would be *their* total whore, gladly.

I hope to find out from your book just how, and if, I fit into the cruel "male world." From other male fantasies I hope to learn why women everywhere feel they are second-class citizens. Women's liberation, I feel, will be men's liberation too.

DAVEY

I am a fourteen-year-old boy. I am very talented in sex. In fact, when any of my friends are troubled about sex, they come to me. My parents think I know nothing about sex, but really I learned the hard way.

There was nothing in your book I did not understand,

for I own many sex books myself. This may come as a surprise to you, but I have this problem which is bluntly I do not know how to kiss. That is my fantasy—to really kiss a girl. Let me explain: Like I know my tongue is supposed to go in her mouth, but where and what do I do?

As you can probably see, being fourteen and not knowing how to kiss can be a problem. I hope you understand and do not laugh at me.

P.S. If you only knew how hard it was for me to write this.

Behind the bravado of their four-letter words, one senses that the inexperienced young men in this chapter are awash with self-questioning: If ever the exciting-but-perilous opportunity should present itself, would they measure up as men? Out of their wide variety of anxieties about The First Time, male virgins invent specific types of fantasy women to meet their special needs:

1. *The Permission Givers.* Enter the older woman, the neighbor; the woman for whom Andrew (above), for instance, baby-sits. These women carry some of mother's authority about the right and wrong of sex. If they initiate the boy, he needn't feel guilty. The obliging married woman also carries an air of nurturance and easy tolerance. She will teach him what to do and not laugh if his efforts seem a bit naive. Being married, she also provides an extra kick: The boy is beating out an older man. Best of all, she is not a virgin. She knows what it is all about. The sight of an erection, his groping hands, are not going to drive her into the fear or fury young men expect from girls their own age.

2. *Wild, Wild Women.* These are often contemporaries; but unlike most females the boy knows, they are aflame for sex. Once again, it is all their idea, their responsibility. Wild women are pictured as living at the very edge of climax, and so there is little or no male worry about performance. Since they often go out hunting for pickups in groups of two or more—so ravenous are Wild, Wild Women for sex—if the young man should tire, they'll bring each other to orgasm. "Yes" from one girl is heaven, but permission from two is even better.

3. *Tame, Tame Women*. This is the sweet girl next door, a cousin who is a year or two younger, the boy's blossoming little sister. Venturing into the unknown world of sexuality, he is anxious lest he meet voracious females he will not be capable of handling. Young girls like the thirteen-year-old swimmers in Milt's fantasy and Shep's niece (both above) reassure by their very familiarity. They are safe, known, homey, less sophisticated than he, allowing him to play the macho stud of his dreams. These girls are so inexperienced, how could they compare him to other, possibly more virile men? If he gets the sexual proceedings wrong, if his technique is not as masterful as he would like, how are these girls to know? Their ignorance of sex is permission all by itself.

These three categories are convenient prototypes; they mustn't be taken as watertight compartments. For instance, Milt has a fantasy of the older woman next door but goes on to another about two wild girls at school. Dale (above) compensates for real rejection by one female by fantasizing about sex with two others. As if to put his timidity to bed forever, he imagines a scene in which a lady judge *orders* him to have sex with his old flame. Finally, to cap it all with the Good Housekeeping Seal of Approval, the judge suddenly becomes a Wild, Wild Woman herself. Lifting her skirts as she gets up from the bench, she joins Dale and Sarah in a trio.

Still a virgin at thirty-three, Foster (above) may not be the statistical norm, but his inability to fuse the good little virgin with the bad older woman into one sexual peer is evidence that keeping women divided into moralistic categories is a way to remain a little boy.

Young women want sex, too, of course, but they want safety even more. In a sense, things are simple for a girl: She sees sex *as* love. Not raised for independence, not comfortable with it, sex for its own sake threatens her with choice and autonomy. She would rather it be the symbiotic glue of eternal love. She offers her boyfriend half a bargain: the sexual liberty her mother forbids *if* accompanied by the commitment forever of which mother approves.

While girls dream of sex as a home away from home, boys see it as a defiant step toward freedom. It is not that they cannot be tender; but with manhood/independence still insecure, love means getting involved, rules, strings: "Don't ever leave me." He is being asked to stop just when he wants to start.

Virgin men also dream of love and hope that someday they will find love *and* sex; but right now the still familiar softness of love is like a letter from home: It weakens the tough stance he has to take if he is ever going to make it, not as a lover, but as a stud. He presses the girl to go further; but for all his hard-won daring, he runs into an old, familiar powerlessness. Sex takes two people; and in the end, the pace is set not by the swifter but by the one who says "No."

Lost somewhere between the nice girls he feels will not accept his sexuality and the bad ones who will (but who are so frighteningly experienced they will render him impotent), Eddie cries out for "the liberated woman the media are always panting about." He sees her as offering him a third alternative, someone who will help him get over his anger at women without smothering him at the same time. Any relationship that falls short of this ideal, he says, "disturbs me so much that I'd rather be alone with my hand," Here are the age-old sorrows of Goethe's Young Werther, the lonely despair we have all felt at fifteen, twenty-two or even thirty-three—as the virginal Foster laments.

Life itself can be a great healer. If so far in this book I seem to have stressed the inhibitions learned in our earliest years, let me add now how much I believe in the remedial powers of experience. We meet other people who see us in a new way, people who ease our anxieties, give us hopeful models of freedom, open doors our parents marked *shut*, people who love us for ourselves and not for being like them. In short, new people, new relationships, give us the chance to practice new ways of being, thinking, and feeling.

As young men even as idealistic as Eddie finally take courage and invite a girl to bed at last, reality teaches a profound lesson. The first time may be scary. The second, less so. And even nice girls can enjoy the proceedings. Repetition and familiarity ease anxiety. In time, mostly pleasure is left. Freud may have made a science of our unconscious fears. He also believed in the reality principle: We can learn.

If Eddie has not yet learned all he needs, he is still young. Struggling against the destructive contradictions of a double standard *he will not accept,* Eddie himself is a sign of change. I think his letter is wonderful.

Here, at the end of these pages, I find that my years of research have confirmed something even the most uninstructed woman takes as given: Inside every adult male is a denied little boy.

He loved his father, but was taught to show that love only through mindless imitation of his father's mindless imitation of *his* father's Victorian authoritarianism.

He loved his mother, but feared her power.

The male principle in society says he is expected to be tough and domineering with women, always in control, and sexually voracious. The female principle is the opposite; when he approaches women, he carries with him all his unconscious memories of mother's awesome powers of retaliation and rejection.

How can he handle the fear and rage that sex means for a man under these conditions? He can't stop, doesn't want to stop, being a man. The frustration is blamed on women, *goddamn them!* Maybe the best thing to do is turn your back on them and forget the whole problem. In the end, it is the man's relentless desire for women that keeps him from this surrender. Fantasies are invented. At least for a sexual moment, magic is called in, reality altered, the perceived nature of women changed; the conflict is healed.

Fantasies are the triumph of love over rage.

There may come a time when society will find ways to have the sexes work together rather than in opposition. In fact, I believe it is beginning now, not through idealism but through economics. As more women go out to work to help support the family, fathers are going to have to share in raising children. Women will reap the rewards of independence, men the pleasures of nurturing. In my opinion, nothing will more effectively reshape our forms of adult sexuality than a society in which children, from the time they are born, are loved, raised, and acculturated by both parents. This will teach daughters and sons that love, tenderness, and compassion can come from either father or mother—as do the harsh disciplines that society and reality demand. Rewards and punishments, love and hate, intimacy and autonomy, will not be taken as dichotomies that run along feminine or masculine lines, but as mixtures that vary with the temperaments of individual mothers and fathers.

I will not comment on fourteen-year-old Davey's letter (above), but close my remarks in this book with a personal message for him:

I have read your P.S., Davey and I know.

A LAST-MINUTE WORD FROM THE AUTHOR

Nancy Friday invites both men and women to contribute to her ongoing research on family relationships. She would welcome your reactions to her comments and any personal experiences you feel are relevant. Please be as specific as possible, stating your age, family background, employment, marital status, and any other biographical information about yourself and any other family members that you feel pertinent. As always, anonymity is guaranteed. Write:

Nancy Friday
P.O. Box 1371
Key West, FL 33041